Nelson Mandela
By Himself

[signature: N Mandela]

THE AUTHORISED BOOK
OF QUOTATIONS

Edited by Sello Hatang and Sahm Venter

MACMILLAN

in association with PQ Blackwell

First produced and originated by PQ Blackwell Limited
116 Symonds Street, Auckland, 1010, New Zealand
www.pqblackwell.com

This edition published in 2013 by
Pan Macmillan South Africa
Private Bag X19
Northlands
Johannesburg
2116
South Africa

www.panmacmillan.co.za

ISBN 978-1-77010-327-6

Text © 2011 Nelson R. Mandela and The Nelson Mandela Foundation
Concept and design © 2011 PQ Blackwell Limited
Cover design: Cameron Gibb
Book design: Cameron Gibb and Sarah Anderson

Printed by 1010 Printing International Limited, China

....

Cover image (handwriting extract) from a notebook belonging to Nelson Mandela, date unknown.
Photograph by Matthew Willman © The Nelson Mandela Foundation.

Contents
....

Introduction

Nelson Rolihlahla Mandela is one of the most quoted – and misquoted – people in the world. This is ironic given that for much of his adult life he could not be quoted at all. In South Africa, quoting Mandela carried with it the threat of a criminal record and a possible prison sentence. Under the apartheid regime, people who were banned or imprisoned could not be quoted, and Mandela was successively banned from December 1952 and was in custody from 5 August 1962 until 11 February 1990.

Of course the words of an accused uttered in open court were exempt from this restriction, and the words he spoke at his October–November 1962 trial and his famous speech from the dock at the Rivonia Trial on 20 April 1964 were quoted in the media. Despite this exemption, people still feared quoting him. The final words in his four-and-a-half-hour-long speech at the Rivonia Trial have become the stuff of legend in the history of the struggle against apartheid:

During my lifetime I have dedicated myself to this struggle of the African people. I have fought against white domination, and I have fought against black domination. I have cherished the ideal of a democratic and free society in which all persons live together in harmony and with equal opportunities. It is an ideal which I hope to live for and to achieve. But if needs be, it is an ideal for which I am prepared to die.

These words characterise the essence of Mandela and his comrades' courage, commitment and leadership in the struggle to end apartheid. In the quarter-century following the end of the trial on 12 June 1964, a silence born out of fear more or less hung over the name Nelson Mandela within South Africa. For decades it was uttered virtually only in secret or in defiance of the increasingly repressive tactics of the apartheid regime and its agents. Some of his words were smuggled out of prison and released by the African National Congress (ANC) in exile, but Mandela had effectively been silenced.

The silence was broken when, speaking from the balcony of the Cape Town City Hall on Sunday 11 February 1990, the newly released Mandela addressed a crowd of thousands of supporters, who had gathered on the Grand Parade to hear his voice, and an audience of millions through television and radio:

Friends, comrades and fellow South Africans, I greet you all in the name of peace, democracy and freedom for all. I stand here before you not as a prophet but as a humble servant of you, the people. Your tireless and heroic sacrifices have made it possible for me to be here today. I therefore place the remaining years of my life in your hands.

This time the whole world heard and read his words and he continued to be widely quoted. His words were publicised internationally: during the period in which he was locked in negotiations alongside his comrades for an end to white minority rule; when he was campaigning for South Africa's first democratic vote; upon his election and inauguration as president; during his travels through South Africa, Africa and the world; when he was carrying out his charity work; and upon his various retirements. Even long after his official 'retirement from retirement' announcement on 1 June 2004, when he famously said, 'Don't call me, I'll call you', we, at the Nelson Mandela Centre of Memory, still process thousands of requests for the authentication of quotations.

We found that many of these, often lifted from websites purporting to contain accurate information about Mandela, were not correct. One of the main 'quotes' by which Mandela is misquoted contains, in actual fact, the words of American author Marianne Williamson from her book *A Return to Love: Reflections on the Principles of a Course in Miracles*. She wrote: 'Our deepest fear is that we are powerful beyond measure.' This quote, and especially Williamson's closing words, 'As we are liberated from our own fear, our presence automatically liberates others', are often incorrectly credited to Mandela.

Our aim in producing this book, therefore, was firstly to provide an accurate and extensive resource for the public and secondly to document in one collection a significant range of Mandela's quotes. The result is a collection of more than sixty years of quotations. In editing this book we were struck as much by the gravitas of his words – expressed when he was facing the death sentence in 1964 and in struggles against apartheid – as by their simplicity.

We were moved by the way in which his words directly link to his values and principles and these are what make Nelson Mandela one of the most loved and admired individuals of the twenty-first century. He chooses his words deliberately, he means what he says and he wants his audience to easily grasp their meaning. As he said on 14 July 2000:

It is never my custom to use words lightly. If twenty-seven years in prison have done anything to us, it was to use the silence of solitude to make us understand how precious words are and how real speech is in its impact on the way people live and die.

His emphasis on the importance of connecting with an audience through the clarity of words is further demonstrated by this quote from a speech he delivered on 21 September 1953:

Long speeches, the shaking of fists, the banging of tables and strongly worded resolutions out of touch with the objective conditions do not bring about mass action and can do a great deal of harm to the organisation and the struggle we serve.

Of course Mandela is also well known for his sense of humour and his ability to find amusement in even the most challenging circumstances. Frequently during our research we came across him making very amusing remarks. In 2005 he explained the value he placed on humour:

You sharpen your ideas by reducing yourself to the level of the people you are with, and a sense of humour and a complete relaxation, even when you're discussing serious things, does help to mobilise friends around you. And I love that.

We have selected more than 2,000 quotations from many thousands more to create sixty-three years of thoughts and sentiments by Mandela. The quotations have been divided into 317 categories within which they appear in chronological order, providing an interesting insight into how his ideas evolved and in many cases remained the same. For example, the following quotations on the principle of non-racialism delivered in 1964 and 2005 respectively:

We of the ANC had always stood for a non-racial democracy, and we shrank from any action which might drive the races further apart than they already were.

and

I hope that our movement will always hold that commitment to non-racialism dear in its thoughts, policies and actions. It is that commitment, even in circumstances where we could have been pardoned for deviating from it, that amongst other things earned us the respect of the world.

Quotations have been selected from his speeches as far back as 1951, recorded interviews from before he was sent to prison, letters dating back to 1948, diary extracts including from his 1962 trip to Africa and the United Kingdom, as well as impromptu remarks, among others. We have, in the main, used full quotations and have provided citations in each case.

We can all honour Nelson Mandela by quoting him correctly and accurately and by recognising the contexts within which his words were uttered.

Sello Hatang and Sahm Venter
EDITORS ON BEHALF OF THE NELSON MANDELA CENTRE OF MEMORY
MARCH 2011

What counts in life is not the mere fact that we have lived. It is what difference we have made to the lives of others that will determine the significance of the life we lead.

NINETIETH BIRTHDAY CELEBRATION OF WALTER SISULU, WALTER SISULU HALL, RANDBURG, JOHANNESBURG, SOUTH AFRICA, 18 MAY 2002

Accountability

The collapse of good conscience and the absence of accountability and public scrutiny have led to crimes against humanity and violations of international law.
RALLY, BLOEMFONTEIN, SOUTH AFRICA, 25 FEBRUARY 1990

Accountability of leaders to the rank and file and the accountability of members to the structures to which they are affiliated is the flip side of the coin of democracy. Such accountability must extend also to the relations existing between the movement as a whole and our people.
RALLY AT THE END OF THE ANC NATIONAL CONSULTATIVE CONFERENCE, SOCCER CITY, SOWETO, SOUTH AFRICA, 16 DECEMBER 1990

If you want to take an action and you are convinced that this is a correct action, you do so and confront that situation.
FROM A CONVERSATION WITH RICHARD STENGEL, 5 APRIL 1993

There is an absence of democratic accountability and control in every sphere of government and the state. To address this debilitating legacy requires determined action and a deep commitment to transforming our society from [a] crisis-ridden present into something all South Africans can be truly proud of.
INTERNATIONAL PRESS INSTITUTE CONGRESS, CAPE TOWN, SOUTH AFRICA, 14 FEBRUARY 1994

We were mindful from the very start of the importance of accountability to democracy. Our experience had made us acutely aware of the possible dangers of a government that is neither transparent nor accountable. To this end our Constitution contains several mechanisms to ensure that government will not be part of the problem, but part of the solution.
AFRICAN REGIONAL WORKSHOP OF THE INTERNATIONAL OMBUDSMAN INSTITUTE, PRETORIA, SOUTH AFRICA, 26 AUGUST 1996

Achievements

Our achievements, however, we know full well, must not be used as an excuse for exaggerating our successes or for ignoring errors committed and weaknesses that require urgent attention.
FROM AN ARTICLE PUBLISHED IN *AFRICA SOUTH, VOL 6.1*, OCTOBER–DECEMBER 1961

Achievements, great and small, will always be acknowledged whether by means of prizes or simple awards. Some people decline such honours, while others accept and then use them selfishly. But there are still others who get them as a result of selfless service to the community, and who tend to use them as an effective instrument in our striving for justice and human dignity.
FROM A LETTER TO DESMOND AND LEAH TUTU, WRITTEN IN VICTOR VERSTER PRISON, PAARL, SOUTH AFRICA, 21 AUGUST 1989

We have learned the lesson that our blemishes speak of what all humanity should not do. We understand this fully that our glories point to the heights of what human genius can achieve.
FIRST STATE OF THE NATION ADDRESS, PARLIAMENT, CAPE TOWN, SOUTH AFRICA, 24 MAY 1994

We must always remain modest about our achievements.
FORTIETH ANNIVERSARY OF THE ESTABLISHMENT OF UMKHONTO WE SIZWE, SOWETO, JOHANNESBURG, SOUTH AFRICA, 16 DECEMBER 2001

Adaptability

The human soul and human body have an infinite capacity of adaptation and it is amazing just how hardened one can come to be, and how concepts which we once treated as relatively unimportant suddenly become meaningful and crucial.

FROM A LETTER TO ADELAIDE TAMBO, WRITTEN ON ROBBEN ISLAND, 1 JANUARY 1970

Human beings have got the ability to adjust to anything.

FROM THE DOCUMENTARY *LEGENDS: NELSON MANDELA*, 2005

Advice

I prefer discussing matters with everyone on a basis of perfect equality, where my views are offered as advice which the person affected is free to accept or reject as it pleases him.

FROM A LETTER TO MAKGATHO MANDELA, WRITTEN ON ROBBEN ISLAND, 28 JULY 1969

[I don't] interfere in the affairs of others, unless I'm asked. Even when I'm asked, my own concern is always to bring people together.

FROM A CONVERSATION WITH RICHARD STENGEL, 3 MAY 1993

Affirmative Action

As a liberation movement, we are committed to the empowerment of the most disadvantaged sections of our people. We believe that this process can begin through a programme of affirmative action and black advancement in areas where racial and gender imbalances exist. We have to break the racial and gender division and domination of intellectual labour by certain racial groups. If we are to effect a meaningful transition to democracy then development of our human resources should begin now.

SIGNING OF A STATEMENT OF INTENT TO SET UP A NATIONAL CAPACITY FOR ECONOMIC RESEARCH AND POLICY FORMULATION, SOUTH AFRICA, 23 NOVEMBER 1991

Affirmative action is not a threat either to standards or to individuals. It is an internationally recognised method of redressing past wrongs. To reject this mechanism is to accept the status quo and to ensure that the fruits of war, colonialism, racism, sexism and oppression continue to be nurtured in our society.

INVESTITURE AS DOCTOR OF LAWS, SOOCHOW UNIVERSITY, TAIWAN, 1 AUGUST 1993

While the democratic state will maintain and develop the market, we envisage occasions when it will be necessary for it to intervene where growth and development require such intervention. Amongst these will be the employment of mechanisms of affirmative action to redress the effects of past discrimination against blacks, against women, people in the rural areas and the physically disabled.

INTERNATIONAL PRESS INSTITUTE CONGRESS, CAPE TOWN, SOUTH AFRICA, 14 FEBRUARY 1994

Affirmative action, which, as we have stated on countless occasions, should benefit all those who were denied rights under apartheid: African, coloured, Indian, women of all races, the disabled, the rural masses and so on.

FORTY-NINTH ANC NATIONAL CONFERENCE, BLOEMFONTEIN, SOUTH AFRICA, 17 DECEMBER 1994

This policy has awakened fears amongst sections of the coloured community. It is sometimes said to be intended to benefit only Africans, and there are claims that there are a few employers who misinterpret it in this way. It is necessary therefore to repeat categorically that anyone who says that affirmative action reserves jobs or opportunities for Africans only, is grossly distorting the policy of the government and the ANC. Anyone denied in this way is denied a right that belongs to all who have been disadvantaged, and they should take it up with the authorities.

INSTITUTE FOR A DEMOCRATIC SOUTH AFRICA NATIONAL CONFERENCE, CAPE TOWN, SOUTH AFRICA, 18 AUGUST 1995

We can neither heal nor build, if we continue to have people in positions of influence and power who, at best, pay lip service to affirmative action, black empowerment and the emancipation of women, or who are, in reality, opposed to these goals; if we have people who continue with blind arrogance to practise racism in the workplaces and schools, despite the appeal we made in our very first address to this Parliament. We must work together to ensure the equitable distribution of wealth, opportunity and power in our society.

STATE OF THE NATION ADDRESS, PARLIAMENT, CAPE TOWN, SOUTH AFRICA, 9 FEBRUARY 1996

Affirmative action as it was intended by the government and the ANC is aimed at providing opportunities for all those previously disadvantaged by apartheid: Africans, coloureds and Indians. We are totally opposed to it being applied for the benefit of Africans only. Nor should it be used to disadvantage those whites who were formerly advantaged. It should create opportunities, not take them away; it is a tool to redress past wrongs, not to create new ones. Properly implemented it will release the immense potential of our people which apartheid left untapped.

MEETING WITH WESTERN CAPE BUSINESS COMMUNITY, CAPE TOWN, SOUTH AFRICA, 6 DECEMBER 1996

We must address the particular fears around affirmative action, teaching, poverty, housing and unemployment. We must know how to distinguish between the racist terms in which some politicians try to exploit these fears and the real underlying feelings of anxiety, as well as the feeling that the ANC is not yet truly a home for the coloured community.

MEETING WITH ANC WESTERN CAPE AND BRANCH EXECUTIVES, CAPE TOWN, SOUTH AFRICA, 8 DECEMBER 1996

On the issue of affirmative action: the government has stated its position over and over again, that what we strive to do is to ensure training, promotion and fair opportunities to a section of our society which was, by law, denied these rights. After years of deliberate neglect and exclusion, any other course of action would be disastrous. In any case, the Constitution enjoins us to undertake this programme.

CLOSING DEBATE ON THE STATE OF THE NATION ADDRESS, PARLIAMENT, CAPE TOWN, SOUTH AFRICA, 12 FEBRUARY 1997

All our students should be able to compete with their counterparts, not only in South Africa but in the rest of the world. While affirmative action helps us redress the neglect of the past, it will not be a permanent feature of our society.

LAUNCH OF THE NATIONAL CAMPAIGN FOR LEARNING AND TEACHING, SOWETO, JOHANNESBURG, SOUTH AFRICA, 20 FEBRUARY 1997

Affirmative action is corrective action. There is no other way of moving away from racial discrimination to true equality.

STATE OF THE NATION ADDRESS, PARLIAMENT, CAPE TOWN, SOUTH AFRICA, 6 FEBRUARY 1998

We know that we can count on unions within our Alliance, as proud custodians of non-racialism, to ensure that this instrument of affirmative action is never used to advance any one group at the expense of others.

MAY DAY RALLY, KIMBERLEY, SOUTH AFRICA, 1 MAY 1998

To change the lives of women and to achieve our goals as a nation, we must also ensure that women participate fully in every sphere of the economic and political life of our country. Democratic government and the policy of affirmative action, is beginning to make an impact.

WORLD RURAL WOMEN'S DAY SYMPOSIUM, MTHATHA, SOUTH AFRICA, 15 OCTOBER 1998

The TRC [Truth and Reconciliation Commission] issues a call, which we strongly endorse, for a recommitment in both public and private sectors, with renewed vigour, to the transformation of our structures and corporations through a combination of affirmative action and employment equity, together with the strengthening of a culture of hard work, efficiency and honesty.

SPECIAL DEBATE ON THE TRC (TRUTH AND RECONCILIATION COMMISSION) REPORT, PARLIAMENT, CAPE TOWN, SOUTH AFRICA, 25 FEBRUARY 1999

Africa

In thinking of the direct enemies of the African people, namely, Great Britain, Spain, France, Portugal, Italy and South Africa, we must never forget the indirect enemy, the infinitely more dangerous enemy who sustains all those with loans, capital and arms. In common with people all over the world, humanity in Africa is fighting these forces.

PRESIDENTIAL ADDRESS TO THE ANNUAL ANC YOUTH LEAGUE CONFERENCE, SOUTH AFRICA, DECEMBER 1951

The future of this continent lies not in the hands of the discredited regimes that have allied themselves with American imperialism. It is in the hands of the common people of Africa functioning in their mass movements.

FROM AN ARTICLE ENTITLED 'A NEW MENACE IN AFRICA', *LIBERATION*, MARCH 1958

The tour of the Continent made a forceful impression on me. For the first time in my life I was a free man: free from white oppression, from the idiocy of apartheid and racial arrogance, from police molestation, from humiliation and indignity. Wherever I went I was treated like a human being.

IN MITIGATION OF SENTENCE AFTER BEING CONVICTED OF INCITING WORKERS TO STRIKE AND LEAVING THE COUNTRY ILLEGALLY, OLD SYNAGOGUE, PRETORIA, SOUTH AFRICA, 7 NOVEMBER 1962

I have always regarded myself, in the first place, as an African patriot.

SPEECH FROM THE DOCK, RIVONIA TRIAL, PALACE OF JUSTICE, PRETORIA, SOUTH AFRICA, 20 APRIL 1964

Western civilisation has not entirely rubbed off my African background.

FROM AN UNPUBLISHED AUTOBIOGRAPHICAL MANUSCRIPT, WRITTEN ON ROBBEN ISLAND, 1975

Although it is always dangerous to make generalisations, it is true to say that the non-aligned world in general, and the people of this continent in particular, have their own distinct approach on many issues that divide the capitalist and socialist countries.

FROM A LETTER TO LORD NICHOLAS BETHELL, WRITTEN IN POLLSMOOR PRISON, CAPE TOWN, SOUTH AFRICA, 1 APRIL 1985

The continent of Africa is well aware of the importance of the environment. But most of the Continent's problems on [the] environment are simply the product of poverty and lack of education. Africa has no resources or skills to deal with desertation [sic], deforestation, soil erosion and pollution.

FROM A NOTEBOOK, DECEMBER 1991

There is definitely a movement in Africa away from authoritarian rule to a multi-party democracy where each party will be free to canvas its own political views. That movement has now taken a very strong form in Africa. It seems to me that very soon it is going to be a flood.

FROM THE DOCUMENTARY *THE LAST MILE: MANDELA, AFRICA AND DEMOCRACY*, 1992

There are concepts of democratic values which in the situation prevailing in Africa have not been easy to apply and there has been a lot of corruption in some of the countries, not all, but in some of the countries in Africa.

IBID

'Africa for the Africans' did not have a racial connotation... Didn't mean to say that the whites who had settled in Africa must be driven out, no. It meant the colonial system must be ended.

FROM A CONVERSATION WITH RICHARD STENGEL, 21 DECEMBER 1992

To say 'Unity, you know, from Cape to Cairo', that was – has always been – a dream and from Morocco to Madagascar. Where they meant one government, I rejected that right from the beginning. When they talked about one Pan-Africanist organisation which could coordinate the efforts of different governments – that I supported. But the concept of one government, I thought that was ridiculous.

IBID

I say that if the development of the African people in this country was not interrupted by the advent of whites, they would have developed just like Europe and reached the same stage, without any contact with anybody.

FROM A CONVERSATION WITH RICHARD STENGEL, 22 DECEMBER 1993

The titanic effort that has brought liberation to South Africa, and ensured the total liberation of Africa, constitutes an act of redemption for the black people of the world. It is a gift of emancipation to those who, because they were white, imposed on themselves the heavy burden of assuming the mantle of rulers of all humanity.

OAU (ORGANISATION OF AFRICAN UNITY) SUMMIT, TUNIS, TUNISIA, 13 JUNE 1994

Africa shed her blood and surrendered the lives of her children so that all her children could be free. She gave of her limited wealth and resources so that all of Africa should be liberated. She opened her heart of hospitality and her head so full of wise counsel, so that we should emerge victorious. A million times, she put her hand to the plough that has now dug up the encrusted burden of oppression that had accumulated for centuries.

IBID

When the history of our struggle is written, it will tell a glorious tale of African solidarity, of Africans' adherence to principles. It will tell a moving story of the sacrifices that the peoples of our continent made, to ensure that that intolerable insult to human dignity, the apartheid crime against humanity, became a thing of the past.

IBID

If freedom was the crown which the fighters of liberation sought to place on the head of mother Africa, let the upliftment, the happiness, prosperity and comfort of her children be the jewel of the crown.

IBID

As a tree will blossom only with care and attention, so our countries and our region will blossom and grow from strength to strength, if we care and work hard. As this tree reaches for the heavens, let it encourage us always to aim higher and higher in meeting the new challenges which face us. As its branches spread, so may the cooperation between us spread out and embrace our whole region and our continent of Africa.

KGOTLA (TRADITIONAL ASSEMBLY), SEROWE, BOTSWANA, 6 SEPTEMBER 1995

The people of the Continent are eager and willing to be among the very best in all areas of endeavour. They are right to pour scorn at any suggestion that they should be judged by lower standards as if they were subhuman. They deserve and are striving for a condition that can be adjudged a better life: in the conduct of politics, in the freedoms they enjoy, in the social conditions under which they live, in the environment which they inhabit.

OAU (ORGANISATION OF AFRICAN UNITY) SUMMIT, YAOUNDE, CAMEROON, 8 JULY 1996

Because of our past, victim to the greed and power of nations from across the oceans, we are justified in demanding a fair share of economic and scientific benefits accrued in large measure at our expense. But because of this past too, we need to exert ourselves that much more and break out of the vicious cycle of dependence imposed on us by the financially powerful, those in command of immense market power and those who dare to fashion the world in their own image.

IBID

For centuries, an ancient continent has bled from many gaping sword wounds. At an earlier time, it lost millions of its most able sons and daughters to a trade in slaves which defined these Africans as fit for slavery because they were African.

ADDRESS TO THE JOINT HOUSES OF PARLIAMENT, WESTMINSTER HALL, LONDON, ENGLAND, 11 JULY 1996

To this day we continue to lose some of the best among ourselves because the lights in the developed world shine brighter.

IBID

Together we have sought peaceful political solutions to some of Africa's conflicts, recognising that conflict threatens not only the gains we have made but also our collective future.

BANQUET IN HONOUR OF PRESIDENT MUSEVENI OF UGANDA, CAPE TOWN, SOUTH AFRICA, 27 MAY 1997

It would be a cruel irony of history if Africa's actions to regenerate the Continent were to unleash a new scramble for Africa which, like that of the nineteenth century, plundered the Continent's wealth and left it once more the poorer.

LECTURE AT THE OXFORD CENTRE FOR ISLAMIC STUDIES, SHELDONIAN THEATRE, OXFORD, ENGLAND, 11 JULY 1997

Africa, more than any other continent, has had to contend with the consequences of conquest in a denial of its own role in history, including the denial that its people had the capacity to bring about change and progress. Today the world knows better. The mists that obscured our vision have all but lifted.

IBID

The attitude of mind and way of life that Biko and his comrades called for are needed today in abundance. They are relevant as we define our being as an African nation on the African continent. They are pertinent in our drive to ward off the temptation to become clones of other people.

COMMEMORATION OF THE TWENTIETH ANNIVERSARY OF THE DEATH IN POLICE DETENTION OF STEVE BIKO, EAST LONDON, SOUTH AFRICA, 1 SEPTEMBER 1997

One destabilising conflict anywhere on the Continent is one too many. And our task, as African peoples and leaders, is not to decry the negative but to seize opportunities that beckon.

PRESENTATION OF THE AFRICA PEACE PRIZE TO MOZAMBIQUE, DURBAN, SOUTH AFRICA, 1 NOVEMBER 1997

Indeed, Africa has what it takes to make her dream of revival come true. We are rising from the ashes of war.

IBID

For as long as the majority of people anywhere on the Continent feel oppressed, are not allowed democratic participation in decision-making processes and cannot elect their own leaders in free and fair elections, there will always be tension and conflict. For as long as legitimate bodies of opinion feel stifled, vile minds will take advantage of justifiable grievances to destroy, to kill and to maim.

IBID

We speak of a continent which, while it led in the very evolution of human life and was a leading centre of learning, technology and the arts in ancient times, has experienced various traumatic epochs, each one of which has pushed her peoples deeper into poverty and backwardness.

OPENING OF THE FIFTIETH ANC NATIONAL CONFERENCE, NORTH-WEST UNIVERSITY, MAFIKENG CAMPUS, SOUTH AFRICA, 16 DECEMBER 1997

The detention without trial of political opponents is contrary to the basic principles of a democratic polity and will not serve to foster confidence in the kind of free political activity to which the Harare Declaration commits us as states of this region.

STATEMENT ON THE ARREST OF FORMER ZAMBIAN PRESIDENT KENNETH KAUNDA, 26 DECEMBER 1997

None of us is a superstar and none can succeed without the success of the other. That common destiny requires that we should treat the question of peace and stability on our Continent as a common challenge.

OAU (ORGANISATION OF AFRICAN UNITY) SUMMIT, OUAGADOUGOU, BURKINA FASO, 8 JUNE 1998

I believe that we must all accept that we cannot abuse the concept of national sovereignty to deny the rest of the Continent the right and duty to intervene when, behind those sovereign boundaries, people are being slaughtered to protect tyranny.

IBID

As we stand on the threshold of a new African era characterised by democracy, sustainable economic development and a reawakening of our rich cultural values and heritage, African unity remains our watchword and the Organisation of African Unity our guide. As we seek to impress upon the world's financial institutions the necessity of lifting the debt burden that impedes Africa's efforts to uplift the poorest of the poor, the need to speak with one continental voice is as great as ever.

BANQUET IN HONOUR OF PRESIDENT RAWLINGS OF GHANA, PRETORIA, SOUTH AFRICA, 9 JULY 1998

Our continent is unfortunately still too much plagued by wars, violent conflicts and instability. In these conditions of instability, ordinary citizens, who have no desire for or part in these conflicts, are the ones that suffer most. Most of them only ask for the opportunity to lead lives of dignity and decency, the central part of which is to provide education for their children and charges.

SADTU (SOUTH AFRICAN DEMOCRATIC TEACHERS' UNION) CONGRESS, JOHANNESBURG, SOUTH AFRICA, 19 JULY 2001

We owe a great debt to our comrades and compatriots on the African continent. If we today talk so insistently of democratic South Africa as in the first place part of Africa, it is also because our liberation movement and army found such [a] hospitable home in so many African countries. Without their support, material and moral, we would not have been where we are today as a movement and a country.

FORTIETH ANNIVERSARY OF THE ESTABLISHMENT OF UMKHONTO WE SIZWE, SOWETO, JOHANNESBURG, SOUTH AFRICA, 16 DECEMBER 2001

There is still too much suffering on our continent that could have been prevented by leadership which put the interests of the people supreme. The conflict, war and instability in many parts of our continent must in great measure be blamed on an absence of leaders who are capable of or willing to subject personal and sectional considerations to the well-being and common good of the people.

UPON RECEIVING THE ORDER OF THE LION OF MALAWI FROM PRESIDENT BAKILI MULUZI, MALAWI, MAY 2002

We need to restore and reaffirm the dignity of the people of Africa and the developing world. We need to place the eradication of poverty at the top of world priorities. We need to know with a fresh conviction that we all share a common humanity and that our diversity in the world is the strength for our future together.

BANQUET CELEBRATING AFRICA'S 100 BEST BOOKS OF THE TWENTIETH CENTURY, CAPE TOWN, SOUTH AFRICA, JULY 2002

We stand at the dawn of an African century, a century where Africa will take its rightful place among the nations of the world.

ROTARY MEETING, PRETORIA EAST, SOUTH AFRICA, NOVEMBER 2003

It is essential for our common future on the planet that the marginalisation of Africa be ended and that all parts of the world be accorded equal attention and focus within our globalised world.

MESSAGE TO THE ROME CONFERENCE ON AFRICA, ROME, ITALY, APRIL 2004

For the sake of Africa and the world, we must act and act now.

FROM THE DOCUMENTARY *HEADLINERS AND LEGENDS: NELSON MANDELA*, 2006

Our continent has progressed tremendously since that visit to the ruins of destroyed Carthage and the beautiful city of rebuilt Tunis. The pessimists have only to read the statistics about new democratic states, the demise of one party states and military dictatorships and the rates with which economies have grown, to realise that Africa is on the rise.

VIDEO MESSAGE FOR THE MO IBRAHIM PRIZE FOR ACHIEVEMENT IN AFRICAN LEADERSHIP AWARDS, ALEXANDRIA, EGYPT, 26 NOVEMBER 2007

Africa: Places

Botswana

Botswana, you see, was quite different from South Africa, and because there were no passes, you couldn't be stopped in the street, you see, for people to demand passes and Africans there exercised a great deal of independence, more independence than we could ever hope for during those days.

FROM A CONVERSATION WITH AHMED KATHRADA, CIRCA 1993/94

On my first-ever visit abroad in 1962, I travelled through this country. Our situations then were in stark contrast. Botswana, or Bechuanaland as it was called, was undergoing her peaceful pre-independence phase. Freedom was beckoning on the horizon. In South Africa, the dark clouds of apartheid repression were descending.

BANQUET HOSTED BY PRESIDENT MASIRE, GABORONE, BOTSWANA, 5 SEPTEMBER 1995

Burundi

There are good men and women in all communities. In particular there are good men and women among the Hutus, Tutsis and the Twa: the duty of a real leader is to identify those good men and women and give them tasks of serving the community.

FROM A PERSONAL FILE, 16 JANUARY 2000

We congratulate the Burundian leaders for responding to the challenge of putting the interests of their long-suffering people ahead of considerations of personal power and sectional sentiments. With your willingness to compromise and preparedness to face the future rather than getting caught in the divisions of your past, you opened an honourable place for yourself and your country in the history of our continent.

INSTALLATION OF THE TRANSITIONAL GOVERNMENT OF BURUNDI, BUJUMBURA, BURUNDI, 1 NOVEMBER 2001

Now it is up to the leadership and the people of Burundi to build a future of peace and security for themselves and future generations. Ultimately it is only you who can make it succeed. The region, the Continent and the international community have pledged their support, but your future is in your own hands.

IBID

Egypt

In spite of plunder by the colonialists, Egypt still is a country of fabulous wealth in ancient art and culture.

FROM AN UNPUBLISHED AUTOBIOGRAPHICAL MANUSCRIPT, WRITTEN ON ROBBEN ISLAND, 1975

Indeed, it is no accident that Africa's greatest city has been a port of call at each stage of our long journey to freedom. I first visited Cairo in 1962 as a freedom fighter when we embarked on our armed struggle. I came again in 1990 when the people of South Africa, together with freedom-loving peoples across the world, had opened the prisons of apartheid. We came then to say that the people of South Africa would never forget the support of the Egyptian Government and people – and today, once again, we thank you from the bottom of our heart.

UPON BEING AWARDED THE COLLAR OF THE NILE BY PRESIDENT HOSNI MUBARAK OF EGYPT AND AWARDING HIM THE ORDER OF GOOD HOPE, CAIRO, EGYPT, 21 OCTOBER 1997

Ghana

My return to Ghana after almost 30 years is a kind of home-coming.

FROM THE DOCUMENTARY *THE LAST MILE: MANDELA, AFRICA AND DEMOCRACY*, 1992

When we think of Ghana, we think of freedom for Africans, African self-determination, pride and dignity of African people. We think of Kwame Nkrumah and his deep love for the people and the continent of Africa, and his passionate belief that we are one people despite national and geographic borders that separate and seek to divide us.

UPON RECEIVING AN HONORARY DEGREE FROM THE UNIVERSITY OF GHANA, JOHANNESBURG, SOUTH AFRICA, 24 APRIL 2002

Libya

The people of Libya shared the trenches with us in our struggle for freedom. You were in the front ranks of those whose selfless and practical support helped assure a victory that was as much yours as it is ours.

BANQUET HOSTED BY MUAMMAR QADDAFI, LIBYA, 22 OCTOBER 1997

It was pure expediency to call on democratic South Africa to turn its back on Libya and Qaddafi, who had assisted us in obtaining democracy at a time when those who now made that call were the friends of the enemies of democracy in South Africa.

LUNCHEON IN HONOUR OF MUAMMAR QADDAFI, CAPE TOWN, SOUTH AFRICA, 13 JUNE 1999

Mozambique

The world is on your side. It cannot and will not betray you. With the support of the world and with the legendary determination of the Mozambican people, you can only emerge victorious.

MESSAGE OF CONDOLENCE ON THE DEATH OF PRESIDENT SAMORA MACHEL, WITH WINNIE MANDELA, 28 OCTOBER 1986

Our grief for the loss of Comrade Samora [Machel] is so deep that it breaks our hearts. Throughout the night we shall join you in the vigil. Throughout the day we shall cry with you for the loss of that powerful soldier, courageous son and noble statesman.

IBID

We must believe that his death will give new strength to your and our determination to someday be free. For you it will be through victory over the immoral and lackey bandits. For us it will be a victory over oppression.

IBID

Rwanda

Tribute is due to the great thinkers of our continent who have been and are trying to move all of us to understand the intimate interconnection between the great issues of our day of peace, stability, democracy, human rights, cooperation and development. Even as we speak, Rwanda stands out as a stern and severe rebuke to all of us for having failed to address these interrelated matters. As a result of that, a terrible slaughter of the innocent is taking place in front of our very eyes.

OAU (ORGANISATION OF AFRICAN UNITY) SUMMIT, TUNIS, TUNISIA, 13 JUNE 1994

The louder and more piercing the cries of despair – even when that despair results in half-a-million dead in Rwanda – the more these cries seem to encourage an instinctive reaction to raise our hands so as to close our eyes and ears.

ADDRESS TO THE JOINT HOUSES OF PARLIAMENT, WESTMINSTER HALL, LONDON, ENGLAND, 11 JULY 1996

Both of us have been part of this unfolding tragedy, watching, waiting, troubled, not knowing what beast born of this superhuman suffering, slouches towards Bethlehem to be born, to borrow the words of an Irish poet. But this we must know, that none of us can insulate ourselves from so catastrophic a scale of human suffering.

IBID

Sahara

Of all the deserts I don't think there is one fearful as the Sahara where there are heaps and heaps of extensive masses of sand visible even when in the air. I never saw a single tree nor a patch of grass.

FROM A LETTER TO WINNIE MANDELA, WRITTEN ON ROBBEN ISLAND, 26 OCTOBER 1976

Tanzania

The people of Tanzania gave unstinting support to the liberation of South Africa. They gave recognition of the most practical kind to the principle that our freedom and theirs were interdependent.

BANQUET IN HONOUR OF JULIUS NYERERE, JOHANNESBURG, SOUTH AFRICA, 17 OCTOBER 1997

Zimbabwe

We watch with sadness the continuing tragedy in Darfur. Nearer to home we had seen the outbreak of violence against fellow Africans in our own country and the tragic failure of leadership in our neighbouring Zimbabwe.

46664 CONCERT, HYDE PARK, LONDON, ENGLAND, 27 JUNE 2008

African National Congress

We have to consider measures to eliminate the looseness and lack of discipline in the movement and also the cultivation of a serious approach to the struggle.

PRESIDENTIAL ADDRESS TO THE ANNUAL ANC YOUTH LEAGUE CONFERENCE, SOUTH AFRICA, DECEMBER 1951

A political movement must keep in touch with reality and the prevailing conditions.

PRESIDENTIAL ADDRESS TO THE ANC TRANSVAAL CONGRESS, ALSO KNOWN AS THE 'NO EASY WALK TO FREEDOM' SPEECH, TRANSVAAL, SOUTH AFRICA, 21 SEPTEMBER 1953

Right at the beginning of my career and experiences as an attorney, I encountered difficulties imposed on me because of the colour of my skin, and further difficulty surrounding me because of my membership and support of the African National Congress.

IN MITIGATION OF SENTENCE AFTER BEING CONVICTED OF INCITING WORKERS TO STRIKE AND LEAVING THE COUNTRY ILLEGALLY, OLD SYNAGOGUE, PRETORIA, SOUTH AFRICA, 7 NOVEMBER 1962

Throughout its fifty years of existence, the African National Congress, for instance, has done everything possible to bring its demands to the attention of successive South African governments. It has sought at all times peaceful solutions for all the country's ills and problems.

IBID

When I reached adult stature, I became a member of the African National Congress. That was in 1944 and I have followed its policy, supported it, and believed in its aims and outlook for eighteen years. Its policy was one which appealed to my deepest inner convictions.

IBID

What has sustained me even in the most grim moments is the knowledge that I am a member of a tried and tested family which has triumphed over many difficulties.

FROM A LETTER TO ADELAIDE TAMBO, WRITTEN ON ROBBEN ISLAND, 31 JANUARY 1970

My association with the African National Congress has taught me that a broad national movement has numerous and divergent contradictions, fundamental and otherwise.

FROM AN UNPUBLISHED AUTOBIOGRAPHICAL MANUSCRIPT, WRITTEN ON ROBBEN ISLAND, 1975

At home I had repeatedly heard that all Thembus were members of Umbutho we Sizwe (National Organisation) because [Chief Jongintaba] Dalindyebo had paid a subscription fee of thirty pounds for his people. But it was first time I heard the name African National Congress, and it was much later that I discovered that this Umbutho we Sizwe was none other than the African National Congress.

IBID

The ANC is part of a powerful alliance in southern Africa involving Frelimo, ZAPU [Zimbabwe African People's Union], the MPLA [People's Movement for the Liberation of Angola] and SWAPO [South West Africa People's Organisation]. We cannot resist being optimistic that the prospects of a new era have been greatly advanced by the liberation of Mozambique and Angola.

FROM AN ESSAY ENTITLED 'CLEAR THE OBSTACLES AND CONFRONT THE ENEMY', WRITTEN ON ROBBEN ISLAND, 1976

The ANC can fulfil its historic mission single-handedly, if need be. It has survived the most ferocious onslaughts from the enemy, launched powerful campaigns from underground, rallied world opinion on our side and is now well poised for the beginning of a new era in the fight against white supremacy in our country.

IBID

In fighting for a non-racial South Africa, the ANC is influenced by its undying love for democracy and by the important fact that the fight is not against a foreign power but against a firmly entrenched white minority in our own country. The staying power of the ANC is enhanced by its ability to adapt quickly to changing conditions.

FROM AN ESSAY ENTITLED 'WHITHER THE BLACK CONSCIOUSNESS MOVEMENT', WRITTEN ON ROBBEN ISLAND, 1978

I am a member of the African National Congress. I have always been a member of the African National Congress and I will remain a member of the African National Congress until the day I die.

RESPONSE TO AN OFFER OF CONDITIONAL FREEDOM, READ BY ZINDZI MANDELA AT A RALLY, JABULANI STADIUM, SOWETO, SOUTH AFRICA, 10 FEBRUARY 1985

There is not a single political organisation in this country, inside and outside Parliament, which can ever compare with the ANC in its total commitment to peace.

FIRST PRESS CONFERENCE AFTER HIS RELEASE, ARCHBISHOP DESMOND TUTU'S RESIDENCE, BISHOPSCOURT, CAPE TOWN, SOUTH AFRICA, 12 FEBRUARY 1990

Everybody now realises that there can be no peaceful settlement in this country without the ANC.

AT HOME, SOWETO, SOUTH AFRICA, 14 FEBRUARY 1990

The ANC offers a home to all who subscribe to the principles of a free, democratic, non-racial and united South Africa. We are committed to building a single nation in our country.

RALLY, KINGS PARK STADIUM, DURBAN, SOUTH AFRICA, 25 FEBRUARY 1990

Any form of violence, any form of coercion, any form of harassment is against the policy of the ANC.

ADDRESS TO YOUTH, SOUTH AFRICA, 13 APRIL 1990

The ANC does not believe in socialism. We are a broad national movement which combines various strands of political thought ranging from the far right to the extreme left, embracing liberal and conservative views.

FROM THE DOCUMENTARY *THE LAST MILE: MANDELA, AFRICA AND DEMOCRACY*, 1992

When you are produced, you see, by a mass movement, like the ANC, you can't avoid thinking about the welfare of your colleagues, because they had sacrificed and some of them had sacrificed much more than some of us had done and for that reason, we made it a point to look after their interests.

FROM A CONVERSATION WITH RICHARD STENGEL, 24 DECEMBER 1992

In the ANC, in addressing any particular problem, we normally start from opposite poles and debate the matter thoroughly. And then reach a consensus which makes our decisions very strong.

FROM A CONVERSATION WITH RICHARD STENGEL, 16 MARCH 1993

It was after '44, after I joined, and once I joined, then I made it my business to know a little more about the type of ideas which were associated with my movement and the struggle for changes in the country.

FROM A CONVERSATION WITH RICHARD STENGEL, CIRCA MARCH 1993

My concern was that we were living under conditions of illegality and it was no longer realistic for us to rely purely on public meetings as we had done in the past. We had now to make sure that we could take a decision nationally and be able to transmit that decision in the very shortest possible time to our membership throughout the country.

FROM A CONVERSATION WITH RICHARD STENGEL, 19 MARCH 1993

You can't divide the organisation. People must be able to come to you and so that you can exercise the role of keeping the organisation together.

FROM A CONVERSATION WITH RICHARD STENGEL, 29 APRIL 1993

Individuals will come and go but the organisation will go on, I believe, forever.

FROM AN INTERVIEW WITH THE BBC (UK), DATE UNKNOWN

Our ability to function as a cohesive force and combative movement depends on the discipline we are all able to master as individuals and as an organisation in our daily work.

SEVENTEENTH ANNIVERSARY OF THE 1976 SOWETO UPRISING, ORLANDO STADIUM, SOWETO, SOUTH AFRICA, 16 JUNE 1993

What we are is enemies of racism and oppression.

ANC NATIONAL CONFERENCE ON RECONSTRUCTION AND STRATEGY, SOUTH AFRICA, 21 JANUARY 1994

I stand before you humbled by your courage, with a heart full of love for all of you. I regard it as the highest honour to lead the ANC at this moment in our history, and that we have been chosen to lead our country into the new century.

ANC ELECTION VICTORY CELEBRATION, CARLTON HOTEL, JOHANNESBURG, SOUTH AFRICA, 2 MAY 1994

I raise a glass to you all for working so hard to achieve what can only be called a small miracle. Let our celebrations be in keeping with the mood set in the elections, peaceful, respectful and disciplined, showing we are a people ready to assume the responsibilities of government.

IBID

To raise our country and its people from the morass of racism and apartheid will require determination and effort. As a government, the ANC will create a legal framework that will assist, rather than impede, the awesome task of reconstruction and development of our battered society.

UPON HIS ELECTION AS PRESIDENT, CITY HALL, CAPE TOWN, SOUTH AFRICA, 9 MAY 1994

It was when I came into the African National Congress that I realised that Xhosas are only a part of the African people. That the task of the ANC was to unite the African people and out of them, build a nation.

FROM A BBC (UK) DOCUMENTARY, 1996

Many among our members see their membership of the ANC as a means to advance their personal ambitions to attain positions of power and access to resources for their own individual gratification.

OPENING OF THE FIFTIETH ANC NATIONAL CONFERENCE, NORTH-WEST UNIVERSITY, MAFIKENG CAMPUS, SOUTH AFRICA, 16 DECEMBER 1997

I will remember this experience fondly for as long as I live. Running like a golden thread through the decisions that we have taken is a reaffirmation of what the ANC has always stood for: to bring fundamental change to the lives of all South Africans, especially the poor; to recognise the actual contradictions in our society and to state them boldly, the better to search for their resolution; to avoid steps that further worsen social conflict; and to build our new nation by continually and consciously exorcising the demon of tribalism, racism and religious intolerance.

CLOSING SESSION OF THE FIFTIETH ANC NATIONAL CONFERENCE, NORTH-WEST UNIVERSITY, MAFIKENG CAMPUS, SOUTH AFRICA, 20 DECEMBER 1997

In the early years when I was all green and raw in the movement's ranks, Constantine Ramohanoe, the Transvaal President of the ANC, took me by train and on foot to visit villages, cities and dorpies, and taught me and my generation never to lose touch with the people.

IBID

More often than not, an epoch creates and nurtures the individuals which are associated with its twists and turns. And so a name becomes the symbol of an era. As we hand over the baton, it is appropriate that I should thank the ANC for shaping me as such a symbol of what it stands for. I know that the love and respect that I have enjoyed is love and respect for the ANC and its ideals. I know that the worldwide appreciation of South Africa's miracle and the dignity of its people is appreciation, first and foremost, of the work of the ANC.

IBID

Let me assure you and the people of our country that, in my humble way, I shall continue to be of service to transformation, and to the ANC, the only movement that is capable of bringing about that transformation.

IBID

If I have been able to help take our country a few steps towards democracy, non-racialism and non-sexism, it is because I am a product of the African National Congress, of the movement for justice, dignity and freedom that produced countless giants in whose shadow we find our glory.

FINAL SITTING OF THE FIRST DEMOCRATICALLY ELECTED PARLIAMENT, CAPE TOWN, SOUTH AFRICA, 26 MARCH 1999

The movement had to gather and regroup in exile and conduct the struggle from foreign and unknown soil. Oliver [Tambo] was already sent abroad to head up the foreign mission of the organisation and it fell on his shoulders to lead the movement in exile.

FIFTH STEVE BIKO LECTURE, UNIVERSITY OF CAPE TOWN, CAPE TOWN, SOUTH AFRICA, 10 SEPTEMBER 2004

Today there are signs of deep divisions in our organisation. Differences and tensions in an organisation are not unusual or abnormal. It is the manner in which we deal with those differences that matters.

MESSAGE TO THE FIFTY-SECOND ANC NATIONAL CONFERENCE, UNIVERSITY OF LIMPOPO, POLOKWANE, SOUTH AFRICA, DECEMBER 2007

I would be nothing without the ANC.

ANC RALLY FOR HIS NINETIETH BIRTHDAY, LOFTUS VERSFELD STADIUM, PRETORIA, SOUTH AFRICA, 2 AUGUST 2008

You are the inheritors of a great organisation, one that has led for almost a century. It is now in your hands to uphold the best and the noblest of that history.

IBID

Let no individual, section, faction or group ever regard itself as greater than the organisation and the common good of all our people.

IBID

I wish the organisation well in its deliberations as it celebrates its past and reflects on its future, both immediate and long term. The primary challenges for our country remain the consolidation and deepening of our democracy and the fundamental improvement of the lives of all South Africans. The role of the ANC in all of this remains crucial.

LAUNCH OF THE ANC ELECTION MANIFESTO 2009 AND NINETY-SEVENTH ANNIVERSARY CELEBRATIONS, ABSA STADIUM, EAST LONDON, SOUTH AFRICA, 10 JANUARY 2009

We once more look to the ANC to provide leadership in creating the circumstances for our people to enjoy and exercise the democratic rights for which we all fought so bravely and with so much sacrifice. Let our organisation at all times conduct itself with the dignity in keeping with its proud history. And let the good of our people always remain supreme in all our considerations.

IBID

African National Congress Youth League

As the guardian of African nationalism, the Congress Youth League and, to a lesser extent, the Senior Congress are undoubtedly the greatest hope that the African people, and indeed all oppressed people, have that they will ever live in a free, independent, united, democratic, and a prosperous South Africa.

PRESIDENTIAL ADDRESS TO THE ANNUAL ANC YOUTH LEAGUE CONFERENCE, SOUTH AFRICA, DECEMBER 1951

I wish to say as emphatically as possible that there is only one African nationalism and that is the African nationalism propounded by the Congress and the Youth League.

IBID

I am a loyal and disciplined member of the ANC. I will carry out whatever instructions they give me.

AT HOME, SOWETO, SOUTH AFRICA, 14 FEBRUARY 1990

The Youth League played such an important role in our own introduction to and entry into national politics that we are greatly honoured to celebrate with the current generation of members of the organisation this landmark occasion.

RALLY TO CELEBRATE THE FIFTY-EIGHTH ANNIVERSARY OF THE ANC YOUTH LEAGUE, SOUTH AFRICA, 27 OCTOBER 2002

It is probably one of the deepest challenges to our Youth League, born out of the liberation struggle, to adapt to and accommodate the needs of a more normalised society in its programmes, projects and message.

IBID

We look to the ANC Youth League to give the lead to the youth of our nation in conducting themselves as self-confident builders of a new society – liberated from a sense of victimhood, secure in the knowledge that we have now taken control over our destiny.

IBID

The history of the ANC Youth League stands as testimony to the constructive role the organised youth of a country can and should play in helping to shape the course of that society.

IBID

African Nationalism

A friend once asked me how I would reconcile my belief in African nationalism and dialectical materialism at one and the same time. There is no contradiction whatsoever between the two ideologies; on the contrary, I have found them complementary.

FROM AN UNPUBLISHED AUTOBIOGRAPHICAL MANUSCRIPT, WRITTEN ON ROBBEN ISLAND, 1975

I am an African nationalist and strive for the unity of the African people, for our emancipation from minority rule and for the right to manage our own affairs.

IBID

African Renaissance

Africa has long traversed past a mindset that seeks to heap all blame on the past and on others. The era of renaissance we are entering is, and should be, based on our own efforts as Africans to change Africa's conditions for the better.

UPON RECEIVING THE AFRICA PEACE AWARD, DURBAN, SOUTH AFRICA, 18 MARCH 1995

No doubt Africa's renaissance is at hand – and our challenge is to steer the Continent through the tide of history. It should not be, that, because of its leaders' own behaviour, anyone should discern any tendency on our part to wallow in the marshes of self-satisfaction with the transient trappings of power.

OAU (ORGANISATION OF AFRICAN UNITY) SUMMIT, YAOUNDE, CAMEROUN, 8 JULY 1996

With all our colours and races combined in one nation, we are an African people. The successes we seek and must achieve in politics, the economy and social development are African successes which must be part of an African renaissance.

ADDRESS TO THE JOINT HOUSES OF PARLIAMENT, WESTMINSTER HALL, LONDON, ENGLAND, 11 JULY 1996

The African rebirth is now more than an idea. Its seeds are being sown in the regional communities we are busy building and in the Continent as a whole.

BANQUET IN HONOUR OF PRESIDENT MUSEVENI OF UGANDA, CAPE TOWN, SOUTH AFRICA, 27 MAY 1997

The time for Africa's renewal, for our continent to occupy the pedestal of the successful, has come to pass. Africa yearns and deserves to redeem her glory, to reassert her centuries-old contribution to economics, politics, culture and the arts, and once more to be a pioneer in the many fields of human endeavour.

PRESENTATION OF THE AFRICA PEACE PRIZE TO MOZAMBIQUE, DURBAN, SOUTH AFRICA, 1 NOVEMBER 1997

As we dream of and work for the regeneration of our continent, we remain conscious that the African Renaissance can only succeed as part of the development of a new and equitable world order in which all the formerly colonised and marginalised take their rightful place, makers of history rather than the possessions of others.

CLOSING ADDRESS TO THE NINETEENTH MEETING OF THE HEADS OF GOVERNMENT OF THE CARICOM
(CARIBBEAN COMMUNITY AND COMMON MARKET), ST LUCIA, 4 JULY 1998

Afrikaners

Honest men are to be found on both sides of the colour line and the Afrikaner is no exception. We have a strong case and the Afrikaner leaders will command undivided support as long as their people are ignorant of the issues at stake. To penetrate their ranks enables us to be informed on trends of thought on current problems and to base our own actions on accurate data and not on mere speculation.

FROM AN ESSAY ENTITLED 'CLEAR THE OBSTACLES AND CONFRONT THE ENEMY', WRITTEN ON
ROBBEN ISLAND, 1976

The response of all communities, black and white, and in particular the Afrikaners, is beyond words. And that is one of the factors which gives us strength, which gives us hope in our future.

FROM THE BRAM FISCHER MEMORIAL LECTURE, MARKET THEATRE, JOHANNESBURG, SOUTH AFRICA,
9 JUNE 1995

I have said on several occasions that the Afrikaners in this country have given us a lot of pain, a lot of suffering. They have been insensitive beyond words. It is difficult to imagine that human beings could do what Afrikaners have done to blacks in this country. But, as an articled clerk, as a lawyer, as a prisoner, as a politician, I discovered one solid fact: that when an Afrikaner changes, he changes completely, he becomes a real friend.

IBID

Many Afrikaners, who once acted with great cruelty and insensitivity towards the majority in our country, to an extent you have to go to jail to understand, have changed completely and become loyal South Africans in whom one can trust. Such changes, in different ways, we must all make if we are to truly heal our nation by working together to address the legacy of our past, especially the poverty that afflicts so many.

REGINA MUNDI CHURCH ON REGINA MUNDI DAY, SOWETO, SOUTH AFRICA, 30 NOVEMBER 1997

Age

Beloved ones have aged rapidly as a result of all kinds of physical and spiritual problems too terrible to mention, bonds of affection tend to weaken whilst the idealist recites the maxim: absence makes the heart grow fonder.

FROM A LETTER TO THOROBETSANE TSHUKUDU [ADELAIDE TAMBO], WRITTEN ON ROBBEN ISLAND, 1 JANUARY 1977

If your knees are becoming stiff, your eyes dim and your head is full of silver, you must take comfort in the knowledge that your own contribution is an important factor in this ferment.

FROM A LETTER TO HILDA BERNSTEIN, WRITTEN IN POLLSMOOR PRISON, CAPE TOWN, SOUTH AFRICA, 8 JULY 1985

There is one respect in which I am head and shoulders above Mr De Klerk and that is in age.

PRESS CONFERENCE, CODESA (CONVENTION FOR A DEMOCRATIC SOUTH AFRICA), KEMPTON PARK, SOUTH AFRICA, 1991

I carry with me the frailties of my age and the fetters of prejudice that are a privilege of my years. And yet my presence here today has given a remarkable youthfulness to my spirit.

PRESENTATION OF THE CAPE TOWN BID AT THE 106TH SESSION OF THE INTERNATIONAL OLYMPIC COMMITTEE, LAUSANNE, SWITZERLAND, 5 SEPTEMBER 1997

There is a complex of positions which those who come after us into the new century and millennium must advance, so that those of us who are weighed down by the burdens of age can say, with conviction, that 'the tree of bitterness has come full leaf' and that the autumn of our lives presages the African spring.

OAU (ORGANISATION OF AFRICAN UNITY) SUMMIT, OUAGADOUGOU, BURKINA FASO, 8 JUNE 1998

One of the advantages of old age is that people respect you just because of your grey hair and say all manner of nice things about you that are not based on who you really are.

EIGHTIETH BIRTHDAY CELEBRATION, GALLAGHER ESTATE, MIDRAND, SOUTH AFRICA, 19 JULY 1998

My frequent assertion that an old man is respected for his grey hair more than for any real achievements, is more and more being proved right.

SUMMIT OF THE GULF COOPERATION COUNCIL, ABU DHABI, UNITED ARAB EMIRATES, 7 DECEMBER 1998

I wish that I had the energy and the fitness of limbs to do a toyi-toyi today.

FUNERAL OF PETER MOKABA, OSCAR MPETHA STADIUM, UNIVERSITY OF THE NORTH, MANKWENG, SOUTH AFRICA, 15 JUNE 2002

We watched each other as our backs bent lower and lower over the years.

UNVEILING OF WALTER SISULU'S TOMBSTONE, NEWCLARE CEMETERY, JOHANNESBURG, SOUTH AFRICA, 16 DECEMBER 2003

I do feel that I am getting old. Time is flying but I am not really worried because people who see me, especially those who see me for the first time, are saying 'Man, you look young'.

REUNION WITH THE MANDELA RECEPTION COMMITTEE, JOHANNESBURG, SOUTH AFRICA, 4 FEBRUARY 2010

I am not sick, I'm old.

JOHANNESBURG, SOUTH AFRICA, 27 JANUARY, 2011

AIDS

AIDS is a major problem to be tackled by the entire world. To deal with it requires resources far beyond the capacity of one continent. No single country has the capacity to deal with it.

FROM A NOTEBOOK, DECEMBER 1991

Many of us find it difficult to talk about sex to our children, but nature's truth is that unless we guide the youth towards safer sex, the alternative is playing into the hands of a killer disease.

NATIONAL CONFERENCE ON AIDS, NASREC, JOHANNESBURG, SOUTH AFRICA, 23 OCTOBER 1992

We already know that AIDS has no cure and no vaccine despite the intensive research efforts. Therefore, prevention remains for us the strategy we must employ.

IBID

The challenge of today, to youth and adults alike, is to make lifestyle choices which help to combat this epidemic.

MESSAGE ON WORLD AIDS DAY, SOUTH AFRICA, 1 DECEMBER 1994

Through our actions let us demonstrate that as a country we are in the forefront of protecting the rights of people with HIV and acting on our responsibilities to stem the epidemic and ensure a caring and supportive environment.

IBID

We need to ensure that we provide the supportive environment to afford people the capacity to protect themselves through increasing access to condoms, drugs for sexually transmitted diseases, access to health care and testing, and counselling facilities. At all times we must speak out against the stigma, blame, shame and denial that has thus far been associated with this epidemic.

IBID

The challenge of AIDS can be overcome if we work together as a global community.

WORLD ECONOMIC FORUM, DAVOS, SWITZERLAND, 3 FEBRUARY 1997

We must repeat over and over again our appeal to young people to abstain from sex as long as possible. If you do decide to engage in sex, then use a condom. We must repeat over and over again our appeal to all men and women to be faithful to one another but otherwise to use condoms.

RALLY ON WORLD AIDS DAY, MTUBATUBA, SOUTH AFRICA, 1 DECEMBER 1998

Let us break the silence by speaking openly and publicly about AIDS, and by bringing an end to discrimination against those living with AIDS; let us care for those living with HIV/AIDS and the orphans, and give them support, with love and compassion.

IBID

Let us say that we will wear the Red Ribbon today, and every day, in remembrance of those who have died and in solidarity with those who are infected. Let us wear it as a sign of our commitment to this pledge.

IBID

The time has come for you to teach your children about safe sex, that a person should have one partner, must have contraceptives and so on. I could see as I was addressing them that I was saying something, you know, which was revolting to them.

BRIEFING TO EDITORS AND OPINION MAKERS, PRETORIA, SOUTH AFRICA, 10 MAY 1999

A massive campaign of education is absolutely necessary to convince the public that they must now abandon old traditions and taboos because this is a disease that attacks the economically active section of the population. It can destroy the economy of the country.

IBID

There must be a number of initiatives educating the public and, of course, making sure that this drug is available, but not at an expensive rate as it still is. It must be affordable and we haven't got resources to be able to give it free of charge.

IBID

Let us not equivocate: a tragedy of unprecedented proportions is unfolding in Africa. AIDS today in Africa is claiming more lives than the sum total of all wars, famines and floods, and the ravages of such deadly diseases as malaria. It is devastating families and communities, overwhelming and depleting health care services, and robbing schools of both students and teachers.

CLOSING ADDRESS AT THE XIII INTERNATIONAL AIDS CONFERENCE, DURBAN, SOUTH AFRICA, 14 JULY 2000

In the face of the grave threat posed by HIV/AIDS, we have to rise above our differences and combine our efforts to save our people. History will judge us harshly if we fail to do so now, and right now.

IBID

We need to break the silence, banish stigma and discrimination, and ensure total inclusiveness within the struggle against AIDS; those who are infected with this terrible disease do not want stigma, they want love.

IBID

The challenge is to move from rhetoric to action, and action at an unprecedented intensity and scale. There is a need for us to focus on what we know works.

IBID

HIV is worse than a war. It is one war where you can make a difference. Talk to your parents, your friends, your teachers about sex and about the dangers of HIV/AIDS.
AIDS PUBLIC SERVICE ANNOUNCEMENT, 1 DECEMBER 2000

Learn about sex before you practise it; learn about safe sex. It is better to wait and grow up before you have sex. When you do have sex think of yourself and others you love. Use a condom.
IBID

You are the future; protect your life and the ones you love by ensuring that HIV/AIDS is not a part of it. Each one of you protect yourself and those you love. I love you and I thank you for caring about your future and about the future of all of us.
IBID

My own belief is that the anti-AIDS message is not succeeding because of one major obstacle: stigmatisation.
ADDRESS TO THE COSATU (CONGRESS OF SOUTH AFRICAN TRADE UNIONS) EXECUTIVE COMMITTEE,
JOHANNESBURG, SOUTH AFRICA, 25 JULY 2001

AIDS is not a curse that we must deny, it is an illness that can be defeated. Resisting the continued stigmatisation of HIV-positive people is not only a compassionate act, it is practical and pragmatic.
IBID

It should start with each member of the Amakhosi talking frankly to his people; it should extend to Members of Parliament devoting the first ten per cent of every speech to this topic, to every doctor talking to their patients during each consultation. Every trade union leader, every shop steward, every employer, every lawyer should, during the course of their daily work, ask: what can we do to stop the spread of HIV?
IBID

This country should develop an army of anti-AIDS campaigners; they should regard AIDS as an enemy against which our country is at war with. They should fight this war every day, from the shop floor, from offices, on sports fields and in classrooms.
IBID

That stigma sometimes is more dangerous than the terminal disease itself. Because you can cure, you can fight and live as long as possible with the assistance of drugs, but a stigma, it destroys your self-confidence.
OPENING OF THE ZOLA CLINIC, SOWETO, SOUTH AFRICA, 7 MARCH 2002

To my mind, nothing can be more heart-rending and in need of urgent attention than the case of AIDS orphans who so often find themselves rejected and ostracised by communities. Personally nothing can shake me more than the sight of these innocent young children suffering physically, socially and emotionally as the consequence of actions and behaviour which they had no control over or part in.
CLOSING ADDRESS TO THE XIV INTERNATIONAL AIDS CONFERENCE, BARCELONA, SPAIN, 12 JULY 2002

As one who had led almost the entirety of his life in a struggle to build a better world, often against odds that were thought insurmountable, I want to say to all of you who are activists in the war against AIDS, 'You have my greatest admiration. Keep on fighting and you will overcome this terrible scourge threatening humankind.'
IBID

We are all human, and the HIV/AIDS epidemic affects us all in the end. If we discard people who are dying from AIDS, then we can no longer call ourselves people.
IBID

Together we can and must win this war against the most serious scourge humankind has faced in centuries.
LAUNCH OF THE NELSON MANDELA/HSRC PRESS STUDY OF AIDS, JOHANNESBURG, SOUTH AFRICA,
SEPTEMBER 2002

The fight against AIDS will indeed require another social revolution. Once more the youth of our country are called upon to play a leading role in a social revolution as they did so heroically in the revolutionary struggle against apartheid.
YOUTH FORUM ON AIDS, UNIVERSITY OF THE WITWATERSRAND, JOHANNESBURG, SOUTH AFRICA,
22 SEPTEMBER 2002

HIV doesn't just happen like getting a cold; it is a consequence of unsafe sex.
We all have to take responsibility for our behaviour. And I want specifically to say to parents: talk openly and often to your children about HIV, sex and relationships.
CEREMONY TO CELEBRATE THE PARTNERSHIP BETWEEN THE NELSON MANDELA FOUNDATION AND
THE KAISER FAMILY FOUNDATION IN SUPPORT OF THE LOVELIFE INITIATIVE, JOHANNESBURG, SOUTH AFRICA,
28 SEPTEMBER 2002

Let us speak openly about sexuality, about relationships, about HIV/AIDS and about how we can contribute to and be part of that battle against the pandemic. The battle starts with awareness.
LAUNCH OF THE AIDS AWARENESS STRATEGY FOR THE CONSTRUCTION INDUSTRY, NELSON MANDELA
NATIONAL MUSEUM, QUNU, SOUTH AFRICA, 21 OCTOBER 2002

We must love, encourage and inspire people who are HIV-positive. This is the greatest contribution we can make in the fight against AIDS.
NOLUNGILE, KHAYELITSHA, CAPE TOWN, SOUTH AFRICA, 12 DECEMBER 2002

The fight against HIV/AIDS offers us the opportunity to once more reach deeply into that pool of humane caring and human compassion that characterised us as a people in our struggle against apartheid. Once more, our people from all backgrounds, genders or age groups shall rally to a call to come together to save our nation from destruction.
YOUTH FORUM ON AIDS, UNIVERSITY OF THE WITWATERSRAND, JOHANNESBURG, SOUTH AFRICA,
22 SEPTEMBER 2003

HIV/AIDS is having a devastating impact on families, communities, societies and economies. Decades have been chopped from life expectancy and young child mortality is expected to more than double in the most severely affected countries of Africa, including South Africa. AIDS is clearly a disaster, effectively wiping out the development gains of the past decades and sabotaging the future.
IBID

We have in our lives fought and won many good battles. Today we are called upon once more to do battle and win the fight against HIV/AIDS as well as that against the inhumane treatment of children. We dare not give up or succumb.
ANNUAL CHILDREN'S CELEBRATIONS, BLOEMFONTEIN, SOUTH AFRICA, 27 SEPTEMBER 2003

Today as we reconstruct and develop our country, we find ourselves faced by an even greater enemy and threat, this time in the form of HIV/AIDS. This pandemic threatens our future in ways and on a scale that we could not have imagined.

PRESS CONFERENCE FOR 46664 CAMPAIGN, ROBBEN ISLAND, CAPE TOWN, SOUTH AFRICA, 28 NOVEMBER 2003

46664 was my prison number. For the eighteen years that I was imprisoned on Robben Island I was supposed to be reduced to that number. Millions of people infected with HIV/AIDS are in danger of being reduced to mere numbers unless we act. They too are serving a prison sentence – for life. So I have allowed my prison number '46664' to help drive this campaign.

46664 CONCERT, GREENPOINT STADIUM, CAPE TOWN, SOUTH AFRICA, 29 NOVEMBER 2003

AIDS is no longer just a disease: it is a human rights issue.

IBID

We must ensure that treatment is made available to those who need it, most especially to those who cannot afford it. Health cannot be a question of income; it is a fundamental human right. We must give people hope that it is possible to lead a healthy, fulfilling life even with HIV/AIDS.

LAUNCH OF SOUTH AFRICA'S FIRST PUBLIC-PRIVATE AIDS TREATMENT SITE, GF JOOSTE HOSPITAL, CAPE TOWN, SOUTH AFRICA, 1 DECEMBER 2003

The most basic dignity, the right to live and to live healthily, is under threat from this destructive pandemic.

TWENTY-EIGHTH INTERNATIONAL RED CROSS AND RED CRESCENT CONFERENCE, GENEVA, SWITZERLAND, 2 DECEMBER 2003

There are medicines that help turn HIV from a death sentence to a chronic illness for those who receive treatment. There are other medicines that keep mothers and pregnant women from passing it on to their newborn.

LAUNCH OF A CD AND DVD FOR 46664 CAMPAIGN, 1 APRIL 2004

The fight against AIDS is one of the greatest challenges the world faces at the start of the twenty-first century.

CLOSING ADDRESS TO THE XV INTERNATIONAL AIDS CONFERENCE, BANGKOK, THAILAND, 16 JULY 2004

In the course of human history, there has never been a greater threat than the HIV/AIDS epidemic. Our attention to this issue cannot be distracted or diverted by problems that are apparently more pressing. History will surely judge us harshly if we do not respond with all the energy and resources that we can bring to bear in the fight against HIV/AIDS.

IBID

My son has died of AIDS.

PRESS CONFERENCE ANNOUNCING THE DEATH OF HIS SON, MAKGATHO, OF AIDS, JOHANNESBURG, SOUTH AFRICA, 6 JANUARY 2005

I hope that as time goes on we will realise that it is important for us to talk openly about people who die from AIDS.

IBID

Let us give publicity to HIV/AIDS and not hide it, because the only way of making it appear to be a normal illness, just like TB [tuberculosis], like cancer, is always to come out and to say somebody has died because of HIV. And people will stop regarding it as something extraordinary, as an illness reserved for people who are going to hell and not to heaven.

IBID

Give a voice to the women of Africa in the fight against HIV and AIDS. Let their voices be heard in the centres of power. Let their voices be heard in the home. Let their voices be heard in the farms and factories, in the towns and villages.

46664 CONCERT, FANCOURT, GEORGE, SOUTH AFRICA, 19 MARCH 2005

We urge you to add your voice to the groundswell that is surely gathering around the world. The more we lack the courage and the will to act, the more we condemn to death our brothers and sisters, our children and our grandchildren. When the history of our times is written, will we be remembered as the generation that turned our backs in a moment of global crisis or will it be recorded that we did the right thing?

46664 CONCERT, TROMSO, NORWAY, 11 JUNE 2005

We live in a world where the AIDS pandemic threatens the very fabric of our lives. Yet we spend more money on weapons than on ensuring treatment and support for the millions infected by HIV. It is a world of great promise and hope. It is also a world of despair, disease and hunger.

LIVE 8 CONCERT, MARY FITZGERALD SQUARE, JOHANNESBURG, SOUTH AFRICA, 2 JULY 2005

AIDS has killed more people than in all the wars and we need to protect ourselves, our children and grandchildren in every possible way against the disease. We cannot allow a disease to destroy the future of our freedom.

RALLY FOR 46664 TORCH RELAY, MIDDELBURG, SOUTH AFRICA, 22 JULY 2005

HIV/AIDS is the greatest challenge facing our nation, which requires a committed, long-term response that coordinates comprehensive prevention, treatment, care and support at all levels.

MEDIA STATEMENT, 5 NOVEMBER 2005

We know that the AIDS pandemic affects us all, and that it is women who bear the most significant burden of HIV and AIDS. As daughters, mothers, sisters and grandmothers, every day they experience and live out the reality of this pandemic. They are the forgotten prisoners of today.

UPON RECEIVING THE AMBASSADOR OF CONSCIENCE AWARD FROM AMNESTY INTERNATIONAL,
NELSON MANDELA FOUNDATION, JOHANNESBURG, SOUTH AFRICA, 1 NOVEMBER 2006

We have to act, we have to act decisively and, above all, we must work together. The answer to turning around the devastating impact of this epidemic lies within us.

MESSAGE FOR WORLD AIDS DAY, 1 DECEMBER 2006

One of the greatest challenges we face is gaping – and growing – disparities in the response to HIV between countries and regions around the world. AIDS-related stigma and discrimination are pervasive and real barriers to stopping the expansion of this disease.

IBID

We are deeply concerned about the devastating HIV/AIDS epidemic and it is our dearest wish that people around the globe will help to get rid of the stigma that surrounds this tragic disease. In doing so, we will assist those living with HIV/AIDS to realise their hopes and dreams for a longer life and a brighter future.

RECORDED MESSAGE FOR SANYA, CHINA, DATE UNKNOWN

AIDS is an exceptional disease and requires an equally exceptional response. It requires strong leadership at international, national and indeed at community level.

RECORDED MESSAGE FOR AN INTERNATIONAL AIDS VACCINE CONFERENCE, DATE UNKNOWN

HIV/AIDS affects and poses a threat to every sector of society but it is the effects on children that are probably the most heart-rending and that pose the greatest challenge to our sense of compassion and caring.

FROM PROMOTIONAL DVD, *THE NELSON MANDELA FOUNDATION*

Apartheid

The African people have raised their voices in condemnation of grinding poverty, the low wages, the acute shortages of land, the inhuman exploitation and the whole policy of white domination. But instead of more freedom, repression began to grow in volume and intensity.

PRESIDENTIAL ADDRESS TO THE ANC TRANSVAAL CONGRESS, ALSO KNOWN AS THE 'NO EASY WALK TO FREEDOM' SPEECH, TRANSVAAL, SOUTH AFRICA, 21 SEPTEMBER 1953

The racial policies of the government have pricked the conscience of all men of goodwill and have aroused their deepest indignation. The feelings of the oppressed people have never been more bitter.

IBID

Every facet of national life is becoming subordinated to the overriding necessity of the party's retention of power. All constitutional safeguards are being thrown overboard and individual liberties are being ruthlessly suppressed.

FROM AN ARTICLE ENTITLED 'PEOPLE ARE DESTROYED', *LIBERATION*, OCTOBER 1955

The breaking up of African homes and families and the forcible separation of children from mothers, the harsh treatment meted out to African prisoners, and the forcible detention of Africans in farm colonies for spurious statutory offences are a few examples of the actual workings of the hideous and pernicious doctrines of racial inequality.

IBID

We cannot for one moment forget that we are up against a fascist government which has built up a massive coercive state apparatus to crush democracy in this country and to silence the voice of all those who cry out against the policy of apartheid and baasskap.

FROM AN ARTICLE ENTITLED 'BANTU EDUCATION GOES TO UNIVERSITY', *LIBERATION*, JUNE 1957

People without votes cannot be expected to go on paying taxes to a government of white domination. People who live in poverty cannot be expected to pay rents under threats of criminal prosecution and imprisonment. Above all, those who are oppressed cannot tolerate a situation where their own people man and maintain the machinery of their own national oppression.

STATEMENT ON BEHALF OF THE NATIONAL ACTION COUNCIL FOLLOWING THE 29–31 MAY 1961 STAY-AT-HOME IN SUPPORT OF A NATIONAL CONVENTION, SOUTH AFRICA, 1961

I consider myself neither legally nor morally bound to obey laws made by a parliament in which I have no representation.

FROM HIS APPLICATION FOR THE RECUSAL OF THE MAGISTRATE MR WA VAN HELSDINGEN, OLD SYNAGOGUE, PRETORIA, SOUTH AFRICA, 22 OCTOBER 1962

In its efforts to keep the African people in a position of perpetual subordination, South Africa must and will fail.

IN MITIGATION OF SENTENCE AFTER BEING CONVICTED OF INCITING WORKERS TO STRIKE AND LEAVING THE COUNTRY ILLEGALLY, OLD SYNAGOGUE, PRETORIA, SOUTH AFRICA, 7 NOVEMBER 1962

I hate the racial arrogance which decrees that the good things of life shall be retained as the exclusive right of a minority of the population to a position of subservience and inferiority, and maintains them as voteless chattels to work where they are told and behave as they are told by the ruling minority.

IBID

The law as it is applied, the law as it has been developed over a long period of history, and especially the law as it is written and designed by the Nationalist government is a law which, in our view, is *immoral, unjust and intolerable*. Our consciences dictate that we must oppose it and that we must attempt to alter it.

IBID

The whites enjoy what may well be the highest standard of living in the world, whilst Africans live in poverty and misery.

SPEECH FROM THE DOCK, RIVONIA TRIAL, PALACE OF JUSTICE, PRETORIA, SOUTH AFRICA, 20 APRIL 1964

The lack of human dignity experienced by Africans is the direct result of the policy of white supremacy.

IBID

Apartheid was conceived as a means of preserving white supremacy forever. But when it became clear that we would resist it to the bitter end and that colonialism was in full retreat everywhere, the regime changed its tune and decided to grant self-government to the Bantustans with a view to ultimate independence.

FROM AN ESSAY ENTITLED 'CLEAR THE OBSTACLES AND CONFRONT THE ENEMY', WRITTEN ON ROBBEN ISLAND, 1976

For three centuries the whites have tried to tell the black man that he has no history, civilisation or identity to be proud of: that only whites have a past, a cultural heritage and a common awareness of their mission in life.

FROM AN ESSAY ENTITLED 'WHITHER THE BLACK CONSCIOUSNESS MOVEMENT', WRITTEN ON ROBBEN ISLAND, 1978

Victory is certain. The revulsion of the world against apartheid is growing and the frontiers of white supremacy are shrinking.

STATEMENT ABOUT THE 1976 SOWETO UPRISING, SMUGGLED OUT OF ROBBEN ISLAND PRISON AND RELEASED BY THE ANC IN EXILE, 1980

That verdict is loud and clear: apartheid has failed. Our people remain unequivocal in its rejection. The young and the old, parent and child, all reject it.

IBID

Apartheid is the rule of the gun and the hangman. The Hippo, the FN rifle and the gallows are its true symbols. These remain the easiest resort, the ever-ready solution of the race-mad rulers of South Africa.

IBID

Apartheid is the embodiment of the racialism, repression and inhumanity of all previous white supremacist regimes. To see the real face of apartheid we must look beneath the veil of constitutional formulas, deceptive phrases and playing with words.

IBID

Despite all the window-dressing and smooth talk, apartheid has become intolerable. This awareness reaches over and beyond the particulars of our enslavement. The measure of this truth is the recognition by our people that under apartheid our lives, individually and collectively, count for nothing.

IBID

Apartheid, which is condemned not only by blacks but also by a substantial section of the whites, is the greatest single source of violence against our people.

FROM A LETTER TO PRESIDENT PW BOTHA, WRITTEN IN POLLSMOOR PRISON, CAPE TOWN, SOUTH AFRICA, 13 FEBRUARY 1985

The apartheid system has devastated the country. Poverty is rampant and endemic. The conditions of life for the people continue to worsen every day.

ADDRESS TO THE FRENCH NATIONAL ASSEMBLY, BOURBON PALACE, PARIS, FRANCE, 7 JUNE 1990

It will forever remain an indelible blight on human history that the apartheid crime ever occurred.

UNITED NATIONS SPECIAL COMMITTEE AGAINST APARTHEID, UNITED NATIONS, NEW YORK CITY, USA, 22 JUNE 1990

It would have been immoral to keep quiet while a racist tyranny sought to reduce an entire people into a status worse than that of the beasts of the forest.

ADDRESS TO THE JOINT SESSION OF THE HOUSE OF CONGRESS, WASHINGTON DC, USA, 26 JUNE 1990

It was impossible to sit still while the obscenity of apartheid was being imposed on our people.

IBID

The sun has begun to set on the evil system of apartheid. We can see the day dawn [when] black people will no longer be condemned to be servants to others simply because these have white skins.

RALLY, MAPUTO, MOZAMBIQUE, 16 JULY 1990

We must move with all possible speed to abolish the apartheid system and to transform South Africa into a united, democratic, non-racial and non-sexist country.

RALLY TO RELAUNCH THE SACP (SOUTH AFRICAN COMMUNIST PARTY), SOUTH AFRICA, 29 JULY 1990

Apartheid, you see, has been something you see; it's a modern form of Nazism where one race claims that it is superior to another and where they rely purely on brute force. Killing people simply because they are demonstrating against what they consider to be injustice and the very fact of using bullets when they are dealing with defenceless crowds, that's a form of Nazism.

FROM A CONVERSATION WITH RICHARD STENGEL, 29 APRIL 1993

You know the brutality of the apartheid regime has been most alarming.

FROM AN INTERVIEW, 1993

Forty years of apartheid have been like forty years of war. Our economy and our social life have been completely devastated, in some respects beyond repair. That was the situation in Europe before the last war. What the Western world did was to mobilise their resources and introduce Marshall Plan aid to ensure that the countries of Europe devastated by war recovered.

SOURCE UNKNOWN

Ours has been a bitterly divided society in which laws and the police were used to defend and maintain an illegitimate system.

NATIONAL DAY OF SAFETY AND SECURITY, VOSLOORUS, SOUTH AFRICA, 15 OCTOBER 1994

Enforced division has engendered in our people a powerful urge towards unity as a condition for freedom and peace.

PRESIDENT'S BUDGET DEBATE IN THE SENATE, CAPE TOWN, SOUTH AFRICA, 18 JUNE 1996

No society emerging out of the grand disaster represented by the apartheid system could afford to carry the blemishes of its past. Had the new South Africa emerged out of nothing, it would not exist. The being it has assumed, dictated by its origins, constitutes a veritable school of learning about what needs to be done, still, to end the system of apartheid.

ADDRESS TO THE JOINT HOUSES OF PARLIAMENT, WESTMINSTER HALL, LONDON, ENGLAND, 11 JULY 1996

We know, and the majority of South Africans know from their daily experiences, that apartheid continues to live with us: in the leaking roofs and corrugated walls of shacks; in the bulging stomachs of hungry children; in the darkness of homes without electricity; and in the heavy pails of dirty water that rural women carry for long distances to cook and to quench their thirst.

FOREIGN CORRESPONDENTS' ASSOCIATION ANNUAL DINNER, JOHANNESBURG, SOUTH AFRICA, 21 NOVEMBER 1997

The apartheid regime had put law and order in disrepute. The human rights of the majority of the population were ruthlessly suppressed, there was detention without trial, torture and murder of political activists, open criticism of the Appeal Court judges who were independent and gave judgement against the regime, and the packing of the judiciary with conservative lawyers.

FROM THE UNPUBLISHED SEQUEL TO HIS AUTOBIOGRAPHY, CIRCA 1998

We are extricating ourselves from a system that insulted our common humanity by dividing us from one another on the basis of race and setting us against each other [as] oppressed and oppressor.

UPON RECEIVING THE REPORT OF THE TRC (TRUTH AND RECONCILIATION COMMISSION), PRETORIA, SOUTH AFRICA, 29 OCTOBER 1998

Together we can continue to replace the darkness of apartheid with the light of freedom, peace and development.

ADDRESS AT THE OPENING OF THE PRESIDENT'S BUDGET DEBATE, PARLIAMENT, CAPE TOWN, SOUTH AFRICA, 2 MARCH 1999

All of us had encountered an illegal, inhuman system called apartheid that sought to suppress our unstoppable yearning to be free in the land of our birth.

ELECTION RALLY, SOWETO, SOUTH AFRICA, 1999

We defeated apartheid because the people of our country decided to work together rather than destroy one another and in the process destroy our entire country.

PRESS CONFERENCE FOR 46664 CAMPAIGN, ROBBEN ISLAND, CAPE TOWN, SOUTH AFRICA, 28 NOVEMBER 2003

We came together as a nation to end the scourge of apartheid. Today we are challenged to end poverty and all its attendant suffering.

ANC RALLY FOR HIS NINETIETH BIRTHDAY, LOFTUS VERSFELD STADIUM, PRETORIA, SOUTH AFRICA, 2 AUGUST 2008

Appearance

A rapidly increasing weight has induced me to cut out lunch and the afternoon snack.

FROM A LETTER TO BRIGADIER KEULDER, COMMANDING OFFICER, WRITTEN IN VICTOR VERSTER PRISON, PAARL, SOUTH AFRICA, 9 OCTOBER 1989

Sometimes you get attached to something, you know? And I just got attached to the beard.

FROM A CONVERSATION WITH AHMED KATHRADA, TALKING ABOUT WHY HE REFUSED TO SHAVE OFF HIS DISTINCTIVE BEARD WHEN HE WAS UNDERGROUND, CIRCA 1993/94

Archbishop [Desmond] Tutu and I discussed this matter. He said to me, '... Mr President, I think you are doing well in everything except the way you dress.' Well, I said to the Archbishop, whom I respect very much, I said, 'Well, let's not enter a discussion where there can be no solution'.

AFTER A VISIT WITH MRS BETSIE VERWOERD, ORANIA, SOUTH AFRICA, 15 AUGUST 1995

Every time I put on that thing I can't even talk. I find it difficult even to talk.

TALKING TO HIS ASSISTANTS WHO WANT HIM TO WEAR A BOW TIE TO THE OFFICIAL INAUGURATION DINNER, FROM THE DOCUMENTARY *MANDELA*, 1996

When one of my famous nephews was asked by the media, 'What do you think of the way in which your uncle dresses?' he said, 'Very disgraceful. A president should always wear a suit, a white shirt, a tie and a hat. My uncle dresses disgracefully. He dresses like a drunkard.'

UPON RECEIVING THE REPORT OF THE TRC (TRUTH AND RECONCILIATION COMMISSION), PRETORIA, SOUTH AFRICA, 29 OCTOBER 1998

If there is anything I can boast about it is that I am taller than the President of the United States of America.

REFERRING TO PRESIDENT JIMMY CARTER AT THE OPENING OF THE ZOLA CLINIC, SOWETO, SOUTH AFRICA, 7 MARCH 2002

It must not disturb my hair, I took an hour combing it.

PUTTING HEADPHONES ON UPSIDE DOWN, FROM THE DOCUMENTARY *MANDELA: THE LIVING LEGEND*, 2003

I have never liked those shoes with pointed noses.

FROM THE DOCUMENTARY *MANDELA AT 90*, 2008

Appreciation

It is always a source of great comfort to know that your efforts are widely appreciated.

FROM A LETTER TO HELEN SUZMAN, WRITTEN ON ROBBEN ISLAND, 1 MARCH 1974

Before I went to jail I was very arrogant, I behaved like an animal to people who were kind to me and I decided that if ever I get a chance, I will make them appreciate what they did to me, they will know that I appreciate it.

FROM THE DOCUMENTARY *MANDELA: THE LIVING LEGEND*, 2003

Armed Struggle

There are many people who feel that the reaction of the government to our stay-at-home: ordering a general mobilisation; arming the white community against tens of thousands of Africans; the show of force throughout the country; notwithstanding our clear declaration that this campaign is being run on peaceful and non-violent lines, closed a chapter as far as our methods of political struggle are concerned.

FROM AN INTERVIEW WITH BRIAN WIDLAKE FOR ITN TELEVISION (UK), JOHANNESBURG, SOUTH AFRICA, 31 MAY 1961

There are many people who feel it is useless and futile for us to continue talking peace and non-violence against a government whose reply is only savage attacks on an unarmed and defenceless people and I think the time has come for us to consider, in the light of our experiences in this stay-at-home, whether the methods which we have applied so far are adequate.

IBID

Even up to the present day the question that is being asked with monotonous regularity up and down the country, is this: is it politically correct to continue preaching peace and non-violence when dealing with a government whose barbaric practices have brought so much suffering and misery to Africans?

STATEMENT ON BEHALF OF THE NATIONAL ACTION COUNCIL FOLLOWING THE 29–31 MAY 1961 STAY-AT-HOME IN SUPPORT OF A NATIONAL CONVENTION, SOUTH AFRICA, 1961

In a country where freedom fighters pay with their very lives and at a time when the most elaborate military preparations are made to crush the people's struggles, planned acts of sabotage against government installations introduce a new phase in the political situation and are a demonstration of the people's unshakeable determination to win freedom whatever the cost may be.

ADDRESS ON BEHALF OF THE ANC DELEGATION TO THE PAFMECA (PAN AFRICAN FREEDOM MOVEMENT OF EAST AND CENTRAL AFRICA) CONFERENCE, ADDIS ABABA, ETHIOPIA, 3 FEBRUARY 1962

They set the scene for violence by relying exclusively on violence with which to answer our people and their demands. The countermeasures which they took clearly reflected growing uneasiness on their part, which grew out of the knowledge that their policy did not enjoy the support of the majority of the people, while ours did.

IN MITIGATION OF SENTENCE AFTER BEING CONVICTED OF INCITING WORKERS TO STRIKE AND LEAVING THE COUNTRY ILLEGALLY, OLD SYNAGOGUE, PRETORIA, SOUTH AFRICA, 7 NOVEMBER 1962

I do not, however, deny that I planned sabotage. I did not plan it in a spirit of recklessness, nor because I have any love of violence. I planned it as a result of a calm and sober assessment of the political situation that had arisen after many years of tyranny, exploitation and oppression of my people by the whites.

SPEECH FROM THE DOCK, RIVONIA TRIAL, PALACE OF JUSTICE, PRETORIA, SOUTH AFRICA, 20 APRIL 1964

We believed that as a result of government policy, violence by the African people had become inevitable, and that unless responsible leadership was given to canalise and control the feelings of our people, there would be outbreaks of terrorism which would produce an intensity of bitterness and hostility between the various races of this country which is not produced even by war.
IBID

We had no doubt that we had to continue the fight. Anything else would have been abject surrender. Our problem was not whether to fight, but was how to continue the fight.
IBID

I started to make a study of the art of war and revolution and, whilst abroad, underwent a course in military training. If there was to be guerrilla warfare, I wanted to be able to stand and fight with my people and to share the hazards of war with them.
IBID

MK [Umkhonto we Sizwe] decided that I should investigate whether facilities were available for the training of soldiers which was the first stage in the preparation for guerrilla warfare.
IBID

At the beginning of June, 1961, after a long and anxious assessment of the South African situation, I and some colleagues, came to the conclusion that, as violence in the country was inevitable, it would be unrealistic and wrong for African leaders to continue preaching peace and non-violence at a time when the government met our peaceful demands with force.
IBID

We first broke the law in a way which avoided any recourse to violence; when this form was legislated against, and then the government resorted to a show of force to crush opposition to its policies, only then did we decide to answer violence with violence.
IBID

All lawful modes of expressing opposition to this principle had been closed by legislation, and we were placed in a position in which we had either to accept a permanent state of inferiority, or to defy the government. We chose to defy the law.
IBID

Sabotage did not involve loss of life, and it offered the best hope for future race relations. Bitterness would be kept to a minimum and, if the policy bore fruit, democratic government could become a reality.
IBID

The avoidance of civil war had dominated our thinking for many years, but when we decided to adopt violence as part of our policy, we realised that we might one day have to face the prospect of such a war.
IBID

Experience convinced us that rebellion would offer the government limitless opportunities for the indiscriminate slaughter of our people. But it was precisely because the soil of South Africa is already drenched with the blood of innocent Africans that we felt it our duty to make preparations as a long-term undertaking to use force in order to defend ourselves against force.

IBID

It was only when all else had failed, when all channels of peaceful protest had been barred to us, that the decision was made to embark on violent forms of political struggle, and to form Umkhonto we Sizwe.

IBID

I can only say that I felt morally obliged to do what I did.

IBID

Umkhonto [we Sizwe] was to perform sabotage, and strict instructions were given to its members right from the start, that on no account were they to injure or kill people in planning or carrying out operations.

IBID

In such a situation resort to violence was the inevitable alternative of freedom fighters who had the courage of their convictions. No men of principle and integrity could have done otherwise. To have folded arms would have been an act of surrender to a government of minority rule and a betrayal of our cause. World history in general, and that of South Africa in particular, teaches that resort to violence may in certain cases be perfectly legitimate.

FROM A LETTER TO THE MINISTER OF JUSTICE, WRITTEN ON ROBBEN ISLAND, APRIL 1969

Few of our men had received professional training in sabotage. On the whole they acquitted themselves well and deserved the praise heaped upon them. However, we were not strong enough to maintain the offensive.

FROM AN ESSAY ENTITLED 'CLEAR THE OBSTACLES AND CONFRONT THE ENEMY', WRITTEN ON ROBBEN ISLAND, 1976

We have always favoured peaceful settlement and urged our people to avoid violence. But the regime took advantage of our desire for peace and burdened us with more repression, forcing us to turn to violence.

IBID

Within twenty-four months the regime had cracked down on us, crippled our organisations and stamped out the acts of sabotage.

IBID

Having been forced to abandon sabotage, which was relatively easy to execute, we now concentrated on the more difficult preparations for the armed struggle. MK [Umkhonto we Sizwe] began sending out recruits for military training in 1962.

IBID

Acts of sabotage were snuffed out because, in our enthusiasm for violence as a weapon to strike at the enemy, we neglected the important work of strengthening the political organisations by recruiting new members, holding branch meetings, conducting political classes and using legal platforms to reach the masses of the people.

IBID

Both the ANC and the PAC [Pan Africanist Congress] have well-trained and disciplined detachments whose mere existence should be a source of pride to us all and which remind us of olden times when we commanded our own armies and could defend our freedom.

IBID

An armed struggle is not a question of simply acquiring a gun and shooting. The people should be drawn in and for every man in the front line there should be ten others to help in the fight.

IBID

From the beginning, the aim should be to develop the armed struggle into a people's war. Victory is impossible if we fail in this.

IBID

The intensification of apartheid, the banning of political organisations and the closing of all channels of peaceful protest conflicted sharply with these principles and forced the ANC to turn to violence.

FROM A LETTER TO PRESIDENT PW BOTHA, WRITTEN IN POLLSMOOR PRISON, CAPE TOWN, SOUTH AFRICA, 13 FEBRUARY 1985

The factors which necessitated the armed struggle still exist today. We have no option but to continue. We express the hope that a climate conducive to a negotiated settlement will be created soon so that there may no longer be the need for the armed struggle.

FIRST SPEECH AFTER HIS RELEASE, CITY HALL, CAPE TOWN, SOUTH AFRICA, 11 FEBRUARY 1990

The armed struggle is merely defensive, is a defensive act against the violence of apartheid.

FIRST PRESS CONFERENCE AFTER HIS RELEASE, ARCHBISHOP DESMOND TÚTU'S RESIDENCE, BISHOPSCOURT, CAPE TOWN, SOUTH AFRICA, 12 FEBRUARY 1990

Until apartheid has been dismantled, there is no reason why we should consider suspending, abandoning the armed struggle. The armed struggle will continue as we announced way back in 1961; it will continue until the basic demands of the people are met.

AT HOME, SOWETO, SOUTH AFRICA, FEBRUARY 1990

If we had peaceful channels of communication, we would never have thought of resorting to violence. If there was not the violence of apartheid, there would never have been violence from our side.

IBID

When we decided to take up arms, it was because the only other choice was to surrender and to submit to slavery.

FORTY-EIGHTH ANC NATIONAL CONFERENCE, DURBAN, SOUTH AFRICA, 2 JULY 1991

If Mr de Klerk promises to do his duty as the head of government, to put an end to the violence, to restrain his security services, to clean the country of hit squads and other elements which are responsible for killing innocent people, then he can come to us and say: I want you to hand over your weapons to us for joint control. But as long as he's playing this double game, he must be clear that we are not going to cooperate with him on this matter. He can do what he likes. We are not going to disband Umkhonto we Sizwe.

RESPONSE TO FW DE KLERK'S FIRST SESSION OF MULTI-PARTY NEGOTIATIONS, WORLD TRADE CENTER, KEMPTON PARK, SOUTH AFRICA, 20 DECEMBER 1991

Although we had no hope of defeating the enemy in the battlefield, nevertheless, we fought back to keep the idea of liberation alive.

FROM A CONVERSATION WITH RICHARD STENGEL, 13 JANUARY 1993

When the only way of making a forward movement, of solving problems, is the use of force, when peaceful methods become inadequate. That is a lesson of history, right down the centuries and in every part of the world.

FROM A CONVERSATION WITH RICHARD STENGEL, 8 FEBRUARY 1993

We want dignified guerrilla warfare, armed struggle where we are guided by principles, where we save lives, where we hit the symbols of oppression. And, if it's a terrorist organisation, it's going to lead to the slaughter of human beings.

FROM A CONVERSATION WITH RICHARD STENGEL, 5 APRIL 1993

Umkhonto [spear] was a powerful weapon amongst the African and they fought their wars with the assegai and they resisted white supremacy for centuries with the spear. And therefore it is something that is very symbolic, very emotional, and we used that.

IBID

The idea was to attack installations, government installations, which were the symbol of oppression. But as the judge said, in the Rivonia Trial, care – that was his finding – care was taken by the MK [Umkhonto we Sizwe] not to injure life, civilian life.

FROM A CONVERSATION WITH RICHARD STENGEL, 9 APRIL 1993

The conditions inside the country were not yet ripe for us to start guerrilla warfare inside the country before these other countries around us are free. I said we must operate from those bases bordering our country, and that is what eventually succeeded.

FROM A CONVERSATION WITH RICHARD STENGEL, 17 APRIL 1993

Umkhonto we Sizwe has, on its own, voluntarily decided to suspend armed action in order to contribute towards the creation of an atmosphere of a climate ideal for a peaceful solution. At first I was not happy about this but when I thought about it at night I thought this was a good tactic and I accepted it and I told Joe [Slovo] that if he raises it in the National Executive I'll support him. That is how the suspension of Umkhonto we Sizwe originated.

FROM A CONVERSATION WITH RICHARD STENGEL, 23 APRIL 1993

When you are going to be a leader of a guerrilla army, you must know what guerrilla warfare means, how it is brought about and you must know how to use a gun and you must know the whole military science. The idea was to fight a war and to change the system by fighting, and the death of human beings you see, was unavoidable.

FROM A CONVERSATION WITH AHMED KATHRADA, CIRCA 1993/94

You can't avoid casualties when you are starting a new method of political activity.

IBID

We were dealing with a strong government, a strong enemy who had the facilities to move around and to be able to detect what was being done on the ground. Under those circumstances, we could only train just a few.

IBID

We wanted to create a force, a military force, which was under a central, political organisation where they took instructions from the political organisation and that is the principle on which it was established.
IBID

It was only when I went to Ethiopia that I actually received military training and also supplemented by training in Morocco.
IBID

We stressed that that training must go hand in hand with political training. They must know why they are going to take up arms and fight. They must be taught that the revolution was not just a question of pulling a trigger and firing – it was an organisation that was intended to take over political power.
IBID

I was then the first Commander of Umkhonto we Sizwe. It was natural that I should be sent out to go and persuade the international community as to the reasons why we took these steps, to train our people and to provide us with resources.
FROM AN INTERVIEW, 1993

We have never been under any misconception that we would be able to achieve a military victory against this regime. We knew we had the advantage of numbers, and therefore the potential to defeat this government in due course. But what we were determined to do was for the oppressed people in this country to be able to stand on their feet and to strike back.
SPEAKING AT THE UNIVERSITY OF KWAZULU-NATAL, DURBAN, SOUTH AFRICA, 1993

In that situation we had no alternative but to resort to armed struggle. But we made it clear, even as we took that decision, that the responsibility rested squarely on the shoulders of the government and that we could refrain from this action even at this eleventh hour if the government agreed to meet and to sit down with us.
FROM A BBC (UK) DOCUMENTARY, 1996

The achievements we have made would not have been possible without the staunch loyalty of our armed forces, without their unwavering dedication to the country and its people.
FREEDOM DAY CELEBRATIONS, MTHATHA, SOUTH AFRICA, 27 APRIL 1999

It was always our view that the methods of the oppressor in the end influenced the resistance methods. And our armed struggle was never simple-minded violence; it was always a politically supervised manner of bringing sanity to those intent upon violently subjecting the people of our country.
INAUGURATION OF A MONUMENT TO THE PASSIVE RESISTANCE CAMPAIGN, UMBILO PARK, DURBAN, SOUTH AFRICA, 27 MAY 2002

Arrest

The world around me literally crumbled, income disappeared and many obligations could not be honoured.
FROM A LETTER TO ZINDZI MANDELA ABOUT BEING ARRESTED FOR TREASON IN 1956, WRITTEN ON ROBBEN ISLAND, 1 MARCH 1981

I realised that to try and get away would be a gamble.

REVISITING THE SITE OF HIS 5 AUGUST 1962 ARREST, HOWICK, SOUTH AFRICA, 15 NOVEMBER 1993

The arrest itself was done very courteously, very politely.

IBID

The policeman was doing his duty, he did it according to the law, he was courteous. He treated me with respect and I had no reason to be bitter at all about a policeman doing his duty. Where we get annoyed is where the police abuse their powers and do things which are impermissible.

IBID

I decided the game was up.

FROM A CONVERSATION WITH AHMED KATHRADA, CIRCA 1993/94

Arts, The

Good use of photography can give even poverty with all its rags, filth and vermin a measure of divineness rarely noticeable in real life.

FROM A LETTER TO ZINDZI MANDELA, WRITTEN ON ROBBEN ISLAND, 27 JANUARY 1980

Good art is invariably universal and timeless.

FROM A LETTER TO ZINDZI MANDELA, WRITTEN ON ROBBEN ISLAND, 10 FEBRUARY 1980

During the worst years of repression, when all avenues of legitimate protest were closed by emergency legislation, it was the arts that articulated the plight and the democratic aspirations of our people. This affirmation was demonstrated through drama, dance, literature, song, film, paintings and sculpture that defied the silence that apartheid sought to impose.

OPENING OF THE CULTURAL DEVELOPMENT CONGRESS AT THE CIVIC THEATRE, JOHANNESBURG, SOUTH AFRICA, 25 APRIL 1993

Few South Africans have not been moved by Miriam Makeba's haunting melodies that have given voice to the pain of exile and dislocation, at the same time inspiring a powerful sense of hope. And many have been inspired by the strains of hope and despair woven into one, in the powerful renditions of Vusi Mahlasela and Johnny Clegg.

PRESIDENT'S BUDGET DEBATE IN THE SENATE, PARLIAMENT, SOUTH AFRICA, 18 JUNE 1996

Our artists and writers have combined a fierce attachment to the particular culture in which they are rooted with an equally strong love of the South African nation as a whole.

IBID

We can only achieve that better life for ordinary people and citizens on our continent if we take seriously and give priority to those simple precepts of humanity that literature, good literature, always deals with. We can achieve that if we ensure that literature and the pursuits of the human spirit are taken seriously and accorded value in our society and our societal pursuits.

BANQUET CELEBRATING AFRICA'S 100 BEST BOOKS OF THE TWENTIETH CENTURY, CAPE TOWN, SOUTH AFRICA, JULY 2002

Assassination

There is no threat from the left-wing, so-called radicals, no. I can move amongst my people here absolutely free without any escort. I have not the slightest doubt that I would be quite safe. All these men would hold themselves responsible for my safety. I cannot say so about the right-wing.

AT HOME, SOWETO, SOUTH AFRICA, 14 FEBRUARY 1990

Well, the death – the assassination of any individual – is never anything pleasant. We would prefer that the community should convey its disapproval of his policies without using methods like assassination.

FROM A CONVERSATION WITH RICHARD STENGEL, 9 DECEMBER 1992

Tonight I am reaching out to every single South African, black and white, from the very depths of my being. A white man, full of prejudice and hate, came to our country and committed a deed so foul that our whole nation now teeters on the brink of disaster. A white woman, of Afrikaner origin, risked her life so that we may know, and bring to justice this assassin.

TELEVISED ADDRESS TO THE NATION AFTER THE ASSASSINATION OF CHRIS HANI, JOHANNESBURG, SOUTH AFRICA, 13 APRIL 1993

Autobiography

What a sweet euphemism for self-praise the English language has evolved! Autobiography.

FROM A LETTER TO FATIMA MEER, WRITTEN ON ROBBEN ISLAND, 1 MARCH 1971

Had I been in a position to write an autobiography, its publication would have been delayed until our bones had been laid.

IBID

A story of one's life should deal frankly with political colleagues, their personalities and their views. The reader would like to know what kind of person the writer is, his relationships with others, and these should emerge not from the epithets used but from the facts themselves.

FROM AN UNPUBLISHED AUTOBIOGRAPHICAL MANUSCRIPT, WRITTEN ON ROBBEN ISLAND, 1975

An autobiography is not merely a catalogue of events and experiences in which a person has been involved, but it also serves as some blueprint on which others may well model their own lives.

FROM THE UNPUBLISHED SEQUEL TO HIS AUTOBIOGRAPHY, CIRCA 1998

Awards

I also dedicate these awards to those millions and millions of ordinary unsung men and women all over the world who throughout this century courageously refused to bow to the baser instincts of our nature and to live their lives in pursuit of peace, tolerance and respect for differences.

ADDRESS TO THE PARLIAMENT OF THE WORLD'S RELIGIONS, CAPE TOWN, SOUTH AFRICA, DECEMBER 1999

I am a simple country boy, and I remain astounded and overawed by the awards and honours that people, for some incomprehensible reason, decide to bestow upon us.

UPON RECEIVING THE PLANET AND HUMANITY AWARD, INTERNATIONAL GEOGRAPHICAL UNION, DURBAN, SOUTH AFRICA, 4 AUGUST 2002

Banning

In short, I found myself treated as a criminal, an unconvicted criminal. I was not allowed to pick my company, to frequent the company of men, to participate in their political activities, to join their organisations. I was not free from constant police surveillance.

IN MITIGATION OF SENTENCE AFTER BEING CONVICTED OF INCITING WORKERS TO STRIKE AND LEAVING THE COUNTRY ILLEGALLY, OLD SYNAGOGUE, PRETORIA, SOUTH AFRICA, 7 NOVEMBER 1962

In 1960, there was a shooting at Sharpeville, which resulted in the proclamation of a state of emergency and the declaration of the ANC as an unlawful organisation. My colleagues and I, after careful consideration, decided that we would not obey this decree.

SPEECH FROM THE DOCK, RIVONIA TRIAL, PALACE OF JUSTICE, PRETORIA, SOUTH AFRICA, 20 APRIL 1964

I made it a point to see the country because I knew that the question of a ban and confinement to a particular area was something that was going to haunt me for the rest of my life as long as I was active politically.

FROM A CONVERSATION WITH RICHARD STENGEL, 24 DECEMBER 1992

Banning not only confines one physically, it imprisons one's spirit. It induces a kind of psychological claustrophobia that makes one yearn for not only freedom of movement but spiritual escape.

FROM LONG WALK TO FREEDOM, 1994

Bhunga

They had what was called the Bhunga which was the political and administrative institution which brought together the leading thinkers and traditional leaders in the area and where they discuss the problems relating to the Transkei. It was a governing body which was unique in the sense that it did not exist anywhere in the country.

FROM A CONVERSATION WITH RICHARD STENGEL, 23 MARCH 1993

Bitterness

I feel as if I have been soaked in gall, every part of me, my flesh, bloodstream, bone and soul, so bitter I am to be completely powerless to help you in the rough and fierce ordeals you are going through.

FROM A LETTER TO WINNIE MANDELA, THEN IN PRETORIA CENTRAL PRISON, WRITTEN ON ROBBEN ISLAND, 1 AUGUST 1970

Perhaps if I was idle and did not have a job to do, I would be as bitter as others. But because I have been given a job to do, I have not had time to think about the cruel experiences I've had. I'm not unique. Others have every reason to be more bitter than I. There are countless people who went to jail and aren't bitter at all, because they can see that their sacrifices were not in vain, and the ideas for which we lived and sacrificed are about to come to fruition. And that removes the bitterness from their hearts.

SOURCE UNKNOWN, 14 JUNE 1993

From this podium, and after a lifetime spent in struggle, we want to echo the Chilean [Pablo Neruda], and express our conviction that the fall of our century will carry away the foliage of bitterness which has accumulated in our hearts, and to which colonialism, neo-colonialism and white minority domination gave birth.

OAU (ORGANISATION OF AFRICAN UNITY) SUMMIT, OUAGADOUGOU, BURKINA FASO, 8 JUNE 1998

Black Consciousness

The observation that emerges from an objective review of the short history and role of the BCM [Black Consciousness Movement] is that, in spite of all its weaknesses and mistakes, the BCM attracted able and serious-minded young people who acquitted themselves well, appreciated the value of unity, and whose main efforts were directed towards this goal. Realists among them accepted that the enemy would not be defeated by fiery speeches, mass campaigns, bare fists, stones and petrol bombs, and that only through a disciplined freedom army, under a unified command, using modern weapons and backed by a united population, will the laurels be ours.

FROM AN ESSAY ENTITLED 'WHITHER THE BLACK CONSCIOUSNESS MOVEMENT', WRITTEN ON ROBBEN ISLAND, 1978

No other movement since the emergence of MK [Umkhonto we Sizwe] had caught the imagination of the youth as the BCM [Black Consciousness Movement] had done, undertaken so many positive mass projects, conducted its campaign with such enduring aggression and handled such a big budget.

IBID

The contribution of the BCM [Black Consciousness Movement] is even more striking if we bear in mind: that when it was launched the enemy had become ruthless in dealing with its opponents; that many activists had been jailed, killed in detention, confined to certain areas or had fled the country; that the liberation movement was seriously crippled and mass political activity had been stamped out.

IBID

Abathwa and Khoikhoi fought for their country and their people. In doing so, they were asserting their identity and love of freedom. That glorious heritage was greatly enriched when, from the second half of the eighteenth century, the Africans took their respective positions in the line of battle. In those patriotic wars our forefathers were in fact saying, 'We are black and we are on our own. This is our land and we shall defend it to the bitter end!'

IBID

One of the greatest legacies of the struggle that [Steve] Biko waged – and for which he died – was the explosion of pride among the victims of apartheid. The value that Black Consciousness placed on culture reverberated across our land, in our prisons, and amongst the communities in exile. Our people, who were once enjoined to look to Europe and America for creative sustenance, turned their eyes to Africa. I speak of culture and creativity because, like truth, they are enduring.

COMMEMORATION OF THE TWENTIETH ANNIVERSARY OF THE DEATH IN POLICE DETENTION OF STEVE BIKO, EAST LONDON, SOUTH AFRICA, 1 SEPTEMBER 1997

From the start, Black Consciousness articulated itself as 'an attitude of mind, a way of life'. In various forms and under various labels, before then and after, this attitude of mind and way of life have coursed through the veins of all the motive forces of struggle; it has fired the determination of leaders and the masses alike.
IBID

The ANC welcomed Black Consciousness as part of the genuine forces of the revolution. We understood that it was helping give organisational form to the popular upsurge of all the oppressed groups of our society. Above all, the liberation movement asserted that in struggle – whether in mass action, underground organisation, armed actions or international mobilisation – the people would most readily develop consciousness of their proud being, of their equality with everyone else, of their capacity to make history.
FIFTH STEVE BIKO LECTURE, UNIVERSITY OF CAPE TOWN, CAPE TOWN, SOUTH AFRICA, 10 SEPTEMBER 2004

The driving thrust of Black Consciousness was to forge pride and unity amongst all the oppressed, to foil the strategy of divide-and-rule, to engender pride amongst the mass of our people and confidence in their ability to throw off their oppression.
IBID

They didn't want to cooperate with the authorities whereas, although we fought questions of principle very firmly, we also believed in order, that there should be order, that prisoners and warders and officials should be able to work together.
TALKING ABOUT BLACK CONSCIOUSNESS MOVEMENT PRISONERS, FROM THE DOCUMENTARY
A SOUTH AFRICAN LOVE STORY: WALTER AND ALBERTINA, 2004

Black Economic Empowerment

We would also like to encourage the greater participation of established financial institutions in the important area of black economic empowerment and support for the development of small and medium business.
FIRST STATE OF THE NATION ADDRESS, PARLIAMENT, CAPE TOWN, SOUTH AFRICA, 24 MAY 1994

If we look at the matter of black economic empowerment, we are right to caution against the creation of a new elite which simply perpetuates inequality. But we must also not lose sight of the fact that against heavy odds, a pioneering entrepreneurial sector is emerging.
TENTH ANNIVERSARY OF THE SOWETAN'S NATION-BUILDING INITIATIVE, JOHANNESBURG, SOUTH AFRICA,
30 JUNE 1998

The private sector and government are profoundly aware that the fruits of our almost miraculous political transition will only be fully realised if all sectors of society also share in the economy, hence this joint drive towards broad-based black economic empowerment.
INVESTEC EVENT, WHITEHALL, LONDON, ENGLAND, 21 OCTOBER 2003

Blame

Blaming things on the past does not make them better.
ROLIHLAHLA PRIMARY SCHOOL, WARRENTON, SOUTH AFRICA, 30 AUGUST 1996

It has been easy to blame all of our troubles on a faceless system: the Crown; the church; hierarchy; globalisation; multinational corporations; the Apartheid state. It is not a hard task to place blame. But we must look within ourselves, become responsible and provide fresh solutions if we ever want to do more than complain, or make excuses.

LAUNCH OF THE FINAL REPORT OF THE WORLD COMMISSION ON DAMS, CABOT HALL, LONDON, ENGLAND, 16 NOVEMBER 2000

No longer shall we seek to place blame for our condition elsewhere or to look to others to take responsibility for our development. We are the masters of our own fate.

BANQUET CELEBRATING AFRICA'S 100 BEST BOOKS OF THE TWENTIETH CENTURY, CAPE TOWN, SOUTH AFRICA, JULY 2002

Body, The

The body is able to look after itself. What you must do, you know, is to encourage the body to have the resources to deal with any indisposition and I believe in that.

FROM A CONVERSATION WITH RICHARD STENGEL, 29 APRIL 1993

Boxing

Boxing is egalitarian. In the ring, rank, age, colour and wealth are irrelevant. When you are circling your opponent, probing his strengths and weaknesses, you are not thinking about his colour or social status.

FROM *LONG WALK TO FREEDOM*, 1994

I did not enjoy the violence of boxing so much as the science of it.

IBID

I would like my friend Evander Holyfield to know that today I feel like the heavyweight boxing champion of the world.

UPON RECEIVING THE CONGRESSIONAL GOLD MEDAL, CONGRESS, WASHINGTON DC, USA, 29 JULY 1998

In its finest form, boxing is an art, a huge spectator interest activity and in many cases a ticket out of poverty.

THIRTY-SIXTH ANNUAL WORLD BOXING COUNCIL CONVENTION, JOHANNESBURG, SOUTH AFRICA, 26 OCTOBER 1998

Perhaps the next best thing to being a world boxing champion, which I never achieved, is to have the privilege of opening a prestigious annual boxing convention.

IBID

I was a fighter.

MEETING WITH BOXER LAILA ALI, NELSON MANDELA FOUNDATION, JOHANNESBURG, SOUTH AFRICA, 30 JANUARY 2006

We support the fact that the women have come forward to challenge the role of men because it has been monopolised by men.

MEETING WITH BOXER, GWENDOLYN O'NEIL, NELSON MANDELA FOUNDATION, JOHANNESBURG, SOUTH AFRICA, 31 JANUARY 2007

Capital Punishment

The answer to the crime problem is not the death penalty, but rather ending the culture of impunity. Committing a crime must bring the certain prospect of arrest, prosecution and punishment.

NATIONAL ECONOMIC DEVELOPMENT AND LABOUR COUNCIL CONFERENCE ON CRIME AND VIOLENCE, JOHANNESBURG, SOUTH AFRICA, 21 NOVEMBER 1996

Calls for the restoration of the death penalty are, in reality, calls to hang those who are black and poor and who, in the main, commit murder among themselves. Those who make this demand seek to deny the fact that it is the dehumanising poverty imposed on the people by the apartheid system which generates this crime.

OPENING OF THE FIFTIETH ANC NATIONAL CONFERENCE, NORTH-WEST UNIVERSITY, MAFIKENG CAMPUS, SOUTH AFRICA, 16 DECEMBER 1997

Caribbean

This region has, in song and verse, in political philosophy and action, long been a source for the articulation of both the lamentations and aspirations of black people everywhere. We are bound by our common African heritage. When Africans were wrenched from their continent, they carried Africa with them and made the Caribbean a part of Africa.

CLOSING ADDRESS TO THE NINETEENTH MEETING OF THE HEADS OF GOVERNMENT OF THE CARICOM (CARIBBEAN COMMUNITY AND COMMON MARKET), ST LUCIA, 4 JULY 1998

Censors

I am hoping that the remorseless fates, that consistently interfere with my correspondence and that have cut me off from my family at such a critical moment, will be induced by considerations of honour and honesty to allow this one through.

FROM A LETTER TO SENATOR DOUGLAS LUKHELE, WRITTEN ON ROBBEN ISLAND, 1 AUGUST 1970

The double standards used in censoring letters is cowardly and calculated to deceive the public into the false impression that our outgoing letters are not censored.

FROM A LETTER WRITTEN ON ROBBEN ISLAND PRISON AND SMUGGLED OUT TO LAWYERS IN DURBAN, SOUTH AFRICA, JANUARY 1977

We have repeatedly requested the censors not to mark returned letters with a ballpoint, but instead to use a pencil.

FROM A LETTER TO MAJOR HARDING, HEAD OF ROBBEN ISLAND PRISON, 23 DECEMBER 1979

Century

Our generation traversed a century that was characterised by conflict, bloodshed, hatred and intolerance: a century which tried but could not fully resolve the problems of disparity between the rich and the poor, between developing and developed countries.

CLOSING SESSION OF THE FIFTIETH ANC NATIONAL CONFERENCE, NORTH-WEST UNIVERSITY, MAFIKENG CAMPUS, SOUTH AFRICA, 20 DECEMBER 1997

Challenges

I am convinced that floods of personal disaster can never drown a determined revolutionary nor can the cumulus of misery that accompanies tragedy suffocate him.

FROM A LETTER TO WINNIE MANDELA, WRITTEN ON ROBBEN ISLAND, 1 AUGUST 1970

Difficulties break some men but make others. No axe is sharp enough to cut the soul of a sinner who keeps on trying, one armed with the hope that he will rise even in the end.

FROM A LETTER TO WINNIE MANDELA, WRITTEN ON ROBBEN ISLAND, 1 FEBRUARY 1975

I approach every problem with optimism.

AT HOME, SOWETO, SOUTH AFRICA, 14 FEBRUARY 1990

I accepted that if you have a problem, you must face it and not gloss over it.

FROM A CONVERSATION WITH RICHARD STENGEL, 29 DECEMBER 1992

This challenge of transformation demands that we reassess the whole framework of our political, social and economic life and root out every vestige of inequality and racism that was imposed by apartheid. It is the only way we can build a new society and realise the vision of peace and prosperity for which innumerable men, women and children were detained, displaced, imprisoned, tortured and murdered.

OPENING OF THE SUB-SAHARAN OIL AND MINERALS CONFERENCE, CAPE TOWN, SOUTH AFRICA, 29–30 NOVEMBER 1993

I hold out a hand of friendship to the leaders of all parties and their members, and ask all of them to join us in working together to tackle the problems we face as a nation.

ANC ELECTION VICTORY CELEBRATION, CARLTON HOTEL, JOHANNESBURG, SOUTH AFRICA, 2 MAY 1994

I know that I am among friends who wish South Africa well, and so I can candidly acknowledge that we do face major challenges. I know that we have a common interest in seeing our new democracy succeed and develop in peace with the help of international capital.

UPON RECEIVING THE FREEDOM OF THE CITY OF LONDON, GUILDHALL, LONDON, ENGLAND, 10 JULY 1996

We do face major challenges, but none are as daunting as those we have already surmounted.

IBID

Can we say with confidence that it is within our reach to declare that never again shall continents, countries or communities be reduced to the smoking battlefields of contending forces of nationality, religion, race or language? Shall we rise to the challenge which history has put before us, of ensuring that the world's prodigious capacity for economic growth benefits all its people and not just the powerful?

LECTURE AT THE OXFORD CENTRE FOR ISLAMIC STUDIES, SHELDONIAN THEATRE, OXFORD, ENGLAND, 11 JULY 1997

We have only just begun this task, whose difficulties we do not underestimate and which will take us years to achieve. But we face the future with confidence, knowing that those who are ready to join hands can overcome the greatest challenges.

UPON RECEIVING AN HONORARY DOCTORATE FROM BEN-GURION UNIVERSITY OF THE NEGEV, CAPE TOWN, SOUTH AFRICA, 19 SEPTEMBER 1997

Now we face a new and even more difficult struggle. In the first years of our freedom we have, as a nation, made a good start. Yet all of us in every community do also know that there is much more still to be done.

INTERCULTURAL EID CELEBRATION, JOHANNESBURG, SOUTH AFRICA, 30 JANUARY 1998

As future leaders who will take over from the older generation to which I belong, you face even greater challenges. Though the world has made much progress in the twentieth century, the lives of much of humanity is still blighted by poverty, violence, hunger, disease and environmental damage.

LAUNCH OF THE CANADIAN FRIENDS OF THE NELSON MANDELA CHILDREN'S FUND, TORONTO, CANADA, 25 SEPTEMBER 1998

It was to be expected, given our past, that we would encounter problems of this kind but not, I believe, how great they would be. Nor that it would be as difficult to mobilise our society in a united effort to eradicate the problems.

OPENING OF THE MORALS SUMMIT, JOHANNESBURG, SOUTH AFRICA, 22 OCTOBER 1998

Every country in the world faces challenges and one of our challenges is to ensure that we deal with poverty, lack of education and also to make sure that our people enjoy good health.

AFTER VOTING, SOUTH AFRICA, DATE UNKNOWN

Though we face many challenges, and though we still have far to go in eradicating the consequences of our past in order to become a fully united and reconciled nation, we have together laid the foundation for doing so.

ADDRESS AT THE OPENING OF THE PRESIDENT'S BUDGET DEBATE, PARLIAMENT, CAPE TOWN, SOUTH AFRICA, 2 MARCH 1999

Every country in the world faces challenges.

AFTER VOTING IN MUNICIPAL ELECTIONS, JOHANNESBURG, SOUTH AFRICA, 11 MARCH 2006

It can be said that there are four basic and primary things that the mass of people in a society wish for: to live in a safe environment, to be able to work and provide for themselves, to have access to good public health and to have sound educational opportunities for their children. Currently we as a society may be struggling in each of those four areas, but we must remain confident that with the personal commitment of each and every one of us we can and will overcome the obstacles towards development.

OPENING OF THE OPRAH WINFREY LEADERSHIP ACADEMY, HENLEY-ON-KLIP, SOUTH AFRICA, 2 JANUARY 2007

As future leaders of this country, your challenge is to foster a nation in which all people, irrespective of race, colour, sex, religion or creed, can assert social cohesion fully. Mindful of your own challenges, you must continue to promote the principle of relentless freedom and democracy as it is the foundation upon which issues of human rights are ingrained.

VIDEO MESSAGE FOR THE NATIONAL YOUTH FESTIVAL, SOUTH AFRICA, JUNE 2008

Change

We can't forget the people who actually have brought about these changes.

FROM AN INTERVIEW WITH THE BBC (UK), 1993

There is a lot of evidence to show that whites in this country support change.
FROM AN INTERVIEW, CIRCA 1994

The change that has taken place is beyond words.
IBID

I think that there is solid evidence that all population groups are for change but of course the minorities have got genuine fears.
IBID

The renewal of nations, the rebirth of continents and the emergence of a new world order are each processes in their own right. But they are also today part of a single transformation of historical significance. Belief in the possibility of change and renewal is perhaps one of the defining characteristics of politics and of religions.
LECTURE AT THE OXFORD CENTRE FOR ISLAMIC STUDIES, SHELDONIAN THEATRE, OXFORD, ENGLAND, 11 JULY 1997

One of the most difficult things is not to change society – but to change yourself.
FROM AN INTERVIEW WITH JOHN BATTERSBY, JOHANNESBURG, SOUTH AFRICA, PUBLISHED IN *THE CHRISTIAN SCIENCE MONITOR*, 10 FEBRUARY 2000

To be an effective agent for peace, you have to seek not only to change the community and the world. What is more difficult is to change yourself before you seek to change others.
UPON RECEIVING THE INAUGURAL LAUREUS LIFETIME ACHIEVEMENT AWARD, SPORTING CLUB, MONACO, MONTE CARLO, 25 MAY 2000

Character

One day we may have on our side the genuine and firm support of an upright and straightforward man, holding high office, who will consider it improper to shirk his duty of protecting the rights and privileges of even his bitter opponents in the battle of ideas that is being fought in our country today.
FROM A LETTER TO WINNIE MANDELA, THEN IN PRETORIA CENTRAL PRISON, WRITTEN ON ROBBEN ISLAND, 1 AUGUST 1970

A good head and a good heart are always a formidable combination.
FROM A LETTER TO FATIMA MEER, WRITTEN ON ROBBEN ISLAND, 1 JANUARY 1976

On which aspect one concentrates in judging others will depend on the character of the particular judge. As we judge others so we are judged by others.
FROM A LETTER TO WINNIE MANDELA, WRITTEN ON ROBBEN ISLAND, 9 DECEMBER 1979

It is what we make out of what we have, not what we are given, that separates one person from another.
FROM *LONG WALK TO FREEDOM*, 1994

I performed in only a few dramas, but I had one memorable role: that of Creon, the king of Thebes, in Sophocles' *Antigone*. I had read some of the classic Greek plays in prison, and found them enormously elevating. What I took out of them was that character was measured by facing up to difficult situations and that a hero was a man who would not break down even under the most trying circumstances.
IBID

It is in the character of growth that we should learn from both pleasant and unpleasant experiences.

FOREIGN CORRESPONDENTS' ASSOCIATION ANNUAL DINNER, JOHANNESBURG, SOUTH AFRICA, 21 NOVEMBER 1997

Chieftaincy

There was a time when, like all peoples on earth, Africans conducted their simple communities through chiefs, advised by tribal councils and mass meetings of the people. In those times, the chiefs were indeed representative governors. Nowhere, however, have such institutions survived the complexities of modern industrial civilisation.

FROM AN ARTICLE ENTITLED 'VERWOERD'S TRIBALISM', *LIBERATION*, MAY 1959

After all, the only heroes I had heard of at that time had almost all been chiefs and the respect enjoyed by the regent from both black and white tended to exaggerate the importance of this institution in my mind.

FROM AN UNPUBLISHED AUTOBIOGRAPHICAL MANUSCRIPT, WRITTEN ON ROBBEN ISLAND, 1975

As descendants of the famous heroes that led us so well during the wars of dispossession and as the traditional leaders in their own right, chiefs are entitled to be treated with respect.

IBID

I saw chieftaincy not only as the pivot around which community life turned but as the key to positions of influence, power and status.

IBID

But if I had stayed at home I would have been a respected chief today, you know? And I would have had a big stomach and a lot of cattle and sheep.

FROM A CONVERSATION WITH RICHARD STENGEL, 3 MAY 1993

Child Abuse

If we want to be the caring society we thought we were striving for during our fight against the iniquities of apartheid, we must eradicate all traces of violence against and abuse of children. No form of violence can ever be excused in a society that wishes to call itself decent, but violence against children must surely rank as the most abominable expression of violence. It subjects the most vulnerable and the weakest to indignity, humiliation, degradation and injury.

SOUTH AFRICA, NOVEMBER 2003

Childhood

I have not forgotten the days of my childhood when we used to gather round community elders to listen to their wealth of wisdom and experience.

FROM AN UNPUBLISHED AUTOBIOGRAPHICAL MANUSCRIPT, WRITTEN ON ROBBEN ISLAND, 1975

I have the most pleasant recollections and dreams about the Transkei of my childhood, where I hunted, played sticks, stole mealies on the cob and where I learnt to count; it is a world which is gone. A well-known English poet had such a world in mind when he exclaimed, 'The things which I have seen I now can see no more'.

FROM A LETTER TO A FRIEND, WRITTEN IN POLLSMOOR PRISON, CAPE TOWN, SOUTH AFRICA, 22 FEBRUARY 1985

One of our favourite pastimes was stick fighting.

FROM A BBC (UK) DOCUMENTARY, 1996

Does my quiet, bucolic childhood seem picturesque in hindsight, especially from this crowded city? I assure you it was not so romantic, or free, back then. All the water we used for farming, cooking and washing – to develop our families and sustain our health – had to be fetched in buckets from the streams and springs.

LAUNCH OF THE FINAL REPORT OF THE WORLD COMMISSION ON DAMS, CABOT HALL, LONDON, ENGLAND, 16 NOVEMBER 2000

Children

Few things make the life of a parent more rewarding and sweet as successful children.

FROM A LETTER TO AMINA CACHALIA, WRITTEN ON ROBBEN ISLAND, 3 MARCH 1981

It would seem that some kind of diaspora is in full swing and children from urban townships and simple country villages alike are scattered all over the world and, in the process, horizons are widened beyond recognition, and new ideas [are] acquired; with this background they return home to an environment not yet ready to accommodate them.

FROM A LETTER TO FRIEDA MATTHEWS, WRITTEN IN POLLSMOOR PRISON, CAPE TOWN, SOUTH AFRICA, 25 FEBRUARY 1987

The mass media, especially television, are today, more than ever before, drawing attention to the plight of the disadvantaged children. Some of the pictures on the set are both touching as well as frightening.

FROM A LETTER TO DR MAMPHELA RAMPHELE, WRITTEN IN POLLSMOOR PRISON, CAPE TOWN, SOUTH AFRICA, 12 AUGUST 1987

The children must, at last, play in the open veld, no longer tortured by the pangs of hunger or ravaged by disease or threatened with the scourge of ignorance, molestation and abuse, and no longer required to engage in deeds whose gravity exceeds the demands of their tender years.

NOBEL PEACE PRIZE AWARD CEREMONY, OSLO, NORWAY, 10 DECEMBER 1993

The reward of which we have spoken will and must also be measured by the happiness and welfare of the mothers and fathers of these children, who must walk the earth without fear of being robbed, killed for political or material profit, or spat upon because they are beggars.

IBID

One of the more shameful chapters of our past has been the devastation of the lives of children.

TENTH ANNIVERSARY CELEBRATION OF THE NEETHLINGSHOF ESTATE, NEETHLINGSHOF ESTATE, STELLENBOSCH, SOUTH AFRICA, 21 APRIL 1995

There can be no keener revelation of a society's soul than the way in which it treats its children.

LAUNCH OF THE NELSON MANDELA CHILDREN'S FUND, MAHLAMBA NDLOPFU, PRETORIA, SOUTH AFRICA, 8 MAY 1995

We come from a past in which the lives of our children were assaulted and devastated in countless ways. It would be no exaggeration to speak of a national abuse of a generation by a society which it should have been able to trust.

IBID

Our children are the rock on which our future will be built, our greatest asset as a nation. They will be the leaders of our country, the creators of our national wealth, those who care for and protect our people.

DEDICATION OF THE QUNU AND NKALANE SCHOOLS, QUNU, SOUTH AFRICA, 3 JUNE 1995

Our children have borne the brunt of apartheid's ravaging deprivation. Most were robbed of their right to a decent education, adequate health care, stable family lives and sometimes of their entire childhood.

OPENING OF CAPE TOWN SOS CHILDREN'S VILLAGE, CAPE TOWN, SOUTH AFRICA, 25 MAY 1996

The children of South Africa have assumed a responsibility beyond their years, both in the freeing of our country and in building its future.

IBID

In the end, the cries of the infant who dies because of hunger or because a machete has slit open its stomach will penetrate the noises of the modern city and its sealed windows to say: am I not human too?

ADDRESS TO THE JOINT HOUSES OF PARLIAMENT, WESTMINSTER HALL, LONDON, ENGLAND, 11 JULY 1996

The children who sleep in the streets, reduced to begging to make a living, are testimony to an unfinished job. The families who live in shacks with no running water, sanitation and electricity are a reminder that the past continues to haunt the present.

SEVENTY-FIFTH ANNIVERSARY OF THE SACP (SOUTH AFRICAN COMMUNIST PARTY), CAPE TOWN, SOUTH AFRICA, 28 JULY 1996

Africa is renowned for its beauty, its rich natural heritage and prolific resources – but equally, the image of its suffering children haunts the conscience of our Continent and the world.

LAUNCH OF THE 'KICK POLIO OUT OF AFRICA' CAMPAIGN, JOHANNESBURG, SOUTH AFRICA, 2 AUGUST 1996

It always gives me great pleasure to be surrounded by the beautiful children of our land. Whenever I am with energetic young people such as yourselves I feel like a recharged battery, confident that our country can look forward to great things. You are the future of this country – you are the people who will lead us into the next century.

FOOD FOR LIFE FESTIVAL, DURBAN, SOUTH AFRICA, 23 APRIL 1997

All of us have a practical responsibility to ensure that our sick children are cared for, in the family and in the community. We have a responsibility to demonstrate our recognition of the value of each person's life, no matter how short, no matter how fragile.

LUNCH FOR THE SPONSORS OF HIS BIRTHDAY PARTY FOR CHILDREN WITH LIFE-THREATENING DISEASES, SOUTH AFRICA, 4 JULY 1997

Let us reach out to the children. Let us do what we can to support their fight to rise above their pain and suffering.

IBID

Together as a nation, we have the obligation to put sunshine into the hearts of our little ones. They are our precious possessions. They deserve what happiness life can offer.
IBID

The true character of a society is revealed in how it treats its children.
LAUNCH OF THE BLUE TRAIN, WORCESTER STATION, WORCESTER, SOUTH AFRICA, 27 SEPTEMBER 1997

Our children are our greatest treasure. They are our future. Those who abuse them tear at the fabric of our society and weaken our nation.
SPEAKING AT A NATIONAL MEN'S MARCH, PRETORIA, SOUTH AFRICA, 22 NOVEMBER 1997

I am the product of Africa and her long-cherished dream of a rebirth that can now be realised so that all of our children may play in the sun.
FINAL SITTING OF THE FIRST DEMOCRATICALLY ELECTED PARLIAMENT, CAPE TOWN, SOUTH AFRICA, 26 MARCH 1999

Be ever vigilant, hold governments accountable, struggle for peace and justice. Do not let up for a moment for there is no circumstance in which the neglect or abuse of children can ever be tolerated.
STATEMENT ON BUILDING A GLOBAL PARTNERSHIP FOR CHILDREN, 6 MAY 2000

In this world of such abundance, surely we can find the means to assure that no child will go hungry, no pregnant woman will be too weak to survive childbirth and that every one of the nearly six million children who will die next year because of malnutrition will be saved.
IBID

There is nothing more terrible than to see children suffering and our hearts go out especially to those infected by HIV/AIDS. As in all wars, they – the children – are the innocent victims that bear the brunt of the suffering.
LAUNCH OF SOS CHILDREN'S VILLAGE FUND-RAISING FOR AIDS PROJECT, SEPTEMBER 2001

There are few experiences in life as painful as that of a parent losing a child to death. No matter what the circumstances are, that loss cuts to the core of our relationships as human beings.
MESSAGE OF CONDOLENCE ON THE DEATH OF ANTON AND HUBERTE RUPERT'S YOUNGEST SON, ANTHONIJ, IN A CAR ACCIDENT, OCTOBER 2001

Giving children a healthy start in life, no matter where they are born or the circumstances of their birth, is the moral obligation of every one of us.
AIDS VACCINE CONFERENCE, SOUTH AFRICA, APRIL 2002

Each of us, as citizens, has a role to play in creating a better world for our children.
LUNCHEON HOSTED BY UNITED NATIONS SECRETARY GENERAL KOFI ANNAN AT THE SPECIAL SESSION OF THE UNITED NATIONS FOR CHILDREN, UNITED NATIONS, NEW YORK CITY, USA, 9 MAY 2002

History will judge us by the difference we make in the everyday lives of children.
IBID

We are at a crucial conjuncture in mobilising the collective energies of humankind towards working together for a more humane, compassionate and just world. And a crucial measure of our compassion will be the manner in which we work for a better life and secure future for our children.
IBID

We understand and promote the notion that while children need to be guided they also have an entrenched right to be whatever they want to be and that they can achieve this only if they are given the space to dream and live out their dreams.

ANNUAL CHILDREN'S CELEBRATIONS, BLOEMFONTEIN, SOUTH AFRICA, 27 SEPTEMBER 2003

Our children are our future and one of our most basic responsibilities is to care for them in the best and most compassionate manner possible.

OPENING OF THE WALTER SISULU PAEDIATRIC CARDIAC CENTRE FOR AFRICA, JOHANNESBURG, SOUTH AFRICA, 7 NOVEMBER 2003

One way that we can build a better future for children is by empowering them through allowing them to speak up for themselves. Of course, we as adults have to guide them and to take ultimate responsibility but that is something quite different from patronising them. The rights of children must, importantly, include the right to be themselves and to talk for themselves.

SPEECH, LOCATION UNKNOWN, SOUTH AFRICA, NOVEMBER 2003

Will you tell the children in your school that I love them?

FROM THE DOCUMENTARY LEGENDS: NELSON MANDELA, 2005

China

The revolution in China was a masterpiece, a *real* masterpiece. If you read how they fought that revolution, you believe in the impossible. It's just miraculous.

FROM A CONVERSATION WITH RICHARD STENGEL, 4 APRIL 1993

Civic Associations

Civic associations in this country play an important role in voicing the aspirations of the people and shaping their thoughts.

FROM A LETTER TO THE PAARL CIVIC ASSOCIATION, WRITTEN IN VICTOR VERSTER PRISON, PAARL, SOUTH AFRICA, 21 AUGUST 1989

Collective Effort

It has been suggested that the advances, the articulateness of our people, the successes which they are achieving here and the recognition which they are winning both here and abroad are in some way the result of my work. I must place on record my belief that I have been only one in a large army of people, to all of whom the credit for any success of achievement is due.

IN MITIGATION OF SENTENCE AFTER BEING CONVICTED OF INCITING WORKERS TO STRIKE AND LEAVING THE COUNTRY ILLEGALLY, OLD SYNAGOGUE, PRETORIA, SOUTH AFRICA, 7 NOVEMBER 1962

As I look back to those days I am inclined to believe that the type of life I led at my home, my experiences in the veld where we worked and played together in groups, introduced me at an early age to the ideas of collective effort.

FROM AN UNPUBLISHED AUTOBIOGRAPHICAL MANUSCRIPT, WRITTEN ON ROBBEN ISLAND, 1975

There is no single individual who can undertake the enormous task of solving the problems of this country. If anybody has acquired any particular status that is due very largely to what the organisation has done.

FROM AN INTERVIEW WITH JAMES ROBBINS OF THE BBC (UK), HIS HOUSE, SOWETO, SOUTH AFRICA, 14 FEBRUARY 1990

These problems cannot be tackled on personal basis, they can only be dealt with through a collective effort. I will not be acting as an individual. I will be acting as a member of a team.

FROM AN INTERVIEW WITH SCOTT MACLEOD OF *TIME* MAGAZINE, SOWETO, SOUTH AFRICA, 26 FEBRUARY 1990

We don't want to raise the role of any particular individual above the collective itself.

FROM A CONVERSATION WITH AHMED KATHRADA, CIRCA 1993/94

What happens when differences arise? We address them, discuss issues on merit, persuade one another and reach a consensus.

FROM AN INTERVIEW WITH THE BBC (UK), 28 OCTOBER 1993

It is in the final analysis, not an individual contribution; it is the collective which is the characteristic feature of our work in the African National Congress.

IBID

You actually appreciate the contribution of others sometimes precisely because they bring a point which you had not thought of.

FROM AN INTERVIEW, DATE UNKNOWN

We are the product of a collective leadership and almost everything we have achieved we have achieved together.

REVISITING ROBBEN ISLAND, CAPE TOWN, SOUTH AFRICA, 11 FEBRUARY 1994

I will not influence them one way or the other because I have confidence in collective leadership and I know that their decision will be absolutely correct.

FROM AN INTERVIEW WITH TOM COHEN AND SAHM VENTER FOR THE ASSOCIATED PRESS, TALKING ABOUT HIS SUCCESSOR, TUYNHUYS, CAPE TOWN, SOUTH AFRICA, 22 SEPTEMBER 1994

To sit down and think at the end of the day and to assess your humble contribution as a member of a team, is an important part of organising and of carrying out your political duties.

CLOSING ADDRESS TO THE FORTY-NINTH ANC NATIONAL CONFERENCE, BLOEMFONTEIN, SOUTH AFRICA, 22 DECEMBER 1994

I would like to be remembered as part of a team, and I would like my contribution to be assessed as somebody who carried out decisions taken by that collective.

FROM AN INTERVIEW WITH JOHN BATTERSBY, JOHANNESBURG, SOUTH AFRICA, PUBLISHED IN *THE CHRISTIAN SCIENCE MONITOR*, 10 FEBRUARY 2000

A cardinal point that we must keep constantly in mind, the lodestar which keeps us on course as we negotiate the uncharted twists and turns of the struggle for liberation, is that the breakthrough is never the result of individual effort. It is always a collective effort and triumph.

FROM A NOTEBOOK, DATE UNKNOWN

Colonialism

It is important for us and for the African people as a whole to realise that, but for the support of American finance it would have been difficult if not impossible for the Western colonial powers to maintain rule in Africa, nor indeed anywhere in the world.

PRESIDENTIAL ADDRESS TO THE ANNUAL ANC YOUTH LEAGUE CONFERENCE, SOUTH AFRICA, DECEMBER 1951

The colonial powers never really developed Africa, in colonies which they ruled. The little infrastructure that was set in motion was always towards the coloniser, not towards the masses of the people in the country.

FROM THE DOCUMENTARY *THE LAST MILE: MANDELA, AFRICA AND DEMOCRACY*, 1992

The expansion of European influence and domination over virtually the entire planet was a central aspect of European ambition in that period of European history.

LECTURE AT THE OXFORD CENTRE FOR ISLAMIC STUDIES, SHELDONIAN THEATRE, OXFORD, ENGLAND, 11 JULY 1997

The nineteenth-century colonisation of the African Continent was in many respects the culmination of the Renaissance-initiated expansion of European dominion over the planet.

IBID

The effects on the colonised continent are too well known to need repetition. Yet, as it has been said, the purpose of studying history is not to deride human action, nor to weep over it or to hate it, but to understand it. And hopefully then to learn from it as we contemplate our future.

IBID

The plundering of indigenous land, exploitation of its mineral wealth and other raw materials, confinement of its people to specific areas and the restriction of their movement have, with notable exceptions, been the cornerstones of colonialism throughout the land.

FROM THE UNPUBLISHED SEQUEL TO HIS AUTOBIOGRAPHY, CIRCA 1998

Colonialism and apartheid have left a sharply polarised society. Until we reduce the wide gaps between the educated and the illiterate, the sheltered and the homeless, and very rich and the poor, we will continue to be deeply divided.

OPENING OF THE 'ONE CITY MANY CULTURES' PROJECT, CAPE TOWN, SOUTH AFRICA, 1 MARCH 1999

The new national boundaries proclaimed in colonial times cut across tribal and clan groupings, across animal migration routes, fragmenting ecosystems and led to biodiversity being destroyed.

MESSAGE TO THE INTERNATIONAL CONFERENCE ON KOREA'S DEMILITARISED ZONE, SEOUL, KOREA, 14–19 JULY 2004

Communication

Not even the most repressive regime can stop human beings from finding ways of communicating and obtaining access to information.

SOURCE UNKNOWN, 1995

Communism

There is no doubt that the Communist Party is behind the movement but, true to form and tradition, they have decided to disguise its true nature and composition in order to deceive the public.

FROM A LETTER TO IB TABATA, 22 MAY 1948 ['MOVEMENT' REFERS TO THE 'FIRST TRANSVAAL–ORANGE FREE STATE PEOPLE'S ASSEMBLY FOR VOTES FOR ALL']

It is perhaps difficult for white South Africans, with an ingrained prejudice against communism, to understand why experienced African politicians so readily accept communists as their friends. But to us the reason is obvious. Theoretical differences amongst those fighting against oppression is a luxury we cannot afford at this stage. What is more, for many decades communists were the only political group in South Africa who were prepared to treat Africans as human beings and their equals, who were prepared to eat with us, talk with us, live with us and work with us.

SPEECH FROM THE DOCK, RIVONIA TRIAL, PALACE OF JUSTICE, PRETORIA, SOUTH AFRICA, 20 APRIL 1964

The alliance with the communist party has been there since the early twenties and it is a simple thing that when you have a common enemy you look for allies.

AT HOME, SOWETO, SOUTH AFRICA, 14 FEBRUARY 1990

The ANC is not a Communist Party. But as a defender of democracy, it has fought and will continue to fight for the right of the Communist Party to exist. As a movement for national liberation, the ANC has no mandate to espouse a Marxist ideology. But as a democratic movement, as a parliament of the people of our country, the ANC has defended and will continue to defend the right of any South African to adhere to the Marxist ideology if that is their wish.

RALLY TO RELAUNCH THE SACP (SOUTH AFRICAN COMMUNIST PARTY), SOWETO, SOUTH AFRICA, 29 JULY 1990

I had discovered that the communists were genuine allies and they had no ulterior motive; their motive was simply to overthrow white domination.

FROM A CONVERSATION WITH RICHARD STENGEL, 18 MARCH 1993

So the fall of the communist party itself had no impact ideologically but from the point of view of us getting arms, that changed the situation.

FROM A CONVERSATION WITH RICHARD STENGEL, 26 APRIL 1993

Community Workers

I have always admired men and women who used their talents to serve the community, and who were highly respected and admired for their efforts and sacrifices, even though they held no office whatsoever in government or society.

FROM THE UNPUBLISHED SEQUEL TO HIS AUTOBIOGRAPHY, CIRCA 1998

Compromise

If you don't intend having a compromise, you don't negotiate at all.

AT HOME, SOWETO, SOUTH AFRICA, 14 FEBRUARY 1990

It is the ANC which will decide what compromises it should make and we are ready for honourable compromises without surrendering our principles.

IBID

Compromises must be made in respect to every issue as long as that compromise is in the interest, not only of one population group but for the country as a whole. That is the nature of compromises.

IBID

Compromise means each of the parties involved should give away something to the other, should accommodate the demands, the fears, of the other party.

FROM AN INTERVIEW WITH SABC (SOUTH AFRICAN BROADCASTING CORPORATION), JOHANNESBURG, SOUTH AFRICA, 15 FEBRUARY 1990

I sensed the government was anxious to overcome the impasse in the country, that they were now convinced they had to depart from their old positions. In ghostly outline, I saw the beginnings of a compromise.

FROM *LONG WALK TO FREEDOM*, 1994

If the experience of South Africa means anything to the world at large, we hope that it is in having demonstrated that where people of goodwill get together and transcend their differences for the common good, peaceful and just solutions can be found even for those problems which seem most intractable.

UPON RECEIVING THE GERMAN MEDIA PRIZE, BADEN-BADEN, GERMANY, 28 JANUARY 1999

It was the common wisdom in the world that South Africans were doomed to self-destruction in a bloody racial confrontation. But the leaders of the different communities and political parties confounded those prophets of doom through their willingness to negotiate and compromise.

IBID

In a world where the strong may seek to impose upon the more vulnerable, and where particular nations or groups of nations may still seek to decide the fate of the planet – in such a world, respect for multilateralism, moderation of public discourse and a patient search for compromise become even more imperative to save the world from debilitating conflict and enduring inequality.

LUNCHEON IN HONOUR OF MUAMMAR QADDAFI, CAPE TOWN, SOUTH AFRICA, 13 JUNE 1999

In every dispute you eventually reach a point where neither party is altogether right or altogether wrong when compromise is the only alternative for those who seriously want peace and stability.

FROM A PERSONAL FILE, 16 JANUARY 2000

With your willingness to compromise and preparedness to face the future rather than getting caught in the divisions of your past, you opened an honourable place for yourself and your country in the history of our Continent.

INSTALLATION OF THE TRANSITIONAL GOVERNMENT, BUJUMBURA, BURUNDI, 1 NOVEMBER 2001

Human beings will always be able to find arguments for confrontation and no compromise. We humans are, however, the beings capable of reason, compassion and change.

MESSAGE TO THE GLOBAL CONVENTION ON PEACE AND NON-VIOLENCE, NEW DELHI, INDIA, 31 JANUARY 2004

Conflict

One of the most important lessons I learnt in my life of struggle for freedom and peace is that in any conflict there comes a point when neither side can claim to be right and the other wrong, no matter how much that might have been the case at the start of a conflict.

VIDEO MESSAGE FOR THE SIGNING OF THE GENEVA ACCORD, DECEMBER 2003

NELSON MANDELA BY HIMSELF

Conscience

This is the dilemma which faced us, and in such a dilemma, men of honesty, men of purpose, and men of public morality and of conscience can only have one answer. They must follow the dictates of their conscience irrespective of the consequences which might overtake them for it.

IN MITIGATION OF SENTENCE AFTER BEING CONVICTED OF INCITING WORKERS TO STRIKE AND LEAVING THE COUNTRY ILLEGALLY, OLD SYNAGOGUE, PRETORIA, SOUTH AFRICA, 7 NOVEMBER 1962

History shows that penalties do not deter men when their conscience is aroused, nor will they deter my people or the colleagues with whom I have worked before.

IBID

I was made, by the law, a criminal, not because of what I had done, but because of what I stood for, because of what I thought, because of my conscience.

IBID

Not just I alone, but all of us are willing to pay the penalties which we may have to pay, which I may have to pay for having followed my conscience in pursuit of what I believe is right. So are we all. Many people in this country have paid the price before me, and many will pay after me.

IBID

I would say that the whole life of any thinking African in this country drives continuously to a conflict between his conscience on the one hand and the law on the other. This is not a conflict peculiar to this country. The conflict arises for men of conscience, for men who think and who feel deeply in every country.

IBID

Even when at times I am plagued with an uneasy conscience I have to acknowledge that my wholehearted commitment to the liberation of our people gives meaning to life and yields for me a sense of national pride and joy.

FROM AN UNPUBLISHED AUTOBIOGRAPHICAL MANUSCRIPT, WRITTEN ON ROBBEN ISLAND, 1975

It will forever remain an accusation and a challenge to all men and women of conscience that it took as long as it has, before all of us stood up to say enough is enough.

ADDRESS TO THE UNITED NATIONS SPECIAL COMMITTEE AGAINST APARTHEID, UNITED NATIONS, NEW YORK CITY, USA, 22 JUNE 1990

The Truth and Reconciliation Commission is an important instrument, not only in dealing with past wrongs, but in freeing all of us to move with a clean conscience into the future.

ANNUAL METHODIST CHURCH CONFERENCE, MTHATHA, SOUTH AFRICA, 18 SEPTEMBER 1994

Constitution of South Africa

The key, therefore, to the protection of any minority is to put core civil and political rights beyond the reach of temporary majorities by guaranteeing them as fundamental human rights, enshrined in a democratic constitution.

INVESTITURE, CLARK UNIVERSITY, ATLANTA, GEORGIA, USA, 10 JULY 1993

We have fought for a democratic constitution since the 1880s. Ours has been a quest for a constitution freely adopted by the people of South Africa, reflecting their wishes and their aspirations.

ADDRESS TO THE PEOPLE OF CAPE TOWN AFTER HIS ELECTION AS PRESIDENT, CITY HALL, CAPE TOWN, SOUTH AFRICA, 9 MAY 1994

We place our vision of a new constitutional order for South Africa on the table not as conquerors, prescribing to the conquered. We speak as fellow citizens to heal the wounds of the past with the intent of constructing a new order based on justice for all.

IBID

One of the most important milestones of our young democracy was the recent adoption of our new Constitution. It lays a firm basis for the religious and cultural freedom of all our people.

MESSAGE FOR JEWISH NEW YEAR (ROSH HASHANAH), SOUTH AFRICA, 13 SEPTEMBER 1996

Let us now, drawing strength from the unity which we have forged, together grasp the opportunities and realise the vision enshrined in this constitution.

SIGNING OF THE NEW CONSTITUTION, SHARPEVILLE, VEREENIGING, SOUTH AFRICA, 10 DECEMBER 1996

We cherish our Constitution and want to ensure that its rights become a living reality for all our people.

FREEDOM DAY CELEBRATIONS, CAPE TOWN, SOUTH AFRICA, 27 APRIL 1998

The government over which I was chosen to preside had to take stock and come to an understanding of the structures and rules that governed our nation and our lives under the perversion of apartheid: to initiate the process of de-legislation and re-legislation; to create a new system of legislation and regulation governed by the supremacy of the Constitution and the rule of law.

FROM AN ARTICLE IN THE *SUNDAY TIMES* (SOUTH AFRICA) MARKING TEN YEARS OF DEMOCRACY, APRIL 2004

The preamble to our Constitution reminds us to honour those who sacrificed for justice and freedom in our land, and to respect those who built and developed our land. Those two phrases represent a profound call to reconciliation amongst the various strands of our often conflicting history.

PRESS CONFERENCE OF THE EX-POLITICAL PRISONERS' COMMITTEE, NELSON MANDELA FOUNDATION, JOHANNESBURG, SOUTH AFRICA, 30 MARCH 2006

Contradictions

Contradictions are an essential part of life and never cease tearing one apart.

FROM A LETTER TO EFFIE SCHULTZ, WRITTEN IN POLLSMOOR PRISON, CAPE TOWN, SOUTH AFRICA, 1 APRIL 1987

Cooperation

You can't avoid having people who are negative, who have not caught the spirit of cooperation.

CONVERSATION WITH TOKYO SEXWALE, FW DE KLERK AND SIVUYILE MIKKI XAYIYA AFTER AGREEING TO APPROACH THE PRIVATE SECTOR FOR FUNDS FOR THE 2004 ELECTION, SOUTH AFRICA, 2004

Corruption

We have learnt now that even those people with whom we fought the struggle against apartheid's corruption can themselves become corrupted.

OPENING OF THE EMTHONJENI YOUTH CENTRE, PRETORIA, SOUTH AFRICA, 25 AUGUST 1998

Having come into government with the declared intention of eliminating the corruption we knew to be endemic, we have in the past four years found that some individuals who fought for freedom have also proved corrupt. Nor should our apartheid past be used as an excuse for such misdemeanours.

OPENING OF THE MORALS SUMMIT, JOHANNESBURG, SOUTH AFRICA, 22 OCTOBER 1998

The symptoms of our spiritual malaise are only too familiar. They include: the extent of corruption in both public and private sector, where office and positions of responsibility are treated as opportunities for self-enrichment; the corruption that occurs within our justice system; violence in interpersonal relations and families, in particular the shameful record of abuse of women and children; and the extent of evasion of tax and refusal to pay for services used.

IBID

It is a measure of how far this rot has spread that we do even find in the religious community individuals who associate with themselves with or abet crime, tax immorality or abuse of women and children. Inasmuch as members of this community should be in the vanguard of dealing with these in the rest of society, the legitimacy of their leadership will also depend on the extent to which they root out these things in their own ranks.

IBID

Frequently erstwhile revolutionaries have easily succumbed to greed, and the tendency to divert public resources for personal enrichment ultimately overwhelmed them.

FROM THE UNPUBLISHED SEQUEL TO HIS AUTOBIOGRAPHY, CIRCA 1998

Our hope for the future depends also on our resolution as a nation in dealing with the scourge of corruption. Success will require an acceptance that, in many respects, we are a sick society.

STATE OF THE NATION ADDRESS, PARLIAMENT, CAPE TOWN, SOUTH AFRICA, 5 FEBRUARY 1999

Countryside

You know that I am essentially a rustic like many of my contemporaries, born and brought up in a country village with its open spaces, lovely scenery and plenty of fresh air.

FROM A LETTER TO SENATOR DOUGLAS LUKHELE, WRITTEN ON ROBBEN ISLAND, 1 AUGUST 1970

Fourteen years of cramped life in South Africa's largest city had not killed the peasant in me and once again I was keen to see that ever-beckoning open veld and the blue mountains, the green grass and bushes, the rolling hills, rich valleys, the rapid streams as they sped across the escarpment into the insatiable sea.

FROM AN UNPUBLISHED AUTOBIOGRAPHICAL MANUSCRIPT, WRITTEN ON ROBBEN ISLAND, 1975

I must have been about five years old when I began going out with other boys to look after sheep and calves and when I was introduced to the exciting love of the veld. Later when I was a bit older I was able to look after cattle as well.

IBID

As compared with the city, life in a rural area is dull and uninspiring, even though we may have been born, grew up there, and even though we may like to be buried there, you would find that a trip abroad is a healthy and rewarding experience.

FROM A LETTER TO KEPU MKENTANE, WRITTEN IN POLLSMOOR PRISON, CAPE TOWN, SOUTH AFRICA, 1 MARCH 1988

I have always found it enjoyable to gaze out of the window while driving. I seemed to have my best ideas while driving through the countryside with the wind whipping through the window.

FROM *LONG WALK TO FREEDOM*, 1994

Courage

I can pretend that I am brave, you know, and [that] I can beat the whole world.

FROM A CONVERSATION WITH RICHARD STENGEL, 18 MARCH 1993

I learned that courage was not the absence of fear, but the triumph over it. I felt fear myself more times than I can remember, but I hid it behind a mask of boldness. The brave man is not he who does not feel afraid, but he who conquers that fear.

FROM *LONG WALK TO FREEDOM*, 1994

I was shaken but pretended that I was supremely confident of the victory of the liberation movement.

FROM THE UNPUBLISHED SEQUEL TO HIS AUTOBIOGRAPHY, CIRCA 1998

Crime

Every community in our country has a fundamental right to be free from fear. Each and every South African has the right to feel secure in their home, to feel safe in the cities, towns and rural areas. People should not fear the night. They must be able to travel to work, to school and other places without danger.

NATIONAL DAY OF SAFETY AND SECURITY, VOSLOORUS, SOUTH AFRICA, 15 OCTOBER 1994

Let us all take responsibility for freeing our communities of crime and violence. Let us not rob ourselves of the freedom which we have so recently won by allowing these evils to continue.

IBID

Attacks on the police are totally unacceptable. The task of the police is to protect and serve communities. The community in turn should help protect the police by denying refuge to criminals who carry out such attacks.

IBID

Freedom would be meaningless without security in the home and in the streets.

FREEDOM DAY CELEBRATIONS, PRETORIA, SOUTH AFRICA, 27 APRIL 1995

Our freedom is also incomplete, dear compatriots, as long as we are denied our security by criminals who prey on our communities, who rob our businesses and undermine our economy, who ply their destructive trade in drugs in our schools, and who do violence against our women and children.

FREEDOM DAY CELEBRATIONS, CAPE TOWN, SOUTH AFRICA, 27 APRIL 1998

Crime is a menace that disturbs any country. It hampers our efforts to build a society in which everyone's rights are respected. While even one person feels insecure in our land, we will not rest.

FIRST TRIANNUAL METHODIST CHURCH OF SOUTH AFRICA CONFERENCE, DURBAN, SOUTH AFRICA, 17 JULY 1998

Criticism

There is a wide difference between constructive criticism that will pave the way to a consensus and mere invective that tends to harden the differences.

FROM AN ESSAY ENTITLED 'CLEAR THE OBSTACLES AND CONFRONT THE ENEMY', WRITTEN ON ROBBEN ISLAND, 1976

Some may prefer not to say a word in regard to the mistakes we have made and the weaknesses shown in the course of our political work. The fact that apartheid institutions are in operation in certain areas is a reflection on us, and a measure of own weaknesses.

IBID

We should concentrate more on constructive self-criticism and on frankly and publicly acknowledging our own mistakes to our own people. Far from being a sign of weakness, it is a measure of one's strength and confidence, which will pay dividends in the end.

IBID

The ANC does not fear self-criticism because we know we have nothing to hide. We are absolutely confident that the tide of history is with us and therefore will not wilt under any form of criticism.

RALLY AT THE END OF THE ANC NATIONAL CONSULTATIVE CONFERENCE, SOCCER CITY, SOWETO, SOUTH AFRICA, 16 DECEMBER 1990

Among ourselves, we could point fingers and apportion blame in all directions. Perhaps that would satisfy an ego. But deflecting criticism, however justified we may be in doing so, would not help resolve the problem.

OPENING OF ANC/INKATHA FREEDOM SUMMIT, DURBAN, SOUTH AFRICA, 29 JANUARY 1991

The question of surrounding yourself, both in structures and in your individual work, with people who are strong and who will resist if you do something wrong is really something worthwhile.

IBID

We have been brought up in this tradition of collective leadership where even the head of the organisation can be subjected to criticism, severe criticism, which he will not resent unless, of course, you are discourteous and so on.

FROM AN INTERVIEW WITH THE BBC (UK), 1993

Criticism must be dignified. We must be factual, we must be realistic, we must be honest but, at the same time, you know, within a certain frame because we are builders.

FROM A CONVERSATION WITH AHMED KATHRADA, CIRCA 1993/94

On a number of occasions they tell me that, 'No, Mr President, with respect, we can't accept this. You are wrong.'

FROM THE DOCUMENTARY COUNTDOWN TO FREEDOM: TEN DAYS THAT CHANGED SOUTH AFRICA, 1994

I have often said that the media are a mirror through which we can see ourselves as others perceive us, warts, blemishes and all. The African National Congress has nothing to fear from criticism. I can promise you, we will not wilt under close scrutiny. It is our considered view that such criticism can only help us to grow, by calling attention to those of our actions and omissions which do not measure up to our people's expectations and the democratic values to which we subscribe.

ADDRESS TO THE INTERNATIONAL FEDERATION OF NEWSPAPER PUBLISHERS CONFERENCE, 14 FEBRUARY 1994

We know too well from our past experiences that robust and honest exchange of opinions and criticism is necessary for any society to be truly democratic and for any government to stay on course.

ADDRESS AT A LUNCHEON AT THE CONFERENCE OF EDITORS, SOUTH AFRICA, 6 SEPTEMBER 1994

South Africa now has a democratic government representative of, and accountable to, all the people. By your fearless commitment to truth and justice, the Methodist Church and other religious bodies helped realise this. But all governments, no matter how democratic, need constructive criticism and advice. I ask you to continue to play your prophetic role, always seeking to hold the nation and all its leaders to the highest standards of integrity and service.

ANNUAL METHODIST CHURCH CONFERENCE, MTHATHA, SOUTH AFRICA, 18 SEPTEMBER 1994

As all our institutions set about defining the part they should play in our new society, there will be moments of difficulty and uncertainty. An institution as central as the mass media is bound to encounter such moments. In this regard, we must commend the vibrancy of public criticism and scrutiny of the working and performance of government at all levels.

PRESIDENT'S BUDGET DEBATE, PARLIAMENT, CAPE TOWN, SOUTH AFRICA, 3 MAY 1995

The strategies, frameworks and plans should be improved through criticism, where necessary, and used for the benefit of the whole country. Ultimately, in debate and in action, now and in the future, we shall always face the option of whether to wallow in the mire of pettiness or to deal with the real issues that face the nation.

ADDRESS AT THE CLOSING OF THE PRESIDENT'S BUDGET DEBATE, PARLIAMENT, CAPE TOWN, SOUTH AFRICA, 21 JUNE 1996

We have raised some of the problems frankly, precisely because we know that the questions raised, the praises rendered and the criticisms offered were part of a robust debate meant to build a better democracy, a better society. They were raised because all of us have confidence that the government is dead serious about mobilising the South African nation to build this into a country of our dreams.

ADDRESS AT THE CLOSING OF THE PRESIDENT'S BUDGET DEBATE, PARLIAMENT, CAPE TOWN, SOUTH AFRICA, 16 APRIL 1997

Do Honourable Members always behave in a way that shows respect for those who elected them, for the public who observe them through the media, for their colleagues and for themselves? And how do we ensure that all the views are freely expressed and given the attention they deserve? On the part of the majority party it means taking opposition criticism of government and considering whether it has merit as something that can help promote the national good.

ADDRESS AT THE CLOSING OF THE PRESIDENT'S BUDGET DEBATE, PARLIAMENT, CAPE TOWN, SOUTH AFRICA, 22 APRIL 1998

Leaders fully appreciate that constructive criticism within the structures of the organisation, however sharp it may be, is one of the most effective methods of addressing internal problems.

FROM THE UNPUBLISHED SEQUEL TO HIS AUTOBIOGRAPHY, CIRCA 1998

We do appreciate criticism. But real leaders are emerging, who are able to see those issues that unite the country: leaders who have a sense of responsibility to ensure that, at the end of each debate, we emerge more united than before.

DEBATE ON THE STATE OF THE NATION ADDRESS, PARLIAMENT, CAPE TOWN, SOUTH AFRICA, 10 FEBRUARY 1999

Obviously there have been mistakes and weaknesses on the part of our government in addressing problems in the country for very obvious reasons. But the overall picture on which we concentrate is that there has been tremendous progress.

BRIEFING TO EDITORS AND OPINION MAKERS, PRETORIA, SOUTH AFRICA, 10 MAY 1999

Cuba

The first country we approached was the United States of America. We could not even succeed to come close to the government, and they refused to assist us. But Cuba, the moment we appealed for assistance they were ready to do so and they did so. Why would we now listen to the Western world when they say we should have nothing to do with Cuba? It is just unreasonable.

FROM THE DOCUMENTARY *MANDELA IN AMERICA*, 1990

I must say that when we wanted to take up arms we approached numerous Western governments for assistance and we were never able to see any but the most junior ministers. When we visited Cuba we were received by the highest officials and were immediately offered whatever we wanted and needed. That was our earliest experience with Cuban internationalism.

SPEECH ON THE THIRTY-EIGHTH ANNIVERSARY OF THE CUBAN REVOLUTION, MATANZAS, CUBA, 26 JULY 1991

The Cuban people hold a special place in the hearts of the people of Africa. The Cuban internationalists have made a contribution to African independence, freedom and justice, unparalleled for its principled and selfless character.

IBID

Custom

I consider myself obliged to pay proper respect to my customs and traditions, provided that such customs and traditions tend to keep us together and do not in any way conflict with the aims and objects of the struggle against racial oppression.

FROM AN UNPUBLISHED AUTOBIOGRAPHICAL MANUSCRIPT, WRITTEN ON ROBBEN ISLAND, 1975

I came to accept that I have no right whatsoever to judge others in terms of my own customs, however much I may be proud of such customs; that to despise others because they have not observed particular customs is a dangerous form of chauvinism.

IBID

I shall neither impose my own customs on others nor follow any practice which will offend my comrades, especially now that freedom has become so costly.

IBID

Mother could neither read nor write and had no means to send me to school. Yet a member of our clan educated me from the elementary school right up to Fort Hare and never expected any refund. According to our custom, I was his child and his responsibility. I have a lot of praise for this institution, not only because it's part of me but also because of its usefulness.

FROM A LETTER TO MRS N THULARE, WRITTEN ON ROBBEN ISLAND, 19 JULY 1977

In our custom and history, the chief is the mouthpiece of his people. He must listen to the complaints of his people. He is the custodian of their hopes and desires. And if any chief decides to be a tyrant, to take decisions for his people, he will come to a tragic end in the sense that we will deal with him.

ADDRESS TO YOUTH, SOUTH AFRICA, 13 APRIL 1990

It is so deeply entrenched that even in prison, prisoners circumcised one another.

FROM A BBC (UK) DOCUMENTARY, TALKING ABOUT THE CUSTOMARY MANHOOD RITE OF PASSAGE OF CIRCUMCISION, 1996

Death

If I must die, let me declare for all to know that I will meet my fate like a man.

FROM A NOTE WRITTEN HOURS BEFORE HIS SENTENCING IN THE RIVONIA TRIAL, PRETORIA, SOUTH AFRICA, 12 JUNE 1964

The death of a human being, whatever may be his station in life, is always a sad and painful affair; that of a noted public figure brings not only grief and mourning to his family and friends but very often entails implications of a wider nature.

FROM A LETTER TO CHIEF MANGOSUTHU BUTHELEZI, WRITTEN ON ROBBEN ISLAND, 4 NOVEMBER 1968

The threat of death evoked no desire in me to play the role of martyr. I was ready to do so if I had to. But the anxiety to live always lingered.

FROM A LETTER TO SEFTON VUTELA, WRITTEN ON ROBBEN ISLAND, 28 JULY 1969

Death is a frightful disaster no matter what the cause and the age of the person affected.

FROM A LETTER TO IRENE BUTHELEZI, UPON RECEIVING THE NEWS OF HIS SON THEMBI'S DEATH, WRITTEN IN VICTOR VERSTER PRISON, PAARL, SOUTH AFRICA, 3 AUGUST 1969

Suddenly my heart seemed to have stopped beating and the warm blood that had freely flown in my veins for the last fifty-one years froze into ice. For some time I could neither think nor talk and my strength appeared to be draining out.

IBID

Old and famous horses keel over like many that went before, some to be forgotten forever and others to be remembered as mere objects of history, and of interest to academicians only.

FROM A LETTER TO ARCHIE GUMEDE, WRITTEN ON ROBBEN ISLAND, 1 JANUARY 1975

The loss of trusted and respected veterans who played such decisive roles in our lives has been a great blow. What was even more heartbreaking is that we were unable to pay homage to them by being present at their gravesides.

FROM A LETTER TO MANGOSUTHU BUTHELEZI, WRITTEN ON ROBBEN ISLAND, 1 OCTOBER 1978

Even as we bow at their graves we remember this: the dead live on as martyrs in our hearts and minds, a reproach to our disunity and the host of shortcomings that accompany divisions among the oppressed, a spur to our efforts to close ranks and a reminder that the freedom of our people is yet to be won.

STATEMENT ABOUT THE 1976 SOWETO UPRISING, SMUGGLED OUT OF ROBBEN ISLAND PRISON AND RELEASED BY THE ANC IN EXILE, 1980

The death of your beloveds and your intimate friends to whom you are linked by countless ties, some going back for several decades; the wide variety of problems to which your family would be exposed in your absence, are personal disasters which are often difficult to endure and, on most occasions, leaving you wondering whether in this kind of life one should have a family, raise children and make firm friendships.

FROM A LETTER TO JOY MOSIELOA, WRITTEN IN POLLSMOOR PRISON, CAPE TOWN, SOUTH AFRICA, 17 FEBRUARY 1986

So many relatives and friends have died over these last twenty years, that it seems the world itself is dying.

FROM A LETTER TO DR AMEEN ARNOLD, WRITTEN IN POLLSMOOR PRISON, CAPE TOWN, SOUTH AFRICA, 10 AUGUST 1987

The death of a gifted veteran is always a tragic affair.

FROM A LETTER TO MRS KINI SIHLALI, WRITTEN ON ROBBEN ISLAND, 4 APRIL 1989

During the last twenty-seven years we have lost so many dear friends and so many noted buildings, that I sometimes fear that by the time I return, the world itself will have disappeared.

FROM A LETTER TO MADANJIT AND MARJORIE KAPITAN, WRITTEN IN VICTOR VERSTER PRISON, PAARL, SOUTH AFRICA, 28 SEPTEMBER 1989

It is a fact of the human condition that each shall, like a meteor, a mere brief passing moment in time and space, flit across the human stage and pass out of existence. Even the golden lads and lasses, as much as the chimney sweepers, come, and tomorrow are no more.

ADDRESS TO THE JOINT SESSION OF THE HOUSE OF CONGRESS, WASHINGTON DC, USA, 26 JUNE 1990

A friendly warder, just as the case was starting, asked me the question, 'Mandela, what do you think the judge is going to do with you in this case?' I said, 'Ag man, they're going to hang us'. I thought he was going to say, 'Ag, they'll never do that' but he stopped, became serious and took his eyes away from me and said, 'You're quite right, they are going to hang you'.

FROM A CONVERSATION WITH RICHARD STENGEL, 3 DECEMBER 1992

There *is* a practice amongst us, when you have been away and you find a close relative has passed away, you go, you are expected to go and pay your respects to his or her grave and it is something I knew would be priority number one when I returned.

FROM A CONVERSATION WITH RICHARD STENGEL, 13 JANUARY 1993

To lose a son, your eldest son, to whom I was very much attached, and I had no opportunity, you know, of paying my respects to his memory by attending the funeral, and seeing to the expenses of the funeral myself, and making sure that he rested very well and peacefully. That was very devastating.

FROM A CONVERSATION WITH RICHARD STENGEL, 9 MARCH 1993

We too will die but that which we collectively contribute to our national cultural identity will live forever beyond us.

OPENING OF THE CULTURAL DEVELOPMENT CONGRESS AT THE CIVIC THEATRE, JOHANNESBURG, SOUTH AFRICA, 25 APRIL 1993

They said [Chief Albert] Luthuli was confined to Groutville, and had become useless, immobilised, [Robert] Sobukwe was in jail and they said [Walter] Sisulu and Mandela are likely to be hanged and it was not very nice to read that you're likely to be hanged.

FROM A CONVERSATION WITH AHMED KATHRADA ABOUT AN EDITORIAL IN THE *RAND DAILY MAIL*, CIRCA 1993/94

We had, in fact, said amongst ourselves, because we were warned by the lawyers to expect a capital sentence at least against some of us and they identified us and we said, 'Let's go down under a cloud of glory'.

FROM A CONVERSATION WITH AHMED KATHRADA, CIRCA 1993/94

We were expecting a death sentence and we had resigned ourselves to it.

IBID

I was prepared for the death penalty. To be truly prepared for something, one must actually expect it. One cannot be prepared for something while secretly believing it will not happen. We were all prepared, not because we were brave but because we were realistic.

FROM *LONG WALK TO FREEDOM*, 1994

Men and women of rare qualities are few and hard to come by. And when they depart, the sense of loss is made the more profound and the more difficult to manage.

FUNERAL OF JOE SLOVO, SOUTH AFRICA, 15 JANUARY 1995

Death is something inevitable. When a man has done what he considers to be his duty to his people and his country, he can rest in peace. I believe I have made that effort and that is, therefore, why I will sleep for the eternity.

FROM THE DOCUMENTARY *MANDELA*, 1996

In eulogies to the departed, the works of the living sometimes bear little relation to reality.

COMMEMORATION OF THE TWENTIETH ANNIVERSARY OF THE DEATH IN POLICE DETENTION OF STEVE BIKO, EAST LONDON, SOUTH AFRICA, 1 SEPTEMBER 1997

If cancer has an upper hand and I leave this world, when I reach the next world the first thing I will do is to look for a branch of the African National Congress and renew my membership.

OPENING OF THE ZOLA CLINIC, SOWETO, SOUTH AFRICA, 7 MARCH 2002

I now know that when my time comes, Walter [Sisulu] will be there to meet me, and I am almost certain he will hold out an enrolment form to register me into the ANC in that world, cajoling me with one of his favourite songs we sang when mobilising people behind the Freedom Charter.

ON THE DEATH OF WALTER SISULU, SOUTH AFRICA, 5 MAY 2003

In the last few years we have walked this road with greater frequency, marching in the procession to bid farewell to the veterans of our movement, paying our last respects to the fallen spears of the nation from a generation now reaching the end of a long and heroic struggle.

FUNERAL OF WALTER SISULU, SOWETO, SOUTH AFRICA, 17 MAY 2003

We shed tears over them because we have walked such a long road together: sharing trials and tribulations; danger, anguish and fear; and also precious moments of joy, gladness and laughter. Their going must leave emptiness with those of us who stay behind.

IBID

They fought a noble battle and lived their lives in pursuit of a better life for all who follow. The democracy, in which we bury them and honour them, is the sweet fruit of their lives of struggle and sacrifice.

IBID

My family's here and I'd like to be buried here at home.

FROM THE DOCUMENTARY *MANDELA: THE LIVING LEGEND*, SPEAKING IN THE FAMILY GRAVEYARD IN QUNU, SOUTH AFRICA, 2003

Even when your parents are old you wish them to continue forever and there are children who died and so it evokes painful memories.

IBID

I would like it to be said that, 'Here lies a man who has done his duty on earth'. That is all.

FROM THE DOCUMENTARY *HEADLINERS AND LEGENDS: NELSON MANDELA*, 2006

Defiance Campaign

Defiance [Campaign] was a step of great political significance. It released strong social forces which affected thousands of our countrymen. It was an effective way of getting the masses to function politically, a powerful method of voicing our indignation against the reactionary policies of the government.

PRESIDENTIAL ADDRESS TO THE ANC TRANSVAAL CONGRESS, ALSO KNOWN AS THE 'NO EASY WALK TO FREEDOM' SPEECH, TRANSVAAL, SOUTH AFRICA, 21 SEPTEMBER 1953

What I took out was the ability to conduct a struggle without violence, in a non-violent manner, peaceful and disciplined. That's what I took out and not even as a principle, but as a tactic.

FROM A CONVERSATION WITH RICHARD STENGEL, 4 DECEMBER 1992

Here were people who were going to jail because of a principle, because they were protesting against a law which they regarded as unjust. Students who were my colleagues left classes and went to defy for the *love* of their people and their country. That had a tremendous impact on me.

FROM A CONVERSATION WITH RICHARD STENGEL, 18 MARCH 1993

The goal was to *break* these six laws and to go to prison and by so doing to focus the attention of the country and the world on our grievances. And that we want to clear everybody from the fear of the white man, which paralysed them, the fear of his courts, his prison, and his police, his army. We wanted people to know that they can actually *challenge* injustice and go to jail and still come out. And we also wanted to instil a spirit of resistance in our people and thirdly, to forge unity.

FROM A CONVERSATION WITH RICHARD STENGEL, CIRCA MARCH 1993

By the standards of the day, it had a tremendous impact, to see people going into jail and coming out alive and even prepared to go back. But it was confined to the towns and we neglected the countryside altogether and that has always been our weakness.
IBID

It was a form of protest, not a means of bringing down the government to its knees immediately.
FROM A CONVERSATION WITH RICHARD STENGEL, 19 MARCH 1993

Some people thought that the Defiance Campaign would actually topple the government and when we said, 'No, there's nothing of the sort', they just did not want to believe us, and wanted us to continue indefinitely. We said, 'You can't do that.' This campaign was merely intended to focus attention on our grievances.
IBID

If a man can challenge a law and go to jail and come out, that man is not likely to be intimidated, you see, by jail life, generally speaking.
FROM A CONVERSATION WITH RICHARD STENGEL, 29 APRIL 1993

We broke those laws and courted jail and, as a result of campaigns of that nature, you got our people now not to fear repression, to be prepared to challenge it.
IBID

The campaign freed me from any lingering sense of doubt or inferiority I might still have felt; it liberated me from the feeling of being overwhelmed by the power and seeming invincibility of the white man and his institutions. But now the white man had felt the power of my punches and I could walk upright like a man, and look everyone in the eye with the dignity that comes from not having succumbed to oppression and fear. I had come of age as a freedom fighter.
FROM LONG WALK TO FREEDOM, 1994

In 1952, we launched the Defiance Campaign where we selected six unjust laws and defied them so that we can go to jail and be able to focus attention on these unjust laws.
FROM A BBC (UK) DOCUMENTARY, 1996

Democracy

All the democratic forces in this country must join in a programme of democratic changes. If they are not prepared to come along with us, they can at least be neutral and leave this government isolated and without friends.
FROM AN ARTICLE ENTITLED 'THE STRUGGLE FOR A NATIONAL CONVENTION', FIGHTING TALK, APRIL 1961

The Africans require the franchise on the basis of one man one vote. They want political independence.
FROM AN INTERVIEW WITH BRIAN WIDLAKE FOR ITN TELEVISION (UK), JOHANNESBURG, SOUTH AFRICA, 31 MAY 1961

We stressed that the strike would be followed by other forms of mass pressure to force the race maniacs who govern our beloved country to make way for a democratic government of the people, by the people and for the people.
FROM THE 'STRUGGLE IS MY LIFE' PRESS STATEMENT, EXPLAINING HIS DECISION TO CARRY ON HIS POLITICAL WORK UNDERGROUND IN ACCORDANCE WITH THE ADVICE OF THE NATIONAL ACTION COUNCIL, SOUTH AFRICA, 26 JUNE 1961

We were inspired by the idea of bringing into being a democratic republic where all South Africans will enjoy human rights without the slightest discrimination: where African and non-African would be able to live together in peace, sharing a common nationality and a common loyalty to this country, which is our homeland.

IN MITIGATION OF SENTENCE AFTER BEING CONVICTED OF INCITING WORKERS TO STRIKE AND LEAVING THE COUNTRY ILLEGALLY, OLD SYNAGOGUE, PRETORIA, SOUTH AFRICA, NOVEMBER 1962

That the will of the people is the basis of the authority of government is a principle universally acknowledged as sacred throughout the civilised world, and constitutes the basic foundations of freedom and justice. It is understandable why citizens, who have the vote as well as the right to direct representation in the country's governing bodies, should be morally and legally bound by the laws governing the country.

IBID

Our main demand is the total abolition of all forms of white supremacy and the extension of the vote to all South Africans.

FROM AN ESSAY ENTITLED 'CLEAR THE OBSTACLES AND CONFRONT THE ENEMY', WRITTEN ON ROBBEN ISLAND, 1976

Our people demand democracy. Our country, which continues to bleed and suffer pain, needs democracy. It cries out for the situation where the law will decree that the freedom to speak of freedom constitutes the very essence of legality and the very thing that makes for the legitimacy of the constitutional order.

ADDRESS TO THE JOINT SESSION OF THE HOUSE OF CONGRESS, WASHINGTON DC, USA, 26 JUNE 1990

The hour of destiny has dawned. The day is not far when our dream of a united, democratic, non-racial and non-sexist South Africa shall be turned into reality.

CONCERT ORGANISED BY THE IRISH ANTI-APARTHEID MOVEMENT, DUBLIN, IRELAND, 1 JULY 1990

It is the solemn responsibility of the most oppressed and exploited to lead South Africa out of the morass and degradation of apartheid into a new era of freedom and democracy for all its people. We extend our arms in friendship to our white compatriots and call upon them to embrace the cause of democracy in their thousands, as the only reliable guarantor of their future. The bright promise of a democratic South Africa demands that they shed their fears and step forward boldly prepared to build a country we can all be proud to call our home.

KEYNOTE ADDRESS TO THE ANC NATIONAL CONSULTATIVE CONFERENCE, JOHANNESBURG, SOUTH AFRICA, 14 DECEMBER 1990

Without democracy there cannot be peace.

SPEAKING AT THE UNIVERSITY COLLEGE OF FORT HARE, ALICE, SOUTH AFRICA, 9 MAY 1992

One of the lessons of our times is that a transfer of power to a democratic organisation does not mean that ordinary people necessarily have the opportunity to exercise their democratic rights.

IBID

It matters very little to me whether I see it or not but it is definitely around the corner and that's what motivates me.

FROM AN INTERVIEW WITH THE BBC (UK), CIRCA 1993

This is a watershed moment for all of us. Our decisions and actions will determine whether we use our pain, our grief and our outrage to move forward to what is the only lasting solution for our country – an elected government of the people, by the people and for the people.

TELEVISED ADDRESS TO THE NATION AFTER THE ASSASSINATION OF CHRIS HANI, SOUTH AFRICA, 13 APRIL 1993

Your right to determine your own destiny was used to deny us to determine our own. Thus history brought our peoples together in its own peculiar ways. That history demands of us that we should strive to achieve what you, through the rediscovery of the practice of democracy, achieved for yourselves.

ADDRESS TO THE HOUSE OF COMMONS, LONDON, ENGLAND, 5 MAY 1993

A democratic order is not based solely on the accepted principle of one person, one vote; it must, in addition, recognise the constitutional right of dissent. It must also ensure that the power of the majority is constrained by constitutional means.

INVESTITURE AS DOCTOR OF LAWS, SOOCHOW UNIVERSITY, TAIWAN, 1 AUGUST 1993

Democracy and human rights are inseparable. We cannot have the one without the other. It is not an easy road that our country is going to travel. The end of apartheid will not guarantee the beginning of democracy. But until apartheid is totally destroyed, there can be no democracy.

IBID

The people of South Africa have waited too long for a government elected by all the people. We must not and we dare not fail them. A democratic government, so elected, can and will address the terrible legacy of apartheid and allow every man, woman and child to walk tall, free and proud in the country of their birth.

REACTING TO THE ANNOUNCEMENT THAT HE HAD BEEN AWARDED THE NOBEL PRIZE FOR PEACE, 15 OCTOBER 1993

Let this, however, be clear: there is no place in a democracy for any community or section of a community to impose its will at the expense the fundamental rights of any other citizen.

ANNOUNCEMENT OF THE ELECTION DATE, MULTI-PARTY NEGOTIATIONS PROCESS, KEMPTON PARK, SOUTH AFRICA, 17 NOVEMBER 1993

The struggle for democracy has never been a matter pursued by one race, class, religious community or gender among South Africans. In honouring those who fought to see this day arrive, we honour the best sons and daughters of all our people. We can count amongst them Africans, coloureds, whites, Indians, Muslims, Christians, Hindus, Jews – all of them united by a common vision of a better life for the people of this country.

ADDRESSING THE PEOPLE OF CAPE TOWN AFTER HIS ELECTION AS PRESIDENT, CITY HALL, CAPE TOWN, SOUTH AFRICA, 9 MAY 1994

Democracy in South Africa has brought new social priorities. It has brought peace with our neighbours. It has exposed our country to the forces of the global economy which is offering new opportunities and challenges, on a larger scale than ever before.

104TH ANNUAL GENERAL MEETING OF THE CHAMBER OF MINES OF SOUTH AFRICA, JOHANNESBURG, SOUTH AFRICA, 8 NOVEMBER 1994

Jawaharlal Nehru taught us that the right to a roof over one's head and affordable services, a job and reasonable income, education and health facilities is more than just a bonus to democracy. It is the essence of democracy itself, the essence of human rights.

RAJIV GANDHI FOUNDATION LECTURE, NEW DELHI, INDIA, 25 JANUARY 1995

Let me restate the obvious: I have long passed my teens; and the distance to my final destination is shorter than the road I have trudged over the years! All of us have to live with this truth, without suffering undue insecurity. That is what nature has decreed.

FROM AN ARTICLE IN THE *SUNDAY TIMES* (SOUTH AFRICA), 22 FEBRUARY 1996

It is not our diversity which divides us; it is not our ethnicity, or religion or culture that divides us. Since we have achieved our freedom, there can only be one division amongst us: between those who cherish democracy and those who do not.

UPON RECEIVING THE FREEDOM OF THE CITY OF DURBAN, DURBAN, SOUTH AFRICA, 16 APRIL 1999

The right of a person to vote freely in democratic elections, to express him or herself without hindrance, to gather and associate as one wishes, to move freely in one's land – these are precious freedoms that lift the human spirit and give expression to our God-given rights.

UPON RECEIVING THE FREEDOM AWARD FROM THE NATIONAL CIVIL RIGHTS MUSEUM, MEMPHIS, TENNESSEE, USA, 22 NOVEMBER 2000

Democratic South Africa remains aware that we have to continuously remain vigilant that the people do in fact govern.

DINNER TO COMMEMORATE THE SIXTH ANNIVERSARY OF THE DEATH OF PREMIER ANDREAS PAPANDREOU OF GREECE, GREECE, 19 JUNE 2001

We have to consolidate and deepen our hard-fought-for democracy: the democratic impulse and practice must live in every fibre of our society.

YOUTH FORUM ON AIDS, JOHANNESBURG, SOUTH AFRICA, 22 SEPTEMBER 2003

An educated, enlightened and informed population is one of the surest ways of promoting the health of a democracy.

ST JOHN'S COLLEGE, JOHANNESBURG, SOUTH AFRICA, 6 OCTOBER 2003

The growth, consolidation and sustained health of our democracy are the responsibilities not only of leaders but also of each and every citizen.

VIDEO MESSAGE TO MARK TEN YEARS OF DEMOCRACY IN SOUTH AFRICA, APRIL 2004

The first decade of democracy was a period of laying the foundations and of consolidation. We can now with some assurance and confidence claim that our democracy is firmly established.

ANC ELECTION RALLY, FIRST NATIONAL BANK STADIUM, SOWETO, SOUTH AFRICA, 4 APRIL 2004

Not only did we avert such racial conflagration, we created amongst ourselves one of the most exemplary and progressive non-racial and non-sexist democratic orders in the contemporary world.

FROM AN ARTICLE IN THE *SUNDAY TIMES* (SOUTH AFRICA) MARKING TEN YEARS OF DEMOCRACY, APRIL 2004

For once history and hope rhymed, a famous poet reminded me and us, speaking of the miracle of our transition and the wonder of our democracy.

IBID

Our democracy must bring its material fruits to all, particularly the poor, marginalised and vulnerable. Our belief in the common good ultimately translates into a deep concern for those that suffer want and deprivation of any kind.

JOINT SITTING OF PARLIAMENT TO MARK TEN YEARS OF DEMOCRACY, PARLIAMENT, CAPE TOWN, SOUTH AFRICA, 10 MAY 2004

Let us refrain from chauvinistic breast-beating, but let [us] also not underrate what we have achieved in establishing a stable and progressive democracy where we take freedoms seriously: in building national unity in spite of decades and centuries of apartheid and colonial rule; and in creating a culture in which we increasingly respect the dignity of all.

IBID

A guiding principle in our search for and establishment of a non-racial inclusive democracy in our country has been that there are good men and women to be found in all groups and from all sectors of society; and that in an open and free society those South Africans will come together to jointly and cooperatively realise the common good.

IBID

We fought hard and sacrificed much for this democracy. Protect, defend, consolidate and advance democracy – within the organisation and in national life. Let us give the lead in demonstrating our respect for the institutions of our democracy – both in our actions and words.

ANC RALLY FOR HIS NINETIETH BIRTHDAY, LOFTUS VERSFELD STADIUM, PRETORIA, SOUTH AFRICA, 2 AUGUST 2008

The freedoms which democracy brings will remain empty shells if they are not accompanied by real and tangible improvements in the material lives of millions of ordinary citizens of those countries.

FROM THE DOCUMENTARY *VIVA MADIBA: A HERO FOR ALL SEASONS*, 2010

Where men and women and children go burdened with hunger, talk of democracy and freedom that does not recognise these material aspects can ring hollow and erode confidence exactly in those values we seek to promote.

IBID

Destiny

People must be allowed to determine their own destiny.

AT HOME, SOWETO, SOUTH AFRICA, 14 FEBRUARY 1990

Determination

There are few misfortunes in this world that you cannot turn into a personal triumph if you have the iron will and the necessary skill.

FROM A LETTER TO ZINDZI MANDELA, WRITTEN ON ROBBEN ISLAND, 25 MARCH 1979

What has kept us all on course is the unquenchable aspiration of our people for equality, dignity, respect and tolerance.

DINNER TO MARK THE ADOPTION OF THE CONSTITUTION, CAPE TOWN, SOUTH AFRICA, 8 MAY 1996

No society emerging out of the grand disaster represented by the apartheid system could afford to carry the blemishes of its past. Had the new South Africa emerged out of nothing, it would not exist. The being it has assumed, dictated by its origins, constitutes a veritable school of learning about what needs to be done, still, to end the system of apartheid.

ADDRESS TO THE JOINT HOUSES OF PARLIAMENT, WESTMINSTER HALL, LONDON, ENGLAND, 11 JULY 1996

If our expectations – if our fondest prayers and dreams – are not realised, then we should all bear in mind that the greatest glory of living lies not in never falling, but in rising every time you fall.

RECEPTION HOSTED BY PRESIDENT BILL CLINTON, THE WHITE HOUSE, WASHINGTON DC, USA, 22 SEPTEMBER 1998

Once a person is determined to help themselves, there is nothing that can stop them.

FATHER'S DAY LUNCH HOSTED BY ZINDZI MANDELA, HYATT WOMEN OF VISION CLUB, JOHANNESBURG, SOUTH AFRICA, 1 JUNE 2002

When people are determined, they can overcome anything.

FROM A CONVERSATION WITH MORGAN FREEMAN, JOHANNESBURG, SOUTH AFRICA, 14 NOVEMBER 2006

Everyone can rise above their circumstances and achieve success if they are dedicated to and passionate about what they do.

FROM A LETTER TO MAKHAYA NTINI ON HIS HUNDREDTH CRICKET TEST FOR SOUTH AFRICA, 17 DECEMBER 2009

Dialogue

Some of the most influential amongst us seriously doubted whether dialogue with the apartheid regime was a feasible option.

FROM AN UNPUBLISHED AUTOBIOGRAPHICAL MANUSCRIPT, WRITTEN ON ROBBEN ISLAND, 1975

The most powerful weapon is not violence but it is talking to people.

FROM AN INTERVIEW WITH THE BBC (UK), 28 OCTOBER 1993

The relative success that we have attained in Southern Africa vindicates our belief that conflicts can and must be resolved peacefully through dialogue.

PRESENTATION OF THE AFRICA PEACE AWARD TO THE NATION OF MOZAMBIQUE, DURBAN, SOUTH AFRICA, 1 NOVEMBER 1997

Unfortunately none of us can escape blame for the situation in which humankind finds itself. In almost every part of the world, human beings find reasons to resort to force and violence in addressing differences that we surely should attempt to resolve through negotiation, dialogue and reason.

MESSAGE TO THE GLOBAL CONVENTION ON PEACE AND NON-VIOLENCE, NEW DELHI, INDIA, 31 JANUARY 2004

Diary of Anne Frank, The

I read the diary before I went to prison but reading books at that time was something totally different from reading the same book inside prison, especially that of Anne Frank because we identified with her in the situation which we were in and, therefore, the lessons of that tragedy sunk more deeply in our souls and also encouraged us in our situation because, if a young girl of thirteen could take such militant action, then we could follow the same example.

FROM AN INTERVIEW, JOHANNESBURG, SOUTH AFRICA, 15 AUGUST 1994

What we took away from that was the invincibility of the human spirit which expresses itself in different ways in different situations. She did it in a remarkable way which encouraged all those who might find themselves in that situation.

IBID

For a young lady of that nature to take a stand is something unique. Her life was one on which young people could model their own lives and that is what was striking about the life of Anne Frank.

IBID

Differences

Our differences are our strength as a species and as a world community.

UPON RECEIVING THE FRANKLIN D ROOSEVELT FOUR FREEDOMS AWARD, 8 JUNE 2002

Dignity

I wish I could tell you more about the courageous band of colleagues with whom I suffer humiliation daily and who nevertheless deport themselves with dignity and determination.

FROM AN UNPUBLISHED AUTOBIOGRAPHICAL MANUSCRIPT, WRITTEN ON ROBBEN ISLAND, 1975

I call in the strongest possible way for us to act with the dignity and discipline that our just struggle for freedom deserves.

WELCOME HOME RALLY, SOCCER CITY, SOWETO, SOUTH AFRICA, 13 FEBRUARY 1990

We come from a people who, because they would not accept to be treated as subhuman, redeemed the dignity of all humanity everywhere.

ADDRESS TO THE PARLIAMENT OF CANADA, OTTAWA, CANADA, 18 JUNE 1990

Our people have the right to hope, the right to a future, the right to life itself. No power on this earth can destroy the thirst for human dignity. Our land cries out for peace. We will only achieve it through adherence to democratic principles and respect for the rights of all.

SPEECH AT KING WILLIAM'S TOWN, BHISHO, SOUTH AFRICA, 8 SEPTEMBER 1992

My government's commitment to create a people-centred society of liberty binds us to the pursuit of the goals of freedom from want, freedom from hunger, freedom from deprivation, freedom from ignorance, freedom from suppression and freedom from fear. These freedoms are fundamental to the guarantee of human dignity.

FIRST STATE OF THE NATION ADDRESS, PARLIAMENT, CAPE TOWN, SOUTH AFRICA, 24 MAY 1994

Our definition of the freedom of the individual must be instructed by the fundamental objective to restore the human dignity of each and every South African.

IBID

Together we won our freedom and dignity. Today we can walk tall and proudly say we are all South Africans.

ELECTION RALLY, SOWETO, SOUTH AFRICA, 1999

The first value quoted in the founding provisions of our Constitution is that of human dignity.

FROM AN ARTICLE IN THE SUNDAY TIMES (SOUTH AFRICA) MARKING TEN YEARS OF DEMOCRACY, APRIL 2004

We accord persons dignity by assuming that they are good, that they share the human qualities we ascribe to ourselves.

JOINT SITTING OF PARLIAMENT TO MARK TEN YEARS OF DEMOCRACY, PARLIAMENT, CAPE TOWN, SOUTH AFRICA, 10 MAY 2004

It was important for you to maintain a certain dignity. Laughing didn't help you to maintain that dignity. You had to be serious.

FROM AN INTERVIEW WITH TIM COUZENS, VERNE HARRIS AND MAC MAHARAJ FOR *MANDELA: THE AUTHORISED PORTRAIT*, 2006, RECALLING HOW AS CHILDREN THEY WERE ENCOURAGED NOT TO LAUGH TOO MUCH, JOHANNESBURG, SOUTH AFRICA, 13 AUGUST 2005

Disability

Disabled children are equally entitled to an exciting and brilliant future.

OPENING OF THE FIRST ANNUAL SOUTH AFRICAN JUNIOR WHEELCHAIR SPORTS CAMP, JOHANNESBURG, SOUTH AFRICA, 4 DECEMBER 1994

I would like to tell you that I also wear hearing aids, just as you do. These little instruments made a big difference to my life. Wherever I go, they help me to listen better, to understand better.

SPEECH AT BARAGWANATH HOSPITAL HEARING AID PROJECT, SOWETO, SOUTH AFRICA, 23 MAY 1997

Human beings regard their mental capacity as the most defining feature of themselves as a species. To respond in a caring manner to the impairment of those capacities in others is to really know ourselves as human beings and to live out our humanness.

ADDRESS AT A FUND-RAISING EVENT FOR THE TAKALANI HOME FOR THE MENTALLY DISABLED, SPARROW SCHOOLS AND LIVING LINK, SOUTH AFRICA, SEPTEMBER 2002

We have tried to give special emphasis to the rights of people living with disability. It is so easy to think of equality demands with reference primarily to race, colour, religion and gender, and to forget, or to relegate to secondary importance, the vast discrimination against disabled persons.

MESSAGE TO THE CONFERENCE FOR THE DISABLED, 4 APRIL 2004

A democracy is an order of social equality and non-discrimination. Our compatriots who are disabled challenge us in a very special way to manifest in real life those values of democracy.

IBID

Disasters

Disasters will always come and go, leaving their victims either completely broken or steeled and seasoned and better able to face the next crop of challenges that may occur.

FROM A LETTER TO WINNIE MANDELA, WRITTEN ON ROBBEN ISLAND, 23 JUNE 1969

Discipline

Human beings like to be associated with a hard-working, disciplined and successful person and, by carefully cultivating these qualities, you will win yourself many friends.

FROM A LETTER TO MAKGATHO MANDELA, WRITTEN ON ROBBEN ISLAND, 28 JULY 1969

As future leaders there are certain responsibilities which we expect you to observe. One of these is utmost discipline. If you are not disciplined, you can never win our confidence.

ADDRESS TO THE YOUTH, SOUTH AFRICA, 13 APRIL 1990

Discrimination

I regarded it as a duty which I owed, not just to my people, but also to my profession, to the practice of law and to justice for all mankind, to cry out against this discrimination, which is essentially unjust and opposed to the whole basis of the attitude towards justice which is part of the tradition of legal training in this country.

IN MITIGATION OF SENTENCE AFTER BEING CONVICTED OF INCITING WORKERS TO STRIKE AND LEAVING THE COUNTRY ILLEGALLY, OLD SYNAGOGUE, PRETORIA, SOUTH AFRICA, 7 NOVEMBER 1962

Discussion

Discussion sharpens one's interest in any subject and accordingly inspires reading and corrects errors.

FROM A LETTER TO THE COMMISSIONER OF PRISONS, WRITTEN ON ROBBEN ISLAND, 10 OCTOBER 1965

In any discussions, especially with politicians, there will be disagreements.

FROM A CONVERSATION WITH RICHARD STENGEL, 22 DECEMBER 1992

I have discovered that in discussions it never helps to take a morally superior tone to one's opponent.

FROM *LONG WALK TO FREEDOM*, 1994

Disease

In this world in which we have the means to cure many of the cancers that only a decade ago were considered lethal, surely we are able to vaccinate all children against child-killing diseases.

STATEMENT ON BUILDING A GLOBAL PARTNERSHIP FOR CHILDREN, 6 MAY 2000

Don't leave it to the government... you, yourself, must take the initiative where you are, to ensure that your neighbours, whatever terminal diseases they are suffering from, are given love, support and whatever means you have in order to make them forget about their illness and to feel that they are human beings; they are loved by those around them.

OPENING OF THE ZOLA CLINIC, SOWETO, SOUTH AFRICA, 7 MARCH 2002

Now, I have suffered from illnesses which have a stigma. When I was in prison I contracted TB and there are many people who do not want to have anything to do with somebody who has tuberculosis. And as you know now, last year, I was found to be a cancer patient. Now, I didn't hide this, I immediately called the press and I told them I have this illness.

IBID

Dreams

The anchor of all my dreams is the collective wisdom of mankind as a whole.

FROM A LETTER TO SENATOR DOUGLAS LUKHELE, WRITTEN ON ROBBEN ISLAND, 1 AUGUST 1970

As we take stock of our accomplishments and shortcomings, we should not, by the slightest of chance, lose sight of our once-ambitious dream for education, total economic participation, democracy and freedom for all.

SPEAKING AT THE NATIONAL YOUTH FESTIVAL, SOUTH AFRICA, JUNE 2008

Duty

To go to prison because of your convictions, and be prepared to suffer for what you believe in, is something worthwhile. It is an achievement for a man to do his duty on earth irrespective of the consequences.

FROM AN INTERVIEW WITH SCOTT MACLEOD OF *TIME* MAGAZINE, SOWETO, SOUTH AFRICA, 26 FEBRUARY 1990

Economy

A form of economy will be decided solely by our determination to make the economy perform fully from the point of view of ensuring full employment, maximum productivity and the development of a social consciousness. Any formula, any option which will enable us to do this, we will adopt.

FROM THE DOCUMENTARY *MANDELA IN AMERICA*, 1990

The democratic project in which we are all interested cannot succeed unless the economy can deliver.

CONFERENCE CONVENED BY THE CONSULTATIVE BUSINESS MOVEMENT ON THE THEME 'OPTIONS FOR BUILDING AN ECONOMIC FUTURE', SOUTH AFRICA, 23 MAY 1990

We have to ensure that the economy serves the interests of the people as a whole, is geared to end the terrible poverty and deprivation that is the legacy of the apartheid system, and grows at a rate and in a manner which will enable all the people to enjoy a decent and rising standard of living.

ADDRESS TO THE EUROPEAN PARLIAMENT, STRASBOURG, FRANCE, 13 JUNE 1990

We are also determined that the political freedom of which we have spoken should go side by side with freedom from hunger, want and suffering. It is therefore of vital importance that we restructure the South African economy so that its wealth is shared by all our people, black and white, to ensure that everybody enjoys a decent and rising standard of living.

ADDRESS TO THE PARLIAMENT OF CANADA, OTTAWA, CANADA, 18 JUNE 1990

We are convinced this economy will have to be restructured, so that it is able to serve the material interests of all our people, and not just the white minority.

MESSAGE TO THE BUSINESS COMMUNITY OF THE USA, 19 JUNE 1990

We require an economy that is able to address the needs of all the people of our country, that can provide food, houses, education, health services, social security and everything that makes human life human, that makes life joyful and not a protracted encounter with hopelessness and despair.

ADDRESS TO THE JOINT SESSION OF THE HOUSE OF CONGRESS, WASHINGTON DC, USA, 26 JUNE 1990

The extent of the deprivation of millions of people has to be seen to be believed. The injury is made that more intolerable by the opulence of our white compatriots and the deliberate distortion of the economy to feed that opulence.

IBID

The struggle we are waging is also for the economic transformation of our country. The system to which we are heirs was designed and operates for the benefit of the white minority at the expense of the black majority. Clearly the situation cannot be allowed to continue in which millions know nothing but the corrosive ache of hunger, in which countless numbers of children die and get deformed as a result of being afflicted by kwashiorkor and other diseases of poverty. Millions are today without jobs and without land. Nothing awaits them except death from starvation and want.

STATEMENT TO THE PARLIAMENT OF THE REPUBLIC OF IRELAND, DUBLIN, REPUBLIC OF IRELAND, 2 JULY 1990

We must reserve the right to use any economic instrument to stimulate growth and effect redistribution to redress historical economic imbalances and injustices.

SIGNING OF A STATEMENT OF INTENT TO SET UP A NATIONAL CAPACITY FOR ECONOMIC RESEARCH AND POLICY FORMULATION, SOUTH AFRICA, 23 NOVEMBER 1991

The biggest threat to democracy, socio-economic justice and economic growth in this country is the monopoly control by a few companies of the whole economy.

IBID

We shall therefore have to apply ourselves with even more discipline and commitment to productivity in order to achieve the economic goals that will help create more jobs and free up resources to deliver services to our people.

INSTALLATION OF PROFESSOR MELCK, UNIVERSITY OF SOUTH AFRICA, PRETORIA, SOUTH AFRICA, 29 MARCH 1999

We must ensure that all South Africans have a sense of ownership in all sectors of society. The long-term stability of our democratic order is also dependent upon all sectors of the population participating meaningfully at all levels of the economy.

ADDRESS AT SOUTH AFRICAN CHAMBER OF BUSINESS (SACOB) DINNER, JOHANNESBURG, SOUTH AFRICA, 23 OCTOBER 2001

Education

We declare our firm belief in the principles enunciated in the Universal Declaration of Human Rights that everyone has the right to education: that education shall be directed to the full development of human personality and to the strengthening of respect for human rights and fundamental freedoms. It shall promote understanding, tolerance and friendship among the nation's racial or religious groups and shall further the activities of the United Nations for the maintenance of peace.

PRESIDENTIAL ADDRESS TO THE ANC TRANSVAAL CONGRESS, ALSO KNOWN AS THE 'NO EASY WALK TO FREEDOM' SPEECH, TRANSVAAL, SOUTH AFRICA, 21 SEPTEMBER 1953

You must defend the right of African parents to decide the kind of education that shall be given to their children. Teach the children that Africans are not one iota inferior to Europeans. Establish your own community schools where the right kind of education will be given to our children. If it becomes dangerous or impossible to have these alternative schools, then again you must make every home, every shack or rickety structure a centre of learning for our children. Never surrender to the inhuman and barbaric theories of Verwoerd.

IBID

Everywhere in the world it is accepted that students, as a thinking and independent-minded section of the population, have the right to freedom of thought and expression of opinion.

STATEMENT TO THE ALL-IN AFRICAN NATIONAL ACTION COUNCIL, 5 SEPTEMBER 1961

The issues that agitate humanity today call for trained minds and the man who is deficient in this respect is crippled because he is not in possession of the tools and equipment necessary to ensure success and victory in the service of country and people.

FROM A LETTER TO MAKGATHO MANDELA, WRITTEN ON ROBBEN ISLAND, 28 JULY 1969

Nobody ever sat with me at regular intervals to give me a clear and connected account of the history of our country, of its geography, natural wealth and problems, of our culture, of how to count, to study weights and measures.

FROM AN UNPUBLISHED AUTOBIOGRAPHICAL MANUSCRIPT, WRITTEN ON ROBBEN ISLAND, 1975

If there is one appeal I could make, it is that young people must take it upon themselves to ensure that they receive the highest education possible so that they can represent us well in future as future leaders.

FROM THE DOCUMENTARY *MANDELA IN AMERICA*, 1990

Children of today are the leaders of tomorrow and education is a very important weapon to prepare children for their future roles as leaders of the community.

AT HOME, SOWETO, SOUTH AFRICA, FEBRUARY 1990

We want all educational institutions to contribute to the creation of the new, democratic, non-racial and non-sexist South Africa. But that does not entail supporting every position of the ANC. We have made mistakes and, perhaps through constructive criticism, scholars at this university can save us from further mistakes. I urge you, therefore, to act as you think is correct and most useful in furthering the overall democratic goals that we share.

SPEAKING AT THE UNIVERSITY COLLEGE OF FORT HARE, ALICE, SOUTH AFRICA, 9 MAY 1992

Education is the great engine of personal development. It is through education that the daughter of a peasant can become a doctor, that the son of a mine worker can become the head of the mine, that a child of farmworkers can become the president of a great nation. It is what we make out of what we have, not what we are given, that separates one person from another.

FROM *LONG WALK TO FREEDOM*, 1994

To our generation, education became a key to unlock the gates of oppression, a tool against the warped logic of the slave-master. Institutions of learning became the centre to challenge colonial domination and injustice. For this, the thorny gown and cap of achievement were detention, death, exile and long terms of imprisonment.

UPON RECEIVING AN HONORARY DOCTORATE FROM SEOUL NATIONAL UNIVERSITY, SEOUL, KOREA, 6 JULY 1995

In the same way that we waged war against apartheid education, government and communities should together combat those factors which militate against effective learning and teaching.

LAUNCH OF THE NATIONAL CAMPAIGN FOR LEARNING AND TEACHING, SOWETO, JOHANNESBURG, SOUTH AFRICA, 20 FEBRUARY 1997

South Africans have made tremendous sacrifices, and many have given their lives, to ensure that you have access to the best education your country can afford. Redeem their sacrifice by acting to ensure that effective learning occurs in our schools.

IBID

You can help educate the nation by participating in the activities of schools and protecting them from vandals, by supporting them, by working with teachers and students, and by constant guidance which ensures that your children always attend school and do their school work.

IBID

We can no longer afford to sit by while some schools are turned into havens of drug abuse, violence or vandalising of valuable property. We can no longer sit and watch while any of our country's children are held back in the mire of ignorance and lack of skills which apartheid decreed should be their lot.

IBID

The majority of our children, especially in rural provinces, still either do not have access to basic education or depend on institutions that lack the teaching media and equipment needed for effective learning and teaching.

EDUCATION AFRICA, PRESIDENTIAL AND PREMIER EDUCATION AWARDS, PRETORIA, SOUTH AFRICA, 22 NOVEMBER 1997

I grew up in an area where education for blacks was very rare indeed. And my parents had never been to school. They were completely illiterate.

LONDON, ENGLAND, 2000

The divide between the rich and the poor, the privileged and the deprived, the powerful and the marginalised has become marked primarily by a differentiation in access to knowledge and information. Those who have access to cutting-edge knowledge hold the advantage in all arenas of social, political and economic life today.

TWENTY-SIXTH INTERNATIONAL CONFERENCE ON IMPROVING UNIVERSITY TEACHING, UNIVERSITY OF JOHANNESBURG, SOUTH AFRICA, JULY 2001

Education is the most powerful weapon we can use to change the world.

ADDRESS AT THE PLANETARIUM, JOHANNESBURG, SOUTH AFRICA, 16 JULY 2003

A nation's future is only as promising as its next generation of citizens, and we commend you for investing in the future of our young ones, by providing children in rural areas with greater access to information technology.

ESKOM DEVELOPMENT FOUNDATION, JOHANNESBURG, SOUTH AFRICA, 11 MARCH 2004

No child in Africa, and in fact anywhere in the world, should be denied education. I know that we can reach this goal.

LAUNCH OF 'A DREAM FOR AFRICA' INTERNATIONAL FUND-RAISING CAMPAIGN, CAPE TOWN, SOUTH AFRICA, 6 DECEMBER 2004

There can be no contentment for any of us when there are children, millions of children, who do not receive an education that provides them with dignity and honour and allows them to live their lives to the full.

RECORDED MESSAGE FOR THE LAUNCH OF THE NELSON MANDELA INSTITUTE FOR EDUCATION AND RURAL DEVELOPMENT, NOVEMBER 2007

It is not beyond our power to create a world in which all children have access to a good education.

IBID

Educating all of our children must be one of our most urgent priorities. We all know that education, more than anything else, improves our chances of building better lives.

MESSAGE FOR 'SCHOOLS FOR AFRICA' CAMPAIGN, JOHANNESBURG, SOUTH AFRICA, 15 MAY 2008

Ego

A blind pursuit of cheap popularity has nothing to do with revolution.

FROM A POLITICAL REPORT OF THE NATIONAL EXECUTIVE COMMITTEE TO THE FORTY-NINTH ANC NATIONAL CONFERENCE, BLOEMFONTEIN, SOUTH AFRICA, 17 DECEMBER 1994

Elders

In my youth in the Transkei, I listened to the elders of my tribe telling stories of the old days. Amongst the tales they related to me were those of wars fought by our ancestors in defence of the fatherland. The names of Dingane and Bambatha, Hintsa and Makana, Squngthi and Dalasile, Moshoeshoe and Sekhukhune were praised as the glory of the entire African nation.

SPEECH FROM THE DOCK, RIVONIA TRIAL, PALACE OF JUSTICE, PRETORIA, SOUTH AFRICA, 20 APRIL 1964

I still respect our elders and like to chat with them about olden times when we had our own government and lived freely.

FROM AN UNPUBLISHED AUTOBIOGRAPHICAL MANUSCRIPT, WRITTEN ON ROBBEN ISLAND, 1975

The old generation that inherited the oral traditions of our ancestors has disappeared or is disappearing and science has developed modern techniques of acquiring knowledge in all fields, but even the younger generation of today still values the experience of elders.

IBID

A society that does not value its older people denies its roots and endangers its future. Let us strive to enhance their capacity to support themselves for as long as possible and, when they cannot do so anymore, to care for them.

MESSAGE ANNOUNCING 1999 AS THE UNITED NATIONS INTERNATIONAL YEAR OF OLDER PERSONS, 17 DECEMBER 1998

Elders, The

Using their collective experience, their moral courage and their ability to rise above the parochial concerns of nation, race and creed, they can help make our planet a more peaceful, healthy and equitable place to live.

LAUNCH OF THE ELDERS, CONSTITUTION HILL, JOHANNESBURG, SOUTH AFRICA, 18 JULY 2008

I believe that, with their experience and their energies, and their profound commitment to building a better world, The Elders can become a fiercely independent and robust force for good, tackling complex and intractable issues, especially those that are not popular.

IBID

Elections

People should be free to form or belong to parties of their choice. There should be regular elections so that the people decide who should be in the driving seat.

CONFERENCE CONVENED BY THE CONSULTATIVE BUSINESS MOVEMENT ON THE THEME 'OPTIONS FOR BUILDING AN ECONOMIC FUTURE', 23 MAY 1990

For the first time in the history of our country, on 27 April 1994, all South Africans, whatever their language, religion and culture, whatever their colour or class, will vote as equal citizens. Millions who were not allowed to vote will do so. I, too, for the first time in my short life, will vote.

ANNOUNCEMENT OF THE ELECTION DATE, MULTI-PARTY NEGOTIATIONS PROCESS, KEMPTON PARK, SOUTH AFRICA, 17 NOVEMBER 1993

The calm and tolerant atmosphere that prevailed during the elections depicts the type of South Africa we can build. It set the tone for the future. We might have our differences, but we are one people with a common destiny in our rich variety of culture and traditions.

ANC ELECTION VICTORY CELEBRATION, CARLTON HOTEL, JOHANNESBURG, SOUTH AFRICA, 2 MAY 1994

When history is finally written, tribute will go to the unsung organiser who trudged the campaign trail to educate our people and prepare them for election day. Tribute will go, above all, to the people themselves who grasped the historic opportunity with both hands and braved the threats from all kinds of quarters. For it is on those momentous days that the saying rang truer than ever before: that the people are their own liberators.

FROM A POLITICAL REPORT OF THE NATIONAL EXECUTIVE COMMITTEE TO THE FORTY-NINTH ANC NATIONAL CONFERENCE, BLOEMFONTEIN, SOUTH AFRICA, 17 DECEMBER 1994

The fact that we have had this election, that it was free and fair, no intimidation, no violence, is a sign of hope in our future.

FROM THE DOCUMENTARY *COUNTDOWN TO FREEDOM: TEN DAYS THAT CHANGED SOUTH AFRICA*, 1994

Emotion

Moodiness is but a common condition that affects many people.

FROM A LETTER TO ZINDZI MANDELA, WRITTEN ON ROBBEN ISLAND, 3 FEBRUARY 1979

I must confess I am unable to describe my emotions. I was completely overwhelmed by the enthusiasm. It is something I did not expect. I would be merely rationalising if I told you that I am able to describe my own feelings – it was breathtaking.

SPEAKING ABOUT THE WELCOME HE RECEIVED UPON HIS RELEASE, FIRST PRESS CONFERENCE AFTER HIS RELEASE, 'BISHOPSCOURT', ARCHBISHOP DESMOND TUTU'S RESIDENCE, CAPE TOWN, SOUTH AFRICA, 12 FEBRUARY 1990

As 'no man is an island', so too are we not men of stone who are not moved by the noble passions of love, friendship and human compassion.

ADDRESS AT THE CATHEDRAL OF UPPSALA, UPPSALA, SWEDEN, 13 MARCH 1990

Well, it would be an exaggeration to say I never become depressed. Many people, of course, may not discover that.

FROM A CONVERSATION WITH RICHARD STENGEL, CIRCA APRIL OR MAY 1993

There were moments when your spirits were down because of what was happening outside but generally speaking one felt that one day I would return.

REVISITING ROBBEN ISLAND, CAPE TOWN, SOUTH AFRICA, 11 FEBRUARY 1994

I find it difficult to personalise the political experiences we had in prison.

IBID

There were many dark moments when my faith in humanity was sorely tested, but I would not and could not give myself up to despair. That way lay defeat and death.

FROM *LONG WALK TO FREEDOM*, 1994

I am not and never have been a man who finds it easy to talk about his feelings in public. I was often asked by reporters how it felt to be free, and I did my best to describe the indescribable, and usually failed.

IBID

Age and a conservative cultural background do not make it easy for me to discuss in public such intimate feelings or emotions.

FROM A PERSONAL FILE, CIRCA 1996

We have a duty to create a conducive environment and to provide the necessary tools and the mechanisms to support people in their endeavours to better themselves.

LAUNCH OF THE NATIONAL CAMPAIGN FOR LEARNING AND TEACHING, SOWETO, JOHANNESBURG, SOUTH AFRICA, 20 FEBRUARY 1997

We are honoured that you wish to celebrate the birthday of a retired old man who no longer has power and influence.

NINETIETH BIRTHDAY RECORDED MESSAGE, 2008

Enemies

We do not underestimate the enemy and in past conflicts against superior odds it has fought courageously and received the admiration of all.

FROM AN UNPUBLISHED AUTOBIOGRAPHICAL MANUSCRIPT, WRITTEN ON ROBBEN ISLAND, 1975

When a man fights, even the enemies, you know, respect you, especially if you fight intelligently.

FROM A CONVERSATION WITH RICHARD STENGEL, CIRCA DECEMBER 1992

If you want to make peace with an enemy, one must work with that enemy and that enemy becomes your partner.

FROM *LONG WALK TO FREEDOM*, 1994

Entitlement

We have also seen the emergence of elitism among some of our members. Notions have surfaced of entitlement to decision-making positions, which have led to a break in the sustained interaction between some of our leaders, on one hand, and our organisation and people, on the other.

OPENING OF THE FIFTIETH ANC NATIONAL CONFERENCE, NORTH-WEST UNIVERSITY, MAFIKENG CAMPUS, SOUTH AFRICA, 16 DECEMBER 1997

Environment

Later, I walked out into the courtyard and the few living things there, the seagulls, wagtails, the plants, small trees and even grass blades were gay and full of smiles. Everything was caught up in the beauty of the day.

FROM A LETTER TO ZINDZI MANDELA, WRITTEN ON ROBBEN ISLAND, 5 MARCH 1978

When I left, at *least* the country was clean. It was a pleasure to look at the veld and to see, you know, to the distant hills, up to the distant hills or horizon, and to see a blade of grass, a green leaf and without the filth that you now found as the result of plastic.

FROM A CONVERSATION WITH RICHARD STENGEL, 13 JANUARY 1993

It's a good thing also to see the day, daybreak, you know, whilst you are on the road and the sun rising, changing, you know, from one time of the night to another.

FROM A CONVERSATION WITH RICHARD STENGEL, 25 MARCH 1993

Each time one of us touches the soil of this land, we feel a sense of personal renewal. The national mood changes as the seasons change. We are moved by a sense of joy and exhilaration when the grass turns green and the flowers bloom.

INAUGURATION AS PRESIDENT OF SOUTH AFRICA, UNION BUILDINGS, PRETORIA, SOUTH AFRICA, 10 MAY 1994

I do not like killing any living thing, even those creatures that fill some people with dread.

FROM *LONG WALK TO FREEDOM*, 1994

I like to see the coming of dawn, the change between day and night, which is always majestic.

IBID

Our future as human beings depends on our intelligent and prudent use of the oceans. And that in turn will depend on the determined efforts of dedicated women and men from all parts of our planet.

FIFTH SESSION OF THE INDEPENDENT WORLD COMMISSION ON THE OCEANS, CAPE TOWN, SOUTH AFRICA, 11 NOVEMBER 1997

I remembered, after our circumcision ritual, washing away my youth in the Mbashe River, and, later, crossing it as a man. Our clean flowing rivers must be known by my grandchildren's grandchildren, many years from now, just as I knew them as a child, many years ago.

LAUNCH OF THE FINAL REPORT OF THE WORLD COMMISSION ON DAMS, CABOT HALL, LONDON, ENGLAND, 16 NOVEMBER 2000

The trees and forests were destroyed exactly because our people were so dependent upon them as sources of energy. And in turn, people are today cold and in want of energy for cooking, cleaning and basic comforts because the trees and forests are destroyed.

UPON RECEIVING THE PLANET AND HUMANITY AWARD, INTERNATIONAL GEOGRAPHICAL UNION, DURBAN, SOUTH AFRICA, 4 AUGUST 2002

The streams of my youth that were places of beauty and inspiration were now clogged up and dirty. I saw the descendants of the mothers of our people bowing down to secure with their bare hands the cleanest of the dirty and dangerous water in those streams and pools.

IBID

Let us stand together to make of our world a sustainable source for our future as humanity on this planet.

IBID

Amongst the many things I learnt, as a president of our country, was the centrality of water in the social, political and economic affairs of the country, Continent and indeed the world.

OPENING OF THE WATER DOME, WORLD SUMMIT FOR SUSTAINABLE DEVELOPMENT, JOHANNESBURG, SOUTH AFRICA, 28 AUGUST 2002

Many of Africa's most beautiful protected areas have their origins in the colonial past, and have a legacy of being 'set aside', thus alienating local people who viewed them as meaningless or even costly.

LAUNCH OF THE WORLD PARKS CONGRESS, JOHANNESBURG, SOUTH AFRICA, 2 SEPTEMBER 2002

The countries of southern Africa are working together to challenge the rigidity of their national boundaries, developing opportunities and potential for both biodiversity, conservation and tourism that would be impossible to reach through individual and uncoordinated efforts.

OPENING OF THE FIFTH WORLD PARKS CONGRESS 'BENEFITS BEYOND BOUNDARIES', DURBAN, SOUTH AFRICA, 8 SEPTEMBER 2003

One must be very far from the hippos, they are the most dangerous.

FROM THE DOCUMENTARY *MANDELA: THE LIVING LEGEND*, 2003

Equality

We are convinced that there are thousands of honest democrats among the white population who are prepared to take up a firm and courageous stand for unconditional equality, for the complete renunciation of 'white supremacy'. To them we extend the hand of sincere friendship and brotherly alliance.

FROM AN ARTICLE ENTITLED 'THE SHIFTING SANDS OF ILLUSION', *LIBERATION*, JUNE 1953

I am influenced more than ever before by the conviction that social equality is the only basis of human happiness.

FROM A LETTER TO SENATOR DOUGLAS LUKHELE, WRITTEN ON ROBBEN ISLAND, 1 AUGUST 1970

I have never regarded any man as my superior, either in my life outside or inside prison.

FROM A LETTER TO GENERAL DU PREEZ, COMMISSIONER OF PRISONS, WRITTEN ON ROBBEN ISLAND, 12 JULY 1976

My respect for human beings is based not on the colour of a man's skin nor authority he may wield, but purely on merit.

IBID

The principle of decolonisation and the acceptance of the rights of all nations to belong to and participate equally in the life of the world community must not be debased so as to oppress other peoples.

UPON RECEIVING THE PRINCE OF ASTURIAS PRIZE OF INTERNATIONAL COOPERATION, SPAIN, 31 OCTOBER 1992

The unprecedented challenge was to restore the human dignity of all our people by removing all forms of racial discrimination, introducing the principle of equality in every sphere of our lives.

FROM THE UNPUBLISHED SEQUEL TO HIS AUTOBIOGRAPHY, CIRCA 1998

Europe: Places

France

In the course of our long, bitter and bloody struggle, we have developed a bond between the people of South Africa and the people of France. We are absolutely convinced that in a post-apartheid South Africa, the friendship, solidarity and cooperation between our two peoples will assume a permanent character.

WELCOME CEREMONY BY PRESIDENT FRANÇOIS MITTERRAND, PARIS, FRANCE, 6 JUNE 1990

The blood of the Huguenots who came to our country in the seventeenth century courses through the veins of many of our people, both black and white. The culture they brought is part of what constitutes the common South African identity.

DINNER HOSTED BY FRENCH PRIME MINISTER MICHEL ROCARD, HOTEL DE MATIGON, PARIS, FRANCE, 7 JUNE 1990

The name France evokes among our people living images of a successful struggle against autocracy, for democracy and justice.

ADDRESS TO THE FRENCH NATIONAL ASSEMBLY, BOURBON PALACE, PARIS, FRANCE, 7 JUNE 1990

Great Britain

I have great respect for British political institutions and for the country's system of justice. I regard the British Parliament as the most democratic institution in the world, and the independence and impartiality of its judiciary never fail to arouse my admiration.

SPEECH FROM THE DOCK, RIVONIA TRIAL, PALACE OF JUSTICE, PRETORIA, SOUTH AFRICA, 20 APRIL 1964

This country has produced men and women whose names are well known in South Africa, because they, together with thousands of others of your citizens, stood up to oppose this evil system and helped to bring us to where we are today, when we can say – at last – freedom is in sight. These Britons acted in the way they did because they realised that they and their country had as much a moral obligation and a strategic imperative to uproot the pernicious system of racism in South Africa, as they had to destroy a similar system in Nazi Germany.

ADDRESS TO THE HOUSE OF COMMONS, LONDON, ENGLAND, 5 MAY 1993

I had quite a lovely time because I saw British politicians, and they welcomed me *very* well.

FROM A CONVERSATION WITH AHMED KATHRADA ABOUT HIS VISIT IN 1962, CIRCA 1993/94

It was, of course, exciting to be in England and [in] the capital of the once-powerful British Empire. I enjoyed that and then in going to their bookshops and so on and getting literature on guerrilla warfare.

FROM A CONVERSATION WITH AHMED KATHRADA, CIRCA 1993/94

I will always cherish this moment, because becoming a citizen of your great city is to me the culmination of a long walk started here in 1962. In a sense, I leave part of my being here.

UPON RECEIVING THE FREEDOM OF THE CITY OF LONDON, GUILDHALL, LONDON, ENGLAND, 10 JULY 1996

As eloquently and passionately, the British rulers of the day spoke in these Houses to say they could not and would not amend their agenda with regard to South Africa, to address the interests of that section of our population which was not white. Despite that rebuff and the terrible cost we had to bear as a consequence, we return to this honoured place neither with pikes, nor a desire for revenge, nor, even, a plea to your distinguished selves to assuage our hunger for bread. We come to you as friends.

ADDRESS TO THE JOINT HOUSES OF PARLIAMENT, WESTMINSTER HALL, LONDON, ENGLAND, 11 JULY 1996

I can never thank the people of Britain enough for their support through those days of the struggle against apartheid.

LAUNCH OF THE 'MAKE POVERTY HISTORY' CAMPAIGN, TRAFALGAR SQUARE, LONDON, ENGLAND, 3 FEBRUARY 2005

I am pleased that the statue will be a representation – and a constant reminder – of South Africa's liberation after many long years of struggle. In Britain you have played an important part in this process. We in South Africa will not forget your efforts to support our liberation struggle – your hospitality to individuals and organisations, your boycotts, your protests, your fund-raising campaigns. We remain profoundly grateful for this support.

RECEPTION FOLLOWING THE UNVEILING OF HIS STATUE, LONDON, ENGLAND, 29 AUGUST 2007

Greece

No democracy in the world can celebrate itself without paying homage to this ancient cradle of democracy. We all owe part of our democratic self-understanding to this heritage.

TOAST TO PRIME MINISTER KONSTANTINOS SIMITIS OF GREECE, GREECE, 18 JUNE 2002

Greece will know as well as any other country in the world that freedom and democracy are never finally achieved states of social existence. Its own history in our times stands as testimony to the fact that human freedom is something that we have to constantly go out and defend, protect, nurture and grow.

DINNER TO COMMEMORATE THE SIXTH ANNIVERSARY OF THE DEATH OF GREEK PREMIER ANDREAS PAPANDREOU, GREECE, 19 JUNE 2002

Ancient Greece, the cradle of democracy and democratic thought, was a constant source of reference and inspiration to us in our struggle for freedom.

IBID

Ireland

The very fact there is today an independent Irish state, however long it took to realise the noble goals of the Irish people by bringing it into being, confirms the fact that we too shall become a free people; we too shall have a country which will, as the great Irish patriots said in The Proclamation of 1916, 'Cherish all the children of the nation equally'.

STATEMENT TO THE PARLIAMENT OF THE REPUBLIC OF IRELAND, DUBLIN, IRELAND, 2 JULY 1990

Sweden

We know and are moved by the fact that among the first to sound the warning bells about the situation in South Africa were Swedish men and women of conscience who had served as missionaries among our people.

ADDRESS AT THE CATHEDRAL OF UPPSALA, UPPSALA, SWEDEN, 13 MARCH 1990

We have become political neighbours who willingly share whatever little bread and salt we may have. The strength this gives us is impossible to measure. It is between us common cause that we have not yet ended the apartheid crime against humanity.

ADDRESS TO THE SWEDISH PARLIAMENT, STOCKHOLM, SWEDEN, 13 MARCH 1990

Evil

Evil ultimately lives in fear of and under threat from the uncompromising commitment to justice, fairness and humane compassion.

BRITISH RED CROSS HUMANITY LECTURE, QUEEN ELIZABETH II CONFERENCE CENTRE, LONDON, ENGLAND, 10 JULY 2003

Exercise

You should also do regular physical exercises, especially trotting in a track-suit. Track running has the advantage of exercising all parts of your body and giving you a feeling of well-being.

FROM A LETTER TO MAKAZIWE MANDELA, WRITTEN ON ROBBEN ISLAND, 31 DECEMBER 1978

Your physical condition, especially the feeling of well-being after a good exercise, is closely related to your academic performance.

FROM A LETTER TO XOLISWA MATANZIMA, WRITTEN ON ROBBEN ISLAND, 23 DECEMBER 1979

I was fit even before I went to prison.

FROM A CONVERSATION WITH RICHARD STENGEL, 29 DECEMBER 1992

Exercises are very good, you know; they give you a feeling of well-being. I've always done them as I get up in the morning, for about an hour.

FROM A CONVERSATION WITH AHMED KATHRADA, CIRCA 1993/94

I was physically fit. Training, physical training, you see, has always been part and parcel of my life and I enjoyed those fatigue marches and the fatigue marches did not take place daily – once in a week, and I did exercises inside the camp and going out sometimes about fourteen miles to the shooting range.

IBID

I have always believed exercise is a key not only to physical health but to peace of mind. Many times in the old days I unleashed my anger and frustration on a punchbag rather than taking it out on a comrade or even a policeman. Exercise dissipates tension, and tension is the enemy of serenity. I found that I worked better and thought more clearly when I was in good physical condition, and so training became one of the inflexible disciplines of my life. In prison, having an outlet for my frustrations was absolutely essential.

FROM LONG WALK TO FREEDOM, 1994

Expectations

If there is anything I kept on stressing it was that people should not have exaggerated expectations, that to address their concerns is not something that can be done overnight.

FROM AN INTERVIEW WITH TOM COHEN AND SAHM VENTER FOR THE ASSOCIATED PRESS, TUYNHUYS, CAPE TOWN, SOUTH AFRICA, 22 SEPTEMBER 1994

People expect me to perform far beyond my ability.

FROM AN INTERVIEW WITH JOHN BATTERSBY, JOHANNESBURG, SOUTH AFRICA, PUBLISHED IN
THE CHRISTIAN SCIENCE MONITOR, 10 FEBRUARY 2000

Eyesight

I must warn you not to allow anybody [to] prescribe reading glasses for you. Many
students, especially those from the rural areas, made that disastrous mistake, and
lived the rest of their lives with weakened and even damaged eyes.

FROM A LETTER TO A GRANDCHILD, WRITTEN IN POLLSMOOR PRISON, CAPE TOWN, SOUTH AFRICA,
11 AUGUST 1988

Fame

When you travel from one place to the other you are surrounded by security.
It's difficult to stop and talk to people as one would like when you visit a new place.

FROM A CONVERSATION WITH RICHARD STENGEL, 23 APRIL 1993

You know, it's a difficult life, this one.

FROM A CONVERSATION WITH AHMED KATHRADA ABOUT BEING RECOGNISED, CIRCA 1993/94

Family

It has not been easy for me during the past period to separate myself from my wife
and children, to say goodbye to the good old days when, at the end of a strenuous
day at an office, I could look forward to joining my family at the dinner table,
and instead to take up the life of a man hunted continuously by the police, living
separated from those who are closest to me, in my own country, facing continually
the hazards of detection and of arrest. This has been infinitely more difficult than
serving a prison sentence. No man in his right senses would voluntarily choose
such a life in preference to the one normal, family, social life which exists in every
civilised community.

IN MITIGATION OF SENTENCE AFTER BEING CONVICTED OF INCITING WORKERS TO STRIKE AND LEAVING
THE COUNTRY ILLEGALLY, OLD SYNAGOGUE, PRETORIA, SOUTH AFRICA, 7 NOVEMBER 1962

From experience I have found that a family photo is everything in prison and you
must have it right from the beginning.

FROM A LETTER TO WINNIE MANDELA, WRITTEN ON ROBBEN ISLAND, 22 JUNE 1969

The dream of every family is to be able to live together happily in a quiet and
peaceful home where parents will have the opportunity of bringing up the children
in the best possible way, or guiding and helping them in choosing careers and of
giving them the love and care which will develop in them a feeling of security
and self-confidence.

FROM A LETTER TO ZINDZI AND ZENI MANDELA, WRITTEN ON ROBBEN ISLAND, 1 JUNE 1970

Physical suffering is nothing compared to the trampling down of those tender bonds
of affection that form the basis of the institution of marriage and the family that
unite man and wife.

FROM A LETTER TO WINNIE MANDELA, WRITTEN ON ROBBEN ISLAND, 1 AUGUST 1970

I have often wondered whether a person is justified in neglecting his own family to fight for opportunities for others.

FROM AN UNPUBLISHED AUTOBIOGRAPHICAL MANUSCRIPT, WRITTEN ON ROBBEN ISLAND, 1975

I like relaxing at the house, reading quietly, taking in the sweet smell that comes from the pots, sitting around the table with the family and taking out my wife and children. When you can no longer enjoy these simple pleasures, something valuable is taken away from your life and you feel it in your daily work.

IBID

I have never welcomed the weakening of family ties by politics or pressure and have always tried to resist that wherever possible.

IBID

I have been fairly successful in putting on a mask behind which I have pined for the family, alone, never rushing for the post when it comes until somebody calls out my name.

FROM A LETTER TO WINNIE MANDELA, WRITTEN ON ROBBEN ISLAND, 26 OCTOBER 1976

Our families are far larger than those of whites and it's always a pure pleasure to be fully accepted throughout a village, district or even several districts occupied by your clan, as a beloved household member, where you can call at any time, completely relax, sleep at ease and freely take part in the discussion of all problems, where you can even be given livestock and land to build free of charge.

FROM A LETTER TO MRS N THULARE, WRITTEN ON ROBBEN ISLAND, 19 JULY 1977

A happy family life is an important pillar to any public man. Few people are as essential or dangerous to the success or downfall of a politician than a good wife or play-girl.

FROM A LETTER TO WINNIE MANDELA, WRITTEN ON ROBBEN ISLAND, 6 MAY 1979

My salutations would be incomplete without expressing my deep appreciation for the strength given to me during my long and lonely years in prison by my beloved wife and family. I am convinced that your pain and suffering was far greater than my own.

FIRST SPEECH AFTER HIS RELEASE, CITY HALL, CAPE TOWN, SOUTH AFRICA, 11 FEBRUARY 1990

We watched our children growing without our guidance... and when we did come out, my children said, 'We thought we had a father and one day he'd come back. But to our dismay, our father came back and he left us alone because he has now become the father of the nation.'

WEDDING OF ZINDZI MANDELA TO ZWELI HLONGWANE, JOHANNESBURG, SOUTH AFRICA, 24 OCTOBER 1992

Our family structure is a large family. If you claim descent from one ancestor, you are a family and you are expected to carry out your duties towards every member of the clan, as to your own children, or sisters or brothers.

FROM A CONVERSATION WITH RICHARD STENGEL, 3 DECEMBER 1992

What I discussed with her was the question of the children... and mentioned the names of friends and people who owed me some money and how to bring up the children, and how it was necessary for her to prepare herself for a hard time.

FROM A CONVERSATION WITH AHMED KATHRADA, TALKING ABOUT A VISIT FROM WINNIE MANDELA AFTER HIS ARREST IN 1962, CIRCA 1993/94

There is the controversy, the contradiction of being committed to your family and wanting to remain with your family so that at the end of the day, you know, you could share the society of your wife and children and to abandon that, you see, was very painful. It gave me a painful feeling.

FROM A CONVERSATION WITH AHMED KATHRADA, CIRCA 1993/94

Whenever anything happened to the family I would come back, you know, from the span, from the quarry and find on my desk a cutting so that I could see what is happening to my family outside.

REVISITING ROBBEN ISLAND, CAPE TOWN, SOUTH AFRICA, 11 FEBRUARY 1994

The next shattering experience was the death of my eldest son in a car accident... He was not only my son but a friend and I was very hurt indeed that I could not pay respects, my last respects to my mother and to my eldest son.

IBID

There are many things that disturb you when children grow without you.

FROM THE DOCUMENTARY MANDELA: THE LIVING LEGEND, 2003

Farming

Farming is not an easy thing.

FROM A CONVERSATION WITH AHMED KATHRADA, CIRCA 1993/94

Fate

Dreams and time schedules prove difficult to fulfil and, where misfortune strikes, fate hardly ever provides golden bridges.

FROM A LETTER TO THOROBETSANE TSHUKUDU [ADELAIDE TAMBO] WRITTEN ON ROBBEN ISLAND, 1 JANUARY 1977

Father

In spite of his friendship with Christians, my father remained aloof from Christianity and instead pinned his own faith on Qamata, the God of his fathers. As the most senior member of the family, he was family priest.

FROM AN UNPUBLISHED AUTOBIOGRAPHICAL MANUSCRIPT, WRITTEN ON ROBBEN ISLAND, 1975

I think he certainly loved and respected his wives and children like any other man. But in maintaining discipline among his children he did not hesitate to use the rod whenever he thought such a course was necessary.

IBID

The acting King who brought me up was appointed, was elected, Acting Paramount Chief by the tribe as a result of the influence of my father.

FROM A CONVERSATION WITH RICHARD STENGEL, 10 MARCH 1993

He kept on calling, 'Nodayimani, give me my tobacco', you see. And this call was persistent, and eventually they gave him, they filled the pipe with tobacco, lit it and gave it to him, and he then smoked and he died smoking.

FROM A CONVERSATION WITH RICHARD STENGEL ABOUT HIS FATHER, 10 MARCH 1993

Fears

We must accept, however, that our statements and declarations alone will not be sufficient to allay the fears of white South Africans. We must clearly demonstrate our goodwill to our white compatriots and convince them by our conduct and arguments that South Africa without apartheid will be a better home for all.

WELCOME HOME RALLY, SOCCER CITY, SOWETO, SOUTH AFRICA, 13 FEBRUARY 1990

We are quite aware of the fears of the whites in the country of being dominated by blacks and we are addressing that very seriously and earnestly.

AT HOME, SOWETO, SOUTH AFRICA, 14 FEBRUARY 1990

It would have been an act of treason against the people and against our conscience to allow fear and the drive towards self-preservation to dominate our behaviour, obliging us to absent ourselves from the struggle for democracy and human rights, not only in our country but throughout the world.

ADDRESS TO THE JOINT SESSION OF THE HOUSE OF CONGRESS, WASHINGTON DC, USA, 26 JUNE 1990

Once you have rid yourself of the fear of the oppressor and his prisons, his police, his army, there is nothing that they can do. You are liberated.

FROM A CONVERSATION WITH RICHARD STENGEL, 9 MARCH 1993

First American Nation

I have received several letters from the First American Nation, the American Indians, and I can assure you that they have left me very disturbed.

FROM THE DOCUMENTARY *MANDELA IN AMERICA*, 1990

Food and Drink

I long for amasi – the food for which I loved to sharpen my teeth and to stretch out my tummy, the one that I really enjoyed, that went straight into my blood and into my heart and produced perfect contentment.

FROM A LETTER TO WINNIE MANDELA, WRITTEN ON ROBBEN ISLAND, 31 AUGUST 1970

A human being, whatever his colour may be, whether he lives under a regime of Christians, Pharisees, hypocrites, heathens or those who choose to flirt with the devil, ought never to be compelled to regard taking meals as a mere duty.

IBID

In town I take skimmed milk but in the Transkei there's no skimmed milk. Milk is milk.

FROM A CONVERSATION WITH RICHARD STENGEL, CIRCA DECEMBER 1992

Today I am prepared to die; I am going to eat it. Yes, I hadn't had eggs and bacon for a long time.

TALKING ABOUT WHEN HE WAS GIVEN BACON AND EGGS AS A PRISONER WHEN HE WAS IN HOSPITAL,
FROM A CONVERSATION WITH RICHARD STENGEL, 3 FEBRUARY 1993

Rooibos tea was my favourite in prison but outside here I have got a lot of love for coffee and hardly take tea.

AFTER A VISIT WITH MRS BETSIE VERWOERD, ORANIA, SOUTH AFRICA, 15 AUGUST 1995

Can we drink whisky?

FROM THE DOCUMENTARY *MANDELA: THE LIVING LEGEND*, AFTER BEING ASKED BY HELICOPTER CREW IF
ANY PASSENGERS HAD QUESTIONS, 2003

Foresight

When a man commits himself to the type of life he has lived for forty-five years, even
though he may well have been aware from the outset of all the attendant hazards, the
actual course of events and the precise manner in which they would influence his life
could never have been clearly foreseeable in every respect.

FROM A LETTER TO JOY MOSIELOA, WRITTEN IN POLLSMOOR PRISON, CAPE TOWN, SOUTH AFRICA,
17 FEBRUARY 1986

If I had been able to foresee all that has since happened, I would certainly have made
the same decision, so I believe at least. But that decision would certainly have been
far more daunting, and some of the tragedies which subsequently followed would
have melted whatever traces of steel were inside me.

IBID

Forgiveness

I am working now with the same people who threw me into jail, persecuted my wife,
hounded my children from one school to the other... and I am one of those who are
saying, 'Let us forget the past, and think of the present'.

FROM A CONVERSATION WITH RICHARD STENGEL, 9 MARCH 1993

We have to forgive the past but, at the same time, ensure that the dignity of the
victims is restored, and their plight properly addressed.

ANNUAL METHODIST CHURCH CONFERENCE, MTHATHA, SOUTH AFRICA, 18 SEPTEMBER 1994

For all people who have found themselves in the position of being in jail and trying
to transform society, forgiveness is natural because you have no time to be retaliative.

FROM AN INTERVIEW WITH JOHN BATTERSBY, JOHANNESBURG, SOUTH AFRICA, PUBLISHED IN *THE CHRISTIAN
SCIENCE MONITOR*, 10 FEBRUARY 2000

Freedom

To overthrow oppression has been sanctioned by humanity and is the highest
aspiration of every free man.

PRESIDENTIAL ADDRESS TO THE ANC TRANSVAAL CONGRESS, ALSO KNOWN AS THE 'NO EASY WALK TO
FREEDOM' SPEECH, TRANSVAAL, SOUTH AFRICA, 21 SEPTEMBER 1953

The magnificent response to the call of the National Action Council for a three-day
strike and the wonderful work done by our organisers and field workers throughout
the country proves once again that no power on earth can stop an oppressed people
determined to win their freedom.

FROM THE 'STRUGGLE IS MY LIFE' PRESS STATEMENT, EXPLAINING HIS DECISION TO CARRY ON HIS POLITICAL
WORK UNDERGROUND IN ACCORDANCE WITH THE ADVICE OF THE NATIONAL ACTION COUNCIL,
SOUTH AFRICA, 26 JUNE 1961

To men, freedom in their own land is the pinnacle of their ambitions, from which nothing can turn men of conviction aside.

IN MITIGATION OF SENTENCE AFTER BEING CONVICTED OF INCITING WORKERS TO STRIKE AND LEAVING THE COUNTRY ILLEGALLY, OLD SYNAGOGUE, PRETORIA, SOUTH AFRICA, 7 NOVEMBER 1962

The purpose of freedom is to create it for others.

FROM A PRISON DESK CALENDAR, WRITTEN ON ROBBEN ISLAND, 2 JUNE 1979

We quickly learned the admonition of a great political thinker and teacher that no people in one part of the world could really be free while their brothers in other parts were still under foreign rule.

FROM A LETTER TO MRS MANORAMA BHALLA, SECRETARY, INDIAN COUNCIL FOR CULTURAL RELATIONS, WRITTEN ON ROBBEN ISLAND, 3 AUGUST 1980

I cherish my own freedom dearly, but I care even more for your freedom.

RESPONSE TO AN OFFER OF CONDITIONAL FREEDOM, READ BY ZINDZI MANDELA AT A RALLY, JABULANI STADIUM, SOWETO, SOUTH AFRICA, 10 FEBRUARY 1985

What freedom am I being offered while the organisation of the people remains banned? What freedom am I being offered when I may be arrested on a pass offence? What freedom am I being offered to live my life as a family with my dear wife who remains in banishment in Brandfort? What freedom am I being offered when I must ask for permission to live in an urban area? What freedom am I being offered when I need a stamp in my pass to seek work? What freedom am I being offered when my very South African citizenship is not respected?

IBID

I will not sell the birthright of my people to be free.

IBID

I cannot and will not give any undertaking at a time when I and you, the people, are not free. Your freedom and mine cannot be separated. I will return.

IBID

Only free men can negotiate. Prisoners cannot enter into contracts.

IBID

We have waited too long for our freedom. We can no longer wait. Now is the time to intensify the struggle on all fronts. To relax our efforts now would be a mistake which generations to come will not be able to forgive. The sight of freedom looming on the horizon should encourage us to redouble our efforts.

FIRST SPEECH AFTER HIS RELEASE, CITY HALL, CAPE TOWN, SOUTH AFRICA, 11 FEBRUARY 1990

Our march to freedom is irreversible. We must not allow fear to stand in our way.

IBID

We want to see the millions of our people build one South African nation whose integrity will be secured by the fact of the freedom of all its members to decide their destiny, speak the language of their choice, enjoy their culture and engage in any religious practice according to their conscience.

MESSAGE TO BIG BUSINESS OF THE USA, 19 JUNE 1990

We have a right to be free. And we shall be free!

CHRISTMAS MESSAGE, 25 DECEMBER 1990

We do not want freedom without bread, nor do we want bread without freedom.
We must provide for all the fundamental rights and freedoms associated with
a democratic society.

INVESTITURE AS DOCTOR OF LAWS, SOOCHOW UNIVERSITY, TAIWAN, 1 AUGUST 1993

It was this desire for the freedom of my people to live their lives with dignity and
self-respect that animated my life, that transformed a frightened young man into
a bold one, that drove a law-abiding attorney to become a criminal, that turned a
family-loving husband into a man without a home, that forced a life-loving man
to live like a monk.

FROM *LONG WALK TO FREEDOM*, 1994

I was not born with a hunger to be free. I was born free – free in every way that
I could know. Free to run in the fields near my mother's hut, free to swim in the
clear stream that ran through my village, free to roast mealies under the stars and
ride the broad backs of slow-moving bulls. As long as I obeyed my father and abided
by the customs of my tribe, I was not troubled by the laws of man or God.

IBID

It was only when I began to learn that my boyhood freedom was an illusion,
when I discovered as a young man that my freedom had already been taken
from me, that I began to hunger for it.

IBID

I have walked that long road to freedom. I have tried not to falter; I have made
missteps along the way. But I have discovered the secret that after climbing a great
hill, one only finds that there are many more hills to climb. I have taken a moment
here to rest, to steal a view of the glorious vista that surrounds me, to look back on
the distance I have come. But I can rest only for a moment, for with freedom comes
responsibilities, and I dare not linger, for my long walk is not yet ended.

IBID

For to be free is not merely to cast off one's chains, but to live in a way that respects
and enhances the freedom of others.

IBID

I knew as well as I knew anything that the oppressor must be liberated just as surely
as the oppressed. A man who takes away another man's freedom is a prisoner of
hatred; he is locked behind the bars of prejudice and narrow-mindedness. I am not
truly free if I am taking away someone else's freedom, just as sure as I am not free
when my humanity is taken from me. The oppressed and the oppressor alike are
robbed of their humanity.

IBID

Mr President, I have come to report to you that South Africa is free today.

SPEECH AT THE GRAVE OF JOHN LANGALIBALELE DUBE, FOUNDING PRESIDENT OF THE ANC, OHLANGE,
SOUTH AFRICA, 27 APRIL 1994

I stand here before you filled with deep pride and joy: pride in the ordinary, humble
people of this country. You have shown such a calm, patient determination to reclaim
this country as your own. And joy that we can loudly proclaim from the rooftops
– free at last!

ANC ELECTION VICTORY CELEBRATION, CARLTON HOTEL, JOHANNESBURG, SOUTH AFRICA, 2 MAY 1994

Never, never and never again shall it be that this beautiful land will again experience the oppression of one by another.

INAUGURATION AS PRESIDENT OF SOUTH AFRICA, UNION BUILDINGS, PRETORIA, SOUTH AFRICA, 10 MAY 1994

We have, at last, achieved our political emancipation. We pledge ourselves to liberate all our people from the continuing bondage of poverty, deprivation, suffering, gender and other discrimination.

IBID

Freedom should not be understood to mean leadership positions or even appointments to top positions. It must be understood as the transformation of the lives of ordinary people in the hostels and the ghettos, in the squatter camps, on the farms and in the mine compounds.

ADDRESS TO THE LEADERS OF THE FREE STATE PROVINCE, SOUTH AFRICA, 17 SEPTEMBER 1994

Tribute will go, above all, to the people themselves who grasped the historic opportunity with both hands and braved the threats from all kinds of quarters. For it is on those momentous days that the saying rang truer than ever before: that the people are their own liberators.

FROM A POLITICAL REPORT OF THE NATIONAL EXECUTIVE COMMITTEE TO THE FORTY-NINTH ANC NATIONAL CONFERENCE, BLOEMFONTEIN, SOUTH AFRICA, 17 DECEMBER 1994

Freedom is meaningless if people cannot put food in their stomachs, if they can have no shelter, if illiteracy and disease continue to dog them.

FROM AN INTERVIEW, CIRCA 1994

A man who takes away another man's freedom is a prisoner of hatred; he is locked behind the bars of prejudice and narrow-mindedness.

IBID

The time has come to accept in our hearts and minds that with freedom comes responsibility.

CLOSING ADDRESS IN THE DEBATE ON THE STATE OF THE NATION ADDRESS, PARLIAMENT, CAPE TOWN, SOUTH AFRICA, 24 FEBRUARY 1995

The feeling of freedom that infuses every South African heart, at last liberated from the yoke of oppression, underlines the fact that we have all, in one way or another, been victims of the system of apartheid.

SPEAKING AT THE FREEDOM DAY CELEBRATIONS, PRETORIA, SOUTH AFRICA, 27 APRIL 1996

We know that the freedom we enjoy is a richly textured gift handcrafted by ordinary folk who would not allow that their own dignity as human beings should be insulted. In the acceptance of that gift is contained an undertaking by our people that we shall never again allow our country to play host to racism. Nor shall our voices be stilled if we see that another, elsewhere in the world, is victim to racial tyranny.

ADDRESS TO THE JOINT HOUSES OF PARLIAMENT, WESTMINSTER HALL, LONDON, ENGLAND, 11 JULY 1996

In centuries of struggle against racial domination, South Africans of all colours and backgrounds proclaimed freedom and justice as their unquenchable aspiration.

SIGNING OF THE NEW CONSTITUTION, SHARPEVILLE, VEREENIGING, SOUTH AFRICA, 10 DECEMBER 1996

We give life to our nation's prayer for freedom regained and continent reborn.

IBID

Those who sought their own freedom in the domination of others were doomed in time to ignominious failure.

IBID

We solemnly honour the pledge we made to ourselves and to the world, that South Africa shall redeem herself and thereby widen the frontiers of human freedom.

IBID

As individuals we have been called upon by history to represent the collective aspirations of a people in bondage, a people in struggle and a people acting out their passions for freedom, reconstruction and development.

ADDRESS AT THE CLOSING OF THE PRESIDENT'S BUDGET DEBATE, PARLIAMENT, CAPE TOWN, SOUTH AFRICA, 22 APRIL 1998

We have been liberated from a system that held us all in its chains, free at last to be who and what we really are, secure in the respect others have for our cultures and religions.

SPEAKING AT THE FREEDOM DAY CELEBRATIONS, CAPE TOWN, SOUTH AFRICA, 27 APRIL 1998

Freedom can never be taken for granted. Each generation must safeguard it and extend it. Your parents and elders sacrificed much so that you should have freedom without suffering what they did. Use this precious right to ensure that the darkness of the past never returns.

ADDRESS AT THE OPENING OF THE PRESIDENT'S BUDGET DEBATE, PARLIAMENT, CAPE TOWN, SOUTH AFRICA, 2 MARCH 1999

Freedom alone is not enough without light to read books at night, without time or access to water to irrigate your farm, without the ability to catch fish to feed your family.

LAUNCH OF THE FINAL REPORT OF THE WORLD COMMISSION ON DAMS, CABOT HALL, LONDON, ENGLAND, 16 NOVEMBER 2000

There is an old saying that freedom and order are constantly in tension with one another in society. Order without freedom leads to totalitarianism. Freedom without order leads to anarchy. It is also said that societies recover quicker and more healthily from too much freedom than they do from totalitarianism.

TENTH ANNIVERSARY CELEBRATION OF THE INSTITUTE FOR THE ADVANCEMENT OF JOURNALISM, JOHANNESBURG, SOUTH AFRICA, 14 JUNE 2002

Freedom in our lifetime was a slogan of hope, encouragement, sustenance and inspiration to generations of our freedom fighters, anti-apartheid activists and the masses of our people suffering oppression, exploitation and degradation.

FROM AN ARTICLE IN THE *SUNDAY TIMES* (SOUTH AFRICA), MARKING TEN YEARS OF DEMOCRACY IN SOUTH AFRICA, APRIL 2004

Freedom is not only the absence of being in jail, just as it is always said that peace is not merely the absence of war.

FROM AN INTERVIEW WITH LORIE KARNATH FOR NOBEL LAUREATES, APRIL 2004

Our nation comes from a history of deep division and strife; let us never through our deeds or words, take our people back down that road.

ANC RALLY FOR HIS NINETIETH BIRTHDAY, LOFTUS VERSFELD STADIUM, PRETORIA, SOUTH AFRICA, 2 AUGUST 2008

Freedom Charter, The

For the first time in the history of our country the democratic forces irrespective of race, ideological conviction, party affiliation or religious belief have renounced and discarded racialism in all its ramifications, clearly defined their aims and objects and united in a common programme of action.

FROM AN ARTICLE ENTITLED 'FREEDOM IN OUR LIFETIME', *LIBERATION*, JUNE 1956

It was for me a matter of joy and pride to be a member of an organisation [ANC] which has proclaimed so democratic a policy and which campaigned for it militantly and fearlessly.

IN MITIGATION OF SENTENCE AFTER BEING CONVICTED OF INCITING WORKERS TO STRIKE AND LEAVING THE COUNTRY ILLEGALLY, OLD SYNAGOGUE, PRETORIA, SOUTH AFRICA, 7 NOVEMBER 1962

We believe that South Africa belongs to all the people who live in it, and not to one group, be it black or white.

SPEECH FROM THE DOCK, RIVONIA TRIAL, PALACE OF JUSTICE, PRETORIA, SOUTH AFRICA, 20 APRIL 1964

The banner that should be hoisted on all the rooftops of our country should declare that South Africa belongs to all who live in it, black and white, and that our country will never be prosperous or free until all our people live in brotherhood, enjoying equal rights and opportunities.

FROM AN ESSAY ENTITLED 'CLEAR THE OBSTACLES AND CONFRONT THE ENEMY' QUOTING THE FREEDOM CHARTER ('SOUTH AFRICA BELONGS TO ALL WHO LIVE IN IT, BLACK AND WHITE'), WRITTEN ON ROBBEN ISLAND, 1976

As reflected in our historic policy document, the Freedom Charter, we are committed to ensure all our citizens enjoy equal rights to their languages, culture and religious freedoms. These provisions, among others, will address the issue of so-called white fears, while meeting the aspirations of the people of South Africa as a whole.

ADDRESS TO THE PARLIAMENT OF CANADA, OTTAWA, CANADA, 18 JUNE 1990

If you study our basic policy document, the Freedom Charter, you will find that it is based on free enterprise.

FROM THE DOCUMENTARY *THE LAST MILE: MANDELA, AFRICA AND DEMOCRACY*, 1992

Before it [the Freedom Charter] was actually taken for ratification by the Congress of the People, it went through our organisation and we made a number of changes. And some of the changes we made disturbed the original drafters. And so it became a collective effort in the proper sense of the word.

FROM A CONVERSATION WITH RICHARD STENGEL, 20 MARCH 1993

Even during the difficult years of the Second World War, when the very survival of democracy in the world was in the balance, the ANC adopted the African Claims, a document inspired by the Atlantic Charter, in which we set our vision of the future. In the midst of the nightmare, called grand apartheid, [we] crafted the Freedom Charter, a political programme born of our struggle and rooted in South African realities, which has received international acclaim as an outstanding human rights document.

INVESTITURE, CLARK UNIVERSITY, ATLANTA, USA, 10 JULY 1993

Freedom Fighters

In the face of the complete failure of the government to heed, to consider, or even to respond to our seriously purposed objections and proposals for a solution to our objections to the forthcoming Republic, what were we to do? Were we to allow the law, which states that you shall not commit an offence by way of protest, to take its course and thus betray our conscience and our belief? Were we to uphold our conscience and our beliefs to strive for all the people who live in this country, both the present generation and for generations to come, and thus transgress against the law?

IN MITIGATION OF SENTENCE AFTER BEING CONVICTED OF INCITING WORKERS TO STRIKE AND LEAVING THE COUNTRY ILLEGALLY, OLD SYNAGOGUE, PRETORIA, SOUTH AFRICA, 7 NOVEMBER 1962

To a freedom fighter hope is what a lifebelt is to a swimmer – a guarantee that one will keep afloat and free from danger.

FROM A LETTER TO WINNIE MANDELA, WRITTEN ON ROBBEN ISLAND, 1 AUGUST 1970

Freedom fighters may choose to court disaster and fight today's revolutions with bows and arrows, shields and spears, or they may be wise and use rifles and ballistic missiles.

FROM AN UNPUBLISHED AUTOBIOGRAPHICAL MANUSCRIPT, WRITTEN ON ROBBEN ISLAND, 1975

Although I was now fully committed and had gained some idea of the hazards that accompanied the life of a freedom fighter, I had not seen any major political campaign by blacks and had not even begun giving serious attention to the question of methods.

IBID

They braved the brutality of the regime regardless of what happened to themselves. For liberation they were prepared to pay the highest price.

FROM THE UNPUBLISHED SEQUEL TO HIS AUTOBIOGRAPHY, WRITEN ON ROBBEN ISLAND, 1975

No self-respecting freedom fighter will take orders from the government on how to wage the freedom struggle against that same government and on who his allies in the freedom struggle should be.

FROM A MEMORANDUM TO PRESIDENT PW BOTHA AHEAD OF A MEETING WITH HIM, WRITTEN IN VICTOR VERSTER PRISON, PAARL, SOUTH AFRICA, JULY 1989

A freedom fighter must take every opportunity to make his case to the people.

SOURCE UNKNOWN, 1994

The names of those who were incarcerated on Robben Island is a roll-call of resistance fighters and democrats spanning over three centuries. If indeed there is a Cape of Good Hope, that hope owes much to the spirit of that legion of fighters and others of their calibre.

ADDRESS FOLLOWING HIS ELECTION AS PRESIDENT, CITY HALL, CAPE TOWN, SOUTH AFRICA, 9 MAY 1994

The place of a freedom fighter is beside his people, not behind bars.

FROM *LONG WALK TO FREEDOM*, 1994

We shall ensure that future generations do not forget the legion of great freedom fighters – communist and non-communist – as we build the better life they envisioned.

SEVENTY-FIFTH ANNIVERSARY OF THE SACP (SOUTH AFRICAN COMMUNIST PARTY), CAPE TOWN, SOUTH AFRICA, 28 JULY 1996

We tried in our simple way to lead our life in a manner that may make a difference to those of others.

UPON RECEIVING THE FRANKLIN D ROOSEVELT FOUR FREEDOMS AWARD, 8 JUNE 2002

Freedom of Expression

One of the tragedies of this country has been the suppression of the press.

PRESS CONFERENCE FOR THE ALTERNATIVE MEDIA, SOWETO, SOUTH AFRICA, 15 FEBRUARY 1990

All views are entitled to be aired. It is through vigorous and constructive debate that together we will chart the path ahead.

OPENING OF THE FORTY-EIGHTH ANC NATIONAL CONFERENCE, UNIVERSITY OF DURBAN-WESTVILLE, DURBAN, SOUTH AFRICA, 2 JULY 1991

I cannot overemphasise the value we place on a free, independent and outspoken press in the democratic South Africa we hope to build.

SPEECH TO THE INTERNATIONAL FEDERATION OF NEWSPAPER PUBLISHERS, PRAGUE, CZECH REPUBLIC, 26 MAY 1992

A critical, independent and investigative press is the lifeblood of any democracy. The press must be free from state interference. It must have the economic strength to stand up to the blandishments of government officials. It must have sufficient independence from vested interests to be bold and inquiring without fear or favour. It must enjoy the protection of the Constitution, so that it can protect our rights as citizens.

INTERNATIONAL PRESS INSTITUTE CONGRESS, CAPE TOWN, SOUTH AFRICA, 14 FEBRUARY 1994

Our commitment to the defence of a free, independent and robustly critical press had been stated over and over since we entered public life after our release from prison, and even more so when we assumed office as president of the country, and equally emphatically every time the occasion arose after our departure from office.

TENTH ANNIVERSARY OF THE INSTITUTE FOR THE ADVANCEMENT OF JOURNALISM, JOHANNESBURG, SOUTH AFRICA, 14 JUNE 2002

South Africa should put the freedom of its press and media at the top of its priorities as a democracy. None of our irritations with the perceived inadequacies of the media should ever allow us to suggest even faintly that the independence of the press could be compromised or coerced. A bad free press is preferable to a technically good subservient press.

IBID

Freedom Struggle

I am surprised at the conditions that the government wants to impose on me. I am not a violent man. My colleagues and I wrote in 1952 to [Daniel] Malan asking for a round-table conference to find a solution to the problems of our country, but that was ignored. When [Johannes] Strijdom was in power, we made the same offer. Again it was ignored. When [Hendrik] Verwoerd was in power we asked for a national convention for all the people in South Africa to decide on their future. This, too, was in vain.

RESPONSE TO AN OFFER OF CONDITIONAL FREEDOM, READ BY ZINDZI MANDELA AT A RALLY, JABULANI STADIUM, SOWETO, SOUTH AFRICA, 10 FEBRUARY 1985

Friendship

My love and respect for our friends inside and outside the country has deepened considerably. I always shudder to think just what would have happened if we are all alone. We would have survived but the task would have been far more difficult.

SOURCE UNKNOWN

Walter [Sisulu] and Kathy [Ahmed Kathrada] share one common feature which forms an essential part of our friendship and which I value very much – they never hesitate to criticise me for my mistakes and throughout my political career have served as a mirror through which I can see myself.

FROM AN UNPUBLISHED AUTOBIOGRAPHICAL MANUSCRIPT, WRITTEN ON ROBBEN ISLAND, 1975

I have a special attachment to the people who befriended me during times of distress.

IBID

I like friends who have independent minds because they tend to make you see problems from all angles.

IBID

Often as I walk up and down the tiny cell, or as I lie on my bed, the mind wanders far and wide, recalling this episode and that mistake. Among these is the thought whether in my best days outside prison I showed sufficient appreciation for the love and kindness of many of those who befriended and even helped me when I was poor and struggling.

FROM A LETTER TO ZINDZI MANDELA, WRITTEN ON ROBBEN ISLAND, 1 MARCH 1981

It is always a source of immense strength to enjoy the support of powerful and faithful friends.

FROM A LETTER TO LORD NICHOLAS BETHELL, WRITTEN IN POLLSMOOR PRISON, CAPE TOWN, SOUTH AFRICA, 1 APRIL 1985

Life to me is, to a large extent, the hope of one day meeting solid friends to hear directly from them about those matters which cannot be squeezed into a short letter.

FROM A LETTER TO DR MAMPHELA RAMPHELE, WRITTEN IN POLLSMOOR PRISON, CAPE TOWN, SOUTH AFRICA, 12 AUGUST 1987

I have always regarded friendship as something very precious. But there are moments in a person's life when it is of singular significance, when it makes you the master of your fate.

FROM A LETTER TO RAY CARTER, WRITTEN IN VICTOR VERSTER PRISON, PAARL, SOUTH AFRICA, 28 FEBRUARY 1989

With such comrades behind you, it is fairly easy to be the captain of one's soul.

FROM A LETTER TO FARIDA OMAR, WRITTEN IN VICTOR VERSTER PRISON, PAARL, SOUTH AFRICA, 28 FEBRUARY 1989

The support of tested and dependable friends gives one the strength to hold on to hope and to endure successfully even the most challenging knocks in life.

FROM A LETTER TO DON MATTERA, WRITTEN IN VICTOR VERSTER PRISON, PAARL, SOUTH AFRICA, 4 APRIL 1989

I have been with Kathy [Ahmed Kathrada] since the late forties. I believe in surrounding myself with strong characters who will tell me when I am wrong, and he is that character.

FROM AN INTERVIEW ABOUT AHMED 'KATHY' KATHRADA, TUYNHUYS, CAPE TOWN, SOUTH AFRICA, 22 AUGUST 1996

Those South Africans who have berated me for being loyal to our friends, literally, they can go and throw themselves in a pool.

PRESS CONFERENCE WITH PRESIDENT BILL CLINTON WHEN ASKED ABOUT HIS RELATIONSHIPS WITH LIBYA, IRAN AND CUBA, CAPE TOWN, SOUTH AFRICA, 27 MARCH 1998

Our moral authority dictates that we should not abandon those who helped us in the darkest hour of the history of this country.

IBID

Our morality does not allow us to desert our friends.

RECEPTION HOSTED BY PRESIDENT BILL CLINTON, THE WHITE HOUSE, WASHINGTON DC, USA, 22 SEPTEMBER 1998

Future

Other people will be driven in the same way in this country, by this very same force of police persecution and of administrative action by the government, to follow my course, of that I am certain.

IN MITIGATION OF SENTENCE AFTER BEING CONVICTED OF INCITING WORKERS TO STRIKE AND LEAVING THE COUNTRY ILLEGALLY, OLD SYNAGOGUE, PRETORIA, SOUTH AFRICA, 7 NOVEMBER 1962

Many people in this country have paid the price before me and many will pay the price after me.

IBID

Someday in the future it'll be possible for humanity to produce saints who will really be upright and venerable, inspired in everything they do by genuine love for humanity and who'll serve all humans selflessly.

FROM A LETTER TO WINNIE MANDELA, WRITTEN ON ROBBEN ISLAND, 19 AUGUST 1976

We face the future with confidence. For the guns that serve apartheid cannot render it unconquerable. Those who live by the gun shall perish by the gun.

STATEMENT ABOUT THE 1976 SOWETO UPRISING, SMUGGLED OUT OF ROBBEN ISLAND PRISON AND RELEASED BY THE ANC IN EXILE, 1980

This knowledge of shared suffering, though formidable in dimension, at the same time keeps alive in us our oneness with mankind, and our own global responsibilities that accrue therefrom. It also helps to strengthen our faith and belief in our future.

FROM A LETTER TO MRS MANORAMA BHALLA, SECRETARY, INDIAN COUNCIL FOR CULTURAL RELATIONS, WRITTEN ON ROBBEN ISLAND, 3 AUGUST 1980

The ideals we cherish, our fondest dreams and fervent hopes may not be realised in our lifetime.

FROM A LETTER TO SHEENA DUNCAN, WRITTEN IN POLLSMOOR PRISON, CAPE TOWN, SOUTH AFRICA, 1 APRIL 1985

Let us together turn into reality the glorious vision of a South Africa free of racism. Free of racial antagonisms among our people. No longer a threat to peace. No longer the skunk of the world. Our common victory is certain.

ADDRESS TO THE INTERNATIONAL LABOUR CONFERENCE, GENEVA, SWITZERLAND, 8 JUNE 1990

When we promised the people freedom, were we offering them a mirage? When we held out a future that will be crowned with happiness and prosperity, were we seeking to blind them to the continuing reality of growing misery and poverty? When we proclaimed that we represent their true interests, were we hiding from the people our inability to deliver what life itself demands?

PATRIOTIC FRONT SUMMIT MEETING, PORT ELIZABETH, SOUTH AFRICA, 29 OCTOBER 1992

We can build a society grounded on friendship and our common humanity – a society founded on tolerance. That is the only road open to us. It is a road to a glorious future in this beautiful country of ours. Let us join hands and march into the future.

ANNOUNCEMENT OF THE ELECTION DATE, MULTI-PARTY NEGOTIATIONS PROCESS, KEMPTON PARK, SOUTH AFRICA, 17 NOVEMBER 1993

We have every reason to look to the future with confidence and a lot of hope because if one considers that the advances that have been made have involved, at one time, no less than twenty-six political parties with different backgrounds, then our achievements have been truly historic.

FROM AN INTERVIEW, CIRCA 1994

The world that we are visualising, is exposed in our Freedom Charter – a land in which the principle is entrenched that South Africa belongs to all its people; a land where there is a Bill of Rights that defends the rights of every individual irrespective of his colour; a multi-party system; regular elections; the proportional representation and the entrenchment of the property, or religious beliefs – that is the world I believe in.

FROM THE DOCUMENTARY *COUNTDOWN TO FREEDOM: TEN DAYS THAT CHANGED SOUTH AFRICA*, 1994

I promise that I will do my best to be worthy of the faith and confidence you have placed in me and my organisation, the African National Congress. Let us build the future together, and toast a better life for all South Africans.

ANC ELECTION VICTORY CELEBRATIONS, CARLTON HOTEL, JOHANNESBURG, SOUTH AFRICA, 2 MAY 1994

All South Africans face the challenge of coming to terms with the past in ways which will enable us to face the future as a united nation at peace with itself.

INTER-FAITH COMMISSIONING SERVICE FOR THE TRC (TRUTH AND RECONCILIATION COMMISSION), ST GEORGE'S CATHEDRAL, CAPE TOWN, SOUTH AFRICA, 13 FEBRUARY 1996

A bright future beckons. The onus is on us, through hard work, honesty and integrity, to reach for the stars.

FREEDOM DAY CELEBRATIONS, PRETORIA, SOUTH AFRICA, 27 APRIL 1996

Our pledge is: never and never again shall the laws of our land rend our people apart or legalise their oppression and repression. Together, we shall march, hand in hand, to a brighter future.

SIGNING OF THE NEW CONSTITUTION, SHARPEVILLE, VEREENIGING, SOUTH AFRICA, 10 DECEMBER 1996

Let us give practical recognition to the injustices of the past, by building a future based on equality and social justice.

IBID

As I sit in Qunu and grow as ancient as its hills, I will continue to entertain the hope that there has emerged a cadre of leaders in my own country and region, on my Continent and in the world, which will not allow that any should be denied their freedom as we were, that any should be turned into refugees as we were, that any should be condemned to grow hungry as we were, that any should be stripped of their human dignity as we were.

ADDRESS TO THE FIFTY-THIRD UNITED NATIONS GENERAL ASSEMBLY, NEW YORK CITY, USA, 21 SEPTEMBER 1998

Our vision for the future is one of renewed dedication by world leaders in all fields of human interaction to a twenty-first century of peace and reconciliation.

UPON RECEIVING THE GERMAN MEDIA PRIZE, BADEN-BADEN, GERMANY, 28 JANUARY 1999

The foundation has been laid – the building is in progress. With a new generation of leaders and a people that rolls up its sleeves in partnerships for change, we can and shall build the country of our dreams!

STATE OF THE NATION ADDRESS, PARLIAMENT, CAPE TOWN, SOUTH AFRICA, 5 FEBRUARY 1999

We shall take not just small steps, but giant leaps to a bright future in the new millennium. As we confounded the prophets of doom, we shall defy today's merchants of cynicism and despair.

IBID

The long walk continues.

FINAL SITTING OF THE FIRST DEMOCRATICALLY ELECTED PARLIAMENT, CAPE TOWN, SOUTH AFRICA, 26 MARCH 1999

The road we have walked has been built by the contribution of all of us; the tools we have used on that road had been fashioned by all of us; the future we face is that of all of us, both in its promises and its demands.

INAUGURATION OF A MONUMENT TO THE PASSIVE RESISTANCE CAMPAIGN, UMBILO PARK, DURBAN, SOUTH AFRICA, 27 MAY 2002

It has to be a better world: one in which the rights of every individual are respected, one that builds on past aspirations for a good life, and one that enables every individual to optimally develop their potential.

MESSAGE TO THE WORLD SOCIAL FORUM, MUMBAI, INDIA, JANUARY 2004

We are too old to pretend to be able to contribute to the resolution of those conflicts and tensions on the international front. It is, therefore, immensely gratifying to note a younger generation of African statespersons emerging. They will be able to speak with authority about a new world order in which people everywhere will live in equality, harmony and peace.

FIFTH ANNUAL NELSON MANDELA LECTURE, LINDER AUDITORIUM, JOHANNESBURG, SOUTH AFRICA, 22 JULY 2007

It is time for new hands to lift the burdens. It is in your hands now.

46664 CONCERT, HYDE PARK, LONDON, ENGLAND, 27 JUNE 2008

It is the task of a new generation to lead and take responsibility; ours has done as well as it could in its time.

LAUNCH OF THE ANC ELECTION MANIFESTO 2009 AND NINETY-SEVENTH ANNIVERSARY CELEBRATIONS, ABSA STADIUM, EAST LONDON, SOUTH AFRICA, 10 JANUARY 2009

Gardening

The Bible tells us that gardens preceded gardeners, but that was not the case at Pollsmoor [Prison], where I cultivated a garden that became one of my happiest diversions. It was my way of escaping from the monolithic concrete world that surrounded us.

FROM *LONG WALK TO FREEDOM*, 1994

I wrote Winnie two letters about a particularly beautiful tomato plant, how I coaxed it from a tender seedling to a robust plant that produced deep red fruit. But, then, either through some mistake or lack of care, the plant began to wither and decline, and nothing I did would bring it back to health. When it finally died, I removed the roots from the soil, washed them and buried them in a corner of the garden.

IBID

Gender Discrimination

Some say that chauvinism is one of my weaknesses. They may be right. True enough, my blood and brain do not often synchronise. Very often reason induces me to approach cautiously what excites my feeling.

FROM A LETTER TO NOMABUTHO BHALA, WRITTEN ON ROBBEN ISLAND, 1 JANUARY 1971

It is now for all of us to redouble our efforts and our commitment to collectively ensure broad-based gender sensitivity and real-life practices of gender equality.

DINNER CELEBRATING WOMEN'S MONTH, JOHANNESBURG COUNTRY CLUB, JOHANNESBURG, SOUTH AFRICA, 25 AUGUST 2003

One of the spectacular achievements of democratic South Africa is the extent to which issues of gender and the role of women had assumed prominence in the public conversation. Too much of this is still only on the rhetorical level, but the fact that few people in our society can claim ideological ignorance or innocence in this matter, is largely due to the consistent and persistent pressure of women.

IBID

No longer are we allowed to put the national question above gender issues; in fact, we are no longer allowed to think of the national question as something apart from the role and place of women in society.

IBID

We need a fundamental change of mindset with regards to the way we speak and behave about sex and sexuality. Boys and men have a particularly critical role in this regard, changing the chauvinist and demeaning ways sexuality and women were traditionally dealt with in both our actions and speaking.

YOUTH FORUM ON HIV/AIDS, UNIVERSITY OF THE WITWATERSRAND, JOHANNESBURG, SOUTH AFRICA, 22 SEPTEMBER 2003

For every woman and girl violently attacked, we reduce our humanity. For every woman forced into unprotected sex because men demand this, we destroy dignity and pride. Every woman who has to sell her life for sex we condemn to a lifetime in prison. For every moment we remain silent, we conspire against our women. For every woman infected by HIV, we destroy a generation.

46664 CONCERT, FANCOURT, GEORGE, SOUTH AFRICA, 19 MARCH 2005

We must be honest and open about the power relationships between men and women in our society, and we must help build a more enabling and supportive environment that puts the role of women centre stage in this struggle. Each one of us – sister and brother, mother and father, teacher and student, priest and parishioner, manager and worker, presidents and prime ministers – must add our voice to this call for action.

IBID

Well, you know, sitting down in jail and reading you discover things which you have never known: makes you realise that some of your ideas in the past were completely wrong.

FROM AN INTERVIEW WITH TIM COUZENS, VERNE HARRIS AND MAC MAHARAJ FOR
MANDELA: THE AUTHORISED PORTRAIT, 2006, JOHANNESBURG, SOUTH AFRICA, 13 AUGUST 2005

Globalisation

It is clear that simultaneously as the process of globalisation grows apace, so does the system of international governance also grow stronger. We have no doubt that this tendency will strengthen rather than weaken.

OPENING OF THE FIFTIETH ANC NATIONAL CONFERENCE, NORTH-WEST UNIVERSITY, MAFIKENG CAMPUS,
SOUTH AFRICA, 16 DECEMBER 1997

Goals

If you have an objective in life, then you want to concentrate on that and not engage in infighting with your enemies. You want to create an atmosphere where you can move everybody towards the goal you have set for yourself – as well as the collective for which you work.

FROM AN INTERVIEW WITH JOHN BATTERSBY, JOHANNESBURG, SOUTH AFRICA, PUBLISHED IN
THE CHRISTIAN SCIENCE MONITOR, 10 FEBRUARY 2000

Going Underground

So far we have been able to anticipate every move the police have made. I have so much work that I don't even think about arrest.

SOURCE UNKNOWN, CIRCA MAY 1961

I have had to separate myself from my dear wife and children, from my mother and sisters, to live as an outlaw in my own land. I have had to close my business, to abandon my profession and live in poverty and misery, as many of my people are doing.

FROM THE 'STRUGGLE IS MY LIFE' PRESS STATEMENT, EXPLAINING HIS DECISION TO CARRY ON HIS POLITICAL
WORK UNDERGROUND, IN ACCORDANCE WITH THE ADVICE OF THE NATIONAL ACTION COUNCIL,
SOUTH AFRICA, 26 JUNE 1961

There comes a time, as it came in my life, when a man is denied that right to live a normal life, when he can only live the life of an outlaw because the Government has so decreed to use the law to impose a state of outlawry upon him. I was driven to this situation, and I do not regret having taken the decisions that I did take.

IN MITIGATION OF SENTENCE AFTER BEING CONVICTED OF INCITING WORKERS TO STRIKE AND LEAVING
THE COUNTRY ILLEGALLY, OLD SYNAGOGUE, PRETORIA, SOUTH AFRICA, 7 NOVEMBER 1962

The ANC refused to dissolve, but instead went underground. We believed it was our duty to preserve this organisation which had been built up with almost 150 years of unremitting toil. I have no doubt that no self-respecting white political organisation would disband itself if declared illegal by a government in which it had no say.

SPEECH FROM THE DOCK, RIVONIA TRIAL, PALACE OF JUSTICE, PRETORIA, SOUTH AFRICA, 20 APRIL 1964

It meant that firstly we should be extremely discreet even in coming together to take decisions because if the organisation is going to operate underground, the first thing we have to do is to create a machinery to enable it to operate underground.

FROM A CONVERSATION WITH RICHARD STENGEL, 5 APRIL 1993

We had already decided to take certain actions, which if we were found out – quite apart from the question of the banning of the ANC – we would have been charged and convicted and the idea of going underground was really to start a new era, the era of violent activities, organised violence.

IBID

I myself did not realise the full implications of the life I had chosen. I knew I was now choosing a career which would bring me and the family formidable problems, but the precise nature in which they would occur I did not anticipate.

FROM AN INTERVIEW, CIRCA 1993

I had a different disguise for the family, for the children and a different disguise, you know, for travelling through town.

FROM AN INTERVIEW, TALKING ABOUT WHEN HE WENT UNDERGROUND ON 29 MARCH 1961 IMMEDIATELY AFTER BEING ACQUITTED IN THE TREASON TRIAL BECAUSE HE HAD EXPECTED TO BE BANNED AGAIN, CIRCA 1993

I had gone underground and it was a new style of life altogether. I had a beard, my dress was totally different. I used to pay attention to new clothing, and so on; I was now wearing a windbreaker, corduroy trousers and sandals and I had long hair, which was not properly combed.

FROM A CONVERSATION WITH AHMED KATHRADA, CIRCA 1993/94

When a man is denied the right to live the life he believes in, he has no choice but to become an outlaw.

SOURCE UNKNOWN, 1994

Our thirst for freedom had turned us into outlaws.

STATE BANQUET HOSTED BY PRESIDENT KETUMILE MASIRE, BOTSWANA, 5 SEPTEMBER 1995

It was felt that somebody should go underground and lead the movement. I accepted the challenge with all its difficulties.

FROM A BBC (UK) DOCUMENTARY, 1996

Goodness

There will always be good men on earth, in all countries, and even here at home.

FROM A LETTER TO WINNIE MANDELA, WRITTEN ON ROBBEN ISLAND, 1 AUGUST 1970

The habit of attending to small things and of appreciating small courtesies is one of the important marks of a good person.

FROM A LETTER TO ZENANI MANDELA, WRITTEN ON ROBBEN ISLAND, 25 MARCH 1979

People will feel I see too much good in people. So it's a criticism I have to put up with and I've tried to adjust to because, whether it is so or not, it is something which I think is profitable.

FROM A CONVERSATION WITH RICHARD STENGEL, 29 DECEMBER 1992

I would venture to say that there is something inherently good in all human beings, deriving from, among other things, the attribute of social consciousness that we all possess. And, yes, there is also something inherently bad in all of us, flesh and blood as we are, with the attendant desire to perpetuate and pamper the self.

PEACE LECTURE OF THE WORLD CONFERENCE ON RELIGION AND PEACE (SOUTH AFRICAN CHAPTER), DURBAN, SOUTH AFRICA, 7 AUGUST 1994

There is a streak of goodness in men that can be buried or hidden and then emerge unexpectedly.

FROM LONG WALK TO FREEDOM, 1994

We signal that good can be achieved amongst human beings who are prepared to trust, prepared to believe in the goodness of people.

JOINT SITTING OF PARLIAMENT TO MARK TEN YEARS OF DEMOCRACY, PARLIAMENT, CAPE TOWN, SOUTH AFRICA, 10 MAY 2004

Goodwill

Currents of goodwill surge forward continually from all points of the compass infusing confidence and hope.

FROM A LETTER TO MANGOSUTHU BUTHELEZI, WRITTEN ON ROBBEN ISLAND, 1 OCTOBER 1978

Greatness

Sometimes it falls upon a generation to be great. You can be that great generation. Let your greatness blossom.

LAUNCH OF THE 'MAKE POVERTY HISTORY' CAMPAIGN, TRAFALGAR SQUARE, LONDON, ENGLAND, 3 FEBRUARY 2005

Guilt

Yet there have been moments when that love and happiness, that trust and hope, have turned into pure agony, when conscience and a sense of guilt have ravaged every part of my being, when I have wondered whether any kind of commitment can ever be sufficient excuse for abandoning a young and inexperienced woman in a pitiless desert, literally throwing her into the hands of highwaymen, a wonderful woman without her pillar of support in times of need.

REVISITING ROBBEN ISLAND, CAPE TOWN, SOUTH AFRICA, TALKING ABOUT WINNIE MANDELA, 11 FEBRUARY 1994

Happiness

There are times of happiness when I laugh alone by thinking of the opportunities I had as well as times of pleasure.

FROM A LETTER TO WINNIE MANDELA, WRITTEN ON ROBBEN ISLAND, 1 OCTOBER 1976

It is a precious virtue to try to make others happy and to forget their worries.

FROM A LETTER TO ZINDZI MANDELA, WRITTEN ON ROBBEN ISLAND, 1 MARCH 1981

Take it upon yourself where you live to make people around you joyful and full of hope.

OPENING OF THE ZOLA CLINIC, SOWETO, SOUTH AFRICA, 7 MARCH 2002

Health

Now and again there have been rumours that my health has broken down and that I am on my last legs.

FROM A LETTER TO AMINA CACHALIA, WRITTEN ON ROBBEN ISLAND, 3 MAY 1981

I feel so well that I could challenge for the heavyweight boxing championship of the world.

FROM A LETTER TO ELAINE KEARNS, WRITTEN IN VICTOR VERSTER PRISON, PAARL, SOUTH AFRICA, 14 FEBRUARY 1989

I feel on top of the world.

JOHANNESBURG, SOUTH AFRICA, 1990

If I have a cold, I just sweat it out because I don't believe very much in medicine.

FROM A CONVERSATION WITH RICHARD STENGEL, CIRCA APRIL/MAY 1993

I thought I should just check with the doctor and he says, 'Well, you will die from everything else except your heart'.

FROM AN INTERVIEW WITH TOM COHEN AND SAHM VENTER FOR THE ASSOCIATED PRESS, TUYNHUYS, CAPE TOWN, SOUTH AFRICA, 22 SEPTEMBER 1994

It is important to follow the prescriptions of the doctor, but it is equally important to be determined to live and not to give in and to do things which will then arouse the spirit of those who are suffering from that illness.

OPENING OF THE ZOLA CLINIC, SOWETO, SOUTH AFRICA, 7 MARCH 2002

I had prostate cancer and then I discussed it with my prison friends, 'Look, I'd better be the one who announces publicly that I have cancer because if I go to a doctor to treat me they are going to go around whispering "did you know that Mandela has cancer?"'

FROM A CONVERSATION WITH MORGAN FREEMAN, JOHANNESBURG, SOUTH AFRICA, 14 NOVEMBER, 2006

Heaven

I am not here to announce any fair departures. And in any case, my family and advisers have warned me not to tell my favourite story about arriving at heaven's door, knocking, providing my name and being sent to the other place. Apparently that story makes too many people morose!

'RETIRING FROM RETIREMENT' ANNOUNCEMENT, NELSON MANDELA FOUNDATION, JOHANNESBURG, SOUTH AFRICA, 1 JUNE 2004

I am sure if I go to heaven and then they say, 'Who are you?' I say, 'No, I'm Madiba' – 'From Qunu?' I say, 'Yes'. They'll say, 'You are daring to come here with all your sins'. They will say, 'Please go away and knock in hell, they might accept you there'.

NINETY-SECOND BIRTHDAY PARTY, HOUGHTON, SOUTH AFRICA, 18 JULY 2010

Heroes

For one thing, those who have no soul, no sense of national pride and no ideals to win can suffer neither humiliation nor defeat; they can evolve no national heritage, are inspired by no sacred mission and can produce no martyrs or national heroes.

FROM A LETTER TO WINNIE MANDELA, WRITTEN ON ROBBEN ISLAND, 23 JUNE 1969

The full story of our past heritage remains incomplete if we forget that line of indigenous heroes who acted as curtain-raisers to the major conflicts that subsequently flamed out, and who acquitted themselves magnificently.

FROM A LETTER TO NOMABUTHO BHALA, WRITTEN ON ROBBEN ISLAND, 1 JANUARY 1971

We are the heirs to a three-stream heritage: an inheritance that inspires us to fight and die for the loftiest ideals in life. The title 'African hero' embraces all these veterans.

IBID

It is certainly quite unreasonable for any man to expect our people to whom we are national heroes, persecuted for striving to win back our country, to forget us in our lifetime at the height of a struggle for a free South Africa.

FROM A LETTER TO GENERAL DU PREEZ, COMMISSIONER OF PRISONS, WRITTEN ON ROBBEN ISLAND, 12 JULY 1976

We salute all of you. We who are confined within the grey walls of the Pretoria regime's walls reach out to our people, with you we count those who have perished by means of the gun and the hangman's rope. We salute all of you – the living, the injured and the dead – for you have dared to rise up against the tyrant's might.

STATEMENT ABOUT THE 1976 SOWETO UPRISING, SMUGGLED OUT OF ROBBEN ISLAND PRISON AND RELEASED BY THE ANC IN EXILE, 1980

Those who are prepared to face problems at eyeball range, and who embrace universal beliefs which have changed the course of history in many societies must, in due course, command solid support and admiration far beyond their own ranks.

FROM A LETTER TO SHEENA DUNCAN, WRITTEN IN POLLSMOOR PRISON, CAPE TOWN, SOUTH AFRICA, 1 APRIL 1985

For thousands of years and one generation after another, the human race has thrown up men and women of love, vision and boundless courage. It is thanks to these towering giants that our humanness has always remained with us and will always remain with us, no matter how difficult the challenges history throws at us from one historic era to another.

ANATOMY OF HATE: RESOLVING CONFLICT THROUGH DIALOGUE AND DEMOCRACY INTERNATIONAL CONFERENCE, OSLO, NORWAY, 26 AUGUST 1990

[Jawaharlal] Nehru was really my hero.

FROM A CONVERSATION WITH AHMED KATHRADA, CIRCA 1993/94

Today's occasion speaks of our resolve: to preserve the memories of our heroes and heroines; to keep alive the flame of patriotism which burnt in the hearts and minds of the likes of Steve Biko; and to redeem the pledge to give a more human face to a society for centuries trampled upon by the jackboot of inhumanity.

COMMEMORATION OF THE TWENTIETH ANNIVERSARY OF THE DEATH IN POLICE DETENTION OF STEVE BIKO, EAST LONDON, SOUTH AFRICA, 1 SEPTEMBER 1997

The names of only very few people are remembered beyond their lives. And some of those are remembered with revulsion for the harm they have done. But there are those who are remembered for their good deeds and the contribution they have made to the society in which they live.

LAUNCH OF THE BRAM FISCHER MEMORIAL TRUST, GREY COLLEGE, BLOEMFONTEIN, SOUTH AFRICA, 28 NOVEMBER 1997

Oliver Tambo was like no one else: a brother and a friend to me. He enriched my own life and intellect; and neither I nor indeed this country can forget this colossus of our history.

CLOSING SESSION OF THE FIFTIETH ANC NATIONAL CONFERENCE, NORTH-WEST UNIVERSITY, MAFIKENG CAMPUS, SOUTH AFRICA, 20 DECEMBER 1997

Heroes like the Khoikhoi leader, Autshumao, Maqoma of the Rharhabe, Bambatha, Cetywayo of the Zulu, Mampuru of the Pedis, Tshivhase of the Vendas and a host of others were in the forefront of the wars of resistance and we speak of them with respect and admiration.

FROM THE UNPUBLISHED SEQUEL TO HIS AUTOBIOGRAPHY, CIRCA 1998

On many occasions, freedom fighters who have been national heroes turn against the masses of the people, they lose the common touch.

ADDRESS TO A GATHERING, SOUTH AFRICA, DATE UNKNOWN

I often say that it is not necessarily the men and women who have titles, it is the humble men and women that you find in all communities but who have chosen the world as the theatre of their operations, who feel the greatest challenges are the socio-economic issues that face the world like poverty, illiteracy, disease, lack of housing, inability to send your children to school – these are my heroes. If any head of state qualifies in this, he is my hero.

CLOSING ADDRESS AT THE XIII INTERNATIONAL AIDS CONFERENCE, DURBAN, SOUTH AFRICA, 14 JULY 2000

Amongst the heroes and heroines of our long struggle for freedom and justice, the name of Joe Slovo will always remain in the front ranks. Few could have been more revered and more universally acclaimed and admired than him.

MEMORIAL FOR JOE SLOVO, AVALON CEMETERY, SOWETO, SOUTH AFRICA, 1 MARCH 2004

Jail walls can never prevent you identifying yourself with the struggle outside prison and, even though we were behind bars, all of us and the leaders of the ANC outside were actually heroes.

FROM THE DOCUMENTARY *LEGENDS: NELSON MANDELA*, 2005

We trust that the statue will be a reminder of the heroes and heroines past as well as an inspiration for continuing struggles against injustice.

UNVEILING OF HIS STATUE, PARLIAMENT SQUARE, LONDON, ENGLAND, 29 AUGUST 2007

The history of struggle in South Africa is rich with the stories of heroes and heroines, some of them leaders, some of them followers. All of them deserve to be remembered.

IBID

It is so easy to break down and destroy. The heroes are those who make peace and build.

SIXTH ANNUAL NELSON MANDELA LECTURE, WALTER SISULU SQUARE, KLIPTOWN, SOWETO, SOUTH AFRICA, 12 JULY 2008

Well, it's a nice feeling for people to talk of you in terms of being a hero. This is not really directed at me. I am used as a peg on which to hang all the adulation.

FROM THE DOCUMENTARY *VIVA MADIBA: A HERO FOR ALL SEASONS*, 2010

Himself, On

The structure and organisation of early African societies in this country fascinated me very much and greatly influenced the evolution of my political outlook.

IN MITIGATION OF SENTENCE AFTER BEING CONVICTED OF INCITING WORKERS TO STRIKE AND LEAVING THE COUNTRY ILLEGALLY, OLD SYNAGOGUE, PRETORIA, SOUTH AFRICA, 7 NOVEMBER 1962

I am one of those who possess scraps of superficial information on a variety of subjects, but who lacks depth and expert knowledge on the one thing in which I ought to have specialised, namely the history of my country and people.

FROM A LETTER TO FATIMA MEER, WRITTEN ON ROBBEN ISLAND, 1 MARCH 1971

I sometimes believe that through me creation intended to give the world the example of a mediocre man in the proper sense of the term.

IBID

I moved in circles where common sense and practical experience were important, and where high academic and practical experience were not necessarily decisive.

FROM AN UNPUBLISHED AUTOBIOGRAPHICAL MANUSCRIPT, WRITTEN ON ROBBEN ISLAND, 1975

My training and experience as a practising lawyer in South Africa's biggest city, Johannesburg, sensitised me at an early age in my political career to what was going on inside the corridors of political power in our country.

IBID

The process of deciding was not simple and straightforward. For some time I hesitated on the sidelines, uncertain what to do. Often I realised the full implications of what I had done, not before, but after taking the step.

IBID

At college I had come to believe that as a graduate I would automatically be at the head, leading my people in all their efforts.

IBID

I developed some inner strength and soon forgot about my difficulties and my poverty and suffering, my loneliness and frustrations.

IBID

I was planning to help correct the errors of South Africa and had forgotten that the first step in doing so was to overcome the weakness of the one South African I knew very well, myself.

IBID

No one had ever briefed me on how we would finally remove the evils of colour prejudice, the books I should read in this connection and the political organisations I should join if I wanted to be part of a disciplined freedom movement. I had to learn all these things by mere chance and through trial and error.

IBID

Even when the clash between you and me has taken the most extreme form, I should like us to fight over principles and ideas and without personal hatred, so that at the end of the battle, whatever the results might be, I can proudly shake hands with you, because I feel I have fought an upright and worthy opponent who has observed the whole code of honour and decency. But when your subordinates continue to use foul methods, then a sense of real bitterness and contempt becomes irresistible.

FROM A LETTER TO GENERAL DU PREEZ, COMMISSIONER OF PRISONS, WRITTEN ON ROBBEN ISLAND, 12 JULY 1976

Sometimes I feel like one who is on the sidelines, who has missed life itself.

FROM A LETTER TO WINNIE MANDELA, WRITTEN ON ROBBEN ISLAND, 21 JANUARY 1979

I am no prophet but I am certainly an optimist and in the case of my discussions with the government, especially with Mr [FW] de Klerk, my optimism has been strengthened.

AT HOME, SOWETO, SOUTH AFRICA, 14 FEBRUARY 1990

Well I do like to think about problems very carefully before I take a decision. But there are some times when you have to take a snap decision. But generally speaking, I would like to think very carefully before I take a decision.

FROM A CONVERSATION WITH RICHARD STENGEL, 14 DECEMBER 1992

I have mellowed, very definitely, and as a young man, you know, I was very radical and using high-flown language, and fighting everybody.

FROM A CONVERSATION WITH RICHARD STENGEL, 3 FEBRUARY 1993

I'm here to serve my community, and if there is somebody who has got problems and who, as a result of his background, cannot cope with his problems, I must immediately help.

FROM A CONVERSATION WITH RICHARD STENGEL, 9 MARCH 1993

I didn't want to be presented in a way that omits the dark spots in my life.

FROM A CONVERSATION WITH RICHARD STENGEL, 16 MARCH 1993

We are a team and if a thing is going to bear my name, normally I would like to have an input in that and also read it very carefully and make sure that I agree with it politically.

FROM A CONVERSATION WITH RICHARD STENGEL, 4 APRIL 1993

My cross-examination ordinarily as a lawyer, was quite gentle because you don't antagonise the witnesses.

FROM A CONVERSATION WITH RICHARD STENGEL, 17 APRIL 1993

I think that I am one of those who believes that revolution interferes with my own personal tastes. I would like to sit down, you know, and to organise my reading as I was doing in prison for example, but the struggle is first and foremost my top priority and I enjoy it.

FROM AN INTERVIEW WITH THE BBC (UK), 28 OCTOBER 1993

I had very little time for social activities.

FROM A CONVERSATION WITH AHMED KATHRAD, CIRCA 1993/94

I was arrogant [in] those days.

FROM A CONVERSATION WITH AHMED KATHRADA ABOUT 1962, CIRCA 1993/94

I must correct a misconception of thinking that an individual can solve problems for the country and bring about democracy.

FROM AN INTERVIEW WITH THE BBC (UK), 1993

I regarded my role in prison as not just the leader of the ANC, but as a promoter of unity, an honest broker, a peacemaker.

FROM *LONG WALK TO FREEDOM*, 1994

There was no particular day on which I said, henceforth I will devote myself to the liberation of my people; instead, I simply found myself doing so, and could not do otherwise.

IBID

A ridiculous notion is sometimes advanced that Mandela has been exclusively responsible for these real achievements of the South African people, particularly our smooth transition. If only to emphasise that I am human, and as fallible as anyone else, let me admit that these accolades do flatter me.

FROM AN ARTICLE IN THE *SUNDAY TIMES* (SOUTH AFRICA), 22 FEBRUARY 1996

On occasion, like other leaders, I have stumbled; and cannot claim to sparkle alone on a glorified perch.

IBID

When I went to school the lady teacher Miss Mdingane asked, 'What is your name?' I told her my African name, Rolihlahla. She says, 'No, I don't want that one; you must have a Christian name.' So I say, 'No, I don't have one.' She says, 'From today you are going to be Nelson.'

FROM THE DOCUMENTARY *MANDELA*, 1996

It will probably shock many people to discover how colossally ignorant I am about simple things the ordinary person takes for granted.

FROM A PERSONAL FILE, CIRCA 1996

As I reflect on the purposes for which we are gathered here today, I seem to arrive more firmly at the conclusion that my own life struggle has had meaning only because, dimly and perhaps incoherently, it has sought to achieve the supreme objective of ensuring that each, without regard to race, colour, gender or social status, could, like every Olympian, have the possibility to reach for the skies.

PRESENTATION OF THE CAPE TOWN BID AT THE 106TH SESSION OF THE INTERNATIONAL OLYMPIC COMMITTEE, LAUSANNE, SWITZERLAND, 5 SEPTEMBER 1997

To join George Washington and Winston Churchill as the other recipients of such an award conferred at a specially convened convocation, the name of an African is now added to those illustrious leaders of the Western world.

UPON RECEIVING AN HONORARY DOCTORATE FROM HARVARD UNIVERSITY, MASSACHUSETTS, USA, 18 SEPTEMBER 1998

I count myself fortunate that, amongst that generation, history permitted me to take part in South Africa's transition from that period into the new era whose foundation we have been laying together.

FINAL SITTING OF THE FIRST DEMOCRATICALLY ELECTED PARLIAMENT, CAPE TOWN, SOUTH AFRICA, 26 MARCH 1999

As for me personally, I belong to the generation of leaders for whom the achievement of democracy was the defining challenge.

IBID

I have, in a small way, done my duty to my country and to my people.

BRIEFING TO EDITORS AND OPINION MAKERS, PRETORIA, SOUTH AFRICA, 10 MAY 1999

I cannot pinpoint a precise moment when I became politicised and knew with a sudden blinding flash that I would spend my life in the liberation struggle. It was rather a process growing out of the oppressive realities of one's life coupled with the formative influences of a variety of people.

REBURIAL CEREMONY FOR ANTON LEMBEDE, MBUMBULU, SOUTH AFRICA, 27 OCTOBER 2002

If I had to live again I would do exactly the same thing. As long as our people were oppressed and deprived of everything to make human beings happy and to enjoy life, it was my duty to be involved and I'd do it all over and over again.

FROM THE DOCUMENTARY *MANDELA: THE LIVING LEGEND*, 2003

When you are answering questions which make many people proud of you, you can actually exaggerate your qualities.

FROM AN INTERVIEW WITH TIM COUZENS, VERNE HARRIS AND MAC MAHARAJ FOR
MANDELA: THE AUTHORISED PORTRAIT, 2006, JOHANNESBURG, SOUTH AFRICA, 13 AUGUST 2005

I go to bed feeling that I have made a humble contribution towards my country and towards my people.

FROM THE DOCUMENTARY *LEGENDS: NELSON MANDELA*, 2005

When Oliver Tambo and I visited Westminster Abbey and Parliament Square in 1962, we half-joked that we hoped that one day a statue of a black person would be erected here alongside General Smuts. Oliver would have been proud today.

IBID

There will be life after Mandela. We have many capable young people in the leadership of the African National Congress. In almost every respect they stand head and shoulders above Mandela.

FROM A DOCUMENTARY BY BEATA LIPMAN, DATE UNKNOWN

What dominates is the feeling of well-being, but of course I am not a young man and the workload is very heavy.

FROM AN INTERVIEW, DATE UNKNOWN

History

Many years ago, when I was a boy brought up in my village in the Transkei, I listened to the elders of the tribe telling stories about the good old days, before the arrival of the white man. Then our people lived peacefully, under the democratic rule of their kings and their amapakati, and moved freely and confidently up and down the country without let or hindrance. Then the country was ours, in our own name and right.

IN MITIGATION OF SENTENCE AFTER BEING CONVICTED OF INCITING WORKERS TO STRIKE AND LEAVING
THE COUNTRY ILLEGALLY, OLD SYNAGOGUE, PRETORIA, SOUTH AFRICA, 7 NOVEMBER 1962

We occupied the land, the forests, the rivers; we extracted the mineral wealth beneath the soil and all the riches of this beautiful country. We set up and operated our own government, we controlled our own armies and we organised our own trade and commerce. The elders would tell tales of the wars fought by our ancestors in defence of the fatherland, as well as the acts of valour performed by generals and soldiers during those epic days.

IBID

Nothing can be as valuable as being part and parcel of the history of a country.

FROM A LETTER TO WINNIE MANDELA, WRITTEN ON ROBBEN ISLAND, 10 JUNE 1969

Since my release, I have become more convinced than ever that the real makers of history are the ordinary men and women of our country; their participation in every decision about the future is the only guarantee of true democracy and freedom.

RALLY, KINGS PARK STADIUM, DURBAN, SOUTH AFRICA, 25 FEBRUARY 1990

Hollywood

Hollywood has tended to stereotype the lives of the people of Africa. As a young man I remember seeing *Tarzan* and being uneasy, even disturbed by this one-dimensional and distorted portrayal. Fortunately over the past few years a few films have sought to partially redress this injustice.

FROM THE DOCUMENTARY *MANDELA IN AMERICA*, 1990

Home

In our home, there were other dependents, boys mainly, and at an early age I drifted away from my parents and moved about, played and ate together with other boys. In fact I hardly remember any occasion when I was ever alone at home.

FROM AN UNPUBLISHED AUTOBIOGRAPHICAL MANUSCRIPT, WRITTEN ON ROBBEN ISLAND, 1975

Home is home even for those who aspire to serve wider interests and who have established their home of choice in distant regions.

IBID

Well, it was an emotive experience to be back home and to enter the bedroom in which I had lived since March 1947.

FROM A CONVERSATION WITH RICHARD STENGEL, 22 APRIL 1993

It was the feeling of satisfaction, of being able to resume a normal life and to join the family and to be able to pick up the old threads and to try and adjust, you know, from an area which, from a place, a spot in the universe which I regarded as my sweet home and where I could sit down and think about the problems of the country.

IBID

There is nothing like returning to a place that remains unchanged to find the ways in which you yourself have altered.

FROM *LONG WALK TO FREEDOM*, 1994

Honour

Honour belongs to those who never forsake the truth even when things seem dark and grim, who try over and over again, who are never discouraged by insults, humiliation and even defeat.

FROM A LETTER TO WINNIE MANDELA, WRITTEN ON ROBBEN ISLAND, 23 JUNE 1969

I should like us to fight over our principles and ideas and without personal hatred so, at the end of the battle, whatever the result might be, I can proudly shake hands with you, because I feel I have fought an upright and worthy opponent who has observed the whole code of honour and decency.

FROM A LETTER WRITTEN ON ROBBEN ISLAND PRISON AND SMUGGLED OUT TO LAWYERS IN DURBAN, SOUTH AFRICA, JANUARY 1977

I learned that to humiliate another person is to make him suffer an unnecessarily cruel fate. Even as a boy, I defeated my opponents without dishonouring them.

FROM *LONG WALK TO FREEDOM*, 1994

Hope

Hope is a powerful weapon, and [one] no one power on earth can deprive you of.

FROM A LETTER TO WINNIE MANDELA, WRITTEN ON ROBBEN ISLAND, 23 JUNE 1969

I never dreamt that time and hope could mean so much to one as they do now.

FROM A LETTER TO ADELAIDE TAMBO, WRITTEN ON ROBBEN ISLAND, 31 JANUARY 1970

I feel my heart pumping hope steadily to every part of my body, warming my blood and pepping up my spirits.

FROM A LETTER TO WINNIE MANDELA, THEN IN PRETORIA CENTRAL PRISON, WRITTEN ON ROBBEN ISLAND, 1 AUGUST 1970

We never lost hope of returning and it was for us to continue our commitment to these founding principles, because to do so we are following in the footsteps of great fighters for human rights.

OPENING OF THE ANNE FRANK MUSEUM AT MUSEUMAFRIKA, JOHANNESBURG, SOUTH AFRICA, 15 AUGUST 1994

There were moments when hope almost vanished but Walter [Sisulu] had enormous capacity to endure and he taught us that it doesn't matter what the situation is, you must hope and be determined that you will triumph in the end.

IBID

Our hopes will become a reality.

STATE OF THE NATION ADDRESS, PARLIAMENT, CAPE TOWN, SOUTH AFRICA, 5 FEBRUARY 1999

Our human compassion binds us the one to the other – not in pity or patronisingly, but as human beings who have learned how to turn our common suffering into hope for the future.

MESSAGE TO THE HEALING AND RECONCILIATION SERVICE 'DEDICATED TO HIV/AIDS SUFFERERS AND FOR THE HEALING OF OUR LAND', 6 DECEMBER 2000

I have spent all my life dreaming of a golden age in which all problems will be solved and our wildest hopes fulfilled.

SOURCE UNKNOWN

Human Rights

You don't have to have education in order to know that you want certain fundamental rights, you have aspirations, you have got claims. It is nothing to do with education.

FROM AN INTERVIEW WITH BRIAN WIDLAKE FOR ITN TELEVISION (UK), JOHANNESBURG, SOUTH AFRICA, 31 MAY 1961

Human rights is still one of the world's burning issues of the day, and the work and achievements of Sir Wilberforce is as relevant now as it was in his time.

FROM A LETTER TO JACK LENNARD, WILBERFORCE COUNCIL, WRITTEN IN VICTOR VERSTER PRISON, PAARL, SOUTH AFRICA, 21 AUGUST 1989

The rights of every citizen to his or her language, culture and religion must also be guaranteed.

ADDRESS TO THE EUROPEAN PARLIAMENT, STRASBOURG, FRANCE, 13 JUNE 1990

Every adult South African must have the right to participate in governing our country through a system of one person, one vote. The human rights of all our citizens must be guaranteed under an entrenched and justiciable bill of rights, which should be enforced by an independent judiciary.

IBID

Given our bitter experience of oppression and repression, we are determined that our country should be a truly thorough-going democracy in which the rights of all its citizens will be inviolable and in which all will be equal before the law.

ADDRESS TO THE PARLIAMENT OF CANADA, OTTAWA, CANADA, 18 JUNE 1990

The basic human rights for all our citizens have to be protected and guaranteed, to ensure the genuine liberty of every individual.

BUSINESS LEADERSHIP MEETING, WORLD TRADE CENTER, NEW YORK CITY, USA, 21 JUNE 1990

To deny people their human rights is to challenge their very humanity. To impose on them a wretched life of hunger and deprivation is to dehumanise them.

ADDRESS TO THE JOINT SESSION OF THE HOUSE OF CONGRESS, WASHINGTON DC, USA, 26 JUNE 1990

To safeguard the freedom of the individual, we will insist that the democratic constitution should be reinforced with an entrenched bill of rights which should be enforced by an independent and representative judiciary.

STATEMENT TO THE PARLIAMENT OF THE REPUBLIC OF IRELAND, DUBLIN, IRELAND, 2 JULY 1990

A bill of rights is an important statement about the nature of power relations in any society. Unlimited executive and legislative power, which still pervades our society under white minority rule, cannot comfortably coexist with a commitment to individual political and civil rights.

INVESTITURE, CLARK UNIVERSITY, ATLANTA, USA, 10 JULY 1993

Our proposals underline the reality that human beings have multiple lives and identities within and across racial and ethnic lines. The key, therefore, to the protection of any minority is to put core civil and political rights beyond the reach of temporary majorities by guaranteeing them as fundamental human rights, enshrined in a democratic constitution.

IBID

Since 1923, when the first-ever bill of rights in South Africa was adopted by the ANC, human rights and the attainment of justice have explicitly been at the centre of our concerns.

IBID

For those who had to fight for our emancipation, such as ourselves, who, with your help, had to free ourselves from the criminal apartheid system, the United Nations Declaration of Human Rights serves as the vindication of the justice of our cause. At the same time, it constituted a challenge to us that our freedom, once achieved, should be dedicated to the implementation of the perspectives contained in the Declaration.

ADDRESS TO THE FIFTY-THIRD UNITED NATIONS GENERAL ASSEMBLY, NEW YORK CITY, USA, 21 SEPTEMBER 1998

We now live in a constitutional state based on the protection and promotion of basic human rights, a state in which the protection of human dignity stands supreme, and in which the Constitution guards over such fundamental values as equality, non-racialism, non-sexism and the rights of all citizens.

RECEPTION DINNER, AIG (AMERICAN INTERNATIONAL GROUP, INC.) BOARD MEETING, TUNIS, TUNISIA, 24 MARCH 2004

As I am former prisoner number 46664, there is a special place in my heart for all those that are denied access to their basic human rights. We urge countries to make the policy changes that are necessary to protect the human rights of those who suffer from unfair discrimination.

CLOSING ADDRESS TO THE XV INTERNATIONAL AIDS CONFERENCE, BANGKOK, THAILAND, 16 JULY 2004

Where there is poverty and sickness, including AIDS, where human beings are being oppressed, there is more work to be done. Our work is for freedom for all.

46664 CONCERT, HYDE PARK, LONDON, ENGLAND, 27 JUNE 2008

Celebrate the nobility of our ideals of creating a non-racial and non-sexist society.

ANC RALLY FOR HIS NINETIETH BIRTHDAY, LOFTUS VERSFELD STADIUM, PRETORIA, SOUTH AFRICA, 2 AUGUST 2008

Let us redouble our efforts to fully realise the ideal of a democratic state and society that secures to all their birthright without distinction of colour, race, sex or belief. Let us live that non-racialism and non-sexism in our every day, deed and word.

IBID

Humanity

The award with which you honour me today is an expression of the common humanity that binds us, one person to another, nation to nation, and people of the North to people of the South. I receive it with pride, as a symbol of partnership for peace, prosperity and equity as we enter the new millennium.

UPON RECEIVING THE CONGRESSIONAL GOLD MEDAL, WASHINGTON DC, USA, 23 SEPTEMBER 1998

In the aftermath of September 11, the world was moved to reflect, amongst other things, about how we live together peacefully and with respect for the differences amongst us.

OPENING CEREMONY OF THE FIRST ANNUAL TRIBECA FILM FESTIVAL, CITY HALL, NEW YORK CITY, USA, 8 MAY 2002

Humility

It is not at all correct to elevate any human being to the position of a god.

AT HOME, SOWETO, SOUTH AFRICA, FEBRUARY 1990

To know that you are the object of such goodwill makes one humble indeed.

FROM A CONVERSATION WITH RICHARD STENGEL, 22 APRIL 1993

Humour

The tradition was not to laugh too much. You had to be serious. Part of leadership was to be a serious person. Not to engage in laughter. That was the tradition in those days.

FROM A CONVERSATION ABOUT HIS YOUTH WITH TIM COUZENS, VERNE HARRIS AND MAC MAHARAJ FOR *MANDELA: THE AUTHORISED PORTRAIT*, 2006, 13 AUGUST 2005

I like, you know, people being relaxed because even when you are discussing a serious matter, relaxation is very important because it encourages your thinking; so I like to make jokes even when examining serious situations. Because when people are relaxed they can think properly.

IBID

We have a sense of humour because we feel it is our duty to make people forget about their problems and to think of things which help them to understand the feelings of the people and their experiences.

IBID

You sharpen your ideas by reducing yourself to the level of the people you are with and a sense of humour and a complete relaxation, even when you're discussing serious things, does help to mobilise friends around you. And I love that.

IBID

Just remember I am looking for a job.

JOKING TO JOURNALISTS ABOUT BEING UNEMPLOYED, JOHANNESBURG, SOUTH AFRICA, 1 APRIL 2006

Hunger Strikes

The human body has got enormous capacity for adjusting, especially if you can link up. You can coordinate your thinking, your whole spiritual approach up to the physical one and if you are convinced that you are doing something right, that you are demonstrating to the authorities, that you can defend your rights and fight back, you don't feel it at all.

FROM A CONVERSATION WITH RICHARD STENGEL, 9 DECEMBER 1992

It was a national tragedy and it didn't matter to me who they were and the fact that the people had decided in principle to starve to death was one, you know, which moved everybody. And I went there in that spirit.

FROM A CONVERSATION WITH RICHARD STENGEL, ABOUT WHY HE VISITED PRISONERS FROM THE ORGANISATION ORDE BOEREVOLK WHO WERE ON HUNGER STRIKE, 26 APRIL 1993

Ideology

I have been influenced in my thinking by both West and East. All this has led me to feel that in my search for a political formula, I should be absolutely impartial and objective. I should tie myself to no particular system of society other than of Socialism. I must leave myself free to borrow the best from the West and from the East.

SPEECH FROM THE DOCK, RIVONIA TRIAL, PALACE OF JUSTICE, PRETORIA, SOUTH AFRICA, 20 APRIL 1964

I had no specific belief except that our cause was just, was very strong and it was winning more and more support.

REVISITING ROBBEN ISLAND, CAPE TOWN, SOUTH AFRICA, 11 FEBRUARY 1994

Illness

It serves no purpose to hide the illness from which you are suffering.

AT HOME, JOHANNESBURG, SOUTH AFRICA, 6 JANUARY 2005

Imperialism

In our experience, the most important thing about imperialism today is that it has gone all over the world subjugating people and exploiting them, bringing death and destruction to millions of people.

FROM EVIDENCE FROM THE TREASON TRIAL, PRETORIA, SOUTH AFRICA, 1956–61

Whilst the influence of the old European powers has sharply declined and whilst the anti-imperialist forces are winning striking victories all over the world, a new danger has arisen and threatens to destroy the newly-won independence of the people of Asia and Africa. It is American imperialism, which must be fought and decisively beaten down if the people of Asia and Africa are to preserve the vital gains they have won in their struggle against subjugation.

FROM AN ARTICLE ENTITLED 'A NEW MENACE IN AFRICA', *LIBERATION*, MARCH 1958

The American brand of imperialism is imperialism all the same in spite of the modern clothing in which it is dressed and in spite of the sweet language spoken by its advocates and agents.

IBID

All over the world the people are astir and the struggle for political progress is gathering momentum by the day. Imperialism has been weighed and found wanting. It has been fought and defeated by the united and concerted action of the common people.

IBID

India

It is precisely India's exemplary role in world affairs that also serves to remind us that our problems, acute as they are, are part of humanity's problems. And no part of the world can dare to consider itself free of them unless and until the day when the last vestige of man-made suffering is eradicated from every corner of the world.

FROM A LETTER TO MRS MANORAMA BHALLA, SECRETARY, INDIAN COUNCIL FOR CULTURAL RELATIONS, WRITTEN ON ROBBEN ISLAND, 3 AUGUST 1980

As much as India is a particle of our country, so are we, too, a particle of India. History has condemned us to seek each other out, to deal with each other as members of the same family.

BANQUET HOSTED BY THE PRESIDENT OF THE REPUBLIC OF INDIA, NEW DELHI, INDIA, 15 OCTOBER 1990

To come to India for us is a homecoming: a pilgrimage to the shrines of great leaders and a great people we shall always admire.

RAJIV GANDHI FOUNDATION LECTURE, NEW DELHI, INDIA, 25 JANUARY 1995

We shall never tire of repeating that India's independence was a victory for all people under colonial rule. It was even more so for South Africans, whose freedom you regarded as essential to your own freedom, whose victory over oppression was also your victory.

BANQUET FOR PRIME MINISTER INDER KUMAR GUJRAL OF INDIA, CAPE TOWN, SOUTH AFRICA, 7 OCTOBER 1997

South Africans have long found inspiration in India, as a nation committed in practice to the universality of human rights.

IBID

You will sense for yourself the extent to which a part of India's soul resides in South Africa, as a revered part of our national life.

IBID

It was India who always stood at the head of the international community's moral, political and material support to our cause to liberate our country from the bondage of racial oppression and racist rule.

SPEECH AT THE PRESIDENTIAL PALACE, NEW DELHI, INDIA, 16 MARCH 2001

Injustice

I believed that in taking up a stand against this injustice, I was upholding the dignity of what should be an honourable profession.

TALKING ABOUT RACIAL DISCRIMINATION AGAINST BLACK LAWYERS DURING HIS TRIAL FOR INCITEMENT AND LEAVING THE COUNTRY ILLEGALLY, PALACE OF JUSTICE, PRETORIA, SOUTH AFRICA, NOVEMBER 1962

Let us give practical recognition to the injustices of the past, by building a future based on equality and social justice.

SIGNING OF THE NEW CONSTITUTION, SHARPEVILLE, VEREENIGING, SOUTH AFRICA, 10 DECEMBER 1996

People, not only in our country but around the world, were inspired to believe that through common human effort, injustice can be overcome and that together a better life for all can be achieved.

FROM A LETTER TO PRESIDENT BARACK OBAMA ON THE OCCASION OF HIS INAUGURATION, 20 JANUARY 2009

Inspiration

My inspiration are men and women who have emerged throughout the globe, and who have chosen the world as the theatre of their operations and who fight socio-economic conditions which do not help towards the advancement of humanity wherever that occurs. Men and women who fight the suppression of the human voice, who fight disease, illiteracy, ignorance, poverty and hunger. Some are known, others are not. Those are the people who have inspired me.

SPEECH AT THE LONDON SCHOOL OF ECONOMICS, LONDON, ENGLAND, 6 APRIL 2000

Integrity

One has made a great deal of progress in developing personal relationships because you assume the basic assumption is that those you deal with are men of integrity. I believe in that.

FROM A CONVERSATION WITH RICHARD STENGEL, 28 DECEMBER 1992

When you are a public figure, you have to accept the integrity of other people until there is evidence to the contrary.

FROM A CONVERSATION WITH RICHARD STENGEL, 3 MAY 1993

Those who conduct themselves with morality, integrity and consistency need not fear the forces of inhumanity and cruelty.

BRITISH RED CROSS HUMANITY LECTURE, QUEEN ELIZABETH II CONFERENCE CENTRE, LONDON, ENGLAND, 10 JULY 2003

International Cooperation

We ask our millions of friends outside South Africa to intensify the boycott and isolation of the government of this country, diplomatically, economically and in every other way. The mines, industries and farms of this country cannot carry on without the labour of Africans imported from elsewhere in Africa.

STATEMENT ON BEHALF OF THE NATIONAL ACTION COUNCIL FOLLOWING THE 29–31 MAY 1961 STAY-AT-HOME IN SUPPORT OF A NATIONAL CONVENTION, SOUTH AFRICA, 1961

We want to build a system of cooperation with all nations so that the liberated South Africa itself becomes a force of peace, friendship and social progress throughout the world.

ADDRESS TO THE INTERNATIONAL LABOUR CONFERENCE, GENEVA, SWITZERLAND, 8 JUNE 1990

In the exercise of that will by this united nation of black and white people, it must surely be that there will be born a country on the southern tip of Africa which you will be proud to call a friend and an ally, because of its contribution to the universal striving towards liberty, human rights, prosperity and peace among the peoples. Let that day come now. Let us keep our arms locked together so that we form a solid phalanx against racism to ensure that that day comes now. By our common actions let us ensure that justice triumphs without delay. When that has come to pass, then shall we all be entitled to acknowledge the salute when others say of us, blessed are the peacemakers.

ADDRESS TO THE JOINT SESSION OF THE HOUSE OF CONGRESS, WASHINGTON DC, USA, 26 JUNE 1990

Out of this cauldron are also born tyrants, dictators and demagogues who not only take away or restrict the rights of the people but also make it impossible to do the things that must be done to bring lasting prosperity to the people. At the same time, the reality can no longer be ignored that we live in an interdependent world which is bound together to a common destiny.

ADDRESS TO THE FORTY-NINTH UNITED NATIONS GENERAL ASSEMBLY, NEW YORK CITY, USA, 3 OCTOBER 1994

The last of our remarks relates to the fact that as consciousness grows about the interdependence of the nations on our planet, so do all major decisions that derive from the system of governance become subject to international review and become dependent for their success on approval and support by an international constituency.

OPENING OF THE FIFTIETH ANC NATIONAL CONFERENCE, NORTH-WEST UNIVERSITY, MAFIKENG CAMPUS, SOUTH AFRICA, 16 DECEMBER 1997

Throughout our struggle for liberation, one of the many things that we learnt from the Communist Party was the importance of international solidarity: that no struggle could be waged effectively in isolation.

UPON RECEIVING THE CHRIS HANI AWARD AT THE TENTH SACP (SOUTH AFRICAN COMMUNIST PARTY) NATIONAL CONGRESS, JOHANNESBURG, SOUTH AFRICA, 1 JULY 1998

In a modern world no country can conduct its affairs in isolation. The problems we face are beyond the capacity of any one nation to solve on its own. What happens in any one country impacts on its neighbours and further afield.

SUMMIT OF THE GULF COOPERATION COUNCIL, ABU DHABI, UNITED ARAB EMIRATES, 7 DECEMBER 1998

What has for me personally been a journey of leave-taking, has also been an encouraging glimpse of a future which can be created as the nations of the world work together to achieve the ideals which they cannot realise separately or in conflict with each other.

IBID

We are at a moment in history where the world can either be drawn into ever-intensifying rounds of global conflict and increasing inequality, or from which it can emerge with a renewed commitment to peace and global cooperation.

UPON RECEIVING THE 'GREATEST SON OF AFRICA' AWARD FROM ROTARY, MALAWI, 23 MAY 2003

In a world still so grossly unequal and divided, both in material terms and in terms of power and influence, our hope for orderly coexistence and for the protection of human dignity lies in global cooperation and an uncompromising multilateral approach to dealing with our problems, conflicts, differences and challenges.

TWENTY-EIGHTH INTERNATIONAL RED CROSS AND RED CRESCENT CONFERENCE, GENEVA, SWITZERLAND, 2 DECEMBER 2003

Interviews

As a general rule, you must get an indication beforehand as to what the interview is all about, prepare for it, be calm and diplomatic and avoid sharp exchanges.

FROM A LETTER TO ZENANI MANDELA, WRITTEN IN POLLSMOOR PRISON, CAPE TOWN, SOUTH AFRICA, 30 JUNE 1987

Islam

As we break free from a bipolar view of the world, the centuries-old discourse about relations between Islam and the West is also naturally giving way to a more multifaceted framework of thought.

LECTURE AT THE OXFORD CENTRE FOR ISLAMIC STUDIES, SHELDONIAN THEATRE, OXFORD, ENGLAND, 11 JULY 1997

Islam has enriched and became part of Africa. In turn, Islam was transformed and Africa became part of it.

IBID

The coming of Islam sometimes meant the imposition of a new political and social order, but also the absorption of Islam into an existing order.

IBID

South Africa's vibrant Islamic heritage is a valued and respected part of our nation.
IBID

Islam has become part of Africa in a process as complex as the history of the Continent itself.
IBID

South Africa's own Islamic heritage has been a vital part of our history.
SUMMIT OF THE GULF COOPERATION COUNCIL, ABU DHABI, UNITED ARAB EMIRATES, 7 DECEMBER 1998

Judiciary

What sort of justice is this that enables the aggrieved to sit in judgement upon those whom they accused, a judiciary controlled entirely by whites and enforcing laws enacted by a white Parliament in which we have no representation: laws, which in most cases are passed in the face of unanimous opposition from Africans.
FROM HIS APPLICATION FOR THE RECUSAL OF THE MAGISTRATE MR WA VAN HELSDINGEN, OLD SYNAGOGUE, PRETORIA, SOUTH AFRICA, 22 OCTOBER 1962

The independence of the judiciary is one of the pillars of our democracy and equally fundamental is the commitment to abide by the decisions of the courts, whether they are in one's favour or not.
ADDRESS AT THE OPENING OF THE PRESIDENT'S BUDGET DEBATE, PARLIAMENT, CAPE TOWN, SOUTH AFRICA, 21 APRIL 1998

I always recall how one of the first judgements in the Constitutional Court was around a matter in which I was involved as president of the country, and the president of the Constitutional Court, regardless of the fact that he once was my lawyer, ruled against me. It was then clear to me that South Africa was in safe hands with that Court standing and operating at the apex of our democracy.
SPECIAL DINNER TO CELEBRATE THE OFFICIAL OPENING OF THE CONSTITUTIONAL COURT BUILDING, CONSTITUTIONAL COURT, JOHANNESBURG, SOUTH AFRICA, 19 MARCH 2004

Justice

Why is it that in this courtroom I face a white magistrate, am confronted by a white prosecutor and escorted into the dock by a white orderly? Can anyone honestly and seriously suggest that in this type of atmosphere the scales of justice are evenly balanced?
FROM HIS APPLICATION FOR THE RECUSAL OF THE MAGISTRATE MR WA VAN HELSDINGEN, OLD SYNAGOGUE, PRETORIA, SOUTH AFRICA, 22 OCTOBER 1962

In the end we must remember that no amount of rules or their enforcement will defeat those who struggle with justice on their side.
AT THE FIFTIETH ANNIVERSARY OF THE GATT (GENERAL AGREEMENT ON TARIFFS AND TRADE), GENEVA, SWITZERLAND, 19 MAY 1998

Killing

Successive white regimes [have] repeatedly massacred unarmed defenceless blacks and wherever and whenever they have pulled out their guns the ferocity of their fire has been trained on the African people.
STATEMENT ABOUT THE 1976 SOWETO UPRISING, SMUGGLED OUT OF ROBBEN ISLAND PRISON AND RELEASED BY THE ANC IN EXILE, 1980

The peaceful and non-violent nature of our struggle never made any impression [on] your government. Innocent and defenceless people were pitilessly massacred in the course of peaceful demonstrations.

FROM A LETTER TO PRESIDENT PW BOTHA, WRITTEN IN POLLSMOOR PRISON, CAPE TOWN, SOUTH AFRICA, 13 FEBRUARY 1985

The stubborn resistance that is everywhere evident in our country today, and the unprecedented loss of lives and detention that are taking place are matters of grave concern to me.

FROM A LETTER TO PROFESSOR SAMUEL DASH, WRITTEN IN POLLSMOOR PRISON, CAPE TOWN, SOUTH AFRICA, 12 MAY 1985

The danger is very great, because although we are determined to do everything to create an atmosphere whereby a peaceful settlement can be reached, we are not prepared to do so indefinitely. We are not prepared to witness the death of our people.

BRIEFING TO THE FIFTH SESSION OF THE OAU'S (ORGANISATION OF AFRICAN UNITY) AD HOC COMMITTEE ON SOUTHERN AFRICA, 8 SEPTEMBER 1990

Those who are determined to destroy the liberation movement have made a serious mistake by killing so many innocent people. They have, in fact, succeeded in bringing us together.

SPEAKING AT KAGISO, WEST RAND, SOUTH AFRICA, CIRCA 1991

There was an unacceptably high incidence of violence in which people were killed. And the arrests and convictions, you see, were few and far between, and it was clear that there was connivance on the part of the security forces.

FROM A CONVERSATION WITH RICHARD STENGEL, 26 APRIL 1993

Few things have angered me as much as this senseless slaughter of innocent people. But whilst I am very angry I must appeal to our people, both black and white, to remain calm and concentrate on the forward movement towards the establishment of a democratic government.

SOURCE UNKNOWN, CIRCA 1993

Landmines

[Landmines] are blind weapons that cannot distinguish between the footfall of a soldier and, that of an old woman gathering firewood. They recognise no cease-fire and, long after the fighting has stopped, they can maim or kill the children and the grandchildren of the soldiers who laid them.

MESSAGE IN SUPPORT OF 'NIGHT OF A THOUSAND DINNERS', ROTARY PRETORIA EAST, PRETORIA, SOUTH AFRICA, NOVEMBER 2003

Language

Afrikaans is the language of a substantial section of the country's blacks and any attempts to deprive them of their language would be dangerous. It is the home language of ninety-five per cent of the coloured population and is used by Indians as well, especially in the country dorps of the Transvaal. It is also widely spoken by the African youth in the urban areas.

FROM AN ESSAY ENTITLED 'WHITHER THE BLACK CONSCIOUSNESS MOVEMENT', WRITTEN ON ROBBEN ISLAND, 1978

Precisely because Afrikaans is the language of the oppressor we should encourage our people to learn it, its literature and history and to watch new trends among Afrikaner writers. To know the strength and weakness of your opponent is one of the elementary rules in a fight.

IBID

While our people are repelled by the crude racism of the Afrikaner, they are attracted by the well-established tradition of liberalism in British political thought and by the fact that Britain has for centuries provided asylum to all kinds of political refugees. However, the English are still important partners in our oppression today. Why should our people not be invited to boycott the English language also and to demand its abolition after liberation?

IBID

Because when you speak a language, English, well many people understand you, including Afrikaners, but when you speak Afrikaans, you know you go straight to their hearts.

FROM A CONVERSATION WITH RICHARD STENGEL, CIRCA DECEMBER1992

The people who speak the language which is regarded as the Xhosa language belong to different tribes.

FROM A CONVERSATION WITH RICHARD STENGEL, 23 MARCH 1993

We do not want to abolish any language; we want to raise the African languages which have been sidelined through the policy of apartheid to equality with English and Afrikaans. That doesn't mean to say that we are actually downgrading Afrikaans and English; we are merely saying that the other languages must be put on the same basis.

FROM A CONVERSATION WITH RICHARD STENGEL, 29 APRIL 1993

I am now more comfortable in English because of the many years I spent here and I've spent in jail and I lost contact, you know, with Xhosa literature.

IBID

We accept that language, culture and religion are important indicators of identity. We, however, totally reject that apartheid-derived assumption that the racial or ethnic group is the basis of all social organisation, and especially that these should define power relations in society.

INVESTITURE, CLARK UNIVERSITY, ATLANTA, USA, 10 JULY 1993

Without language, one cannot talk to people and understand them; one cannot share their hopes and aspirations, grasp their history, appreciate their poetry or savour their songs.

FROM *LONG WALK TO FREEDOM*, 1994

Unfortunately me English no speak.

FROM THE DOCUMENTARY *MANDELA: THE LIVING LEGEND*, 2003

I spoke Afrikaans better in jail because I could practise it every day.

FROM AN INTERVIEW WITH VERNE HARRIS FOR THE CENTRE OF MEMORY, JOHANNESBURG, SOUTH AFRICA, 2005

Leadership

The spirit of the people cannot be crushed and, no matter what happens to the present leadership, new leaders will arise like mushrooms till full victory is won.

PRESIDENTIAL ADDRESS TO THE ANNUAL ANC YOUTH LEAGUE CONFERENCE, SOUTH AFRICA, DECEMBER 1951

A leadership commits a crime against its own people if it hesitates to sharpen its political weapons where they have become less effective.

ADDRESS ON BEHALF OF THE ANC DELEGATION TO THE PAFMECA (PAN AFRICAN FREEDOM MOVEMENT OF EAST AND CENTRAL AFRICA) CONFERENCE, ADDIS ABABA, ETHIOPIA, 3 FEBRUARY 1962

A man who rises to the position of premier in any country must be a man of ability, forceful personality and uprightness in his public life.

FROM AN UNPUBLISHED AUTOBIOGRAPHICAL MANUSCRIPT, WRITTEN ON ROBBEN ISLAND, 1975

No worthy leaders of a freedom movement will ever submit to conditions which are essentially terms of surrender dictated by a victorious commander to a beaten enemy, and which are really intended to weaken the organisation and to humiliate its leadership.

FROM A MEMORANDUM TO PRESIDENT PW BOTHA, WRITTEN IN VICTOR VERSTER PRISON, PAARL, SOUTH AFRICA, JULY 1989

The world is full of people with natural leadership qualities. The traditional leaders, who led the independence struggle from the seventeenth century, were such men. But times have changed and education has become a very powerful weapon in the struggle to produce a well-developed person.

FROM A LETTER TO MAKHI JOMO DALASILE, WRITTEN IN VICTOR VERSTER PRISON, PAARL, SOUTH AFRICA, 14 AUGUST 1989

Only leaders of a special calibre and integrity are able to see the basic problems that affect us all, and who tend to avoid the sterile polemics that limit the vision of many activists.

FROM A LETTER TO JAMES MNDAWENI, WRITTEN IN VICTOR VERSTER PRISON, PAARL, SOUTH AFRICA, 21 AUGUST 1989

There are various standards by which to measure the significance of an organisation. One of the most important of these standards is the calibre of its leadership.

FROM A LETTER TO REVEREND ANDREW HUNTER, WRITTEN IN VICTOR VERSTER PRISON, PAARL, SOUTH AFRICA, 21 AUGUST 1989

Chiefly office is not something that history has given to certain individuals to use or abuse as they see fit. Like all forms of leadership, it places specific responsibilities on its holders. As [Chief Albert] Luthuli, himself a chief, put it, 'A chief is primarily a servant of the people. He is the voice of his people.'

RALLY, KINGS PARK STADIUM, DURBAN, SOUTH AFRICA, 25 FEBRUARY 1990

There's nothing as bad as a leader making a demand which you know can *never* succeed.

FROM A CONVERSATION WITH RICHARD STENGEL, CIRCA DECEMBER 1992

A common touch is of immense advantage, especially on the part of a head of state.

FROM A CONVERSATION WITH RICHARD STENGEL, 2 FEBRUARY 1993

It is absolutely necessary at times for the leader to take an independent action without consulting anybody and to present what he has done to the organisation.
IBID

Our approach was to empower the organisation to be effective in its leadership.
FROM A CONVERSATION WITH RICHARD STENGEL, 25 MARCH 1993

You learn that you don't have to have a degree to have the qualities of a leader, the qualities of a man who wants to fight injustice wherever he is.
FROM A CONVERSATION WITH RICHARD STENGEL, 29 APRIL 1993

The leader's first task is to create a vision. His second is to create a following to help him implement the vision and to manage the process through effective teams. The people being led know where they are going because the leader has communicated the vision and his followers have bought into the goal he has set as well as the process of getting there.
FROM A NOTEBOOK, CIRCA 1993

I always remember the regent's axiom: a leader, he said, is like a shepherd. He stays behind the flock letting the most nimble go on ahead, whereupon the others follow, not realising that all along they are being directed from behind.
FROM *LONG WALK TO FREEDOM*, 1994

There are times when a leader can show sorrow in public, and that it will not diminish him in the eyes of his people.
IBID

It is the dictate of history to bring to the fore the kind of leaders who seize the moment, who cohere the wishes and aspirations of the oppressed. Such was Steve Biko, a fitting product of his time, a proud representative of the reawakening of a people.
COMMEMORATION OF THE TWENTIETH ANNIVERSARY OF THE DEATH IN POLICE DETENTION OF STEVE BIKO, EAST LONDON, SOUTH AFRICA, 1 SEPTEMBER 1997

It is also the fate of leadership to be misunderstood: for historians, academics, writers and journalists to reflect great lives according to their own subjective canon. This is all the more evident in a country where the interpreters have a much greater pool of resources to publish views regarding the quest for dignity and nationhood.
IBID

One of the temptations of a leader who has been elected unopposed is that he may use that powerful position to settle scores with his detractors, marginalise them and in certain cases, get rid of them. And surround himself with 'yes men and women'.
CLOSING SESSION OF THE FIFTIETH ANC NATIONAL CONFERENCE, NORTH-WEST UNIVERSITY, MAFIKENG CAMPUS, SOUTH AFRICA, 20 DECEMBER 1997

There is a contradiction in leadership because the leader must keep the forces that lead his organisation together. But you can't do that unless you allow dissent, that any subject should be discussed from all angles and people should even be able to criticise the leader without fear or favour. Only in that case are you likely to keep your colleagues together.
IBID

Real leaders must be ready to sacrifice all for the freedom of their people.

CHIEF ALBERT LUTHULI CENTENARY CELEBRATIONS, KWADUKUZA, SOUTH AFRICA, 25 APRIL 1998

The mark of great leaders is the ability to understand the context in which they are operating and act accordingly. As a brave and dedicated fighter for liberation, comrade Chris [Hani] pursued the mission of our organisation which at all moments he participated in defining.

UPON RECEIVING THE CHRIS HANI AWARD AT THE TENTH SACP (SOUTH AFRICAN COMMUNIST PARTY) NATIONAL CONGRESS, JOHANNESBURG, SOUTH AFRICA, 1 JULY 1998

Good leaders fully appreciate that the removal of tensions in society, of whatever nature, puts creative thinkers on centre stage by creating an ideal environment for men and women of vision to influence society.

FROM THE UNPUBLISHED SEQUEL TO HIS AUTOBIOGRAPHY, CIRCA 1998

It is a grave error for any leader to be oversensitive in the face of criticism, to conduct discussions as if he or she is a schoolmaster talking to less informed and inexperienced learners.

IBID

Many of our traditional leaders are also not aware of the lessons of history. They do not seem to know that there were once absolute monarchs in the world who did not share power with their subjects.

IBID

We must never forget that the institution of traditional leaders is sanctified by African law and custom, by our culture and tradition. No attempt must be made to abolish it. We must find an amicable solution based on democratic principles, and which allows traditional leaders to play a meaningful role in levels of government.

IBID

Leaders will have to give clear and decisive leadership towards a world of tolerance and respect for difference, and an uncompromising commitment to peaceful solutions of conflicts and disputes.

UPON RECEIVING THE GERMAN MEDIA PRIZE, BADEN-BADEN, GERMANY, 28 JANUARY 1999

To the extent that your leadership helps improve the lives of the people, to the extent that it fosters the best of African culture and tradition, and above all to the extent it fosters unity and peace amongst the people, my days will be filled with contentment.

INSTALLATION OF CHIEF SANGO PHATHEKILE HOLOMISA, MQANDULI DISTRICT, TRANSKEI, SOUTH AFRICA, 17 APRIL 1999

A true leader must work hard to ease tensions, especially when dealing with sensitive and complicated issues. Extremists normally thrive when there is tension, and pure emotion tends to supersede rational thinking.

FROM A PERSONAL NOTEBOOK, 16 JANUARY 2000

A real leader uses every issue, no matter how serious and sensitive, to ensure that at the end of the debate we should emerge stronger and more united than ever before.

IBID

I have full confidence in our collective leadership. But this does not mean there may not be differences of opinion and even disappointments amongst us. If there are, they must be debated fully but let everyone accept the derision of the majority and work hard to implement it.

ANC GENERAL COUNCIL MEETING, PORT ELIZABETH, SOUTH AFRICA, 12 JULY 2000

We need the commitment of leaders at all levels in order to achieve the better life for all that we promised our people.

IBID

Amongst my generation there are many that could have taken my place if circumstance and history had determined differently. Where I gave leadership it was because of those that surrounded me and formed me.

UPON RECEIVING AN HONORARY FELLOWSHIP OF MAGDALENE COLLEGE, CAMBRIDGE UNIVERSITY, ENGLAND, 2 MAY 2001

I know that the world often refers to me as one such example of leadership. I can only accept those accolades in the knowledge that I am one of a collective my country and its history produced.

IBID

The quality of change in our society will greatly depend upon the quality of leadership that is exercised in the various sectors and activities of our communities, organisations and public life.

DINNER AT THE BLACK MANAGEMENT FORUM ANNUAL CONFERENCE, SOUTH AFRICA, OCTOBER 2002

By ancestry, I was born to rule. Xhamela [Walter Sisulu] helped me understand that my real vocation was to be a servant of the people.

ON THE DEATH OF WALTER SISULU, SOUTH AFRICA, 5 MAY 2003

As we have so often observed: many of us had gained positions, received honours and accolades and had been acclaimed in many places. None of us, however, can match the leadership and the humanity of this man, Walter Sisulu, who chose not to draw upon himself the spotlight but always built and praised others. When there was work and battle to be done, he was in the forefront. When acclaim was offered, he stood back.

OPENING OF MANDELA HOUSE, JOHANNESBURG, SOUTH AFRICA, 6 MAY 2003

Good wise leaders respect the law and basic values of their society.

ANNUAL CHILDREN'S CELEBRATIONS, BLOEMFONTEIN, SOUTH AFRICA, 27 SEPTEMBER 2003

If I am your leader, you have to listen to me and if you don't want to listen to me, then drop me as your leader.

FROM THE DOCUMENTARY MANDELA: THE LIVING LEGEND, RECALLING SPEAKING AT A RALLY AT KINGS PARK STADIUM WHERE HIS ENTREATIES FOR PEACE WERE NOT WELL RECEIVED BY THE CROWD, DURBAN, SOUTH AFRICA, 2003

I am often deeply under the impression of how our celebration of the not inconsiderable achievements of democratic South Africa tends to focus on the contributions and roles of such as Mandela and [Govan] Mbeki, who had the privilege of being founding presidents, and others who enjoyed prominence during the transitional negotiations.

FIFTH STEVE BIKO LECTURE, UNIVERSITY OF CAPE TOWN, CAPE TOWN, SOUTH AFRICA, 10 SEPTEMBER 2004

The baton of leadership had been passed on and we wish that honours would celebrate those that have taken over so excellently from our generation.

UPON RECEIVING THE FREEDOM OF THE CITY OF TSHWANE, NELSON MANDELA FOUNDATION, JOHANNESBURG, SOUTH AFRICA, 13 MAY 2008

Now – as much as ever in our history – we require disciplined leaders and members with respect for their organisation, who care equally for all South Africans and for all people who live within our borders.

ANC RALLY FOR HIS NINETIETH BIRTHDAY, LOFTUS VERSFELD STADIUM, PRETORIA, SOUTH AFRICA, 2 AUGUST 2008

If you don't take precautions it is easy to forget that you have been put into that position by the poorest of the poor.

ADDRESS TO A GATHERING, SOUTH AFRICA, DATE UNKNOWN

Leadership falls into two categories. Those who are inconsistent, whose actions cannot be predicted, who agree today on a major [issue] and repudiate it the following day. Those who are consistent, who have a sense of honour, a vision.

FROM A NOTEBOOK, DATE UNKNOWN

We have been brought up in the tradition of collective leadership. We discuss matters thoroughly, differ sometimes very sharply but eventually we reach a consensus.

FROM THE DOCUMENTARY VIVA MADIBA: A HERO FOR ALL SEASONS, 2010

Legacy

I have done whatever I did, both as an individual and as a leader of my people, because of my own experience in South Africa and my own proudly felt African background.

SPEECH FROM THE DOCK, RIVONIA TRIAL, PALACE OF JUSTICE, PRETORIA, SOUTH AFRICA, 20 APRIL 1964

Next to my wife's affection and that of the family as a whole, few things have inspired me more than the knowledge that in spite of all that the enemy is doing to isolate and discredit us people everywhere never forget us.

FROM AN UNPUBLISHED AUTOBIOGRAPHICAL MANUSCRIPT, WRITTEN ON ROBBEN ISLAND, 1975

The knowledge that in your day you did your duty, and lived up to the expectations of your fellow men is in itself a rewarding experience and magnificent achievement.

FROM A LETTER TO SHEENA DUNCAN, WRITTEN IN POLLSMOOR PRISON, CAPE TOWN, SOUTH AFRICA, 1 APRIL 1985

Nothing brings more pride and satisfaction to the old guard than to know that the ideas for which they have sacrificed so much are coming to fruition at last.

FROM A LETTER TO FRANKLIN SONN, WRITTEN IN VICTOR VERSTER PRISON, PAARL, SOUTH AFRICA, 21 AUGUST 1989

Men and women, all over the world, right down the centuries, come and go. Some leave nothing behind, not even their names. It would seem they never existed at all.

FROM THE UNPUBLISHED SEQUEL TO HIS AUTOBIOGRAPHY, CIRCA 1998

Liberation Movement

The common man who for generations has been the tool of insane politicians and governments, who has suffered privations and sorrow in wars that were of profit to tiny privileged groups, is today rising from being the object of history to becoming the subject of history.

PRESIDENTIAL ADDRESS TO THE ANNUAL ANC YOUTH LEAGUE CONFERENCE, SOUTH AFRICA, DECEMBER 1951

Whilst the dark and sinister forces in the world are organising a desperate and last-minute fight to defend a decadent and bankrupt civilisation, the common people, full of confidence and buoyant hope, struggle for the creation of a new, united and prosperous human family.

IBID

True, the struggle will be a bitter one. Leaders will be deported, imprisoned and even shot. The government will terrorise the people and their leaders in an effort to halt the forward march; ordinary forms of organisation will be rendered impossible.

IBID

We learned that when the masses of the people were on the march, even if we had genuine principled objections to the move, we must never be against the mass movement of the people. We learned that always a true fighter must be on the side of the people against the oppressor.

IBID

Sons and daughters of Africa, our tasks are mighty indeed, but I have abundant faith in our ability to reply to the challenge posed by the situation. Under the slogan of 'Full Democratic Rights in South Africa Now', we must march forward into victory.

IBID

For the ordinary men and women in the world, the oppressed all over the world are becoming the conscious creators of their own history.

IBID

The theory that we can sit with folded arms and wait for a future Parliament to legislate for the essential dignity of every human being irrespective of race, colour or creed is crass perversion of elementary principles of political struggle.

FROM AN ARTICLE ENTITLED 'THE SHIFTING SANDS OF ILLUSION', *LIBERATION*, JUNE 1953

The day of reckoning between the forces of freedom and those of reaction is not very far off. I have not the slightest doubt that, when that day comes, truth and justice will prevail.

PRESIDENTIAL ADDRESS TO THE ANC TRANSVAAL CONGRESS, ALSO KNOWN AS THE 'NO EASY WALK TO FREEDOM' SPEECH, TRANSVAAL, SOUTH AFRICA, 21 SEPTEMBER 1953

If the ruling circles seek to maintain their position by such inhuman methods, then a clash between the forces of freedom and those of reaction is certain. The grave plight of the people compels them to resist to the death the stinking policies of the gangsters that rule our country.

IBID

You can see that 'there is no easy walk to freedom anywhere' and many of us will have to pass through the valley of the shadow of death again and again before we reach the mountain tops of our desires.

QUOTING JAWAHARLAL NEHRU, PRESIDENTIAL ADDRESS TO THE ANC TRANSVAAL CONGRESS, ALSO KNOWN AS THE 'NO EASY WALK TO FREEDOM' SPEECH, TRANSVAAL, SOUTH AFRICA, 21 SEPTEMBER 1953

We cannot for one moment forget that we are up against a fascist government which has built up a massive coercive state apparatus to crush democracy in this country and to silence the voice of all those who cry out against the policy of apartheid and baasskap.

FROM AN ARTICLE ENTITLED 'BANTU EDUCATION GOES TO UNIVERSITY', *LIBERATION*, JUNE 1957

In its struggle for the attainment of its demands the liberation movement avails itself of various political weapons, one of which might (but not necessarily) be the boycott. It is, therefore, a serious error to regard the boycott as a weapon that must be employed at all times and in all conditions.

FROM AN ARTICLE ENTITLED 'OUR STRUGGLE NEEDS MANY TACTICS', *LIBERATION*, FEBRUARY 1958

The forces of liberation are strong and powerful and their numbers are growing. The morale is high and we look forward to the future with perfect confidence.

STATEMENT ON BEHALF OF THE NATIONAL ACTION COUNCIL FOLLOWING THE 29–31 MAY 1961 STAY-AT-HOME IN SUPPORT OF A NATIONAL CONVENTION, SOUTH AFRICA, 1961

We are the people of this country. We produce the wealth of the gold mines, of the farms and of industry. Non-collaboration is the weapon we must use to bring down the government. We have decided to use it fully and without reservation.

IBID

Non-collaboration is a dynamic weapon. We must refuse. We must use it to send the government to the grave.

FROM THE 'STRUGGLE IS MY LIFE' PRESS STATEMENT, EXPLAINING HIS DECISION TO CARRY ON HIS POLITICAL WORK UNDERGROUND IN ACCORDANCE WITH THE ADVICE OF THE NATIONAL ACTION COUNCIL, SOUTH AFRICA, 26 JUNE 1961

We plan to make government impossible.

IBID

When a government seeks to suppress a peaceful demonstration of an unarmed people by mobilising the entire resources of the state, military and otherwise, it concedes powerful mass support for such a demonstration. Could there be any other evidence to prove that we have become a power to be reckoned with and the strongest opposition to the government?

IBID

I will not leave South Africa, nor will I surrender. Only through hardship, sacrifice and militant action can freedom be won. The struggle is my life. I will continue fighting for freedom until the end of my days.

IBID

I shall fight the Government side by side with you, inch by inch, and mile by mile, until victory is won.

IBID

I should assure you that the African people of South Africa, notwithstanding fierce persecution and untold suffering, in their ever-increasing courage will not for one single moment be diverted from the historic mission of liberating their country and winning freedom, lasting peace and happiness.

ADDRESS ON BEHALF OF THE ANC DELEGATION TO THE PAFMECA (PAN AFRICAN FREEDOM MOVEMENT OF EAST AND CENTRAL AFRICA) CONFERENCE, ADDIS ABABA, ETHIOPIA, 3 FEBRUARY 1962

Uneasy lies the head that wears the crown of white supremacy in South Africa. The banning and confinement of leaders, banishments and deportations, imprisonment and even death, have never deterred South African compatriots.

IBID

The freedom movement in South Africa believes that hard and swift blows should be delivered with the full weight of the masses of the people, who alone furnish us with one absolute guarantee that the freedom flames now burning in this country shall never be extinguished.

IBID

Men, I think, are not capable of doing nothing, of saying nothing, of not reacting to injustice, of not protesting against oppression, of not striving for the good society and the good life in the ways they see it.

IN MITIGATION OF SENTENCE AFTER BEING CONVICTED OF INCITING WORKERS TO STRIKE AND LEAVING THE COUNTRY ILLEGALLY, OLD SYNAGOGUE, PRETORIA, SOUTH AFRICA, 7 NOVEMBER 1962

I have done my duty to my people and to South Africa. I have no doubt that posterity will pronounce that I was innocent and that the criminals that should have been brought before this court are the members of the Verwoerd Government.

IBID

Whatever sentence Your Worship sees fit to impose upon me for the crime for which I have been convicted before this court, may it rest assured that when my sentence has been completed, I will still be moved, as men are always moved by their conscience; I will still be moved by my dislike of the race discrimination against my people when I come out from serving my sentence, to take up again, as best I can, the struggle for the removal of those injustices until they are finally abolished once and for all.

IBID

If I had my time over I would do the same again. So would any man who dares call himself a man.

IBID

I hoped and vowed then that, among the treasures that life might offer me, would be the opportunity to serve my people and make my own humble contribution to their freedom struggles.

IBID

During my lifetime I have dedicated myself to this struggle of the African people. I have fought against white domination, and I have fought against black domination. I have cherished the ideal of a democratic and free society in which all persons live together in harmony and with equal opportunities. It is an ideal which I hope to live for and to achieve. But if needs be, it is an ideal for which I am prepared to die.

SPEECH FROM THE DOCK, RIVONIA TRIAL, PALACE OF JUSTICE, PRETORIA, SOUTH AFRICA, 20 APRIL 1964

Our fight is against real, and not imaginary, hardships or, to use the language of the State Prosecutor, 'so-called hardships'. Basically, we fight against two features which are the hallmarks of African life in South Africa and which are entrenched by legislation which we seek to have repealed. These features are poverty and lack of human dignity, and we do not need communists or so-called 'agitators' to teach us about these things.

IBID

I hoped that life might offer me the opportunity to serve my people and make my own humble contribution to their freedom struggle.

IBID

As disciplined and dedicated comrades fighting for a worthy cause, we should be ready to undertake any tasks which history might assign to us, however high the price to be paid may be.

FROM A LETTER TO SEFTON VUTELA, WRITTEN ON ROBBEN ISLAND, 28 JULY 1969

We are heirs to a three-stream heritage: an inheritance that inspires us to fight and die for the loftiest ideals in life.

FROM A LETTER TO NOMABUTHO BHALA, WRITTEN ON ROBBEN ISLAND, 1 JANUARY 1971

The wheel of life is there and national heroes throughout our history from Autshumao to [Chief Albert] Luthuli, in fact the entire people of our country have been working for it for more than three centuries. It is clogged with dry wax and rust but we have managed to make it creak and move backwards and forwards and we live in the hope and confidence that one day we'll be able to turn it full circle so that the exalted will crumble and the despised be exalted, no – so that all men – the exalted and the wretched of the earth can live as equals.

FROM AN UNPUBLISHED AUTOBIOGRAPHICAL MANUSCRIPT, WRITTEN ON ROBBEN ISLAND, 1975

I will strenuously fight for the respect of the national independence of a free and democratic South Africa and will resist aggression against its territorial integrity or interference in its domestic affairs.

IBID

I have to acknowledge that my whole-hearted commitment to the liberation of our people gives meaning to life and yields for me a sense of national pride and real joy.

IBID

The anti-apartheid forces are strong and vocal both inside and outside Parliament. Their continued existence during such a critical period and the rise of new organisations in place of those that have been driven underground show that the masses refuse to accept white supremacy and that, in spite of the great damage the enemy has done, ultimate victory will certainly be ours.

FROM AN ESSAY ENTITLED 'CLEAR THE OBSTACLES AND CONFRONT THE ENEMY', WRITTEN ON ROBBEN ISLAND, 1976

South African whites are making a fine contribution to the struggle. Since 1962 no less than forty-five of them have been jailed for a variety of political offences ranging from sabotage to furthering the aims of a banned organisation.

IBID

It is true that the South African revolution will be victorious only if the Africans take the lead, and if the African masses are fully mobilised. But the true story of our struggle shows that the fight against racial oppression is not the monopoly of the black man.

FROM AN ESSAY ENTITLED 'WHITHER THE BLACK CONSCIOUSNESS MOVEMENT', WRITTEN ON ROBBEN ISLAND, 1978

Experience tells us that the road to liberation is not an easy, romantic wish, but a practical and complicated undertaking that calls for clear thinking and proper planning.

IBID

Those who creep in darkness will not sleep till the bird flies or till they crush its head with a kerrie.

FROM A LETTER TO WINNIE MANDELA, WRITTEN ON ROBBEN ISLAND, 17 DECEMBER 1978

We are proud of the fact that we have liberated not only coloureds, Indians and Africans, we have liberated whites as well.

FROM AN INTERVIEW, DATE UNKNOWN

Our march to freedom is long and difficult, but both within and beyond our borders the prospects of victory grow bright.

STATEMENT ABOUT THE 1976 SOWETO UPRISING, SMUGGLED OUT OF ROBBEN ISLAND PRISON AND RELEASED BY THE ANC IN EXILE, 10 JUNE 1980

The rattle of gunfire and the rumbling of Hippo armoured vehicles since June 1976 have once again torn aside that veil. Spread across the face of our country, in black townships, the racist army and police have been pouring a hail of bullets killing and maiming hundreds of black men, women and children. The toll of the dead and injured already surpasses that of all past massacres carried out by this regime.

IBID

The resistance of the black man to white colonial intrusion was crushed by the gun. Our struggle to liberate ourselves from white domination is held in check by force of arms. From conquest to the present the story is the same. Successive white regimes have repeatedly massacred unarmed defenceless blacks. And wherever and whenever they have pulled out their guns the ferocity of their fire has been trained on the African people.

IBID

Unite, mobilise, fight on. Between the anvil of united mass action and the hammer of the armed struggle we shall crush apartheid and white minority racist rule.

IBID

Our people – African, Indian, coloured and democratic whites – must be united into a single massive and solid wall of resistance, of united mass action.

IBID

The struggle is our life and, even though the moment of victory may not be at hand, we can nevertheless make the freedom fight either immensely enriching or absolutely disastrous.

FROM A LETTER TO MANGOSUTHU BUTHELEZI, WRITTEN IN VICTOR VERSTER PRISON, PAARL, SOUTH AFRICA, 3 FEBRUARY 1989

Through the years oppressed people have fought for their birthright by peaceful means, where that was possible, and through force where peaceful channels were closed.

FROM A MEMORANDUM TO PRESIDENT PW BOTHA, WRITTEN IN VICTOR VERSTER PRISON, PAARL, SOUTH AFRICA, JULY 1989

Our struggle has won the participation of every language and colour, every stripe and hue in this country.

RALLY, KINGS PARK STADIUM, DURBAN, SOUTH AFRICA, 25 FEBRUARY 1990

We have stood fearless before the guns of apartheid. The blood of our martyrs has stained the floors and walls of apartheid jails. Yet we have never faltered in our quest to create a South Africa where freedom, peace, justice and equality prevail.

RALLY, BLOEMFONTEIN, SOUTH AFRICA, 25 FEBRUARY 1990

What impels us to act is the daily picture we see, of black children who are dead when they should have been alive, of stunted adults who should have been as fit as athletes, of bullet-riddled bodies of patriots who should have been alive except that they elected to be counted among the peacemakers.

ADDRESS TO THE EUROPEAN PARLIAMENT, STRASBOURG, FRANCE, 13 JUNE 1990

An entire people has learnt not to mourn the death of heroes and heroines, but to steel itself for new battles.

ADDRESS TO THE PARLIAMENT OF CANADA, OTTAWA, CANADA, 18 JUNE 1990

Nothing can stop the evolution of humanity towards the condition of greater and ever-expanding freedom. While the voice of an individual can be condemned to silence by death, imprisonment and confinement, the spirit that drives people to seek liberty can never be stilled.

STATEMENT TO THE PARLIAMENT OF THE REPUBLIC OF IRELAND, DUBLIN, IRELAND, 2 JULY 1990

We are in struggle because we value life and love all humanity. The liberated South Africa we envision is one in which all our people, both black and white, will be one to the other, brother and sister. We see being born a united South African nation of equal compatriots, enriched by the diversity of the colour and culture of the citizens who make up the whole.

IBID

Our activists were compelled to live as outlaws. We were hounded out of our jobs and our homes. Others were driven into exile. Yet the enemy failed to crush us.

RALLY AT THE END OF THE ANC NATIONAL CONSULTATIVE CONFERENCE, SOCCER CITY, SOWETO, SOUTH AFRICA, 16 DECEMBER 1990

It is necessary that no one who has participated in the liberation struggle remain in prison; none should languish in exile; and none within the country should be required to live clandestinely and in fear of arrest for actions they carried out in order to bring about the destruction of apartheid.

STATEMENT ON OPERATION VULINDLELA, 22 JULY 1991

We literally had to walk through a garden of thorns, and we are still wading across rivers of blood.

INSTALLATION OF MANDELA AS CHANCELLOR OF THE UNIVERSITY OF THE NORTH, UNIVERSITY OF THE NORTH, TURFLOOP, SOUTH AFRICA, 25 APRIL 1992

It is the combination of non-violent struggles and military action that inspired our people to carry on struggling under the most heinous conditions.

UNVEILING OF GANDHI MEMORIAL, SOUTH AFRICA, 6 JUNE 1993

We are not the first liberation movement to take power without experience.

FROM AN INTERVIEW WITH THE BBC (UK), 28 OCTOBER 1993

I reminded people again and again that the liberation struggle was not a battle against any one group or colour, but a fight against a system of repression. At every opportunity, I said all South Africans must now unite and join hands and say we are one country, one nation, one people, marching together into the future.

FROM *LONG WALK TO FREEDOM*, 1994

December 16 was the anniversary of that bloody battle on the banks of the river Ncome, as warriors fought to stave off the persistent incursion into ancestral lands, into their freedom and their dignity. Many perished in honour, as have thousands before and after them.

FROM A POLITICAL REPORT OF THE NATIONAL EXECUTIVE COMMITTEE, FORTY-NINTH ANC NATIONAL CONFERENCE, BLOEMFONTEIN, SOUTH AFRICA, 17 DECEMBER 1994

All that we can do is to ensure that the new battle that we are fighting, of ensuring a better life to all our people, that battle is fought and won.

ROBBEN ISLAND REUNION CONFERENCE, UNIVERSITY OF THE WESTERN CAPE, BELLVILLE, SOUTH AFRICA, 12 FEBRUARY 1995

If there was something unique about our freedom struggle, it was in the fact that it enjoyed support from virtually all political parties in all parts of the world.

SUMMIT OF THE GULF COOPERATION COUNCIL, ABU DHABI, UNITED ARAB EMIRATES, 7 DECEMBER 1998

History and circumstances privileged me to be a part of an inspiring and highly supportive collective of leaders, a member of a liberation movement that with consistency and discipline championed the cause of our people for more than eight decades. I was likewise privileged to be born in a country whose people courageously resisted one of the cruellest systems of racial oppression and domination this century has witnessed.

UPON RECEIVING THE GERMAN MEDIA PRIZE, BADEN-BADEN, GERMANY, 28 JANUARY 1999

It is AZAPO [Azanian People's Organisation], it is the PAC [Pan Africanist Congress], it is the ANC that destroyed white supremacy.

BRIEFING TO EDITORS AND OPINION MAKERS, PRETORIA, SOUTH AFRICA, 10 MAY 1999

Let us remember that despite oppression, despite hangings, bannings, imprisonments and exile, our Liberation Movement united like no other in the world.

ANC GENERAL COUNCIL MEETING, PORT ELIZABETH, SOUTH AFRICA, 12 JULY 2000

Our cause was now supported by the entire world and apartheid South Africa was a polecat of the world, was completely isolated.

SPEAKING ABOUT THE FIRST 46664 CONCERT AT WEMBLEY STADIUM, FROM THE DOCUMENTARY *MANDELA: THE LIVING LEGEND*, 2003

I know that there are many members of the ANC who suffered far more than I have done for the liberation of South Africa.

OPENING OF THE NELSON MANDELA BRIDGE, JOHANNESBURG, SOUTH AFRICA, 20 JULY 2003

We defeated apartheid because the people of our country decided to work together rather than destroy one another and in the process destroy our entire country.

PRESS CONFERENCE FOR 46664 CAMPAIGN, ROBBEN ISLAND, CAPE TOWN, SOUTH AFRICA, 28 NOVEMBER 2003

Our work is far from complete.

46664 CONCERT, HYDE PARK, LONDON, ENGLAND, 27 JUNE 2008

Life

The process of illusion and disillusionment is part of life and goes on endlessly.

FROM AN UNPUBLISHED AUTOBIOGRAPHICAL MANUSCRIPT, WRITTEN ON ROBBEN ISLAND, 1975

What counts in life is not the mere fact that we have lived. It is what difference we have made to the lives of others that will determine the significance of the life we lead.

NINETIETH BIRTHDAY CELEBRATION OF WALTER SISULU, WALTER SISULU HALL, RANDBURG, JOHANNESBURG, SOUTH AFRICA, 18 MAY 2002

I must be satisfied with my life as it is.

FROM THE DOCUMENTARY *MANDELA: THE LIVING LEGEND*, 2003

Listening

In a position which I hold, your main task is to keep different factions together and therefore you must listen very carefully when somebody comes to explain a problem to you.

FROM A CONVERSATION WITH RICHARD STENGEL, 29 APRIL 1993

As a leader, I have always followed the principles I first saw demonstrated by the regent at the Great Place [Mqhekezweni]. I have always endeavoured to listen to what each and every person in a discussion had to say before venturing my own opinion.

FROM *LONG WALK TO FREEDOM*, 1994

Love

May the knowledge that you are loved sharpen interest in your work and bring you rich reward at the end of the year.

FROM A BIRTHDAY CARD TO NANDI MANDELA, WRITTEN IN POLLSMOOR PRISON, CAPE TOWN, SOUTH AFRICA, 23 JUNE 1988

Comrade Nomzamo [Winnie Mandela] accepted the onerous burden of raising our children on her own. She was more fortunate than other single mothers in that she enjoyed the moral and material support of both the South African and the international community. She endured the persecutions heaped upon her by the government with exemplary fortitude and never wavered from her commitment to the struggle for freedom. Her tenacity reinforced my personal respect, love and growing affection. It also attracted the admiration of the world at large. My love for her remains undiminished.

ANNOUNCING HIS SEPARATION FROM WINNIE MANDELA, JOHANNESBURG, SOUTH AFRICA, 13 APRIL 1992

The people will kill me out of love because everybody wants to touch me, wants to embrace me and so on and I have to be protected from people who are my fans, who are my admirers and that is a source of great strength.

FROM AN INTERVIEW WITH TOM COHEN AND SAHM VENTER FOR THE ASSOCIATED PRESS, TUYNHUYS, CAPE TOWN, SOUTH AFRICA, 22 SEPTEMBER 1994

This young man loves each and every one of you; as a matter of fact, had I big pockets, I would take each and every one of you and put you in my pockets and return with you to South Africa.

FROM THE BALCONY OF SOUTH AFRICA HOUSE, TRAFALGAR SQUARE, LONDON, ENGLAND, JULY 1996

I love each and every one of you. I wish I could put every single one of you in my pocket to show you how much I love you. Each one of you: protect yourself and those you love.

MESSAGE TO THE YOUNG PEOPLE OF SOUTH AFRICA ON WORLD AIDS DAY, 1 DECEMBER 2000

Our society needs to re-establish a culture of caring.

FATHER'S DAY LUNCH HOSTED BY ZINDZI MANDELA, HYATT WOMEN OF VISION CLUB, JOHANNESBURG, SOUTH AFRICA, 1 JUNE 2001

The path of those who preach love, and not hatred, is not easy. They often have to wear a crown of thorns.

MESSAGE TO THE GLOBAL CONVENTION ON PEACE AND NON-VIOLENCE, NEW DELHI, INDIA, 31 JANUARY 2004

I would hope that the average individual experiences one of the highest levels of emotional attachments, satisfaction and happiness when in love.

FROM A PERSONAL FILE, DATE UNKNOWN

Mandela Day

We are humbled by the call for an annual Mandela Day in our honour.

NELSON MANDELA FOUNDATION, JOHANNESBURG, SOUTH AFRICA, 30 JUNE 2009

Our struggle for freedom and justice was a collective effort. Mandela Day is no different.

IBID

It is in your hands to create a better world for all who live in it. Mandela Day will not be a holiday but a day devoted to service.

IBID

It is our hope that people will dedicate their time and effort to improve the conditions within their own communities. We thank you for participating in Mandela Day.

IBID

Mandela Rhodes Foundation

A new generation of potential leaders is beginning to emerge on the African continent. The Mandela Rhodes Foundation will nurture these young people, helping to stimulate their creativity, even as they acquire the skills that will help reshape the destiny of our continent.

RECORDED MESSAGE FOR A GALA DINNER IN MONACO 'UNITED FOR A BETTER WORLD', 1 DECEMBER 2004

Marriage

A happy marriage is the ambition of all human beings, and that you found your life partner gave me real joy.

FROM A LETTER TO LEABIE PILISO [HIS SISTER], WRITTEN ON ROBBEN ISLAND, 1 JUNE 1970

Physical suffering is nothing compared to the trampling down of those tender bonds that form the basis of the institution of marriage and the family that unite man and wife.

FROM A LETTER TO WINNIE MANDELA, WRITTEN ON ROBBEN ISLAND, 1 AUGUST 1970

Comrade Nomzamo [Winnie Mandela] and myself contracted our marriage at a critical time in the struggle for liberation in our country. Owing to the pressures of our shared commitment to the ANC and the struggle to end apartheid, we were unable to enjoy a normal family life. Despite these pressures, our love for each other and our devotion to our marriage grew and intensified.

ANNOUNCING HIS SEPARATION FROM WINNIE MANDELA, JOHANNESBURG, SOUTH AFRICA, 13 APRIL 1992

The most pleasant memory when a man returns to his home after almost twenty-eight years is when you close the bedroom door and to try and assure my wife that I am back and that her problems will now be shared.

FROM THE DOCUMENTARY *VIVA MADIBA: A HERO FOR ALL SEASONS*, 2010

Martyrs

The Abathwa and the Khoikhoi opened the patriotic wars that raged until the end of the nineteenth century and produced martyrs which today's freedom fighters, themselves born and bred in a racist environment, hardly ever mention in their speeches and writings on the struggle of our people against foreign aggression.

FROM AN ESSAY ENTITLED 'WHITHER THE BLACK CONSCIOUSNESS MOVEMENT', WRITTEN ON ROBBEN ISLAND, 1978

As far back as 1965, John Harris, a white member of the Liberal Party and the ARM (African Resistance Movement) was executed after committing an act of sabotage. What more can a white man do to identify himself with the black man's struggle than to buy freedom with his own life? To dismiss such martyrs as oppressors is a crime most South African freedom fighters find difficult to excuse.

IBID

The memory of Ruth First and countless others who died that we may be free, lives in our hearts. They will never be forgotten.

TENTH ANNIVERSARY OF RUTH FIRST'S DEATH, 17 AUGUST 1992

We are a nation in mourning. Our pain and anger is real. Yet, we must not permit ourselves to be provoked by those who seek to deny us the very freedom Chris Hani gave his life for.

ADDRESS TO THE NATION AFTER THE ASSASSINATION OF CHRIS HANI, SOUTH AFRICA, 10 APRIL 1993

It is through their unflinching sacrifice in the face of a vicious, ruthless and racist government that today we remain firmly on the road to a better life for all.

FUNERAL OF MRS NOKUZOLA BIKO, GINSBERG, KING WILLIAM'S TOWN, SOUTH AFRICA, 26 NOVEMBER 1995

Steve [Biko] was not another statistic. His death helped highlight the plight of detainees who were daily subjected to gruesome methods of torture, death and unending spells in detention without trial.
IBID

Media

It was the press that kept the memory of those who had been imprisoned for offences committed in the course of their political activities. It was the press that never forgot us and we are therefore indebted to you.
FIRST PRESS CONFERENCE AFTER HIS RELEASE, ARCHBISHOP DESMOND TUTU'S RESIDENCE, BISHOPSCOURT, CAPE TOWN, SOUTH AFRICA, 12 FEBRUARY 1990

It is your duty to examine the conduct of public figures and to place them in the spotlight – that is your duty.
TALKING TO JOURNALISTS IN RESPONSE TO A QUESTION ABOUT HIS PENDING SEPARATION, SOUTH AFRICA, 1992

We in the African National Congress believe in a free and vigorous press because the press can serve as a mirror in which we can see ourselves, be consciously aware of our weaknesses and mistakes.
FROM THE DOCUMENTARY *THE LAST MILE: MANDELA, AFRICA AND DEMOCRACY*, 1992

The media was very hostile to us and they were actually calling for our hanging.
FROM A CONVERSATION WITH RICHARD STENGEL ABOUT THE RIVONIA TRIAL, 17 APRIL 1993

Newspapers are only a poor shadow of reality; their information is important to a freedom fighter not because it reveals the truth, but because it discloses the biases and perceptions of both those who produce the paper and those who read it.
FROM *LONG WALK TO FREEDOM*, 1994

The media fraternity is more than just a critical observer of history in the making. At least in our young democracy, it contributes not merely by being a watchdog. It is a builder; it is an active participant.
CAPE TOWN PRESS CLUB'S TWENTY-FIRST ANNIVERSARY CELEBRATION, CAPE TOWN, SOUTH AFRICA, 31 OCTOBER 1996

I always relish the opportunity to be with journalists, knowing that I am among people who are brutally frank with me and my colleagues, and people who I know relish our frankness too.
SOURCE AND DATE UNKNOWN

Today I wish merely to thank you for your dedicated loyalty to the South African story, for your efforts to place South Africa on the world map, and for the battles with your media houses to appreciate that the hard slog of reconstruction and development is as exciting as the tremors of conflict.
FOREIGN CORRESPONDENTS' ASSOCIATION ANNUAL DINNER, JOHANNESBURG, SOUTH AFRICA, 21 NOVEMBER 1997

Instrumental in keeping us in touch and informed: in the dissemination of both the good news and the bad, the sensational and the mundane, has been the media. I wish to pay tribute on this occasion to their unflinching, and often ill-appreciated, commitment to their task and their contribution to a more-informed, and hence, a better world.

CLOSING SESSION OF THE FIFTIETH ANC NATIONAL CONFERENCE, NORTH-WEST UNIVERSITY, MAFIKENG CAMPUS, SOUTH AFRICA, 20 DECEMBER 1997

The media is one of the principal figures in ensuring that we develop our country, we unite our people, we promote reconciliation.

BRIEFING TO EDITORS AND OPINION MAKERS, PRETORIA, SOUTH AFRICA, 10 MAY 1999

In all my years in public life my favourite ladies and gentlemen were exactly members of the media. You were always the ones with the most courage to remind and reprimand me when I was acting less than a gentleman.

PRESS CONFERENCE FOR 46664 CAMPAIGN, ROBBEN ISLAND, CAPE TOWN, SOUTH AFRICA, 28 NOVEMBER 2003

Newspapers allow us to hold a mirror up to ourselves, and we must be brave enough to look squarely at the reflections.

MESSAGE TO THE CONGRESS OF THE WORLD ASSOCIATION OF NEWSPAPERS; FOURTEENTH CONGRESS OF THE WORLD EDITORS FORUM, CASTLE OF GOOD HOPE, CAPE TOWN, SOUTH AFRICA, 3 JUNE 2007

Meditation

The cell gives you the opportunity to look daily into your entire conduct, to overcome the bad and develop whatever is good in you. Regular meditation, say about fifteen minutes a day before you turn in, can be very fruitful in this regard.

FROM A LETTER TO WINNIE MANDELA, THEN IN KROONSTAD PRISON, SOUTH AFRICA, WRITTEN ON ROBBEN ISLAND, 1 FEBRUARY 1975

Memory

Few things have inspired me more than the knowledge that in spite of all that the enemy is doing to isolate and discredit us, people everywhere never forget us.

FROM AN UNPUBLISHED AUTOBIOGRAPHICAL MANUSCRIPT, WRITTEN ON ROBBEN ISLAND, 1975

Long absence from a place can be disastrous, obliterating as it often does, some of the fondest memories.

FROM A LETTER TO MR KHALAKE SELLO, WRITTEN ON ROBBEN ISLAND, 26 OCTOBER 1980

Until I was jailed I never fully appreciated the capacity of memory, the endless string of information the head can carry.

FROM A LETTER TO HILDA BERNSTEIN, WRITTEN IN POLLSMOOR PRISON, CAPE TOWN, SOUTH AFRICA, 8 JULY 1985

The time will come when our nation will honour the memory of all the sons, the daughters, the mothers, the fathers, the youth and the children who, by their thoughts and deeds, gave us the right to assert with pride that we are South Africans, that we are Africans and that we are citizens of the world.

FIRST STATE OF THE NATION ADDRESS, PARLIAMENT, CAPE TOWN, SOUTH AFRICA, 24 MAY 1994

We should never forget those on whose shoulders we stand and those who paid the supreme price for freedom.

UPON RECEIVING THE FREEDOM OF HOWICK, HOWICK SPORTS GROUNDS, HOWICK, SOUTH AFRICA, 12 DECEMBER 1996

Whatever my wishes might be, I cannot bind future generations to remember me in the particular way I would like.

FROM AN INTERVIEW WITH JOHN BATTERSBY, JOHANNESBURG, SOUTH AFRICA, PUBLISHED IN *THE CHRISTIAN SCIENCE MONITOR*, 10 FEBRUARY 2000

The memory of a history of division and hate, injustice and suffering, inhumanity of person against person should inspire us to celebrate our own demonstration of the capacity of human beings to progress, to go forward, to improve, to do better.

JOINT SITTING OF PARLIAMENT TO MARK TEN YEARS OF DEMOCRACY, PARLIAMENT, CAPE TOWN, SOUTH AFRICA, 10 MAY 2004

All of us have a powerful moral obligation to the many voices and stories either marginalised or suppressed during the apartheid era.

LAUNCH OF THE CENTRE OF MEMORY, JOHANNESBURG, SOUTH AFRICA, 21 SEPTEMBER 2004

The history of our country is characterised by too much forgetting. A forgetting which served the powerful and dispossessed the weak.

IBID

One of our challenges as we build and extend democracy is the need to ensure that our youth know where we have come from, what we have done to break the shackles of oppression and how we have pursued the journey to freedom and dignity for all. We will fail our youth if we leave them in ignorance of what has given them the opportunities they now enjoy. At the same time, for those of us who are older and have lived through the transition from apartheid to democracy, the processes of remembering offer us healing and a means of respecting the many comrades who made it possible.

IBID

In our view the work of archives in the South Africa of today is potentially one of the most critical contributions to restoration and reconciliation. All of us have a powerful moral obligation to the many voices and stories either marginalised or suppressed during the apartheid era.

IBID

May we never forget those generations who challenged the apartheid regime, and who made our freedom possible through many years of struggle.

LAUNCH OF '466/64: A PRISONER WORKING IN THE GARDEN EXHIBITION', CONSTITUTION HILL, JOHANNESBURG, SOUTH AFRICA, 16 MARCH 2005

All of us tend to associate archives and museums with a remembering of the past. But that is only part of their work. If justice is their most important shaping influence, then they are also about making the future.

IBID

In the life of any individual, family, community or society, memory is of fundamental importance. It is the fabric of identity.

FROM *A PRISONER IN THE GARDEN: OPENING NELSON MANDELA'S PRISON ARCHIVE*, 2005

The struggle against apartheid can be typified as the pitting of memory against forgetting. It was in our determination to remember our ancestors, our stories, our values and our dreams that we found comradeship.

IBID

At the heart of every oppressive tool developed by the apartheid regime was a determination to control, distort, weaken and even erase people's memories.

FROM *A PRISONER IN THE GARDEN: OPENING NELSON MANDELA'S PRISON ARCHIVE*, 2005

Institutions of Memory, such as the Nelson Mandela Centre of Memory project, have a significant role to play in finding the stories that are sidelined by power... We are grateful to the Nelson Mandela Foundation and its Centre of Memory project for the important work that it is doing in ensuring that our histories are not lost.

LAUNCH OF THE IZIPHO EXHIBITION, BOOK AND COMIC SERIES, NELSON MANDELA FOUNDATION, JOHANNESBURG, SOUTH AFRICA, 14 JULY 2005

Middle East, The

As a movement we recognise the legitimacy of Palestinian nationalism just as we recognise the legitimacy of Zionism as a Jewish nationalism. We insist on the right of the State of Israel to exist within secure borders but with equal vigour support the Palestinian right to national self-determination.

THIRTY-SEVENTH CONGRESS OF THE SOUTH AFRICAN JEWISH BOARD OF DEPUTIES, CARLTON HOTEL, JOHANNESBURG, SOUTH AFRICA, 21 AUGUST 1993

It is my hope that the peace process in the Middle East will continue, and that it will bear fruit. Our experience has taught us that with goodwill a negotiated solution can be found for even the most profound problems.

MESSAGE ON JEWISH NEW YEAR (ROSH HASHANAH), SOUTH AFRICA, 13 SEPTEMBER 1996

Today, at the end of a century which has seen such a desert of devastation caused by horrific wars, a century which at last has gained much experience in the peaceful resolution of conflicts, we must ask: is this a time for war; is this a time for sending young men to their death?

UPON RECEIVING AN HONORARY DOCTORATE FROM BEN-GURION UNIVERSITY OF THE NEGEV, CAPE TOWN, SOUTH AFRICA, 19 SEPTEMBER 1997

The temptation in our situation is to speak in muffled tones about an issue such as the right of the people of Palestine to a state of their own. We can easily be enticed to read reconciliation and fairness as meaning parity between justice and injustice. Having achieved our own freedom, we can fall into the trap of washing our hands of difficulties that others face. Yet we would be less than human if we did so.

INTERNATIONAL DAY OF SOLIDARITY WITH THE PALESTINIAN PEOPLE, PRETORIA, SOUTH AFRICA, 4 DECEMBER 1997

Palestinian and Israeli campaigners for peace know that security for any nation is not abstract, neither is it exclusive. It depends on the security of others; it depends on mutual respect and trust. Indeed, these soldiers of peace know that their destiny is bound together, and that none can be at peace while others wallow in poverty and insecurity.

IBID

Soldiers of peace recognise that the world we live in is rising above the trappings of religious and racial hatred and conflict. They recognise that the spurning of agreements reached in good faith and the forceful occupation of land can only fan the flames of conflict. They know from their own experience that, it is in a situation such as this, that extremists on all sides thrive, fed by the blood lust of centuries gone by.
IBID

All of us need to do more in supporting the struggle of the people of Palestine for self-determination, in supporting the quest for peace, security and friendship in this region.
IBID

When, in 1977, the United Nations passed the resolution inaugurating the International Day of Solidarity with the Palestinian people, it was asserting the recognition that injustice and gross human rights violations were being perpetrated in Palestine. In the same period, the UN took a strong stand against apartheid and over the years, an international consensus was built, which helped to bring an end to this iniquitous system. But we know too well that our freedom is incomplete without the freedom of the Palestinians, without the resolution of conflicts in East Timor, the Sudan and other parts of the world.
IBID

South Africa is proud to be part of the international consensus affirming the right of Palestine to self-determination and statehood. We are committed to playing our humble part, within the limits of our resource, to help ensure that Palestine assumes its rightful position in the global arena.
BANQUET FOR PRESIDENT YASSER ARAFAT OF PALESTINE, CAPE TOWN, SOUTH AFRICA, 11 AUGUST 1998

South Africans understand the suffering of the Palestinian people. Palestinians continue to suffer humiliation and economic hardship. Those who live in exile as refugees have for long been sustained by their hope for an end to the conflict and the dawning of a better future.
SPEECH DELIVERED BY FOREIGN MINISTER ALFRED NZO ON BEHALF OF PRESIDENT MANDELA ON THE INTERNATIONAL DAY OF SOLIDARITY WITH THE PALESTINIAN PEOPLE, SOUTH AFRICA, 25 NOVEMBER 1998

The people of Palestine and the whole region need our support for their efforts to put an end to this conflict which has plagued the world for so long.
IBID

We remain convinced that the only means of ending conflict and bringing peace and security to Palestine, Israel and the region is through negotiations and the faithful implementation of agreements reached so far.
IBID

It would be nothing short of tragic if failure to abide by agreements, including the release of political prisoners, again frustrated the aspirations of the Palestinian people for justice and the yearning of the whole region and the world for peace in the Middle East.
SUMMIT OF THE GULF COOPERATION COUNCIL, ABU DHABI, UNITED ARAB EMIRATES, 7 DECEMBER 1998

We should condemn both [Tony] Blair and [George W] Bush and let them know in no uncertain terms that what they are doing is wrong.
SPEAKING AT A CONFERENCE OF THE INTERNATIONAL WOMEN'S FORUM, TOKYO, JAPAN, 30 JANUARY 2003

We have found ourselves compelled to speak out strongly in recent months against the rise of unilateralism in world affairs. We publicly and in private expressed our sharp differences on this matter with Prime Minister [Tony] Blair and President [George W] Bush, both young leaders whom we otherwise hold in high regard.

BRITISH RED CROSS HUMANITY LECTURE, QUEEN ELIZABETH II CONFERENCE CENTRE, LONDON, ENGLAND, 10 JULY 2003

You, the people of Israel and Palestine, must now give the lead to your leaders, taking your societies beyond hatred and fear; recognising the peaceful coexistence between a sovereign and viable state of Palestine and a safe and secure state of Israel is your responsibility.

STATEMENT ABOUT THE SIGNING OF THE GENEVA ACCORD, NOVEMBER 2003

We warned against the invasion of Iraq, and observe the terrible suffering in that country.

46664 CONCERT, HYDE PARK, LONDON, ENGLAND, 27 JUNE 2008

We look back at much human progress, but we sadly note so much failing as well. In our time we spoke out on the situation in Palestine and Israel, and that conflict continues unabated.

IBID

Millennium, The

Let us join hands to ensure that, as we enter the new millennium, the political rights that the twentieth century has recognised, and the independence that nations have gained, shall be translated into peace, prosperity and equity for all.

CORONATION OF KING LETSIE III, MASERU, LESOTHO, 31 OCTOBER 1997

Mistakes

Only armchair politicians are immune from committing mistakes. Errors are inherent in political action. Those who are in the centre of political struggle, who have to deal with practical and pressing problems, are afforded little time for reflection and no precedents to guide them and are bound to slip up many times.

FROM AN UNPUBLISHED AUTOBIOGRAPHICAL MANUSCRIPT, WRITTEN ON ROBBEN ISLAND, 1975

I don't want to be frightened by the fact that a person has made certain mistakes and he has got human frailties.

FROM A CONVERSATION WITH RICHARD STENGEL, 3 MAY 1993

Monarchy

Even at the height of the severe repression by the apartheid regime there were courageous monarchs like Sabata of the Thembus and Cyprian of the Zulus who refused to betray their people.

FROM THE UNPUBLISHED SEQUEL TO HIS AUTOBIOGRAPHY, CIRCA 1998

Morality

A movement without a vision would be a movement without moral foundation.

INVESTITURE AS DOCTOR OF LAWS, SOOCHOW UNIVERSITY, TAIWAN, 1 AUGUST 1993

We are in this modern globalised world each the keeper of our brother and sister. We have too often failed that moral calling.

BRITISH RED CROSS HUMANITY LECTURE, QUEEN ELIZABETH II CONFERENCE CENTRE, LONDON, ENGLAND, 10 JULY 2003

Mother

Her visits had always excited me and the news of her death hit me hard. I at once felt lonely and empty.

FROM A LETTER TO KD MATANZIMA, WRITTEN ON ROBBEN ISLAND, 14 OCTOBER 1968

I had never dreamt that I would never be able to bury ma.

FROM A LETTER TO NOPHIKELA MADIKIZELA, WRITTEN ON ROBBEN ISLAND, 4 MAY 1969

She spent all her life in the countryside and became attached to its plains and hills, to its fine people and simple ways.

IBID

I watched her as she walked away slowly to the boat that would take her back to the mainland, and I feared I had seen her for the last time.

IBID

I have done my best at all times to bring a measure of ease and comfort into my mother's life.

FROM AN UNPUBLISHED AUTOBIOGRAPHICAL MANUSCRIPT, WRITTEN ON ROBBEN ISLAND, 1975

Being together with my mother in her home filled me with boyish excitement.

IBID

My mother was just a simple peasant lady and she was alright when my father was alive, but she was depending on herself, ploughing her field... the life in the countryside is very hard.

FROM A CONVERSATION WITH RICHARD STENGEL, 25 MARCH 1993

One of the saddest moments in my life in prison was the death of my mother... She came a couple of times to visit me but the last time she came to see me it was in 1968; I could see that she wasn't well. As she left I looked at her as she walked to the harbour. I had the feeling that I had seen her for the last time and that was the case. She died and I tried to get permission from the authorities to go and bury her but they refused.

REVISITING ROBBEN ISLAND, CAPE TOWN, SOUTH AFRICA, 11 FEBRUARY 1994

My mother, she was my first friend in the proper sense of the word. She was not an emotional person, she was completely controlled, calm, at peace with herself and with the world.

FROM THE DOCUMENTARY MANDELA, 1996

A lady who never went to school, who could not read and write but who was able to listen to the enlightened Christians in the village and became a Christian in spite of the fact that my father wouldn't come near Christianity.

IBID

Music

African music is something that goes straight to your heart and it tells the story of your own life, your living conditions, your aspirations.

FROM A CONVERSATION WITH RICHARD STENGEL, 25 MARCH 1993

The curious beauty of African music is that it uplifts even as it tells a sad tale. You may be poor, you may only have a ramshackle house, you may have lost your job, but that song gives you hope.

FROM *LONG WALK TO FREEDOM*, 1994

We have spent many years of our life in the isolation of a prison island. I suppose it is difficult for others to imagine just how much solace we drew in those years from the knowledge and remembrance of the great works of music that emanated from this city. Its resonance kept on reminding us of the ultimate unity of the human soul and the indestructibility of the human spirit.

SPEECH, VIENNA, AUSTRIA, 22/23 OCTOBER 2003

Mythology

After supper we would listen enthralled to my mother and sometimes my aunt telling us stories, legends, myths and fables which have come down from countless generations, and all of which tended to stimulate the imagination and contained some valuable moral lesson.

FROM AN UNPUBLISHED AUTOBIOGRAPHICAL MANUSCRIPT, WRITTEN ON ROBBEN ISLAND, 1975

As for mythology my interest in that particular field has a long history, my mother having fed me on it from the earliest days of my childhood.

FROM A LETTER TO FATIMA MEER, WRITTEN ON ROBBEN ISLAND, 1 JANUARY 1976

Nazism

The millions of graves strewn across Europe which are the result of the tyranny of Nazism, the decimation of the native peoples of the Americas and Australia, the destructive trail of the apartheid crime against humanity – all these are like a haunting question that floats in the wind: why did we allow these to happen?

ADDRESS TO THE JOINT HOUSES OF PARLIAMENT, WESTMINSTER HALL, LONDON, ENGLAND, 11 JULY 1996

Negotiation

When we have fought it out and reduced this country to ashes it will still be necessary for us to sit down together and talk about the problems of reconstruction – the black man and the white man, the African and the Afrikaner.

FROM AN ESSAY ENTITLED 'CLEAR THE OBSTACLES AND CONFRONT THE ENEMY', WRITTEN ON ROBBEN ISLAND, 1976

I am prepared to play my role in efforts to normalise the situation, and to negotiate over the mechanics of transferring power to all South Africans.

FROM A LETTER TO PROFESSOR SAMUEL DASH, WRITTEN IN POLLSMOOR PRISON, CAPE TOWN, SOUTH AFRICA, 12 MAY 1986

The step I am taking should, therefore, not be seen as the beginning of actual negotiations between the government and the ANC. My task is a very limited one, and that is to bring the country's two major political bodies to the negotiating table.

FROM A LETTER TO PRESIDENT PW BOTHA, WRITTEN IN VICTOR VERSTER PRISON, PAARL, SOUTH AFRICA, JULY 1989

We have not as yet begun discussing the basic demands of the struggle. I wish to stress that I myself have at no time entered into negotiations about the future of our country except to insist on a meeting between the ANC and the government.

FIRST SPEECH AFTER HIS RELEASE, CITY HALL, CAPE TOWN, SOUTH AFRICA, 11 FEBRUARY 1990

Negotiations on the dismantling of apartheid will have to address the overwhelming demand of our people for a democratic, non-racial and unitary South Africa.

IBID

We are marching to a new future based on strong foundations of respect for each other achieved through bona fide negotiations.

RALLY, SOWETO, SOUTH AFRICA, 13 FEBRUARY 1990

I was a facilitator only when I was in prison; once I leave prison the whole task of conducting negotiations is that of the National Executive in Lusaka.

AT HOME, SOWETO, SOUTH AFRICA, 14 FEBRUARY 1990

I sincerely hope that in future we are going to move away from the situation of conflict and confrontation to that of peaceful negotiations.

IBID

Well, if you decide to settle problems through negotiation, then you must be prepared to compromise, and compromise, as I understand it, is not in regard to peripheral issues.

FROM AN INTERVIEW WITH THE SOUTH AFRICAN BROADCASTING CORPORATION, JOHANNESBURG, SOUTH AFRICA, 15 FEBRUARY 1990

We are the people who initiated discussions which were calculated to get the government and the ANC to sit down and to explore a political solution.

PRESS CONFERENCE, CAPE TOWN, SOUTH AFRICA, APRIL 1990

If you are negotiating you must do so in a spirit of reconciliation, not from the point of view of issuing ultimatums.

ADDRESSING THE MEDIA AFTER MEETING WITH PRESIDENT FW DE KLERK ABOUT VIOLENCE ON THE EAST RAND, UNION BUILDINGS, CAPE TOWN, SOUTH AFRICA, CIRCA EARLY 1990s

The ANC has taken the initiative to get the government and the ANC to sit down together and hammer out a peaceful solution.

PRESS CONFERENCE, CAPE TOWN, SOUTH AFRICA, 4 MAY 1990

The carrying on of negotiations and rhetoric on peace while at the same time the government is conducting a war against us is a position we cannot accept. We have warned the government several times on this matter and if they fail to take effective action, the whole of South Africa, unfortunately and very much against our will, will be drowned in blood.

BRIEFING TO THE FIFTH SESSION OF THE OAU'S (ORGANISATION OF AFRICAN UNITY) AD HOC COMMITTEE ON SOUTHERN AFRICA, 8 SEPTEMBER 1990

Again I must warn that unless the government takes immediate steps to stop this violence there is no question of negotiations at all. But if they do take visible measures to end the violence the ANC will never be found wanting because we are the people who started the peace process and we are determined that it should succeed.

SPEAKING AT KAGISO, WEST RAND, SOUTH AFRICA, CIRCA 1991

Today will be indelibly imprinted in the history of our country. If we, who are gathered here, respond to the challenge before us, today will mark the commencement of the transition from apartheid to democracy. Our people, from every corner of our country, have expressed their yearning for democracy and peace. CODESA represents the historical opportunity to translate that yearning into reality.

OPENING OF CODESA (CONVENTION FOR A DEMOCRATIC SOUTH AFRICA), WORLD TRADE CENTER, KEMPTON PARK, SOUTH AFRICA, 20 DECEMBER 1991

You want to discuss problems with people soberly, because the people would like to know how you express yourself, and then they can have an idea of how you are handling important issues in the course of those negotiations.

FROM A CONVERSATION WITH RICHARD STENGEL, 3 FEBRUARY 1993

A softer approach, especially when you are confident of a case, brings about results far more than aggression.

FROM A CONVERSATION WITH RICHARD STENGEL, 8 FEBRUARY 1993

So what I decided to do was to start negotiations without telling them, and then confront them with a fait accompli.

FROM A CONVERSATION WITH RICHARD STENGEL, 8 MARCH 1993

Those first talks were very frank, friendly and Thabo Mbeki explained it very well in a meeting which he addressed subsequent to that meeting of the two delegations when he said that there we were and found that none of us had horns.

FROM A CONVERSATION WITH RICHARD STENGEL, 22 APRIL 1993

When we met, you see, we discovered that in actual fact these were ordinary human beings who could respond very constructively and in a humane manner; the policy was still there, very harsh, but the human beings were totally different.

IBID

Negotiations must be viewed as the culmination of all our collective efforts on different levels, through the use of a variety of methods, under different conditions, to achieve our strategic objective – the transfer of power from the minority to the majority.

UMKHONTO WE SIZWE NATIONAL CONFERENCE, EASTERN TRANSVAAL, 3 SEPTEMBER 1993

Often, the most discouraging moments are precisely the time to launch an initiative. At such times, people are searching for a way out of their dilemma.

FROM LONG WALK TO FREEDOM, 1994

Our observation is that men and women throughout the world want peace, want security, want to get on with their lives and the very fact that parties that have been in conflict are sitting down to talk sends a message of hope to many people, not only in the area affected but throughout the world.

AFTER MEETING SINN FEIN LEADER GERRY ADAMS, SHELL HOUSE, JOHANNESBURG, SOUTH AFRICA, 19 JUNE 1995

Our experience has taught us that with goodwill a negotiated solution can be found for even the most profound problems.

MESSAGE FOR JEWISH NEW YEAR (ROSH HASHANAH), SOUTH AFRICA, 13 SEPTEMBER 1996

South Africa does not believe it can solve the problems of others. But we do believe that our own humble experience has shown that negotiated solutions can be found even to conflicts that have come to seem intractable and that such solutions emerge when those who have been divided reach out to find the common ground.

UPON RECEIVING AN HONORARY DOCTORATE FROM BEN-GURION UNIVERSITY OF THE NEGEV, CAPE TOWN, SOUTH AFRICA, 19 SEPTEMBER 1997

Even during the days of negotiations, our own experience taught us that the pursuit of human fraternity and equality – irrespective of race or religion – should stand at the centre of our peaceful endeavours.

INTERNATIONAL DAY OF SOLIDARITY WITH THE PALESTINIAN PEOPLE, PRETORIA, SOUTH AFRICA, 4 DECEMBER 1997

Our own humble experience has shown that negotiated solutions can be found even to conflict that the world has come to regard as insoluble. It has taught us that such solutions emerge when former opponents reach out to find common ground.

BANQUET FOR PRESIDENT YASSER ARAFAT OF PALESTINE, CAPE TOWN, SOUTH AFRICA, 11 AUGUST 1998

Negotiation and discussion are the greatest weapons we have for promoting peace and development.

SUMMIT OF THE GULF COOPERATION COUNCIL, ABU DHABI, UNITED ARAB EMIRATES, 7 DECEMBER 1998

I approached the government without even telling my fellow prisoners.

FROM THE UNPUBLISHED SEQUEL TO HIS AUTOBIOGRAPHY, CIRCA 1998

No problem is so deep that it cannot be overcome, given the will of all parties, through discussion and negotiation rather than force and violence.

ADDRESS AT THE OPENING OF THE PRESIDENT'S BUDGET DEBATE, PARLIAMENT, CAPE TOWN, SOUTH AFRICA, 2 MARCH 1999

Amongst the principles which the liberation movement pursued from the beginning of negotiations is that out of any debate we must emerge stronger and more united, and that there should be no winners or losers.

FINAL SITTING OF THE FIRST DEMOCRATICALLY ELECTED PARLIAMENT, CAPE TOWN, SOUTH AFRICA, 26 MARCH 1999

We as the ANC had the courage and the vision to know that without talking to our enemies at the time, we would never be able to bring about that transformation and so we had the courage of going to them and saying, 'Why must we be slaughtering one another when we could sit down and sort out our problems peacefully?' Fortunately, amongst our enemies, there were people who also had the foresight and the courage to say, 'Let's forget the past' and we sat down and spoke. That is what has given me real pride.

BRIEFING TO EDITORS AND OPINION MAKERS, PRETORIA, SOUTH AFRICA, 10 MAY 1999

We could never have brought about this peaceful change without sitting down and talking to our enemy.

IBID

The leaders of the liberation movement had the vision and commitment to put rational considerations above the emotional impulses that would have us refuse to talk to the enemy.

BLACK MANAGEMENT FORUM ANNUAL CONFERENCE, SOUTH AFRICA, OCTOBER 2002

We were expected to destroy one another and ourselves collectively in the worst racial conflagration. Instead, we as a people chose the path of negotiation, compromise and peaceful settlement. Instead of hatred and revenge we chose reconciliation and nation-building.

SPEAKING AT NOBEL SQUARE, CAPE TOWN, SOUTH AFRICA, 14 DECEMBER 2003

The best weapon is to sit down and talk.

FROM THE DOCUMENTARY *MANDELA: THE LIVING LEGEND*, 2003

Our leaders confounded all the predictions of doom by sitting down to negotiate a peaceful settlement of our differences. If we could do that, it should be possible in other situations as well.

FROM AN INTERVIEW WITH LORIE KARNATH FOR NOBEL LAUREATES, APRIL 2004

Historical enemies succeeded in negotiating a peaceful transition from apartheid to democracy exactly because we were prepared to accept the inherent capacity for goodness in the other.

JOINT SITTING OF PARLIAMENT TO MARK TEN YEARS OF DEMOCRACY, PARLIAMENT, CAPE TOWN, SOUTH AFRICA, 10 MAY 2004

South Africa continues to be an example of what can be achieved in circumstances of conflict if there is the will and commitment to finding peaceful solutions.

BIRTHDAY CELEBRATIONS FOR ARCHBISHOP DESMOND TUTU, JOHANNESBURG, SOUTH AFRICA, 7 DECEMBER 2006

To talk to one another as South Africans, to negotiate under circumstances that did not demean any of the involved parties, to seek solutions through honourable compromise: these approaches were always a central part of the thinking of the liberation movement.

NATIONAL CIVIL SOCIETY CONFERENCE, SOUTH AFRICA, 24 APRIL 2010

By starting negotiations from jail, I was not starting anything new; we had made this decision already in December 1961.

FROM AN INTERVIEW, DATE UNKNOWN

Nelson Mandela Children's Fund

Our love for children is undiminished. Their innocence and energy, their happiness and welfare must be protected and treasured. It is their laughter that I yearned for while in prison. My Children's Fund will continue to bring hope to children and young people.

RECORDED MESSAGE FOR A GALA DINNER IN MONACO 'UNITED FOR A BETTER WORLD', 1 DECEMBER 2004

Nelson Mandela Foundation

Memory is a vital force in the life of people and nations and can help unite divided societies. My Foundation will continue to bring people together, providing a safe space, especially for those who disagree, to listen and talk to each other.

RECORDED MESSAGE FOR A GALA DINNER IN MONACO 'UNITED FOR A BETTER WORLD', 1 DECEMBER 2004

Nobel Peace Prize

That South Africa has once again been given the Nobel Peace Prize is a tribute to all South Africans. It is an expression of the profound confidence the international community has vested in us that we can collectively address the enormous problems our country faces without recourse to violence and coercion.

UPON THE ANNOUNCEMENT OF THE AWARD OF THE NOBEL PRIZE FOR PEACE, 15 OCTOBER 1993

I am keenly aware that the Nobel Peace Prize imposes an even greater obligation on me personally to strive even harder, in the interests of all South Africans, for peace, justice and democracy.

IBID

Let it never be said by future generations that indifference, cynicism or selfishness made us fail to live up to the ideals of humanism which the Nobel Peace Prize encapsulates. Let the strivings of us all prove Martin Luther King Jr to have been correct, when he said that humanity can no longer be tragically bound to the starless midnight of racism and war.

NOBEL PEACE PRIZE AWARD CEREMONY, OSLO, NORWAY, 10 DECEMBER 1993

I have never cared very much for personal prizes. A man does not become a freedom fighter in the hope of winning awards, but when I was notified that I had won the 1993 Nobel Peace Prize jointly with Mr de Klerk, I was deeply moved.

FROM *LONG WALK TO FREEDOM*, 1994

Non-racialism

We have made it very clear in our policy that South Africa is a country of many races. There is room for all the various races in this country.

FROM AN INTERVIEW WITH BRIAN WIDLAKE FOR ITN TELEVISION (UK), JOHANNESBURG, SOUTH AFRICA, 31 MAY 1961

In the African states I saw black and white mingling peacefully and happily in hotels, cinemas, trading in the same areas, using the same public transport and living in the same residential areas.

IN MITIGATION OF SENTENCE AFTER BEING CONVICTED OF INCITING WORKERS TO STRIKE AND LEAVING THE COUNTRY ILLEGALLY, OLD SYNAGOGUE, PRETORIA, SOUTH AFRICA, 7 NOVEMBER 1962

We of the ANC had always stood for a non-racial democracy, and we shrank from any action which might drive the races further apart than they already were. But the hard facts were that fifty years of non-violence had brought the African people nothing but more and more repressive legislation, and fewer and fewer rights.

SPEECH FROM THE DOCK, RIVONIA TRIAL, PALACE OF JUSTICE, PRETORIA, SOUTH AFRICA, 20 APRIL 1964

We are redoubling our efforts to get the whites to accept that we are brothers, we are sisters, we are children of God just as they are and there is no reason whatsoever why there should be any feeling of hostility or suspicion between black and white in this country.

AT HOME, SOWETO, SOUTH AFRICA, 14 FEBRUARY 1990

Bound together by their common destiny, there will be neither white nor black, but just South Africans, free and proud. Proud to be members of the human family.

CONCERT ORGANISED BY THE IRISH ANTI-APARTHEID MOVEMENT, DUBLIN, IRELAND, 1 JULY 1990

We are seriously committed to a new, non-racial, democratic South Africa. It is an ideal for which many of us went to prison, for which many have died in prison cells, on the gallows, and on the killing fields of our towns, townships and in the countries of southern Africa.

STATEMENT TO THE PARTY PARLIAMENTARY GROUP ON SOUTH AFRICA, COMMITTEE ROOM, PARLIAMENT, LONDON, ENGLAND, 3 JULY 1990

We are a non-racial organisation and we want that our meetings, our structures reflect this non-racial character.

SPEAKING AT KAGISO, WEST RAND, SOUTH AFRICA, CIRCA 1991

The attempts to divide our people along ethnic lines, to turn their rich variety into a danger with which to pierce their hearts, must be made to fail.

ANC/INKATHA SUMMIT, DURBAN, SOUTH AFRICA, 29 JANUARY 1991

There can be no salvation for our beleaguered country but the realisation by all and sundry that we are one people – black and white. Cast in a mould that can be different, but one interdependent people all the same – irrespective of the political and ideological creed that each one of us might hold dear.

IBID

The ANC is committed to non-racialism, to having all the people of South Africa live in peace and friendship.

SPEAKING AT THE UNIVERSITY OF PRETORIA, PRETORIA, SOUTH AFRICA, 29 APRIL 1991

The non-racial unity of our country is non-negotiable, and may not be compromised.

SPEAKING AT THE UNIVERSITY OF DURBAN-WESTVILLE, DURBAN, SOUTH AFRICA, 6 JULY 1991

We are fighting for a society where people will cease thinking in terms of colour.

FROM A CONVERSATION WITH RICHARD STENGEL, 8 MARCH 1993

We have never accepted really multiracialism. Our demand is for a non-racial society, because when you talk of multiracialism, you are multiplying the races.

FROM A CONVERSATION WITH RICHARD STENGEL, 9 MARCH 1993

I did feel that the South African Jews had less colour consciousness than the other white groups.

FROM A CONVERSATION WITH RICHARD STENGEL, 16 MARCH 1993

The question of a non-racial society has always been the standpoint of the African National Congress, especially since 1955 when we published the Freedom Charter. It became an established policy of the ANC.

FROM A CONVERSATION WITH RICHARD STENGEL, 28 APRIL 1993

I have stood firmly throughout my life in the belief that we are one country, we are one people: coloured, Indian, African and white. One country, one people.

REVISITING ROBBEN ISLAND, CAPE TOWN, SOUTH AFRICA, 11 FEBRUARY 1994

One of the striking features in the world is the emergence of men and women in every continent who have decided to take up socio-economic issues in every part of the world, no matter what the ethnic group of the person suffering is.

OPENING OF THE ZOLA CLINIC, SOWETO, SOUTH AFRICA, 7 MARCH 2002

The non-racial character of our struggle and of the society we are building today owes much to the efforts and contributions of persons like Rusty Bernstein. He made a deliberate and considered choice to forego what could have been a life of comfort and ease to join forces with his fellow South Africans in the fight for democracy and freedom.

ON THE DEATH OF RUSTY BERNSTEIN, JOHANNESBURG, SOUTH AFRICA, 24 JUNE 2002

As we lead the transformation of our country making sure that black people take their rightful places as full participants in all sectors and at all levels of society, the guiding principle should be clearly seen and heard that we are building a non-racial society.

BLACK MANAGEMENT FORUM ANNUAL CONFERENCE, SOUTH AFRICA, OCTOBER 2002

I hope that our movement will always hold that commitment to non-racialism dear in its thoughts, policies and actions. It is that commitment, even in circumstances where we could have been pardoned for deviating from it, that amongst other things earned us the respect of the world.

COMMEMORATION OF THE LIVES OF YUSUF CACHALIA AND BRAM FISCHER, JOHANNESBURG METROPOLITAN CENTRE, JOHANNESBURG, SOUTH AFRICA, 5 JUNE 2005

Non-violence

Non-violence, as effective as it had been, could never actually deliver the goods because we are dealing with a government which is completely insensitive, which has no culture of democracy.

FROM A CONVERSATION WITH RICHARD STENGEL, 19 MARCH 1993

We took up the attitude that we would stick to non-violence only insofar as the conditions permitted that. Once the conditions were against that we would automatically abandon non-violence and use the methods which were dictated by the conditions.

FROM A CONVERSATION WITH RICHARD STENGEL, 25 MARCH 1993

We have always believed in non-violence as a tactic. Where the conditions demanded that we should use non-violence we would do so; where the conditions demanded that we should depart from non-violence we would do so.

FROM A CONVERSATION WITH RICHARD STENGEL, 5 APRIL 1993

For me, non-violence was not a moral principle but a strategy; there is no moral goodness in using an ineffective weapon.

FROM *LONG WALK TO FREEDOM*, 1994

Opportunity

You have to carefully choose the opportunity and make sure that history would be on your side.

FROM A CONVERSATION WITH RICHARD STENGEL, 5 APRIL 1993

We pass through this world but once and opportunities you miss will never be available to you again.

FROM A NOTEBOOK, DATE UNKNOWN

Oppression

Gone forever are the days when harsh and wicked laws provide the oppressors with years of peace and quiet.

PRESIDENTIAL ADDRESS TO THE ANC TRANSVAAL CONGRESS, ALSO KNOWN AS THE
'NO EASY WALK TO FREEDOM' SPEECH, TRANSVAAL, SOUTH AFRICA, 21 SEPTEMBER 1953

We have been conditioned by the history of white government in this country to accept the fact that Africans, when they make their demands to have some chance of success, will be met by force and terror on the part of the government. This is not something we have taught the African people; this is something the African people have learnt from their own bitter experience.

IN MITIGATION OF SENTENCE AFTER BEING CONVICTED OF INCITING WORKERS TO STRIKE AND LEAVING
THE COUNTRY ILLEGALLY, OLD SYNAGOGUE, PRETORIA, SOUTH AFRICA, 7 NOVEMBER 1962

Optimism

I am fundamentally an optimist. Whether that comes from nature or nurture, I cannot say. Part of being optimistic is keeping one's head pointed towards the sun, one's feet moving forward.

FROM *LONG WALK TO FREEDOM*, 1994

Organisation of African Unity

It will never happen again that our country should seek to dominate another through force of arms, economic might or subversion. We are determined to remain true to the vision which you held out for South Africa as you joined the offensive to destroy the system of apartheid.

OAU (ORGANISATION OF AFRICAN UNITY) SUMMIT, TUNIS, TUNISIA, 13 JUNE 1994

Today, at the lower reaches of the Sahara, under whose majestic sands hides much of our ancient African origins and the things that link the African North and South, I have the honour to present my valediction to a conclave, which was the midwife of our freedom, which has been our teacher as we have striven to learn what we should do with that freedom.

OAU (ORGANISATION OF AFRICAN UNITY) SUMMIT, OUAGADOUGOU, BURKINA FASO, 8 JUNE 1998

Pain

Wounds which cannot be seen are more painful than the ones that you can see which can be cured by a doctor.

REVISITING ROBBEN ISLAND, CAPE TOWN, SOUTH AFRICA, 11 FEBRUARY 1994

I spent a terrible time without sharing my pain with anybody.

IBID

Passive Resistance

The Gandhian philosophy of peace, tolerance and non-violence began in South Africa as a powerful instrument of social change.

OPENING OF THE GANDHI HALL, LENASIA, SOUTH AFRICA, 27 SEPTEMBER 1992

Past, The

In my present circumstances thinking about the past can be more exacting than contemplating the present and predicting the course of future events.

FROM A LETTER TO HILDA BERNSTEIN, WRITTEN IN POLLSMOOR PRISON, CAPE TOWN, SOUTH AFRICA,
8 JULY 1985

The past is a rich resource on which we can draw in order to make decisions for the future, but it does not dictate our choices. We should look back at the past and select what is good, and leave behind what is bad.

RALLY, KINGS PARK STADIUM, DURBAN, SOUTH AFRICA, 25 FEBRUARY 1990

While we can all agree that the past should not be permitted to become a burden that impairs the ability of our country and its people to move forward, it would be extremely short-sighted to dismiss it and try to forget it as if it only had one single, brutal dimension.

THIRTY-SEVENTH CONGRESS OF THE SOUTH AFRICAN JEWISH BOARD OF DEPUTIES, CARLTON HOTEL,
JOHANNESBURG, SOUTH AFRICA, 21 AUGUST 1993

There are still some within our country who wrongly believe they can make a contribution to the cause of justice and peace by clinging to the shibboleths that have been proved to spell nothing but disaster. It remains our hope that these, too, will be blessed with sufficient reason to realise that history will not be denied and that the new society cannot be created by reproducing the repugnant past, however refined or enticingly repackaged.

NOBEL PEACE PRIZE AWARD CEREMONY, OSLO, NORWAY, 10 DECEMBER 1993

I think we will all agree that it is not the most pleasant thing to revive bitter memories, to invoke the pain and suffering of the past but, like the people of the Netherlands and others in Europe, we experienced the harsh realities of Nazism and Fascism. Like the people of the developing world who lived under the brutality of colonialism, we in South Africa know too well that we cannot move forward with confidence if we ignore the past.

OPENING OF THE ANNE FRANK MUSEUM AT MUSEUMAFRIKA, JOHANNESBURG, SOUTH AFRICA, 15 AUGUST 1994

There is a view that the past is best forgotten. Some criticise us when we say that whilst we can forgive, we can never forget. They do not agree that perpetrators of human rights violations should make full disclosure and acknowledge what they have done before they can be granted amnesty.

INTER-FAITH COMMISSIONING SERVICE FOR THE TRC (TRUTH AND RECONCILIATION COMMISSION),
ST GEORGE'S CATHEDRAL, CAPE TOWN, SOUTH AFRICA, 13 FEBRUARY 1996

Ordinary South Africans are determined that the past be known, the better to ensure that it is not repeated. They seek this, not out of vengeance, but so that we can move into the future together. The choice of our nation is not whether the past should be revealed, but rather to ensure that it comes to be known in a way which promotes reconciliation and peace.

IBID

There are monuments which stand as mute pointers to a fixed and ever-receding past. Devoid of life, they have little meaning outside the history books and the minds of learned people.

REDEDICATION OF THE 1820 SETTLERS MONUMENT, GRAHAMSTOWN, SOUTH AFRICA, 16 MAY 1996

As we seek to know the truth about our divided past, nothing is more painful than confronting the terrible hurts that we inflicted on each other during the last decades of apartheid rule.

FREEDOM DAY CELEBRATIONS, UPINGTON, SOUTH AFRICA, 27 APRIL 1997

We recall our terrible past so that we can deal with it, to forgive where forgiveness is necessary, without forgetting, to ensure that never again will such inhumanity tear us apart and to move ourselves to eradicate a legacy that lurks dangerously as a threat to our democracy.

SPECIAL DEBATE ON THE TRC (TRUTH AND RECONCILIATION COMMISSION) REPORT, PARLIAMENT, CAPE TOWN, SOUTH AFRICA, 25 FEBRUARY 1999

Let us not dwell too parochially on that past. Let it inspire us to make the intellectual and cultural contributions to the thinking and understanding of our common humanity that can make of the world a better place for all.

BANQUET CELEBRATING AFRICA'S 100 BEST BOOKS OF THE TWENTIETH CENTURY, CAPE TOWN, SOUTH AFRICA, JULY 2002

Let us never be unmindful of the terrible past from which we come – that memory not as a means to keep us shackled to the past in a negative manner, but rather as a joyous reminder of how far we have come and how much we have achieved.

JOINT SITTING OF PARLIAMENT TO MARK TEN YEARS OF DEMOCRACY, PARLIAMENT, CAPE TOWN, SOUTH AFRICA, 10 MAY 2004

We are pleased that the truth about the past is starting to come out.

FROM THE DOCUMENTARY *HEADLINERS AND LEGENDS: NELSON MANDELA*, 2006

Remember the horror from which we come; never forget the greatness of a nation that could overcome its divisions and bring itself to where it is; and let us never again descend into destructive decisiveness no matter what the considerations are.

UPON RECEIVING THE FREEDOM OF THE CITY OF TSHWANE, NELSON MANDELA FOUNDATION, JOHANNESBURG, SOUTH AFRICA, 13 MAY 2008

Peace

People throughout the world are coming to understand how closely the struggle for peace and against the menace of war is linked with the preservation of the right of the nation and the individual to a peaceful existence.

NATAL PEACE CONFERENCE, SOUTH AFRICA, 23 AUGUST 1953

It may well be that the days when nations will turn mighty armies into powerful peace movements, and deadly weapons into harmless ploughshares are still years away. But it is a source of real hope that there are today world organisations, governments, heads of state, influential groups and individuals who are striving earnestly and courageously for world peace.

FROM A LETTER TO LORD NICHOLAS BETHELL, WRITTEN IN POLLSMOOR PRISON, CAPE TOWN, SOUTH AFRICA, 4 JUNE 1986

We remain committed to peace and, if the government gives us the opportunity, if they normalise the situation, we are ready to make a positive contribution towards the peaceful settlement of the problems of this country.

FIRST PRESS CONFERENCE AFTER HIS RELEASE, ARCHBISHOP DESMOND TUTU'S RESIDENCE, BISHOPSCOURT, CAPE TOWN, SOUTH AFRICA, 12 FEBRUARY 1990

I have committed myself to the promotion of peace in the country but I have done so as part and parcel of the decisions and campaigns which have been taken and launched by the ANC.

IBID

We want to move away from the atmosphere of conflict. We would like that our established policy of settling problems through peaceful means should again be restored.

AT HOME, SOWETO, SOUTH AFRICA, 14 FEBRUARY 1990

Our own fate, born by a succession of generations that reach backwards into centuries, has been nothing but tension, conflict and death. In a sense we do not know the meaning of peace except in the imagination. But because we have not known true peace in its real meaning, because, for centuries, generations have had to bury the victims of state violence, we have fought for the right to experience peace.

ADDRESS TO THE JOINT SESSION OF THE HOUSE OF CONGRESS, WASHINGTON DC, USA, 26 JUNE 1990

There cannot be peace while our people lack basic social facilities, including basic health care. There cannot be peace, while the overwhelming number of doctors and medical facilities are concentrated in areas accessible only to a small section of the population.

GRADUATION CEREMONY, MEDICAL UNIVERSITY OF SOUTH AFRICA, SOUTH AFRICA, 23 MARCH 1991

Through peace you will be able to convert, you see, the most determined people, the most committed to the question of violence.

FROM A CONVERSATION WITH RICHARD STENGEL, 16 MARCH 1993

What was important was to make sure that the message of peace went down deeply in the thinking and approach of our people.

IBID

For it is not merely good logic but the reality of life that, in the end, society's freedom from hunger, ignorance and disease is more often than not the dividing line between war and peace.

UPON RECEIVING THE AFRICA PEACE AWARD, DURBAN, SOUTH AFRICA, 18 MARCH 1995

Soldiers of peace recognise that the world we live in is rising above the trappings of religious and racial hatred and conflict. They recognise that the spurning of agreements reached in good faith and the forceful occupation of land can only fan the flames of conflict.

INTERNATIONAL DAY OF SOLIDARITY WITH THE PALESTINIAN PEOPLE, PRETORIA, SOUTH AFRICA, 4 DECEMBER 1997

We live in a world and in times in which it is recognised that peace is the most powerful weapon any community or people has to bring about stability and progress through development.

UPON RECEIVING AN HONORARY DOCTORATE FROM THE UNIVERSITY OF KWAZULU-NATAL, KWAZULU-NATAL, SOUTH AFRICA, 30 MAY 1998

South Africa's concern with peace across the globe is not just a selfless one. It is in the deep interests of our country to ensure that the same principles of freedom and democracy that we hold to be true find resonance in other parts of the world.

UPON RECEIVING THE CHRIS HANI AWARD AT THE TENTH SACP (SOUTH AFRICAN COMMUNIST PARTY), NATIONAL CONGRESS, JOHANNESBURG, SOUTH AFRICA, 1 JULY 1998

Peace is the greatest weapon for development that any people can have.

ADDRESS TO THE NATIONAL EXECUTIVE COMMITTEE OF CHAMA CHA MAPINDUZI (RULING PARTY OF TANZANIA), DAR ES SALAAM, TANZANIA, 17 NOVEMBER 1998

The spilling of blood creates a climate that undermines the peace process.

FUNERAL OF PRINCE CYRIL MFUNAFUTHI ZULU, DURBAN, SOUTH AFRICA, 14 NOVEMBER 1999

There can be no greater cause in the world today than the quest for peace. Nothing is going to stop the peace process in this country.

JOHANNESBURG PRESS CLUB 'NEWSMAKER OF THE DECADE' GALA DINNER, JOHANNESBURG, SOUTH AFRICA, 31 OCTOBER 2001

We need to continue emphasising the fact of the overwhelming existence of such common decency and desire to live in peace with one another in the world. Ordinary women, men and children across the globe, irrespective of different backgrounds, histories or persuasions, merely desire for the opportunities to live lives of dignity.

IBID

Peace is not just the absence of conflict; peace is the creation of an environment where all can flourish regardless of race, colour, creed, religion, gender, class, caste or any other social markers of difference.

MESSAGE TO THE GLOBAL CONVENTION ON PEACE AND NON-VIOLENCE, NEW DELHI, INDIA, 31 JANUARY 2004

Development and peace are indivisible. Without peace and international security, nations cannot focus on the upliftment of the most underprivileged of their citizens.

IBID

Our strongest weapon which the enemy can never be able to resist is peace.

FROM A CONVERSATION WITH AHMED KATHRADA AND MAC MAHARAJ, JOHANNESBURG, SOUTH AFRICA, 27 JULY 2006

In a world riven by violence and strife, Gandhi's message of peace and non-violence holds the key to human survival in the twenty-first century. He rightly believed in the efficacy of pitting the soul force of the Satyagraha against the brute force of the oppressor and, in effect, converting the oppressor to the right and moral point of view.

VIDEO MESSAGE TO THE SATYAGRAHA CENTENARY CONFERENCE, NEW DELHI, INDIA, 29–30 JANUARY 2007

The most peaceful method of resolving issues is peace.

FROM THE DOCUMENTARY *MANDELA AT 90*, 2008

When I came out I stressed the question of reconciliation and peace which is important. I mean you gain nothing by conflict and tension. It is better to preach peace.

IBID

No serious political organisation will ever talk peace when an aggressive war is being waged against it.

CAPE TOWN, SOUTH AFRICA, DATE UNKNOWN

People

Since the dawn of history, mankind has honoured and respected brave and honest people.

FROM A LETTER TO WINNIE MANDELA, WRITTEN ON ROBBEN ISLAND, 23 JUNE 1969

In real life we deal, not with gods, but with ordinary humans like ourselves: men and women who are full of contradictions, who are stable and fickle, strong and weak, famous and infamous, people in whose bloodstream the muckworm battles daily with potent pesticides.

FROM A LETTER TO WINNIE MANDELA, WRITTEN ON ROBBEN ISLAND, 9 DECEMBER 1979

One benefits a great deal by meeting people from different walks of life and that conversations with people from such differing environments tend to widen one's general knowledge.

FROM A LETTER TO MAKAZIWE MANDELA, WRITTEN ON ROBBEN ISLAND, 31 JANUARY 1981

Few people are ever satisfied with watching from the sidelines, unable to help influence the course of events.

FROM A LETTER TO EFFIE SCHULTZ, WRITTEN IN POLLSMOOR PRISON, CAPE TOWN, SOUTH AFRICA, 1 APRIL 1987

You have to recognise that people are produced by the mud in the society in which you live and that therefore they are human beings. They have got good points, they have got weak points. Your duty is to work with human beings as human beings, not because you think they are angels.

FROM A CONVERSATION WITH RICHARD STENGEL, 29 APRIL 1993

All men, even the most seemingly cold-blooded, have a core of decency, and if their hearts are touched, they are capable of changing.

FROM *LONG WALK TO FREEDOM*, 1994

Our most valued treasure is our people, especially the youth. It is our human resources that enable us to reap the benefits of all our other assets.

LAUNCH OF THE NATIONAL CAMPAIGN FOR LEARNING AND TEACHING, SOWETO, JOHANNESBURG, SOUTH AFRICA, 20 FEBRUARY 1997

There is universal respect and even admiration for those who are humble and simple by nature, and who have absolute confidence in all human beings irrespective of their social status.

FROM THE UNPUBLISHED SEQUEL TO HIS AUTOBIOGRAPHY, CIRCA 1998

During my political career, I have discovered that in all communities, African, coloured, Indian and whites, and in all political organisations without exception, there are good men and women who fervently wish to go on with their lives, who yearn for peace and stability, who want a decent income, good houses and to send their children to the best schools, who respect and want to maintain the social fabric of society.

IBID

Our freedom can never be complete or our democracy stable unless the basic needs of our people are met.

UPON RECEIVING THE FREEDOM OF THE CITY OF DURBAN, DURBAN, SOUTH AFRICA, 16 APRIL 1999

It was the ordinary people, not kings and generals, it was the ordinary people, some of whom were not known in their own villages, who put an end to those tyrants – to those dictators.

ADDRESS TO THE PARLIAMENT OF THE WORLD'S RELIGIONS, CAPE TOWN, SOUTH AFRICA, DECEMBER 1999

People are human beings, produced by the society in which they live. You encourage people by seeing the good in them.

FROM AN INTERVIEW, DATE UNKNOWN

There are good men and women in any community and in all political parties or persuasions. It is when those men and women get together that the builders rather than the destroyers triumph. It is then that our common humanity is reaffirmed.

PEACE FESTIVAL, CENTRE JEUNES KAMENGE, BUJUMBURA, BURUNDI, DECEMBER 2000

Let us remind ourselves that it is ordinary people – men and women, boys and girls – that make the world a special place.

NMCF (NELSON MANDELA CHILDREN'S FUND) ANNUAL CHILDREN'S CELEBRATION AND THE SOUTHERN AFRICAN YOUTH IN PARLIAMENT FORUM, FRENCH SCHOOL LYCÉE FRANÇAIS JULES VERNE, JOHANNESBURG, SOUTH AFRICA, 9 JULY 2008

Perceptions

We always think that others have got horns before you actually meet them.

AFTER A VISIT WITH MRS BETSIE VERWOERD, ORANIA, SOUTH AFRICA, 15 AUGUST 1995

Persecution

It's been a valuable experience for me to watch powerful organisations and highly placed individuals clubbing together for the specific purpose of destroying a virtually widowed woman; how all these can stoop so low as to bring to my notice all sorts of details calculated to dim the clear image I have about the most wonderful friend I have in life completely baffles me.

FROM A LETTER TO WINNIE MANDELA, WRITTEN ON ROBBEN ISLAND, 19 AUGUST 1976

The question of my wife being harassed and persecuted by the police, and sometimes being assaulted, and I was not there to defend her. That was a very difficult moment for me.

FROM A CONVERSATION WITH RICHARD STENGEL, 9 MARCH 1993

Personal Development

To work hard and systematically in your studies throughout the year, will in the end bring you coveted prizes and much personal happiness.

FROM A LETTER TO MAKGATHO MANDELA, WRITTEN ON ROBBEN ISLAND, 28 JULY 1969

In judging our progress as individuals we tend to concentrate on external factors such as one's social position, influence and popularity, wealth and standard of education. These are, of course, important in measuring one's success in material matters and it is perfectly understandable if many people exert themselves mainly to achieve all these. But internal factors may be even more crucial in assessing our development as a human being. Honesty, sincerity, simplicity, humility, pure generosity, absence of vanity, readiness to serve others – qualities which are within easy reach of every soul – are the foundation of one's spiritual life.

FROM A LETTER TO WINNIE MANDELA, WRITTEN ON ROBBEN ISLAND, 1 FEBRUARY 1975

The important thing to remember is that no single person can do everything.

FATHER'S DAY LUNCH HOSTED BY ZINDZI MANDELA, HYATT WOMEN OF VISION CLUB, JOHANNESBURG, SOUTH AFRICA, 1 JUNE 2001

Personal Responsibility

We can neither heal nor build if, on the one hand, the rich in our society see the poor as hordes of irritants or if, on the other hand, the poor sit back, expecting charity. All of us must take responsibility for the upliftment of our conditions, prepared to give our best to the benefit of all.

STATE OF THE NATION ADDRESS, PARLIAMENT, CAPE TOWN, SOUTH AFRICA, 9 FEBRUARY 1995

It behoves all South Africans, themselves erstwhile beneficiaries of generous international support, to stand up and be counted among those contributing actively to the cause of freedom and justice.

ADDRESS AT THE INTERNATIONAL DAY OF SOLIDARITY WITH THE PALESTINIAN PEOPLE, PRETORIA, SOUTH AFRICA, 4 DECEMBER 1997

All of us should ask ourselves the question: have I done everything in my power to bring about lasting peace and prosperity in my city and my country?

UPON RECEIVING THE FREEDOM OF DURBAN, SOUTH AFRICA, 16 APRIL 1999

Planning

Significant progress is always possible if we ourselves try to plan every detail of our lives and actions and allow the intervention of fate only on our own terms.

FROM A LETTER TO THOROBETSANE TSHUKUDU (ADELAIDE TAMBO), WRITTEN ON ROBBEN ISLAND, 1 JANUARY 1977

Preparing a master plan and applying it are two different things.

FROM AN ESSAY ENTITLED 'WHITHER THE BLACK CONSCIOUSNESS MOVEMENT', WRITTEN ON ROBBEN ISLAND, 1978

The advantage of organisation and sound planning in family affairs, in the factories and on social and other spheres is that institutions and organisations can work well through teamwork, even though individuals in those institutions may come and go.

FROM A LETTER TO MATLALA A TSHUKUDU (ADELAIDE TAMBO), WRITTEN ON ROBBEN ISLAND, 9 NOVEMBER 1980

Pleasure

Delayed enjoyment can be immensely sweet.

FROM A LETTER TO FRIEDA MATTHEWS, WRITTEN IN POLLSMOOR PRISON, CAPE TOWN, SOUTH AFRICA, 10 MARCH 1986

Political Prisoners

The only way to avert disaster is not to keep innocent men in jail but to abandon your provocative actions and to pursue sane and enlightened policies.

FROM A LETTER TO THE MINISTER OF JUSTICE, WRITTEN ON ROBBEN ISLAND, 22 APRIL 1969

We have sat in prison with great African patriots and noble examples of the human race who faced torture and did not flinch, who met the hangman's noose with songs of freedom, who accepted their cells as but a school out of which they would emerge with their convictions, their determination and willingness to sacrifice immeasurably strengthened.

ADDRESS TO THE PARLIAMENT OF CANADA, OTTAWA, CANADA, 18 JUNE 1990

The government wanted to restrict the *meaning* of a political prisoner as somebody who had left the country without documents, you know, they tried to restrict it so that only a *few* people should qualify. But we said, 'Any person whose offence was politically motivated, it may be any kind of offence, it may be sedition, it may be treason, it may be theft, it may be assault, as long as it was politically motivated.'

FROM A CONVERSATION WITH RICHARD STENGEL, 22 APRIL 1993

I had to go and persuade them that, 'Look, come out, we want you outside, want you to come and help us. There is no point in you remaining in jail when you can be free.'

FROM A CONVERSATION WITH RICHARD STENGEL ABOUT PRISONERS WHO WANTED TO COME OUT OF JAIL ONLY AS THE RESULT OF A 'BATTLEFIELD' VICTORY, 23 APRIL 1993

Politics

Those who are in the centre of political struggle, who have to deal with practical and pressing problems, are afforded little time for reflection and no precedents to guide them and are bound to slip up many times.

FROM AN UNPUBLISHED AUTOBIOGRAPHICAL MANUSCRIPT, WRITTEN ON ROBBEN ISLAND, 1975

I was backward politically and I was dealing with chaps, you see, who knew politics, who could discuss what was happening in South Africa and outside South Africa.

FROM A CONVERSATION WITH RICHARD STENGEL ABOUT HIS INITIAL NERVOUSNESS AT PARTICIPATING IN POLITICAL MEETINGS IN THE 1940s, 16 MARCH 1993

Success in politics demands that you must take your people into confidence about your views and state them very clearly, very politely, very calmly, but nevertheless state them openly.

FROM A CONVERSATION WITH RICHARD STENGEL, 29 APRIL 1993

When I came to varsity, to school, especially high school, then I came… to be aware that there was something like a political organisation and a political struggle.

FROM A CONVERSATION WITH RICHARD STENGEL, 3 MAY 1993

A philosopher once noted that something is odd if a person is not liberal when he is young and conservative when he is old.

FROM *LONG WALK TO FREEDOM*, 1994

Polygamy

Polygamy is part of the history of our people, especially the Ngunis, where one man takes a number of wives, especially members of the Royal Family.

FROM A CONVERSATION WITH RICHARD STENGEL, 10 MARCH 1993

The Chief would then marry as many wives as he could afford. Each wife would have her own separate kraal, and sometimes they would be separated by twenty miles, as my family, for example.

IBID

My father was a polygamist with four wives, nine children. I grew up in that atmosphere where we played together, fought against one another but ate from one dish.

FROM THE DOCUMENTARY *MANDELA*, 1996

Poverty

There are two ways to break out of poverty. The first is by formal education, and the second is by the worker acquiring greater skill at his work and thus higher wages. As far as Africans are concerned, both these avenues of advancement are deliberately curtailed by legislation.

SPEECH FROM THE DOCK, RIVONIA TRIAL, PALACE OF JUSTICE, PRETORIA, SOUTH AFRICA, 20 APRIL 1964

In that first year in Johannesburg I learnt more about poverty than I did during my childhood days at Qunu.

FROM AN UNPUBLISHED AUTOBIOGRAPHICAL MANUSCRIPT, WRITTEN ON ROBBEN ISLAND, 1975

Open the cooking pots and ask the men why there is so little food inside. When the rains come into your homes, place the hands of your men in the pools on the floor, and ask them, why? There is only one answer, and that answer is our common deprivation.

RALLY, KINGS PARK STADIUM, DURBAN, SOUTH AFRICA, 25 FEBRUARY 1990

We must also make the point very firmly that the political settlement, and democracy itself, cannot survive unless the material needs of the people, the bread and butter issues, are addressed as part of the process of change and as a matter of urgency. It should never be that the anger of the poor should be the finger of accusation pointed at all of us because we failed to respond to the cries of the people for food, for shelter, for the dignity of the individual.

ADDRESS TO THE JOINT SESSION OF THE HOUSE OF CONGRESS, WASHINGTON DC, USA, 26 JUNE 1990

To be poor is a terrible thing.

FROM A CONVERSATION WITH AHMED KATHRADA, CIRCA 1993/94

We now undertake that we cannot rest while millions of our people suffer the pain and indignity of poverty in all its forms.

ADDRESS TO THE FORTY-NINTH UNITED NATIONS GENERAL ASSEMBLY, NEW YORK CITY, USA, 3 OCTOBER 1994

Without socio-economic changes to improve the living conditions of especially the poor, our newly achieved democracy will be hollow.

DINNER OF THE FEDERATION OF INDIAN CHAMBERS OF COMMERCE, CONFEDERATION OF INDIAN INDUSTRIES AND JOINT BUSINESS COUNCILS, DELHI, INDIA, 26 JANUARY 1995

What challenges us, who define ourselves as states-persons, is the clarion call to dare to think that what we are about is people – the proverbial man and woman in the street. These, the poor, the hungry, the victims of petty tyrants, the objectives of policy, demand change.

SPECIAL COMMEMORATIVE MEETING OF THE UNITED NATIONS GENERAL ASSEMBLY ON THE FIFTIETH ANNIVERSARY OF THE UNITED NATIONS, NEW YORK CITY, USA, 23 OCTOBER 1995

As long as many of our people still live in utter poverty, as long as children still live under plastic covers, as long as many of our people are still without jobs, no South African should rest and wallow in the joy of freedom.

THANKSGIVING SERVICE UPON ARCHBISHOP DESMOND TUTU'S RETIREMENT, ST GEORGE'S CATHEDRAL, CAPE TOWN, SOUTH AFRICA, 23 JUNE 1996

We should not allow South African politics to be relegated to trivialities chosen precisely because they salve the consciences of the rich and powerful, and conceal the plight of the poor and powerless.

SEVENTY-FIFTH ANNIVERSARY OF THE SACP (SOUTH AFRICAN COMMUNIST PARTY), CAPE TOWN, SOUTH AFRICA, 28 JULY 1996

The children who sleep in the streets, reduced to begging to make a living, are testimony to an unfinished job. The families who live in shacks with no running water, sanitation and electricity are a reminder that the past continues to haunt the present.

IBID

As the world frees itself from the dominance of bipolar power the stark division of the world's people into rich and poor comes all the more clearly into view. And within that division Sub-Saharan Africa occupies the most extreme position.

LECTURE AT THE OXFORD CENTRE FOR ISLAMIC STUDIES, SHELDONIAN THEATRE, OXFORD, ENGLAND, 11 JULY 1997

Will future generations say of us: 'Indeed, they did lay the foundations for the eradication of world poverty; they succeeded in establishing a new world order based on mutual respect, partnership and equity'?

IBID

Poverty and material inequality are enemies of lasting peace and stability.

CLOSING SESSION OF THE FIFTIETH ANC NATIONAL CONFERENCE, NORTH-WEST UNIVERSITY, MAFIKENG CAMPUS, SOUTH AFRICA, 20 DECEMBER 1997

We are proud of the achievements we have made. But the poverty that continues to stalk millions, the problems of education, housing, health, landlessness and lack of jobs that continue to afflict the majority of our citizens – all these are reminders that the mission of meaningful freedom, democracy and human rights is yet to be fulfilled.

ADDRESS AT THE CLOSING OF THE PRESIDENT'S BUDGET DEBATE, PARLIAMENT, CAPE TOWN, SOUTH AFRICA, 22 APRIL 1998

Our freedom and our rights will only gain their full meaning as we succeed together in overcoming the divisions and inequalities of our past and in improving the lives of especially the poor.

FREEDOM DAY CELEBRATIONS, CAPE TOWN, SOUTH AFRICA, 27 APRIL 1998

The needs of the poor and the previously disadvantaged are great.

UPON RECEIVING AN HONORARY DOCTORATE FROM THE UNIVERSITY OF ZULULAND, SOUTH AFRICA, 30 MAY 1998

The very right to be human is denied every day to hundreds of millions of people as a result of poverty, the unavailability of basic necessities such as food, jobs, water and shelter, education, health care and a healthy environment.

ADDRESS TO THE FIFTY-THIRD UNITED NATIONS GENERAL ASSEMBLY, NEW YORK CITY, USA, 21 SEPTEMBER 1998

Put starkly, we have a situation in which the further accumulation of wealth, rather than contributing to the improvement of the quality of life of all humanity, is generating poverty at a frighteningly accelerated pace.

IBID

We must continue, with still greater speed, to change the lives of our people, especially the poorest of the poor, by eradicating what remains of apartheid and its legacy.

ADDRESS TO THE JOINT SESSION OF THE PARLIAMENT OF PAKISTAN, ISLAMABAD, PAKISTAN, 4 MAY 1999

We must ensure that globalisation benefits not only the powerful but also the men, women and children whose lives are ravaged by poverty.

SPEAKING AT THE UNIVERSITY OF BEIJING, BEIJING, CHINA, 6 MAY 1999

If we are to build a democracy worthy of the name, then we shall have to ensure that it brings real material improvements in the lives of the majority of South Africans whose poverty is the legacy of their oppression.

IBID

We need not be ashamed in admitting that poverty is still with us. It is not enough to say that we have inherited it. It is more important to take steps as a matter of the utmost urgency to put an end to it. We do not need careerists or opportunists in the various levels of government.

ANC GENERAL COUNCIL MEETING, PORT ELIZABETH, SOUTH AFRICA, 12 JULY 2000

Abject poverty is demeaning, is an assault on the dignity of those that suffer it. In the end it demeans us all. It makes the freedom of all of us less meaningful.

UPON RECEIVING THE FREEDOM AWARD FROM THE NATIONAL CIVIL RIGHTS MUSEUM, MEMPHIS, TENNESSEE, USA, 22 NOVEMBER 2000

A secure future for humanity depends as much as anything else on the rapid narrowing of the gap between the rich and the poor within single nations and amongst nations.

TWENTY-SIXTH INTERNATIONAL CONFERENCE ON IMPROVING UNIVERSITY TEACHING, UNIVERSITY OF JOHANNESBURG, JOHANNESBURG, SOUTH AFRICA, JULY 2001

We have a long way to go in our country before we can proclaim that we have achieved our objectives. Poverty and its attendant phenomena of suffering and deprivation are still too much with us before we can claim victories over the legacies of oppression and discrimination.

RECEPTION DINNER, AIG (AMERICAN INTERNATIONAL GROUP, INC.) BOARD MEETING, TUNIS, TUNISIA, 24 MARCH 2004

Too many people in our country are still suffering the hardships and deprivations of poverty. One of the root causes of that poverty is the absence of jobs; nothing can be more of an assault on a person's dignity than the inability to find work and gainful employment.

VIDEO MESSAGE TO MARK TEN YEARS OF DEMOCRACY IN SOUTH AFRICA, APRIL 2004

Like slavery and apartheid, poverty is not natural. It is man-made and it can be overcome and eradicated by the actions of human beings.

LAUNCH OF THE 'MAKE POVERTY HISTORY' CAMPAIGN, TRAFALGAR SQUARE, LONDON, ENGLAND, 3 FEBRUARY 2005

In this new century, millions of people in the world's poorest countries remain imprisoned, enslaved and in chains. They are trapped in the prison of poverty. It is time to set them free.

IBID

Where poverty exists, there is not true freedom.

IBID

As long as poverty, injustice and gross inequality persist in our world, none of us can truly rest.

IBID

Massive poverty and obscene inequality are such terrible scourges of our time – times in which the world boasts breathtaking advances in science and technology, industry and wealth accumulation – that they have to rank alongside slavery and apartheid as social ills.

IBID

As long as abject poverty persists globally as a manifestation of gross inequality, the struggle that I and my comrades and compatriots and all our international solidarity partners conducted is not over.

G7 FINANCE MINISTERS MEETING, GLENEAGLES, SCOTLAND, 4 FEBRUARY 2005

Overcoming poverty is not a gesture of charity. It is an act of justice. It is the protection of a fundamental human right, the right to dignity and a decent life.

LIVE 8 CONCERT, MARY FITZGERALD SQUARE, JOHANNESBURG, SOUTH AFRICA, 2 JULY 2005

Poverty and deprivation in our midst demean all of us. Let us mobilise in one great cooperative national effort the enormous energy of our society in order to overcome and eliminate poverty.

ANC RALLY FOR HIS NINETIETH BIRTHDAY, LOFTUS VERSFELD STADIUM, PRETORIA, SOUTH AFRICA, 2 AUGUST 2008

Today we are challenged to end poverty and its attendant suffering.

IBID

There is little to be said in favour of poverty, but it was often an incubator of true friendship. Many people will appear to befriend you when you are wealthy, but precious few will do the same when you are poor. If wealth is a magnet, poverty is a kind of repellent. Yet poverty often brings out the true generosity in others.

SOURCE UNKNOWN

Practicality

Whilst political consciousness is vital in the formation of an army and in mobilising mass support, practical matters must not be lost sight of.

FROM A NOTEBOOK, 1962

President

I, Nelson Rolihlahla Mandela, do hereby swear to devote myself to the well-being of the Republic of South Africa and all its people.

OATH OF OFFICE, INAUGURATION AS PRESIDENT OF SOUTH AFRICA, UNION BUILDINGS, PRETORIA, SOUTH AFRICA, 10 MAY 1994

I am committed to ensuring that the president of a country like ours must not live in a style which is totally different from that of the masses of the people who put him in power.

FROM AN INTERVIEW WITH TOM COHEN AND SAHM VENTER FOR THE ASSOCIATED PRESS, TUYNHUYS, CAPE TOWN, SOUTH AFRICA, 22 SEPTEMBER 1994

My installation as the first democratically elected president of the Republic of South Africa was imposed on me much against my advice.

FROM THE UNPUBLISHED SEQUEL TO HIS AUTOBIOGRAPHY, CIRCA 1998

Now the former terrorist had the task of uniting South Africa, of implementing the core principle of the Freedom Charter which declares that South Africa belongs to all its people, black and white.

IBID

I urged three senior leaders that I would prefer to serve without holding any position in the organisation or government.

IBID

Shortly after I became president I publicly announced that I would serve one term only and would not seek re-election.

IBID

Next time, at the end of the next five years, when I challenge for the presidency, I will make sure that I select people who will make it possible for me to be a president for life.

MAKING A JOKE AT HIS FAREWELL BANQUET HOSTED BY PRESIDENT THABO MBEKI, PRETORIA, SOUTH AFRICA, 16 JUNE 1999

Pride

Often in normal life, when happy and free, we build for ourselves ivory towers into which we retreat and within which we swell with pride and conceit and treat with indifference and even contempt the generosity and affection of friends.

FROM A LETTER TO SEFTON VUTELA, WRITTEN ON ROBBEN ISLAND, 28 JULY 1969

No proud people will ever obey orders from those who have humiliated and dishonoured them for so long.

CAPE TOWN, SOUTH AFRICA, DATE UNKNOWN

Prison

I can't remember losing my sense of control; after all, in that situation you can only survive if you keep calm and cool.

AT HOME, SOWETO, SOUTH AFRICA, 14 FEBRUARY 1990

You have to start from the bottom in a new prison because they are told, 'These are political prisoners, you must treat them nicely', but to do so, their conception of how to treat a black prisoner nicely, it's very different from what our conception of nice treatment is.

FROM A CONVERSATION WITH RICHARD STENGEL, 30 DECEMBER 1992

Prison: Comrades

I was with brave colleagues; they appeared to be braver than myself. I would like to put that on record.

FROM A CONVERSATION WITH AHMED KATHRADA, CIRCA 1993/94

In prison we were thrown together and we fought daily against prison policy, and therefore interaction became the order of the day, as against what used to happen outside where we hardly ever met.

FROM A CONVERSATION WITH RICHARD STENGEL, 9 MARCH 1993

It was difficult to concentrate on the negative aspect of your life. The important thing is that I was in the company of men of great experience and great talent.

REVISITING ROBBEN ISLAND, CAPE TOWN, SOUTH AFRICA, 11 FEBRUARY 1994

Of course we had very lovely moments. I was in the company of great comrades both inside the ANC and outside... When you sat down with them to have discussions, you felt you were a new man.

IBID

My comrades in prison were men of honesty and principle.

FROM THE UNPUBLISHED SEQUEL TO HIS AUTOBIOGRAPHY, CIRCA 1998

Prison: Conditions

Every winter season has become a nightmare to us and we hope that we might not have to endure another spell of winter with the present outfit which does not afford us any protection against the cold.

FROM A MEMORANDUM TO HELEN SUZMAN, WRITTEN ON ROBBEN ISLAND, 23 FEBRUARY 1967

No pillows are provided and we are forced to use other articles such as the jacket and pair of trousers as a pillow. Our blankets were issued in 1964 (with the exception naturally of those who arrived later) and we have not been issued new ones ever since.

IBID

Right from the beginning we decided that we would seek to improve prison conditions by discussing our problems directly with the authorities.

IBID

I am a prisoner serving a sentence of life imprisonment and there is not the slightest danger that I might in the meantime continue to practise as an attorney.

FROM A LETTER TO THE STATE ATTORNEY MR JH DU TOIT, WRITTEN ON ROBBEN ISLAND, 6 DECEMBER 1967

Many people who ponder on the problems of the average prisoner tend to concentrate more on the lengthy sentences still to be served, the hard labour to which we are condemned, the coarse and tasteless menus, the grim and tedious boredom that stalks every prisoner and the frightful frustrations of a life in which human beings move in complete circles, landing today exactly at the point where you started the day before. But some of us have had experiences much more painful than these, because these experiences eat too deeply into one's being, into one's soul.

FROM A LETTER TO IRENE NOLUSAPHO MKWAYI, WRITTEN ON ROBBEN ISLAND, 19 NOVEMBER 1969

I am not in a position to identify any single factor which I can say impressed me, but firstly there *was* the policy of the government which was ruthless and very brutal and you have to go to jail to discover what the real policy of a government is.

FROM A CONVERSATION WITH RICHARD STENGEL, 29 APRIL 1992

They are very small, no windows, very unhealthy.

FROM A CONVERSATION WITH RICHARD STENGEL DESCRIBING HIS CELL ON ROBBEN ISLAND IN 1964, 3 DECEMBER 1992

It was June and it was very cold. And our clothing was a short pair of trousers and a khaki shirt and a cotton jacket. And then open-toe sandals. And our work was to crush stones. And we were outside and it was very cold, without any protection. Very cold. So cold that you felt it in your bones.

IBID

There were bright moments where some warders would treat you, you know, as human beings.

FROM A CONVERSATION WITH RICHARD STENGEL, 4 DECEMBER 1992

I cleaned my bucket every day and I had no problem, you see, in cleaning the bucket of another.

FROM A CONVERSATION WITH RICHARD STENGEL, 14 DECEMBER 1992

It is impossible for people to endure torture under the conditions where they were *completely* cut off from the outside, where they had no opportunity of appealing to anybody.

FROM A CONVERSATION WITH RICHARD STENGEL, 21 DECEMBER 1992

We were not allowed to read newspapers and I remember very well how successful we were in smuggling newspapers.

REVISITING ROBBEN ISLAND, CAPE TOWN, SOUTH AFRICA, 11 FEBRUARY 1994

It was hard at first because our hands were not used to work and some of us developed blisters.

IBID

The cell was small but we appreciated the privacy.

FROM THE DOCUMENTARY *LEGENDS: NELSON MANDELA*, 2005

Prison: Dreams

My dream life became very rich, and I seemed to pass entire nights reliving the high and low times of the old days.

FROM *LONG WALK TO FREEDOM*, 1994

One of the dreams I constantly had in prison was me going home and getting out in the middle of the city and having to walk from town to Soweto and reaching home, finding that the house was open, that there was nobody at home and being concerned as to what had happened to Winnie and the children.

FROM A BBC (UK) DOCUMENTARY, 1996

Prison: Endurance

It has been said a thousand and one times that what matters is not so much what happens to a person than the way such person takes it.

FROM A LETTER TO TIM MAHARAJ, WRITTEN ON ROBBEN ISLAND, 1 FEBRUARY 1971

I'm beginning to feel that no metal, not even gold or diamond, is free from the corroding effects of rust.

FROM A LETTER TO THOROBETSANE TSHUKUDU (ADELAIDE TAMBO), WRITTEN ON ROBBEN ISLAND, 1 JANUARY 1977

If we continue to enjoy good health, and if our spirits remain high, it has not necessarily been due to any special consideration or care taken by the Department of Prisons.

FROM A LETTER TO PRESIDENT PW BOTHA, WRITTEN IN POLLSMOOR PRISON, CAPE TOWN, SOUTH AFRICA, 13 FEBRUARY 1985

We saw that no prison walls or guard dogs or even the cold seas that are like a deadly moat surrounding Robben Island prison, could ever succeed to frustrate the desires of all humanity. We drew strength and sustenance from the knowledge that we were part of a greater humanity than our jailers could claim.

ADDRESS AT THE CATHEDRAL OF UPPSALA, UPPSALA, SWEDEN, 13 MARCH 1990

Prison – far from breaking our spirits – made us more determined to continue with this battle until victory was won.

FROM A CONVERSATION WITH RICHARD STENGEL, 10 MARCH 1993

Prison is itself a tremendous education in the need for patience and perseverance. It is, above all, a test of one's commitment. Those who passed through that school have all acquired a firmness, tempered by a remarkable resilience.

REVISITING ROBBEN ISLAND, CAPE TOWN, SOUTH AFRICA, 11 FEBRUARY 1994

Prison and the authorities conspire to rob each man of his dignity. In and of itself, that assured that I would survive, for any man or institution that tries to rob me of my dignity will lose because I will not part with it at any price or under any pressure.

FROM *LONG WALK TO FREEDOM*, 1994

Prison was a kind of crucible that tested a man's character. Some men, under the pressure of incarceration, showed true mettle, while others revealed themselves as less than what they had appeared to be.

IBID

I believe the way in which you will be treated by the prison authorities depends on your demeanour and you must fight that battle and win it on the very first day.

FROM A BBC (UK) DOCUMENTARY, 1996

If you obey them in carrying out humiliating things that will remain with you throughout your stay in prison, it is better to take a stand right from the beginning.

FROM THE DOCUMENTARY MANDELA: THE LIVING LEGEND, 2003

We didn't compromise at all, we challenged them throughout.

FROM AN INTERVIEW WITH VERNE HARRIS ABOUT CHALLENGING THE PRISON AUTHORITIES, JOHANNESBURG, SOUTH AFRICA, 2005

Prison: Escape

As a prisoner, I would take any opportunity to escape, but when dealing with a particular individual whom you respected, you would not like to put [them] into trouble.

FROM A CONVERSATION WITH AHMED KATHRADA TALKING ABOUT WHY HE DIDN'T TAKE OPPORTUNITIES TO ESCAPE IF IT MEANT A PRISON WARDER HE RESPECTED WOULD HAVE BEEN PUNISHED FOR HIS ACTIONS, CIRCA 1993/94

I never contemplated escaping, especially when people are kind to you. I would always look for an opportunity where I could do it alone without taking advantage of the trust which people put in me. It never occurred to me to run away.

IBID

Unlikely a prospect as it might have seemed, I nevertheless thought about escape the entire time I was on the island.

FROM LONG WALK TO FREEDOM, 1994

Prison: Hard Labour

When we arrived, they asked us to crush stones to make gravel. They bring big stones, they had one on the ground and then you have a hammer and you break the stones on this big stone.

FROM A CONVERSATION WITH RICHARD STENGEL, 5 DECEMBER 1993

Prison: Loneliness

My main problem since I left home is my sleeping without you next to me and my waking up without you close to me, the passing of the day without my having seen you and with that audible voice of yours. The letters I write to you and those you write to me are an ointment to the wounds of our separation.

FROM A LETTER TO WINNIE MANDELA, WRITTEN ON ROBBEN ISLAND, 26 OCTOBER 1976

A reprimand is always a disarming affair, even when one is surrounded by lifelong friends and plenty of comfort. But in the loneliness of a prison cell a rebuke from a loved couple can be as painful as a dart going through the heart.

FROM A LETTER TO AMINA CACHALIA, WRITTEN IN POLLSMOOR PRISON, CAPE TOWN, SOUTH AFRICA, 1 MARCH 1988

To be alone in prison is a difficulty. You must never try it.

FROM A CONVERSATION WITH RICHARD STENGEL, 6 APRIL 1993

Although I am a gregarious person, I love solitude even more. I welcome the opportunity to be by myself, to plan, to think, to plot. But one can have too much solitude. I was terribly lonesome for my wife and my family.

REVISITING ROBBEN ISLAND, CAPE TOWN, SOUTH AFRICA, 11 FEBRUARY 1994

Prison: Mistreatment

It is our considered opinion that our treatment in this prison is in any respects not compatible with the spirit and provisions of the Prisons Act and the prisons regulations.

FROM A MEMORANDUM TO HELEN SUZMAN, WRITTEN ON ROBBEN ISLAND, 23 FEBRUARY 1967

We consider it to be a violation of the fundamental principles of justice and fairness and incompatible with the Christian spirit for the Prisons Department to discriminate on grounds of race in fixing the diet scales of its prison population.

IBID

Victimisation of prisoners for one reason or another is a daily affair in the prison.

IBID

I hate being moved from one prison to another. It involves much inconvenience and degrading treatment.

FROM AN UNPUBLISHED AUTOBIOGRAPHICAL MANUSCRIPT, WRITTEN ON ROBBEN ISLAND, 1975

The inhumanity of the average South African warder still remains; only it has been diverted into other channels and has taken the subtle form of psychological persecution, a field in which some of your local officials are striving to become specialists.

FROM A LETTER TO GENERAL DU PREEZ, COMMISSIONER OF PRISONS, WRITTEN ON ROBBEN ISLAND, 12 JULY 1976

In this country only white prisoners have the right to sleep in pyjamas with the exception of those fellow prisoners who are hospitalised locally and who are provided with a nightshirt which in many cases barely reaches one's knees. Black prisoners here sleep naked with only blankets as a cover.

IBID

My experience during the last fifteen years of my imprisonment has taught me that, when dealing with prisoners, the average prison officer does not at all consider it improper to transgress the law, to plot secretly and to brush aside the moral code.

FROM A LETTER TO THE HEAD OF ROBBEN ISLAND PRISON, 18 SEPTEMBER 1977

Indeed it is common knowledge that in the course of our long imprisonment, especially during the first years, the prison authorities had implemented a deliberate policy of doing everything to break our morale. We were subject to harsh, if not brutal, treatment, and permanent physical and spiritual harm was caused to many prisoners.

FROM A LETTER TO PRESIDENT PW BOTHA, WRITTEN IN POLLSMOOR PRISON, CAPE TOWN, SOUTH AFRICA, 13 FEBRUARY 1985

We had very harsh experiences; we got used to them and, in later years, speaking about myself and the colleagues who were convicted with me in the Rivonia Trial, things improved to such an extent that we forget about those harsh experiences.

AT HOME, SOWETO, SOUTH AFRICA, 14 FEBRUARY 1990

We went through very harsh experiences at the beginning of our life imprisonment. I was never brutally assaulted, but many of my colleagues around me were.

FROM AN INTERVIEW WITH SCOTT MACLEOD OF *TIME* MAGAZINE, SOWETO, SOUTH AFRICA, 26 FEBRUARY 1990

They wanted to show us that to come to jail is not an easy thing, it's not a picnic and you must never come to jail again. They wanted to break our spirits.

FROM A CONVERSATION WITH RICHARD STENGEL, 3 DECEMBER 1992

We were concerned, not with fighting individual warders, however bad a warder was, we were concerned with fighting the *policy* of the Prisons Department.

FROM A CONVERSATION WITH RICHARD STENGEL, 29 DECEMBER 1992

Well, you don't want to be assaulted, you don't want to be hurt, and you feel the pain and humiliation. But nevertheless you reckon that these are the type of things, this is the price you have to pay in order to assert your views, your ideas.

FROM A CONVERSATION WITH RICHARD STENGEL, 9 MARCH 1993

A nation should not be judged by how it treats its highest citizens, but its lowest ones... and South Africa treated its imprisoned African citizens like animals.

FROM *LONG WALK TO FREEDOM*, 1994

The meanness of the prison officials was staggering but we were not surprised.

FROM THE DOCUMENTARY *MANDELA: THE LIVING LEGEND*, 2003

Prison: Outlook

Throughout my imprisonment my heart and soul have always been somewhere far beyond this place, in the veld and the bushes.

FROM A LETTER TO SENATOR DOUGLAS LUKHELE, WRITTEN ON ROBBEN ISLAND, 1 AUGUST 1970

It is only my flesh and bones that are shut up behind these tight walls. Otherwise I remain cosmopolitan in my outlook; in my thoughts I am as free as a falcon.

IBID

Even behind prison walls I can see the heavy clouds and the blue sky over the horizon.

FROM AN UNPUBLISHED AUTOBIOGRAPHICAL MANUSCRIPT, WRITTEN ON ROBBEN ISLAND, 1975

I knew from the very first day of our incarceration that in the end it would prove impossible for the apartheid system to keep us in its dungeons.

ADDRESS TO THE INTERNATIONAL LABOUR CONFERENCE, GENEVA, SWITZERLAND, 8 JUNE 1990

To survive in prison, one must develop ways to take satisfaction in one's daily life. One can feel fulfilled by washing one's clothes so that they are particularly clean, by sweeping a corridor so that it is free of dust, by organising one's cell to conserve as much space as possible. The same pride one takes in more consequential tasks outside prison one can find in doing small things inside prison.

FROM *LONG WALK TO FREEDOM*, 1994

I felt like a curious tourist in a strange and remarkable land.

IBID

Prison: Pollsmoor Prison

To be moved to another place was really upsetting, but we soon got used to it.

FROM A CONVERSATION WITH RICHARD STENGEL, 29 DECEMBER 1992

Prison: Reflections

The cell is an ideal place to learn to know yourself, to search realistically and regularly the process of your own mind and feelings.

FROM A LETTER TO WINNIE MANDELA, THEN IN KROONSTAD PRISON, SOUTH AFRICA, WRITTEN ON ROBBEN ISLAND, 1 FEBRUARY 1975

Prison, especially for those who stay in single cells, provides many moments to reflect on problems too numerous to be listed down on paper.

FROM A LETTER TO ZINDZI MANDELA, WRITTEN ON ROBBEN ISLAND, 1 MARCH 1981

To spend twenty-seven years in prison, you see, you lose a lot, but at the same time although prison is not a place for any human being, one was able to reflect, to think, and this has been rewarding.

AT HOME, SOWETO, SOUTH AFRICA, 14 FEBRUARY 1990

I had had in prison the opportunity to stand at a distance and I was able to look at myself from a distance, as well as my organisation, and to reflect very calmly on these mistakes and weaknesses – mistakes made and weaknesses which were shown in the course of our political work.

FROM A CONVERSATION WITH RICHARD STENGEL, 10 MARCH 1993

As far as I am concerned, I have come back with the same views I had before I went to jail, and with the same enthusiasm for my political work and for serving our people.

IBID

I don't think I was fundamentally different from what I was before I went to jail, except that in jail I had a lot of time to think about problems and to see the mistakes that we had committed. I came out mature.

FROM A CONVERSATION WITH RICHARD STENGEL, CIRCA MARCH 1993

I went for a long holiday for twenty-seven years and it was a time to stand away from myself, and from ourselves and to look at our work. Although it was a tragic experience, it was also very helpful because we were able quietly to reassess our work, the mistakes that we had made, the achievements and we came out better prepared to carry on our work and to face new challenges.

REVISITING THE SITE OF HIS 5 AUGUST 1962 ARREST, HOWICK, SOUTH AFRICA, 15 NOVEMBER 1993

Prison provided the time – much more than enough time – to reflect on what one had done and not done.

FROM *LONG WALK TO FREEDOM*, 1994

In prison, one has time to review the past, and memory becomes both a friend and a foe. My memory transported me into moments of both great joy and sadness.

IBID

One had very shattering experiences but the dominating thing is also the positive things that occurred here. One of these was the ability to think about problems; that's the one thing we don't have now that we are locked up in struggle.
IBID

Of the aspects of prison life I appreciated, in spite of the tragedy of being imprisoned, especially for a long term of years, in prison for many years, is the fact that one got the opportunity to sit down and think.
CLOSING ADDRESS TO THE FORTY-NINTH ANC NATIONAL CONFERENCE, BLOEMFONTEIN, SOUTH AFRICA, 22 DECEMBER 1994

Never, never again shall South Africa imprison its citizens simply because they disagree with the government of the day.
ROBBEN ISLAND REUNION CONFERENCE, UNIVERSITY OF THE WESTERN CAPE, BELLVILLE, SOUTH AFRICA, 12 FEBRUARY 1995

The fact that you could sit alone and think gave us a wonderful opportunity to change ourselves.
FROM A BBC (UK) DOCUMENTARY, 1996

One was angry at what was happening – the humiliation, the loss of our human dignity. We tended to react in accordance with anger and our emotion rather than sitting down and thinking about things properly. But in jail, especially for those who stayed in single cells, you had enough opportunity to sit down and think.
FROM AN INTERVIEW WITH JOHN BATTERSBY, JOHANNESBURG, SOUTH AFRICA, PUBLISHED IN
THE CHRISTIAN SCIENCE MONITOR, 10 FEBRUARY 2000

Thinking is one of the most important weapons in dealing with problems... and we didn't have that outside.
IBID

One of the things most difficult for me to comprehend is that we spent such a long time here.
FROM THE DOCUMENTARY MANDELA: THE LIVING LEGEND, SPEAKING IN HIS CELL ON ROBBEN ISLAND, 2003

One of the things that made me long to be back in prison was that I had so little opportunity for reading, thinking and quiet reflection after my release.
'RETIRING FROM RETIREMENT' ANNOUNCEMENT, NELSON MANDELA FOUNDATION, JOHANNESBURG, SOUTH AFRICA, 1 JUNE 2004

You could be in your cell the whole night, you are able to sit down and think and you could stand away from yourself and look at your performance before you went to prison.
FROM THE DOCUMENTARY LEGENDS: NELSON MANDELA, 2005

Prison: Rehabilitation

Prisons, as they have existed and still exist in our country, are not conducive to the rehabilitation of the prisoners.
OPENING OF THE EKUSENI YOUTH CENTRE, NEWCASTLE, SOUTH AFRICA, 19 NOVEMBER 1996

Prison: Rejection of Release

We will, under no circumstances, accept being released to the Transkei or any other Bantustan. You know full well that we have spent the latter part of our lives in prison exactly because we are opposed to the very idea of separate development, which makes us foreigners in our own country, and which enables the government to perpetuate our oppression to this very day.

FROM A LETTER TO WINNIE MANDELA, QUOTING A LETTER TO KD MATANZIMA, WRITTEN IN POLLSMOOR PRISON, CAPE TOWN, SOUTH AFRICA, 27 DECEMBER 1984

If there is any one amongst you who cherishes my freedom, Oliver Tambo cherishes it more, and I know that he would give his life to see me free. There is no difference between his views and mine.

RESPONSE TO AN OFFER OF CONDITIONAL FREEDOM, READ BY ZINDZI MANDELA AT A RALLY, JABULANI STADIUM, SOWETO, SOUTH AFRICA, 10 FEBRUARY 1985

Let [President PW] Botha show that he is different to [Daniel] Malan, [Johannes] Strijdom and [Hendrik] Verwoerd. Let him renounce violence. Let him say that he will dismantle apartheid. Let him unban the people's organisation, the African National Congress. Let him free all who have been imprisoned, banished or exiled for their opposition to apartheid. Let him guarantee free political activity so that people may decide who will govern them.

IBID

No self-respecting human being will demean and humiliate himself by making a commitment of the nature you demand. You ought not to perpetuate our imprisonment by the simple expedient of setting conditions which, to your own knowledge, we will never under any circumstances accept.

FROM A LETTER TO PRESIDENT PW BOTHA, WRITTEN IN POLLSMOOR PRISON, CAPE TOWN, SOUTH AFRICA, 13 FEBRUARY 1985

Prison: Release

I am also aware that massive efforts have been made here and abroad for my release and that of other political prisoners, a campaign which has given us much inspiration and shown us that we have hundreds of thousands of friends.

FROM AN UNPUBLISHED AUTOBIOGRAPHICAL MANUSCRIPT, WRITTEN ON ROBBEN ISLAND, 1975

However inspiring it is to know that our friends are insisting on our release, a realistic approach clearly shows that we must rule out completely the possibility that such a demand will succeed.

IBID

In my lifetime I shall step out into the sunshine, walk with firm feet because that event will be brought about by the strength of my organisation and the sheer determination of our people.

IBID

Friends, comrades and fellow South Africans, I greet you all in the name of peace, democracy and freedom for all! I stand here before you not as a prophet but as a humble servant of you, the people. Your tireless and heroic sacrifices have made it possible for me to be here today. I therefore place the remaining years of my life in your hands.

FIRST SPEECH AFTER HIS RELEASE, CITY HALL, CAPE TOWN, SOUTH AFRICA, 11 FEBRUARY 1990

I am absolutely excited to be out.

FIRST PRESS CONFERENCE AFTER HIS RELEASE, ARCHBISHOP DESMOND TUTU'S RESIDENCE, BISHOPSCOURT, CAPE TOWN, SOUTH AFRICA, 12 FEBRUARY 1990

I was excited to be free and to see the crowds that had come to welcome me, although I had not expected such a turnout.

AT HOME, SOWETO, SOUTH AFRICA, 14 FEBRUARY 1990

These people had come to welcome us; they wanted to share the joy of seeing a prisoner released, to return to his people.

IBID

The demand has never been the release of Mandela as an individual, the demand has been the release of all political prisoners in the country.

IBID

Our own liberation from prison is taken as a signal that the people will soon liberate themselves from the larger prison represented by the apartheid system.

ADDRESS TO THE INTERNATIONAL LABOUR CONFERENCE, GENEVA, SWITZERLAND, 8 JUNE 1990

I had asked the prison authorities to make sure that the warders who worked with me in the section of the prison where I was kept should assemble at the gate with their families so that I could have the opportunity of thanking them and I was expecting no more than twenty to thirty people because they were working in shifts and so on and I was expecting no more than thirty people. I was surprised then to see the crowd I never even had the opportunity of seeing the warders because of the crowd, both inside the gate and outside.

FROM A CONVERSATION WITH RICHARD STENGEL, 22 APRIL 1993

Those were very anxious moments because the crowd just surrounded us... At one time the car was threatening to tilt and I was very much concerned. They tried very hard to open, to enable the car to go forward, it could not go forward, it could not go backwards. And people like Allan Boesak and others tried hard to open some space for me.

IBID

Well I'm happy to be back home, it is a very rewarding and enriching experience to resume normal life and to hear the laughter of the children and to be able to guide them as they grow.

FROM AN INTERVIEW, CIRCA 1993

Now it was most strange that a prisoner who is serving a long term should argue to remain in prison when the jailer says, 'Go out'. But I was concerned because they said, 'Well, we'll fly you from here to a place in the Transvaal and then late on Sunday night we will take you to your home.' Now I didn't want to come back like that. I wanted that there should be some publicity when I come back.

FROM AN INTERVIEW WITH THE BBC (UK), 28 OCTOBER 1993

It was a wonderful day to be free and to be able to participate in the political activities in the country. I had said both to Mr PW Botha when I saw him in July 1989 and then on the two occasions on which I met [FW] de Klerk that if they want to release me to play a constructive role, they must unban my organisation.

REVISITING ROBBEN ISLAND, CAPE TOWN, SOUTH AFRICA, 11 FEBRUARY 1994

When I was released from prison there was a little bit of irony in the sense that Mr [FW] de Klerk told me on 9 February that I would be released on Sunday. I said please give me two weeks so I can arrange with my people outside. I was afraid that the release would be chaotic.

IBID

I was coming to the unknown and naturally I was very much concerned as to how I am going to be received, how I am going to be treated, what type of life I was going to spend.

IBID

When I saw the crowd it aroused feelings of excitement I couldn't control, I couldn't describe. I now had to be with my family and children and there was a new world that was open to me which was shut when I was in prison.

FROM THE DOCUMENTARY *MANDELA: THE LIVING LEGEND*, 2003

When I came out of jail I arrived in a country which was totally different from the one that sent me to jail and we have to welcome that because people who stood far from us now realise how important the struggle was. Because we have liberated not only the oppressed but even the oppressor. They can now move amongst us without any concern or protection.

EIGHTY-EIGHTH BIRTHDAY CELEBRATIONS, NELSON MANDELA CHILDREN'S FUND, JOHANNESBURG, SOUTH AFRICA, JULY 2006

I came out with mixed feelings: there was the joy and excitement of meeting my beloved wife; I also would have the opportunity of helping my children and grandchildren grow. I had the opportunity of meeting my comrades who had kept the fires alive during these twenty-seven years. It was when I came out, however, that I felt the full impact of the challenge that faced my comrades and I.

FROM AN INTERVIEW, DATE UNKNOWN

Prison: Reputation

Hardly had we set foot on the Island when the prisoners' grapevine buzzed with the news of our arrival.

FROM AN UNPUBLISHED AUTOBIOGRAPHICAL MANUSCRIPT, WRITTEN ON ROBBEN ISLAND, 1975

To the extent that I have been able to achieve anything, I know that this is because I am the product of the people of South Africa.

FINAL SITTING OF THE FIRST DEMOCRATICALLY ELECTED PARLIAMENT, CAPE TOWN, SOUTH AFRICA, 26 MARCH 1999

I never imagined that the world would give us the support we enjoyed and to be known as a miracle country. I never expected that, but that gave us a lot of pride.

FROM THE DOCUMENTARY *MANDELA: THE LIVING LEGEND*, 2003

We indeed have much to be proud of and grateful for. We now live in a stable and inclusive democracy under a constitution that is the envy of many the world over. Our nation has come together in non-racial unity that surprised the world.

FAREWELL BANQUET FOR SOUTH AFRICA'S 2010 SOCCER WORLD CUP BID COMMITTEE, VODAWORLD, MIDRAND, SOUTH AFRICA, 10 MAY 2004

In a cynical world we have become an inspiration to many. We signal that good can be achieved amongst human beings who are prepared to trust, prepared to believe in the goodness of people.

JOINT SITTING OF PARLIAMENT TO MARK TEN YEARS OF DEMOCRACY, PARLIAMENT, CAPE TOWN, SOUTH AFRICA, 10 MAY 2004

Prison: Robben Island Prison

I was excited at the prospect of seeing Robben Island, a place that I had heard about since the days of my childhood, a place that our people talked of as esiqithini – the Island.

FROM AN UNPUBLISHED AUTOBIOGRAPHICAL MANUSCRIPT, WRITTEN ON ROBBEN ISLAND, 1975

Autshumao was banished by Van Riebeeck to Robben Island at the end of the 1658 War between the Khoikhoi and the Dutch. The honour is even more fitting in that Autshumao was also the first and so far the only person to successfully escape from the Island. After several attempts he finally succeeded in making his break in an old boat that was ridden with holes and considered completely unseaworthy.

IBID

I have never been able to ascertain why after just two weeks on Robben Island I was transferred back to Pretoria... The transfer certainly had no connection with the fact that I was subsequently charged in the Rivonia Trial because the arrest which eventually led to that case took place on the 11th July 1963, almost a month after I was removed from the Island.

IBID

On some days the weather on the island is quite beautiful.

FROM A LETTER TO A FRIEND, WRITTEN ON ROBBEN ISLAND, 5 MARCH 1978

Our first years were very hard indeed but we drew a distinction between the system against which we were fighting and the individuals who carried out that policy.

FROM AN INTERVIEW WITH JAMES ROBBINS FOR THE BBC (UK), HIS HOUSE, SOWETO, SOUTH AFRICA, 14 FEBRUARY 1990

It was a very nice atmosphere.

FROM A CONVERSATION WITH RICHARD STENGEL ABOUT THE JOURNEY TO ROBBEN ISLAND AFTER BEING SENTENCED TO LIFE IMPRISONMENT, 3 DECEMBER 1992

In 1947, I spent a holiday in Cape Town and then I went ... up on Table Mountain, which is the highest point in Cape Town, and from Table Mountain I could see Robben Island. I never dreamt that one day I would be there.

FROM A CONVERSATION WITH RICHARD STENGEL, 3 DECEMBER 1993

It evokes all kinds of memories – but I'm concentrating on the pleasant ones.

AFTER REPORTING TO ROBBEN ISLAND PRISONERS ABOUT PROGRESS IN TALKS TO HAVE THEM RELEASED, 9 OCTOBER 1990

I am confident that we will together find a way to combine the many dimensions of the Island, and that we will do so in a manner that recognises above all its pre-eminent character as a symbol of the victory of the human spirit over political oppression and of reconciliation over enforced division.

HERITAGE DAY CELEBRATION, ROBBEN ISLAND, CAPE TOWN, SOUTH AFRICA, 24 SEPTEMBER 1997

How do we reflect the fact that the people of South Africa as a whole, together with the international community, turned one of the world's most notorious symbols of racist oppression into a worldwide icon of the universality of human rights: of hope, peace and reconciliation.

IBID

Robben Island is a vital part of South Africa's collective heritage.

IBID

Esiqithini – the Island – a place of pain and banishment for centuries and now of triumph – presents us with the rich challenge of heritage; its future has been the subject of intense and wide-ranging debate.

IBID

The Island has become a monument of the struggle for democracy, part of a heritage that will always inspire our children and our friends from other lands as we strive to build a just and prosperous nation.

IBID

They used to treat us very tough but when there was an important visitor coming then they would relax. They would say, 'Oh no no, you don't have to work continuously, you can just take a walk, if you want to, around the quarry'. Then we knew that a visitor is coming, but once the visitor is gone, the same cruelty would be mobilised.

FROM AN INTERVIEW WITH VERNE HARRIS, JOHANNESBURG, SOUTH AFRICA, 2005

You know, Robben Island, I like it very much, although when I was a prisoner it was not my favourite. But now when I look back I say, no, that was a good place. No, the experience you know? Because it was a totally different experience from what we know and what we would like, but I was happy that I went through it.

FROM THE DOCUMENTARY MANDELA AT 90, 2008

Prison: Routine

Routine is the supreme law of a prison in every country of the world almost, and every day is for all practical purposes like the day before.

FROM A LETTER TO FRIEDA MATTHEWS, WRITTEN IN POLLSMOOR PRISON, CAPE TOWN, SOUTH AFRICA, 25 FEBRUARY 1987

Prison: Singing

They wanted to break our spirits. So what we did was to sing freedom songs as we were working and everybody was inspired.

FROM A CONVERSATION WITH RICHARD STENGEL, 8 DECEMBER 1992

There were some fellows, you know, who were good singers. I was not one of them, but I enjoyed singing.

FROM A CONVERSATION WITH RICHARD STENGEL, 14 DECEMBER 1992

We sang freedom songs as we worked, the spirit was very high. Then the authorities, in order to make us feel the hard work, they prohibited us from singing.

REVISITING ROBBEN ISLAND, CAPE TOWN, SOUTH AFRICA, 11 FEBRUARY 1994

Prison: Study

Going to jail really helped me because you see I would do, for example, a BA [Bachelor of Arts degree] and the ANC says, 'No, no, stop with those things. We want you to do this – something political for the movement'. So there was interference and I only made progress when I was in jail.

FROM THE DOCUMENTARY *MANDELA AT 90*, 2008

Prison: Suffering

Too many have died since I went to prison. Too many have suffered for the love of freedom. I owe it to their widows, to their orphans, to their mothers and to their fathers who have grieved and wept for them. Not only I have suffered during these long, lonely, wasted years. I am not less life-loving than you are.

RESPONSE TO AN OFFER OF CONDITIONAL FREEDOM, READ BY ZINDZI MANDELA AT A RALLY, JABULANI STADIUM, SOWETO, SOUTH AFRICA, 10 FEBRUARY 1985

I must say that it is a matter of grave concern to sit on the sidelines and be a mere spectator in the tragic turmoil that is tearing our country apart, and that is generating such dangerous passions.

FROM A LETTER TO LORD NICHOLAS BETHELL, WRITTEN IN POLLSMOOR PRISON, CAPE TOWN, SOUTH AFRICA, 4 JUNE 1986

During the twenty-six years of incarceration, the inability to respond meaningfully to deserving appeals for financial help has indeed been a harrowing experience for me.

FROM A LETTER TO THE REVEREND AUSTEN MASSEY, WRITTEN IN VICTOR VERSTER PRISON, PAARL, SOUTH AFRICA, 17 JANUARY 1989

Prison not only robs you of your freedom, it attempts to take away your identity.

FROM *LONG WALK TO FREEDOM*, 1994

I had no time to brood. I enjoyed reading and writing letters and that occupied my mind completely, except of course that when I learned of the harsh experiences of my family, that naturally disturbed me.

REVISITING ROBBEN ISLAND, CAPE TOWN, SOUTH AFRICA, 11 FEBRUARY 1994

Of course there were painful moments because the apartheid regime was expert in persecuting people psychologically.

FROM THE DOCUMENTARY *MANDELA: THE LIVING LEGEND*, 2003

Prison: Support for Release

We never felt a sense of hopelessness because we went to jail under a cloud of praise and support and demands for our release by heads of states, by governments, by parliaments, which gave us, which were a source of inspiration for us.

FROM AN INTERVIEW WITH JAMES ROBBINS FOR THE BBC (UK), HIS HOUSE, SOWETO, SOUTH AFRICA, 14 FEBRUARY 1990

Every day we heard your voices ring – 'free the political prisoners!' We heard your voices sing – 'let my people go!' As we heard that vibrant and invigorating cry of human concern, we knew that we would be free.

ADDRESS AT THE CATHEDRAL OF UPPSALA, UPPSALA, SWEDEN, 13 MARCH 1990

In the end, the high and mighty also heard the voice of the little people. They too discovered that buried away in the dungeons of the Pretoria regime were men and women who should never have been arrested in the first place. They too joined the noble chorus – 'free the political prisoners'.

IBID

During all the days we spent buried in the apartheid dungeons, we never lost our confidence in the certainty of our release and our victory over the apartheid system. This was because we knew that not even the hard-hearted men of Pretoria could withstand the enormous strength represented by the concerted effort of the peoples of South Africa and the rest of the world.

CONCERT, WEMBLEY STADIUM, LONDON, ENGLAND, 16 APRIL 1990

After one has been in prison it is the small things that one appreciates – the feeling of being able to take a walk whenever one wants, to cross a road, to go into a shop and buy a newspaper, to speak or choose to remain silent – the simple act of being able to control one's person.

FROM A CONVERSATION WITH AHMED KATHRADA, CIRCA 1993/94

There is nothing as encouraging to a prisoner who feels that his life has not been wasted, to see his comrades outside prison keeping the fires burning.

REVISITING ROBBEN ISLAND, CAPE TOWN, SOUTH AFRICA, 11 FEBRUARY 1994

We shall never forget how millions of people around the world joined us in solidarity to fight the injustice of our oppression while we were incarcerated.

LIVE 8 CONCERT, MARY FITZGERALD SQUARE, JOHANNESBURG, SOUTH AFRICA, 2 JULY 2005

Prison: Unity

In Robben Island we had members of the ANC, of the PAC [Pan Africanist Congress], of AZAPO [Azanian People's Organisation] and together we were able to solve the problems which faced us as prisoners.

REVISITING ROBBEN ISLAND, CAPE TOWN, SOUTH AFRICA, 11 FEBRUARY 1994

One of the advantages of prison… is firstly the fact that we were put together as members of different political organisations; we could now start a debate on the question of unity and a common approach to problems.

IBID

Prison: Victor Verster Prison

I am also enjoying life on this farm, far away from the concrete jungle that has surrounded me all these years. Here I can breathe relatively clean air.

FROM A LETTER TO EVON KEARNS, WRITTEN IN VICTOR VERSTER PRISON, PAARL, SOUTH AFRICA, 28 FEBRUARY 1989

The only thing that indicated that this was a prison was that there was a security wall around the building but otherwise I was free.

SPEAKING ABOUT VICTOR VERSTER PRISON WHILE REVISITING ROBBEN ISLAND, CAPE TOWN, SOUTH AFRICA, 11 FEBRUARY 1994

I used to go under a tree there and relax where I think I am free and yet they had a microphone in the tree.

FROM AN INTERVIEW WITH VERNE HARRIS, JOHANNESBURG, SOUTH AFRICA, 2005

Although it was meant as a punishment originally, I grew to love it because the rest of the prisoners were in a building for prisoners and that isolation, in putting me in a house, was something of a privilege.

IBID

The warders were not allowed to swim but they would have a guard and then swim; we would swim together.

IBID

Prison: Visitors

A visit in prison, no matter under what conditions, is not something a person can ever praise. Any set-up where you can only speak to your beloved family for a limited period, and where there is no privacy whatsoever, is a depressing experience.

FROM A LETTER TO PRINCE THUMBUMUZI DLAMINI, WRITTEN IN POLLSMOOR PRISON, CAPE TOWN, SOUTH AFRICA, 5 AUGUST 1985

A visit to a prisoner always has significance difficult to put into words.

FROM A LETTER TO FRIEDA MATTHEWS, WRITTEN IN POLLSMOOR PRISON, CAPE TOWN, SOUTH AFRICA, 25 FEBRUARY 1987

You had a glass partition and your visitor stood on one side and you were on the other side and there was a warder behind you, there was a warder behind your visitor, to make sure that you talked only about family matters.

FROM A CONVERSATION WITH RICHARD STENGEL, 4 DECEMBER 1992

Prison: Warders

I don't want us to create the impression that all warders were just animals, rogues, no. Right from the beginning, there were warders who felt that we should be treated correctly.

FROM A CONVERSATION WITH RICHARD STENGEL, 4 DECEMBER 1992

As prisoners, we used our individual and collective positions to make friends with some of our jailers.

FROM AN INTERVIEW WITH JOHN BATTERSBY, JOHANNESBURG, SOUTH AFRICA, PUBLISHED IN THE CHRISTIAN SCIENCE MONITOR, 10 FEBRUARY 2000

I had a garden which I looked after and when the tomatoes were ready the warders would be very friendly and come and get some tomatoes from the garden.

FROM AN INTERVIEW WITH VERNE HARRIS, JOHANNESBURG, SOUTH AFRICA, 2005

Privacy

There are affairs in life where third parties, no matter who they are, should not be let in at all.

FROM A LETTER TO WINNIE MANDELA, WRITTEN ON ROBBEN ISLAND, 1 FEBRUARY 1975

You should not discuss your domestic problems and religious views with others even if they are your intimate friends.

FROM A LETTER TO MAKAZIWE MANDELA, WRITTEN ON ROBBEN ISLAND, 11 MARCH 1979

Promises

It is easy to make promises but never go to action.

LIVE 8 CONCERT, MARY FITZGERALD SQUARE, JOHANNESBURG, SOUTH AFRICA, 2 JULY 2005

Protest Action

Mass action has got the capacity to overthrow governments. Because if we can so organise that people will stay at home and have a massive prolonged industrial action, that is capable of bringing down a government.

FROM A CONVERSATION WITH RICHARD STENGEL, 29 APRIL 1993

Public Service

Whether you change the linen or stitch up wounds, cook the food or dispense the medicines, it is in your hands to help build a public service worthy of all those who gave their lives for the dream of democracy.

NAMING OF THE TAMBO MEMORIAL HOSPITAL, BOKSBURG, SOUTH AFRICA, 16 APRIL 1998

Racism

I want at once to make it clear that I am no racialist, and I detest racialism, because I regard it as a barbaric thing, whether it comes from a black man or from a white man.

FROM HIS APPLICATION FOR THE RECUSAL OF THE MAGISTRATE MR WA VAN HELSDINGEN, OLD SYNAGOGUE, PRETORIA, SOUTH AFRICA, 22 OCTOBER 1962

In relationship with us, South African whites regard as fair and just to pursue policies which have outraged the conscience of mankind, and of honest and upright men throughout the civilised world. They suppress our aspirations, bar our way to freedom and deny us opportunities in our moral and material progress, to secure ourselves from fear and want.

IBID

I hate racial discrimination most intensely and in all its manifestations. I have fought it all during my life; I fight it now, and I will do so until the end of my days. Even though I now happen to be tried by one whose opinion I hold in high esteem, I detest most violently the set-up that surrounds me here. It makes me feel that I am a black man in a white man's court. This should not be.

IBID

Whatever he himself may say in his defence, the white man's moral standards in this country must be judged by the extent to which he has condemned the vast majority of its citizens to serfdom and inferiority.

IBID

All the good things of life are reserved for the white folk, and we blacks are expected to be content to nourish our bodies with pieces of food as they drop from the tables of men with a white skin.

IBID

I hate the practice of race discrimination, and in my hatred I am sustained by the fact that the overwhelming majority of mankind hate it equally... Nothing that this court can do to me will change in any way that hatred in me, which can only be removed by the removal of the injustice and the inhumanity which I have sought to remove from the political and social life of this country.

IN MITIGATION OF SENTENCE AFTER BEING CONVICTED OF INCITING WORKERS TO STRIKE AND LEAVING THE COUNTRY ILLEGALLY, OLD SYNAGOGUE, PRETORIA, SOUTH AFRICA, 7 NOVEMBER 1962

I hate the systematic inculcation of children with colour prejudice and I am sustained in that hatred by the fact that the overwhelming majority of mankind here, and abroad, are with me in that.

IBID

The lack of human dignity experienced by Africans is the direct result of the policy of white supremacy. White supremacy implies black inferiority. Legislation designed to preserve white supremacy entrenches this notion. Menial tasks in South Africa are invariably performed by Africans.

SPEECH FROM THE DOCK, RIVONIA TRIAL, PALACE OF JUSTICE, PRETORIA, SOUTH AFRICA, 20 APRIL 1964

It is not true that the enfranchisement of all will result in racial domination. Political division, based on colour, is entirely artificial and, when it disappears, so will the domination of one colour group by another. The ANC has spent half a century fighting against racialism. When it triumphs it will not change that policy.

IBID

I detest white supremacy and will fight it with every weapon in my hands.

FROM A LETTER TO GENERAL DU PREEZ, COMMISSIONER OF PRISONS, WRITTEN ON ROBBEN ISLAND, 12 JULY 1976

I will further ask for an order restraining you and your officials from preaching racialism to prisoners of different population groups in the single cell section where I am kept, and from trying to foment feelings of hostility amongst us.

FROM A LETTER TO COLONEL ROELOFSE, COMMANDING OFFICER ROBBEN ISLAND, WRITTEN ON ROBBEN ISLAND, 11 OCTOBER 1976

We have consistently condemned the colour bar and maintained no man of principle could surrender his dignity and submit to it.

FROM AN ESSAY ENTITLED 'CLEAR THE OBSTACLES AND CONFRONT THE ENEMY', WRITTEN ON ROBBEN ISLAND, 1976

Science and experience have also shown that no race is inherently superior to others, and this myth has been equally exploded whenever blacks and whites are given equal opportunity for development.

FROM AN ESSAY ENTITLED 'WHITHER THE BLACK CONSCIOUSNESS MOVEMENT', WRITTEN ON ROBBEN ISLAND, 1978

Those who help to perpetuate white supremacy are the enemies of the people, even if they are black, while those who oppose all forms of racism form part of the people irrespective of their colour.

IBID

It is our sacred duty to warn you not to drag the country into civil war merely to defend racial oppression.

FROM A LETTER TO LOUIS LE GRANGE, MINISTER OF PRISONS AND POLICE, WRITTEN ON ROBBEN ISLAND, 4 SEPTEMBER 1979

It will be important to ensure that within South Africa, as in Germany after the Second World War, the necessary democratic institutions are put in place so that racial tyranny does not raise its ugly head again.

ADDRESS TO THE INTERNATIONAL LABOUR CONFERENCE, GENEVA, SWITZERLAND, 8 JUNE 1990

Never should racism in our country and from whatever quarter, raise its ugly head again. All of us South Africans, both black and white, must build a common sense of nationhood in which all ideas of vengeance and retribution are impermissible.

ADDRESS TO THE PARLIAMENT OF CANADA, OTTAWA, CANADA, 18 JUNE 1990

To destroy racism in the world, we, together, must expunge apartheid racism in South Africa. Justice and liberty must be our tool, prosperity and happiness our weapon.

ADDRESS TO THE JOINT SESSION OF THE HOUSE OF CONGRESS, WASHINGTON DC, USA, 26 JUNE 1990

No institution committed to the pursuit of truth can flourish in a social order committed to the pursuit of racism and the preservation of racial domination.

UPON RECEIVING AN HONORARY LLD DEGREE, UNIVERSITY OF THE WITWATERSRAND, JOHANNESBURG, SOUTH AFRICA, 6 SEPTEMBER 1991

A bill of rights cannot be associated with the political or economic subordination of either the majority or the minority. If there is one lesson we can learn from the struggle against racism, in our country as well as yours, it is that racism must be consciously combatted, and not discreetly tolerated.

INVESTITURE, CLARK UNIVERSITY, ATLANTA, USA, 10 JULY 1993

Each and every one of us have felt brandished as subhuman by the fact that some could treat others as though they were no more than disposable garbage. In the end, there was nobody of conscience who could stand by and do nothing in the search for an end to the apartheid crime against humanity.

SPEAKING AT THE UNITED NATIONS, NEW YORK CITY, USA, 24 SEPTEMBER 1993

It will perhaps come to be that we who have harboured in our country the worst example of racism since the defeat of Nazism, will make a contribution to human civilisation by ordering our affairs in such a manner that we strike an effective and lasting blow against racism everywhere.

ADDRESS TO THE FORTY-NINTH UNITED NATIONS GENERAL ASSEMBLY, NEW YORK CITY, USA, 3 OCTOBER 1994

In all we do, we have to ensure the healing of the wounds inflicted on all our people across the great dividing line imposed on our society by centuries of colonialism and apartheid. We must ensure that colour, race and gender become only a God-given gift to each one of us and not an indelible mark or attribute that accords a special status to any.

IBID

Whatever the time it will take, we will not tire. The very fact that racism degrades both the perpetrator and the victim commands that, if we are true to our commitment to protect human dignity, we fight on until victory is achieved.

IBID

All of us know how stubbornly racism can cling to the mind and how deeply it can infect the human soul. Where it is sustained by the racial ordering of the material world, as in the case in our country, that stubbornness can multiply a hundredfold.

IBID

No one is born hating another person because of the colour of his skin, or his background, or his religion. People must learn to hate, and if they can learn to hate, they can be taught to love, for love comes more naturally to the human heart than its opposite.

FROM *LONG WALK TO FREEDOM*, 1994

You have to see the way in which people live to really understand the evil of racial oppression in this country. How evil is it for human beings to be so cruel to other human beings?

FROM AN INTERVIEW WITH ADRIAN HADLAND FOR *THE STAR* AND SAHM VENTER FOR THE ASSOCIATED PRESS, QUNU, MTHATHA, SOUTH AFRICA, 25 DECEMBER 1995

Racism is a blight on the human conscience. The idea that any people can be inferior to another, to the point where those who consider themselves superior define and treat the rest as subhuman, denies the humanity even of those who elevate themselves to the status of gods.

ADDRESS TO THE JOINT HOUSES OF PARLIAMENT, WESTMINSTER HALL, LONDON, ENGLAND, 11 JULY 1996

Can we continue to tolerate our ancestors being shown as people locked in time? Such degrading forms of representation inhibit our children's appreciation of the value and strength of our democracy, of tolerance and of human rights. They demean the victims and warp the minds of the perpetrators.

HERITAGE DAY CELEBRATION, ROBBEN ISLAND, CAPE TOWN, SOUTH AFRICA, 24 SEPTEMBER 1997

We have not fallen from heaven into this new South Africa; we all come crawling from the mud of a deeply racially divided past. And as we go towards that brighter future and stumble on the way, it is incumbent upon each of us to pick the other up and mutually cleanse ourselves.

SPEAKING AT THE UNIVERSITY OF PRETORIA, PRETORIA, SOUTH AFRICA, 4 DECEMBER 1997

We slaughter one another in our words and attitudes. We slaughter one another in the stereotypes and mistrust that linger in our heads, and the words of hate we spew from our lips.

STATE OF THE NATION ADDRESS, PARLIAMENT, CAPE TOWN, SOUTH AFRICA, 5 FEBRUARY 1999

Our struggle was against white supremacy, not against white people.

FORTIETH ANNIVERSARY OF THE ESTABLISHMENT OF UMKHONTO WE SIZWE, SOWETO, JOHANNESBURG, SOUTH AFRICA, 16 DECEMBER 2001

We tried to remove the prism of race from the way people look at the world.

VIDEO RECORDED MESSAGE PLAYED AT THE LAUNCH OF THE EXHIBITION 'DEAR MR MANDELA, DEAR MRS PARKS: CHILDREN'S LETTERS, GLOBAL LESSONS', NELSON MANDELA NATIONAL MUSEUM, QUNU, SOUTH AFRICA, 19 JULY 2008

Discrimination against and the stigmatisation of one part of the population devalued the humanity not only of the victims but of all the people of our country.

STATEMENT READ AT THE OFFICIAL OPENING CEREMONY OF THE DURBAN REVIEW CONFERENCE, GENEVA, SWITZERLAND, 20 APRIL 2009

We must, however, not allow differences of opinion to ever paralyse our efforts towards attaining a world free of racial bigotry, hatred, discrimination and intolerance.

IBID

Throughout our life we have fought against white domination and have fought against black domination; we intend to remain true to this principle to the end of our days.

SOURCE UNKNOWN

Rainbow Nation

If we are able today to speak proudly of a rainbow nation, united in its diversity of culture, religion, race, language and ethnicity, it is in part because the world set us a moral example which we dared to follow. This achievement is bound to last because it is founded on the realisation that reconciliation and nation-building mean, among other things, that we should set out to know the truth about the terrible past and ensure it does not recur.

RAJIV GANDHI FOUNDATION LECTURE, NEW DELHI, INDIA, 25 JANUARY 1995

Reading

There are certain precautions you should take to prepare yourself for a fruitful study career. You must brush up your knowledge through systematic reading of literature and newspapers.

FROM A LETTER TO MAKAZIWE MANDELA, WRITTEN ON ROBBEN ISLAND, 31 DECEMBER 1978

When you read works of that nature you become encouraged. It puts life in you.

FROM A CONVERSATION WITH RICHARD STENGEL, ABOUT THE POEM 'INVICTUS' BY WILLIAM ERNEST HENLEY (1875), CIRCA MARCH 1993

I used to like reading as you know, during those days; before I was really busy, I liked reading.

FROM A CONVERSATION WITH RICHARD STENGEL, 19 MARCH 1993

I was reading and I discovered that there was a world which I did not know, whose doors opened to me and the influences of these men must be reckoned as against that background.

FROM A CONVERSATION WITH RICHARD STENGEL, 3 MAY 1993

There is not a single political prisoner during my time on Robben Island who contributed as *much* as Mac Maharaj in introducing political literature into Robben Island.

FROM A CONVERSATION WITH RICHARD STENGEL, 22 DECEMBER 1993

It is one of the greatest experiences… you can have, you know, to read a Greek tragedy and Greek literature in general.

FROM A CONVERSATION WITH RICHARD STENGEL, 23 DECEMBER 1993

It is always a special pleasure to talk to children about my favourite pastime: reading.

LAUNCH OF *MADIBA, THE RAINBOW MAN*, 27 NOVEMBER 1997

When we read we are able to travel to many places, meet many people and understand the world. We can also learn how to deal with problems we are having by learning from the lessons of the past.

IBID

One of the sad realities today is that very few people, especially young people, read books. Unless we can find imaginative ways of addressing this reality, future generations are in danger of losing their history.

LAUNCH OF THE IZIPHO EXHIBITION, BOOK AND COMIC SERIES, NELSON MANDELA FOUNDATION, JOHANNESBURG, SOUTH AFRICA, 14 JULY 2005

Not a day goes by when I don't read every newspaper I can lay my hands on, wherever I am.

MESSAGE TO THE CONGRESS OF THE WORLD ASSOCIATION OF NEWSPAPERS, FOURTEENTH CONGRESS OF THE WORLD EDITORS FORUM, CASTLE OF GOOD HOPE, CAPE TOWN, SOUTH AFRICA, 3 JUNE 2007

Realists

The realist, however shocked and disappointed by the frailties of those he adores, will look at human behaviour from all sides objectively and will concentrate on those qualities in a person which are edifying, which lift your spirit [and] kindle one's enthusiasm to live.

FROM A LETTER TO WINNIE MANDELA, WRITTEN ON ROBBEN ISLAND, 9 DECEMBER 1979

Reconciliation

There are many who did not understand that to heal we had to lance the boil. There are many who still do not understand that the obedient silence of the enslaved is not the reward of peace which is our due. There are some who cannot comprehend that the right to rebellion against tyranny is the very guarantee of the permanence of freedom.

FUNERAL OF OLIVER TAMBO, FNB (FIRST NATIONAL BANK) STADIUM, SOWETO, JOHANNESBURG, SOUTH AFRICA, 2 MAY 1993

The time for healing of the wounds has come. The moment to bridge the chasm that divides us has come. The time to build is upon us.

INAUGURATION AS PRESIDENT OF SOUTH AFRICA, UNION BUILDINGS, PRETORIA, SOUTH AFRICA, 10 MAY 1994

This is a practical way of forgetting the past and of building our country.

TEA PARTY FOR THE WIVES AND WIDOWS OF FORMER FREEDOM FIGHTERS AND FORMER PRESIDENTS AND PREMIERS OF SOUTH AFRICA, PRETORIA, SOUTH AFRICA, 23 JULY 1994

In the end, reconciliation is a spiritual process, which requires more than just a legal framework. It has to happen in the hearts and minds of people.

ANNUAL METHODIST CHURCH CONFERENCE, MTHATHA, SOUTH AFRICA, 18 SEPTEMBER 1994

Our watchwords must be justice, peace, reconciliation and nation-building in the pursuit of a democratic, non-racial and non-sexist country. In all we do, we have to ensure the healing of the wounds inflicted on all our people across the great dividing line imposed on our society by centuries of colonialism and apartheid.

ADDRESS TO THE FORTY-NINTH UNITED NATIONS GENERAL ASSEMBLY, NEW YORK CITY, USA, 3 OCTOBER 1994

Reconciliation means working together to correct the legacy of past injustice.

NATIONAL RECONCILIATION DAY, SOUTH AFRICA, 16 DECEMBER 1995

The first founding stone of our new country is national reconciliation and national unity. The fact that it has settled in its mortar needs no advertising. If it were not so, the blood in the streets would trumpet it loudly that we had failed to achieve acceptance of the need for all our people, black and white, to live together in peace, as equals and as citizens bound together by a common destiny.

ADDRESS TO THE JOINT HOUSES OF PARLIAMENT, WESTMINSTER HALL, LONDON, ENGLAND, 11 JULY 1996

Being latecomers to freedom and democracy, we have the benefit of the experience of others. Through them, we understand that formal political rights will remain an empty shell and democracy fragile, without real improvement in the lives of people and without an all-inclusive approach that reconciles the beneficiaries of the old order with those who seek improvement from the new.

LECTURE AT THE OXFORD CENTRE FOR ISLAMIC STUDIES, SHELDONIAN THEATRE, OXFORD, ENGLAND, 11 JULY 1997

Inasmuch as reconciliation touches on every aspect of our lives, it is our nation's lifeline.

SPECIAL DEBATE ON THE TRC (TRUTH AND RECONCILIATION COMMISSION) REPORT, PARLIAMENT, CAPE TOWN, SOUTH AFRICA, 25 FEBRUARY 1999

The quest for reconciliation was the spur that gave life to our difficult negotiations process and the agreements that emerged from it.

IBID

Reconciliation is central to that vision which moved millions of men and women to risk all, including their lives, in the struggle against apartheid and white domination. It is inseparable from the achievement of a non-racial, democratic and united nation affording common citizenship, rights and obligations to each and every person, and respecting the rich diversity of our people.

IBID

It is, that if we are one nation with one destiny, then our first task is the collective eradication of the legacy of the inhuman system of apartheid as a necessary step towards the reconciliation of our nation.

ADDRESS AT THE OPENING OF THE PRESIDENT'S BUDGET DEBATE, PARLIAMENT, CAPE TOWN, SOUTH AFRICA, 2 MARCH 1999

Reconciliation was not an afterthought or an add-on of our struggle and our eventual triumph. It was always imbedded in our struggle. Reconciliation was a means of struggle as much as it was the end goal of our struggle.

SPEAKING AT A CONFERENCE OF THE INTERNATIONAL WOMEN'S FORUM, TOKYO, JAPAN, 30 JANUARY 2003

We need to celebrate ourselves and our achievement as often as we can. And we must, as you have chosen to do with this project, continue to build on that achievement, promoting and furthering the cause of national reconciliation.

SPEAKING AT NOBEL SQUARE, CAPE TOWN, SOUTH AFRICA, 14 DECEMBER 2003

Perhaps we should call on all South Africans, in all walks of life... to find within their communities, localities or towns a concrete opportunity to reach out and make national reconciliation real... Make national reconciliation work in your own life.

IBID

If we don't forgive them, then that feeling of bitterness and revenge will be there and we are saying, 'Let us forget the past, let's concern ourselves with the present and the future' but to say the atrocities of the past will never be allowed to happen again.

FROM THE DOCUMENTARY MANDELA: THE LIVING LEGEND, 2003

I was born and brought up in South Africa and was able to see very clearly what the response of South Africans would be to the message of nation building and reconciliation.

FROM THE DOCUMENTARY *LEGENDS: NELSON MANDELA*, 2005

Reconstruction and Development

The reality, however, is that as much as our political liberation was not easy to achieve, so it will not be an easy walk to arrive at the point of the socio-economic upliftment of all the people of our country. We must therefore approach the challenge of reconstruction and development and with both feet firmly planted on the ground.

ANC NATIONAL CONFERENCE ON RECONSTRUCTION AND STRATEGY, NASREC, JOHANNESBURG, SOUTH AFRICA, 21 JANUARY 1994

Consistent with our objective of creating a people-centred society and effectively to address the critical questions of growth, reconstruction and development, we will, together with organised labour and the private sector, pay special attention to the issue of human resource development.

FIRST STATE OF THE NATION ADDRESS, PARLIAMENT, CAPE TOWN, SOUTH AFRICA, 24 MAY 1994

We have achieved our freedom. But formal liberation will be an empty shell if we do not immediately start addressing the social conditions bred by apartheid. The Reconstruction and Development Programme must be implemented without delay.

ANNIVERSARY OF THE SOWETO UPRISING ON 16 JUNE 1976, SOUTH AFRICA, 16 JUNE 1994

Success in the implementation of reconstruction and development is the sure guarantee for lasting peace and stability.

ADDRESS AT A LUNCHEON AT THE CONFERENCE OF EDITORS, SOUTH AFRICA, 6 SEPTEMBER 1994

Reconstruction and development entails more than just creating jobs or building houses. It means the fundamental restructuring of society as a whole, including relations at the workplace.

MESSAGE TO THE FIFTH NATIONAL CONGRESS OF COSATU (CONGRESS OF SOUTH AFRICAN TRADE UNIONS), SOWETO, SOUTH AFRICA, 7 SEPTEMBER 1994

We cannot build or heal our nation, if – in both the private and public sectors, in the schools and universities, in the hospitals and on the land, in dealing with crime and social dislocation – we continue with business as usual, wallowing in notions of the past. Everywhere and in everything we do, what is now required is boldness in thinking, firmness in resolve and consistency in action.

STATE OF THE NATION ADDRESS, PARLIAMENT, CAPE TOWN, SOUTH AFRICA, 9 FEBRUARY 1995

Reconciliation cannot be attained without reconstruction and development, and vice versa.

FROM AN ARTICLE IN THE *SUNDAY TIMES* (SOUTH AFRICA), 22 FEBRUARY 1996

In the same way that the liberation of South Africa from apartheid was an achievement of Africa, the reconstruction and development of our country is part of the rebirth of the Continent.

LECTURE AT THE OXFORD CENTRE FOR ISLAMIC STUDIES, SHELDONIAN THEATRE, OXFORD, ENGLAND, 11 JULY 1997

Oliver Tambo led us to freedom. Now we are engaged in an even more difficult and demanding struggle, the struggle to rebuild and develop our country so that all should enjoy a better life.

NAMING OF THE TAMBO MEMORIAL HOSPITAL, SOUTH AFRICA, 16 APRIL 1998

We have steadily increased budget allocations to special, targeted poverty-relief and employment-creating programmes. Ours is therefore a broad-ranging programme for meeting social and developmental needs. It focuses not on a few communities, but on all deprived communities. It is a broad-based and many-sided approach to reconstruction and development.

ADDRESS AT THE OPENING OF THE PRESIDENT'S BUDGET DEBATE, PARLIAMENT, CAPE TOWN, SOUTH AFRICA, 2 MARCH 1999

Sustained economic growth is indispensable to the achievement of our goals of reconstruction and development, in particular the eradication of poverty.

ADDRESS TO THE PARLIAMENT OF THE NETHERLANDS, THE HAGUE, THE NETHERLANDS, 12 MARCH 1999

To the extent that I have been able to take our country forward to this new era, it is because I am the product of the people of the world who have cherished the vision of a better life for all people everywhere.

FINAL SITTING OF THE FIRST DEMOCRATICALLY ELECTED PARLIAMENT, CAPE TOWN, SOUTH AFRICA, 26 MARCH 1999

We had miraculously – as many said – transcended the deep divisions of our past to create a new inclusive democratic order; we had confidence that as a nation we would similarly confront and deal with the challenges of reconstruction and development.

JOINT SITTING OF PARLIAMENT TO MARK TEN YEARS OF DEMOCRACY, PARLIAMENT, CAPE TOWN, SOUTH AFRICA, 10 MAY 2004

Red Cross

The improvements in the conditions of our imprisonment at Robben Island were to a large measure due to the pressure that the mere presence of the Red Cross brought to bear on our jailer-regime.

BRITISH RED CROSS HUMANITY LECTURE, QUEEN ELIZABETH II CONFERENCE CENTRE, LONDON, ENGLAND, 10 JULY 2003

In the midst of bloodshed and war, of animosity and pain, hatred and conflict, the Red Cross has carried the flag of the belief in our common humanity and lived out that belief in action in conditions and circumstances where the opposite sentiment dominated.

IBID

Regret

There is one regret I have had throughout my life: that I never became the boxing heavyweight champion of the world.

EVENT WITH PRESIDENT BILL CLINTON, WASHINGTON DC, USA, 1990

I shall personally never regret the life Comrade Nomzamo [Winnie Mandela] and I tried to share together. Circumstances beyond our control, however, dictated it should be otherwise. I part from my wife with no recriminations. I embrace her with all the love and affection I have nursed for her inside and outside prison from the moment I first met her.

ANNOUNCING HIS SEPARATION FROM WINNIE MANDELA, JOHANNESBURG, SOUTH AFRICA, 13 APRIL 1992

I regret that there are many men who brought about this day but who did not live to see the new South Africa arrive.

ROBBEN ISLAND REUNION CONFERENCE, UNIVERSITY OF THE WESTERN CAPE, BELLVILLE, SOUTH AFRICA, 12 FEBRUARY 1995

While in prison I often reflected upon the things one neglected and omitted. I always then thought about the people I neglected to thank and pay tribute to for what they meant in one's life. And quite often one neglected the families and loved ones of those with whom you were associated in struggle.

COMMEMORATION OF THE LIVES OF YUSUF CACHALIA AND BRAM FISCHER, JOHANNESBURG METROPOLITAN CENTRE, JOHANNESBURG, SOUTH AFRICA, 5 JUNE 2005

Relationships

I would think that people who subscribe to the same values, who share a common vision and who accept each other's integrity have laid a basis for a good relationship.

FROM A PERSONAL FILE, DATE UNKNOWN

Religion

Spiritual weapons can be dynamic and often have an impact difficult to appreciate except in the light of actual experience in given situations. In a way they make prisoners free men, turn commoners into monarchs and dirt into pure gold.

FROM A LETTER TO SENATOR DOUGLAS LUKHELE, WRITTEN ON ROBBEN ISLAND, 1 AUGUST 1970

The two influences that dominated my thoughts and actions during those days were chieftaincy and the church.

FROM AN UNPUBLISHED AUTOBIOGRAPHICAL MANUSCRIPT, WRITTEN ON ROBBEN ISLAND, 1975

We, who were brought up in religious homes, and who studied in missionary schools, experienced the acute spiritual conflict that occurred in us when we saw the way of life we considered sacred being challenged by new philosophies and when we realised that amongst those who dismissed our beliefs as opium were clear thinkers whose integrity and love of their fellow men was beyond doubt.

FROM A LETTER TO FATIMA MEER, WRITTEN ON ROBBEN ISLAND, 1 JANUARY 1976

The simple lesson of all religions, of all philosophies and of life itself is that, although evil may be on the rampage temporarily, the good must win the laurels in the end.

IBID

I have my own beliefs as to the existence or non-existence of a Supreme Being and it is possible that one could easily explain why mankind has from time immemorial believed in the existence of a god.

FROM A LETTER TO MAKAZIWE MANDELA, WRITTEN ON ROBBEN ISLAND, 27 MARCH 1977

At Fort Hare I even became a Sunday School teacher.

IBID

I was of course, baptised in the Wesleyan Church, and went to its missionary schools. Outside and here I remain a staunch member but one's church outlook tends to broaden and to welcome efforts towards denominational unity.

FROM A LETTER TO MRS N THULARE, WRITTEN ON ROBBEN ISLAND, 19 JULY 1977

Always make religion a personal and private affair confined to yourself. Do not burden others with your religious and other personal affairs.

FROM A LETTER TO MAKAZIWE MANDELA, WRITTEN ON ROBBEN ISLAND, 21 DECEMBER 1978

I've always regarded the multiplicity of gods in Greek mythology as yet another manifestation of the widespread belief that the destiny of all natural and human affairs is in the hands of the divinities whose superhuman excellence is a source of inspiration and hope to all creation, an excellence which will ultimately rule the world.

FROM A LETTER TO FATIMA MEER, WRITTEN ON ROBBEN ISLAND, 1 JANUARY 1979

At least there was one thing in which both the adherents of the scriptures as well as atheists were agreed: belief in the existence of beings with superhuman powers indicates what man would like to be and how throughout the centuries he has fought against all kinds of evil and strived for a virtuous life.

IBID

Men of vision have proclaimed the gospel that we live in one world, face common social problems and that justice and peace bring security and joy to men.

FROM A LETTER TO HELEN JOSEPH, WRITTEN ON ROBBEN ISLAND, 11 MARCH 1979

Religion, especially belief in the existence of a Supreme Being, has always been a controversial subject that splits nations and even families. But it is always best to treat the relationship between a man and his god as a purely personal affair, a question of faith and not of logic. No one has the right to prescribe to others what they should or should not believe in.

FROM A LETTER TO MRS DEBORAH OPITZ, WRITTEN IN VICTOR VERSTER PRISON, PAARL, SOUTH AFRICA, 10 MAY 1989

The South African churches have made a substantial contribution to the struggle for real change in this country and the Church of the Province has pride of place in that historic line-up. Its consistency and forthrightness on national issues inspires us all.

FROM A LETTER TO ARCHBISHOP DESMOND AND LEAH TUTU, WRITTEN IN VICTOR VERSTER PRISON, PAARL, SOUTH AFRICA, 21 AUGUST 1989

Few people will deny that the Church of the Province has produced heroes and martyrs of the highest integrity.

FROM A LETTER TO REVEREND ANDREW HUNTER, WRITTEN IN VICTOR VERSTER PRISON, PAARL, SOUTH AFRICA, 21 AUGUST 1989

Indeed our priests, religious organisations are doing a wonderful job in trying to help to make it possible for our people to live in peace and security.

SPEAKING AT KAGISO, WEST RAND, SOUTH AFRICA, CIRCA 1991

We are committed to building bridges and helping to embrace all of humanity under one umbrella and move forward in strength and confidence to a better future. We believe that this is not different from what Hindu scriptures have also been saying.

DIWALI CELEBRATION, DURBAN, SOUTH AFRICA, 3 NOVEMBER 1991

Religion depends on *belief*, not on logic and – but sometimes, you would like to investigate the origin of an idea in the Bible and what lessons you can draw from the experiences which are outlined in the Bible and *when* there is a scientific basis, it throws a new light, because the Bible itself is a great – a very great literature.

FROM A CONVERSATION WITH RICHARD STENGEL, 21 DECEMBER 1992

There was a chap who prayed, Reverend Japhta, who made a rather remarkable prayer and he said, 'God, we have been praying to you, pleading with you, asking you to liberate us. Now we are instructing you to liberate us.'

FROM A CONVERSATION WITH RICHARD STENGEL, 5 APRIL 1993

South Africans of Jewish descent have historically been disproportionately represented among our white compatriots in the liberation struggle.

THIRTY-SEVENTH CONGRESS OF THE SOUTH AFRICAN JEWISH BOARD OF DEPUTIES, JOHANNESBURG, SOUTH AFRICA, 21 AUGUST 1993

Religion is about mutual love and respect for one another and for life itself. It is about the dignity and equality of humankind made in the image of God.

FROM AN INTERVIEW WITH CHARLES VILLA-VICENCIO, JOHANNESBURG, SOUTH AFRICA, 1993

To share the sacrament as part of the tradition of my Church was important for me. It gave me a sense of inner quiet and calm. I used to come away from these services feeling a new man.

IBID

I am not particularly religious or spiritual. Let's say I am interested in all attempts to discover the meaning and purpose of life. Religion is an important part of this exercise.

IBID

I never abandoned my Christian beliefs.

FROM A CONVERSATION WITH AHMED KATHRADA, CIRCA 1993/94

Many people, you see, who nevertheless accept scientific explanations, nevertheless are devout Christians, have got religious convictions.

IBID

The sense of social responsibility that the religious community has always upheld found expression in your immense contribution to the efforts to rid our country of the scourge of racism and apartheid. When pronouncements and actions against the powers-that-be meant persecution and even death, you dared to stand up to the tyrants.

ANNUAL METHODIST CHURCH CONFERENCE, MTHATHA, SOUTH AFRICA, 18 SEPTEMBER 1994

I cannot overemphasise the role that the Methodist Church has played in my own life.

IBID

The Church, with its message of forgiveness, has a special role to play in national reconciliation.

IBID

Those who enjoyed the fruits of unjust privilege must be helped to find a new spirit of sharing.

IBID

The spirit of reconciliation and the goodwill within the nation can, to a great measure, be attributed to the moral and spiritual interventions of the religious community.

IBID

All South Africans must be free to practise any religion of their choice.

TWENTY-THIRD ANNIVERSARY CONFERENCE OF THE GOSPEL CHURCH OF POWER OF RSA (REPUBLIC OF SOUTH AFRICA), BHISHO, SOUTH AFRICA, 10 SEPTEMBER 1995

What challenges us, is to ensure that none should enjoy lesser rights and none tormented because they are born different, hold contrary political views or pray to God in a different manner.

SPECIAL COMMEMORATIVE MEETING OF THE UNITED NATIONS GENERAL ASSEMBLY ON THE FIFTIETH ANNIVERSARY OF THE UNITED NATIONS, NEW YORK CITY, USA, 23 OCTOBER 1995

All the major religions teach the importance of peace and reconciliation. But they also insist that with reconciliation must come an end to injustice.

OPENING OF THE YOUNG CHRISTIAN WORKERS WORLD COUNCIL, OUKASIE, SOUTH AFRICA, 26 NOVEMBER 1995

In the building of our new nation, reconstruction goes hand in hand with reconciliation. We look to the Church, with its message of justice, peace, forgiveness and healing, to play a key role in helping our people, of every colour, to move from the divisions of the past to a future that is united in a commitment to correct wrongs and restore a just order.

THANKSGIVING SERVICE UPON ARCHBISHOP DESMOND TUTU'S RETIREMENT, ST GEORGE'S CATHEDRAL, CAPE TOWN, SOUTH AFRICA, 23 JUNE 1996

People of all religions, teachers and students, in our cities, towns and rural areas, from north to south and east to west – let us join hands for peace and prosperity.

SIGNING OF THE NEW CONSTITUTION, SHARPEVILLE, VEREENIGING, SOUTH AFRICA, 10 DECEMBER 1996

There is no power on earth that can compare with religion, that's why I respect it.

FROM A BBC (UK) DOCUMENTARY, 1996

As with other aspects of its heritage, African traditional religion is increasingly recognised for its contribution to the world. No longer seen as despised superstition which had to be superseded by superior forms of belief: today its enrichment of humanity's spiritual heritage is acknowledged.

LECTURE AT THE OXFORD CENTRE FOR ISLAMIC STUDIES, SHELDONIAN THEATRE, OXFORD, ENGLAND, 11 JULY 1997

As in the new global order, no country, region or continent can any longer operate in isolation from the rest of the world. No social movement in any country or continent can isolate itself from similar movements coexisting within it. This would apply to religion as much as anything else living in a society.

IBID

The strength of inter-religious solidarity in action against apartheid, rather than mere harmony or coexistence, was critical in bringing that evil system to an end. This approach, rather than verbally competing claims, enabled each tradition to bring its best forward and place it at the service of all.

IBID

We need religious institutions to continue to be the conscience of society, a moral custodian and a fearless champion of the interests of the weak and downtrodden. We need religious organisations to be part of a civil society mobilised to campaign for justice and the protection of basic human rights.

REGINA MUNDI DAY, REGINA MUNDI CHURCH, SOWETO, SOUTH AFRICA, 30 NOVEMBER 1997

The freedom which we won with the active participation of the religious community, indeed the majority of South Africans, has given us a constitution which guarantees to all South Africans their religious freedom.

IBID

Religious organisations also played a key role in exposing apartheid for what it was – a fraud and a heresy. It was encouraging to hear of the God who did not tolerate oppression, but who stood with the oppressed.

FIRST TRIANNUAL METHODIST CHURCH OF SOUTH AFRICA CONFERENCE, DURBAN, SOUTH AFRICA, 17 JULY 1998

Whenever the noble ideals and values of religion have been joined with practical action to realise them, it has strengthened us and at the same time nurtured those ideals within the liberation movement.

FIFTIETH ANNIVERSARY OF THE WORLD COUNCIL OF CHURCHES, HARARE, ZIMBABWE, 13 DECEMBER 1998

The moral decay of some communities in various parts of the world reveals itself among others in the use of the name of God to justify the maintenance of actions which are condemned by the entire world as crimes against humanity.

FROM THE UNPUBLISHED SEQUEL TO HIS AUTOBIOGRAPHY, CIRCA 1998

We shall have to reach deep into the wells of our human faith as we approach the new century. No less than in any other period of history, religion will have a crucial role to play in guiding and inspiring humanity to meet the enormous challenges that we face.

ADDRESS TO THE PARLIAMENT OF THE WORLD'S RELIGIONS, CAPE TOWN, SOUTH AFRICA, DECEMBER 1999

Without the church, without religious institutions, I would never have been here today.

IBID

I do appreciate the importance of religion... you'd have to have been in a South African jail under apartheid where you could see the cruelty of human beings to each other in its naked form. But it was again, religious institutions, Hindus, Muslims, leaders of the Jewish faith, Christians, it was them who gave us hope that one day we would come out. We would return.

IBID

Our religious leaders were in the forefront of keeping the spirit of resistance alive amongst our people in those days when repression intensified and took on horrendous proportions intended to cow the people into submission.

SEVENTY-FIFTH BIRTHDAY OF ARCHBISHOP DESMOND TUTU, JOHANNESBURG, SOUTH AFRICA, 8 OCTOBER 2006

Repression

Repression had swept the country clear of all visible organisation of the people. But at each turn of history, apartheid was bound to spawn resistance; it was destined to bring to life the forces that would guarantee its death.

COMMEMORATION OF THE TWENTIETH ANNIVERSARY OF THE DEATH IN POLICE DETENTION OF STEVE BIKO, EAST LONDON, SOUTH AFRICA, 1 SEPTEMBER 1997

Resolutions

At the beginning of the year, I used to take resolutions that this is what I would do, then I find that I can't even stick to that resolution for two days.

FROM A CONVERSATION WITH RICHARD STENGEL, 3 MAY 1993

Respect

The police did have some respect for me because I was already an attorney, I was a lawyer and they had some respect for me and they knew my background also.

FROM A CONVERSATION WITH RICHARD STENGEL, 18 MARCH 1993

Retirement

There will be life after this president has gone. Not only will there be life but you will see dramatic changes, at a much faster pace than I am able to do at the present moment.

SPEAKING TO THE MEDIA OUTSIDE 10 DOWNING STREET AFTER A MEETING WITH PRIME MINISTER JOHN MAJOR, LONDON, ENGLAND, 10 JULY 1996

Here are the reins of the movement – protect and guard its precious legacy; defend its unity and integrity as committed disciples of change; pursue its popular objectives like true revolutionaries who seek only to serve the nation.

CLOSING SESSION OF THE FIFTIETH ANC NATIONAL CONFERENCE, NORTH-WEST UNIVERSITY, MAFIKENG CAMPUS, SOUTH AFRICA, 20 DECEMBER 1997

The time has come to hand over the baton. And I personally relish the moment when my fellow veterans, whom you have seen here, and I shall be able to observe from near and judge from afar. As 1999 approaches, I will endeavour as State President to delegate more and more responsibility, so as to ensure a smooth transition to the new presidency. Thus I will be able to have that opportunity in my last years to spoil my grandchildren and try in various ways to assist all South African children, especially those who have been the hapless victims of a system that did not care.

IBID

The time has come for me to take leave. The time has come to hand over the baton in a relay that started more than eighty-five years ago in Mangaung, nay more, centuries ago when the warriors of Autshumao, Makana, Mzilikazi, Moshoeshoe, Khama, Sekhukhune, Labotsibeni, Cetshwayo, Nghunghunyane, Uithalder and Ramabulana, laid down their lives to defend the dignity and integrity of their being as a people.

IBID

Born as the First World War came to a close and departing from public life as the world marks half-a-century of the Universal Declaration of Human Rights, I have reached that part of the long walk when the opportunity is granted, as it should be to all men and women, to retire to some rest and tranquility in the village of my birth.

ADDRESS TO THE FIFTY-THIRD UNITED NATIONS GENERAL ASSEMBLY, NEW YORK CITY, USA, 21 SEPTEMBER 1998

It is a great privilege for me, as my public life draws to a close, to be allowed to share these thoughts and dreams for a better world with you. I do so filled with hope, knowing that I am amongst men and women who have chosen to make the world the theatre of their operations in pursuit of freedom and justice. It is as a peaceful and equitable world takes shape that I and the legions across the globe who dedicated their lives in striving for a better life for all, will be able to retire in contentment and at peace.

FIFTIETH ANNIVERSARY OF THE WORLD COUNCIL OF CHURCHES, HARARE, ZIMBABWE, DECEMBER 1998

I will count myself as amongst the aged of our society: as one of the rural population; as one concerned for the children and youth of our country; and as a citizen of the world committed, as long as I have strength, to work for a better life for all people everywhere. And as I have always done, I will do what I can within the discipline of the broad movement for peace and democracy to which I belong.

FINAL SITTING OF THE FIRST DEMOCRATICALLY ELECTED PARLIAMENT, CAPE TOWN, SOUTH AFRICA, 26 MARCH 1999

For my part, I wish to say that it has been a profound privilege to be accountable to this Parliament. Though there is sadness in leave-taking, I am filled with contentment by the sounds of voices that I have heard in the many debates that I have attended.

IBID

Mr [Thabo] Mbeki knows so clearly what he has to do better than this old man.

BRIEFING TO EDITORS AND OPINION MAKERS, PRETORIA, SOUTH AFRICA, 10 MAY 1999

I don't want to reach 100 years whilst I am still trying to bring about a solution in some complicated international issue.

IBID

I welcome the possibility of revelling in obscurity as I am going to do when I step down.

IBID

It is no easy thing to rest while millions still bear the burden of poverty and insecurity. But my days will be filled with contentment to the extent that hands are joined across social divides and national boundaries, between continents and over oceans, to give effect to that common humanity in whose name we have together made the long walk to where we are today.

FAREWELL BANQUET HOSTED BY PRESIDENT THABO MBEKI, PRETORIA, SOUTH AFRICA, 16 JUNE 1999

It would be tempting to sit back in retirement, but we all have a responsibility to contribute the little we are able to.

DINNER IN HONOUR OF NELSON MANDELA AND GRAÇA MACHEL, STANHOPE HOTEL, NEW YORK CITY, USA, 6 MAY 2002

It was a matter of great comfort and consolation to me when the very young Bill Clinton joined me in the ranks of retired and discarded former presidents, now without office or power.

PRE-RECORDED MESSAGE TO THE CLINTON FOUNDATION, 1 MARCH 2004

Thank you for being kind to an old man – allowing him to take a rest, even if many of you may feel that after loafing somewhere on an island and other places for twenty-seven years, the rest is not really deserved.

'RETIRING FROM RETIREMENT' ANNOUNCEMENT, NELSON MANDELA FOUNDATION, JOHANNESBURG, SOUTH AFRICA, 1 JUNE 2004

When I told one of my advisers a few months ago that I wanted to retire, he growled at me, 'You are retired'. If that is really the case, then I should say I now announce that I am retiring from retirement.

IBID

I do not intend to hide away totally from the public, but henceforth I want to be in the position of calling you to ask whether I would be welcome, rather than being called upon to do things and participate in events. The appeal therefore is don't call me, I'll call you.

IBID

We have fought for peace and reconciliation, for social justice, for all men, women and children to live together in harmony and with equal opportunities. These are ideals I still believe in, ideals that I still live for but the time has come to fully hand over my work to my charities: the Nelson Mandela Foundation, the Nelson Mandela Children's Fund and the Mandela Rhodes Foundation.

RECORDED MESSAGE FOR THE PASTEUR FOUNDATION, 1 DECEMBER 2004

I am no longer in politics, I'm just watching from a distance and when people come to me and say, 'What do we do with a situation like this?' I say, 'No, go to people in politics, I am no longer in politics, I've retired'.

FROM THE DOCUMENTARY MANDELA AT 90, 2008

I am proud to be here at this ground-breaking first meeting of The Global Elders. As I have said, I am trying to take my retirement seriously and, though I will not be able to participate in the really exciting part of the work, analysing problems, seeking solutions, searching out partners, I will be with you in spirit.

ADDRESS TO THE ELDERS, ULUSABA PRIVATE GAME RESERVE, SOUTH AFRICA, 26 MAY 2008

Rivonia Trial

The Rivonia Trial aroused emotions tremendously and the way we conducted the trial where the government was hoping to put us in the dock, we put the government in the dock; right from our plea, we made it clear that this was a unique trial and we said it is the government that should be in the dock, not us. We plead not guilty.

FROM A CONVERSATION WITH RICHARD STENGEL, 3 DECEMBER 1992

I read that speech, which was *challenging* to the authorities, where I said I have done these things – I have done them because I am a man of principle and therefore I did so consciously because I cannot accept to be treated as inferior to anybody else. So that, more or less, put me in the spotlight.

FROM A CONVERSATION WITH RICHARD STENGEL, 10 MARCH 1993

That my guilt was quite clear and that it would not be politically correct for me to deny some of the allegations and that I should make them myself before I am cross-examined and justify what I did.

FROM A CONVERSATION WITH RICHARD STENGEL ABOUT WHY HE GAVE A SPEECH FROM THE DOCK INSTEAD OF TESTIFYING IN THE RIVONIA TRIAL, WHICH WOULD HAVE OPENED HIM TO CROSS-EXAMINATION, 17 APRIL 1993

We never pleaded guilty in the Rivonia Trial. We pleaded not guilty, remember? We said that it is the government that is the criminal.

FROM A CONVERSATION WITH AHMED KATHRADA, CIRCA 1993/94

Routine

When you have got a programme to apply, whatever the merits of that programme, it is difficult to concentrate on the negative aspects of your life.

REVISITING ROBBEN ISLAND, CAPE TOWN, SOUTH AFRICA, 11 FEBRUARY 1994

Saints and Sinners

Never forget that a saint is a sinner who keeps on trying.

FROM A LETTER TO WINNIE MANDELA, WRITTEN ON ROBBEN ISLAND, 1 FEBRUARY 1975

We are told that a saint is a sinner who keeps on trying to be clean. One may be a villain for three-quarters of his life and be canonised because he lived a holy life for the remaining quarter of that life.

FROM A LETTER TO WINNIE MANDELA, WRITTEN ON ROBBEN ISLAND, 9 DECEMBER 1979

One issue that deeply worried me in prison was the false image that I unwittingly projected to the outside world: of being regarded as a saint. I never was one, even on the basis of an earthly definition of a saint as a sinner who keeps on trying.

FROM THE UNPUBLISHED SEQUEL TO HIS AUTOBIOGRAPHY, CIRCA 1998

If you come across as a saint, people can become very discouraged.

FROM AN INTERVIEW WITH JOHN BATTERSBY, JOHANNESBURG, SOUTH AFRICA, PUBLISHED IN *THE CHRISTIAN SCIENCE MONITOR*, 10 FEBRUARY 2000

What always worried me in prison was [that I could acquire] the image of someone who is always 100 per cent correct and can never do any wrong.

IBID

The impression that you are a demigod worried me. I wanted to be like an ordinary human being with virtues and vices.

FROM THE DOCUMENTARY *MANDELA: THE LIVING LEGEND*, 2003

Sanctions

It is because of sanctions that such enormous progress has been made.

FROM THE DOCUMENTARY *MANDELA IN AMERICA*, 1990

We have been forced to adopt sanctions because it was the only way, apart from the armed struggle, in which there can be movement forward.

AT HOME, SOWETO, SOUTH AFRICA, 14 FEBRUARY 1990

As far as we are concerned, sanctions have worked very well.

IBID

Science

You may unconsciously offend a lot of people by trying to sell them ideas they regard as unscientific and pure fiction.

FROM A LETTER TO MAKAZIWE MANDELA, WRITTEN ON ROBBEN ISLAND, 27 MARCH 1977

You will be safe if you always try to seek a scientific explanation for all that happens, even if you come to a wrong conclusion.

FROM A LETTER TO ZINDZI MANDELA, WRITTEN ON ROBBEN ISLAND, 26 NOVEMBER 1978

I don't like miracles that always occur in distant lands, especially if they are not capable of scientific explanation.

FROM A LETTER TO ZINDZI MANDELA, WRITTEN ON ROBBEN ISLAND, 25 MARCH 1979

The role of scientific knowledge is to ensure that decisions are made based on fact and knowledge rather than belief, myth and superstition.

SECOND INTERNATIONAL AIDS SOCIETY CONFERENCE ON HIV PATHOGENESIS AND TREATMENT, PARIS, FRANCE, 13 JULY 2003

Self-control

I was brought up in high schools, boarding schools, where you were without women for almost six months, and you exercised discipline of yourself.

FROM A CONVERSATION WITH RICHARD STENGEL, 9 MARCH 1993

He had caused me to violate my self-control and I considered that a defeat at the hands of my opponent.

FROM LONG WALK TO FREEDOM, TALKING ABOUT A PRISON WARDER, 1994

Selflessness

I am prepared to pay the penalty even though I know how bitter and desperate is the situation of an African in the prisons of this country.

IN MITIGATION OF SENTENCE AFTER BEING CONVICTED OF INCITING WORKERS TO STRIKE AND LEAVING THE COUNTRY ILLEGALLY, OLD SYNAGOGUE, PRETORIA, SOUTH AFRICA, 7 NOVEMBER 1962

Honesty, sincerity, simplicity, humility, pure generosity, absence of vanity, readiness to serve others – qualities which are within easy reach of every soul – are the foundation of one's spiritual life.

FROM A LETTER TO WINNIE MANDELA, WRITTEN ON ROBBEN ISLAND, 1 FEBRUARY 1975

There can be no greater gift than that of giving one's time and energy to help others without expecting anything in return.

CEREMONY TO ACKNOWLEDGE FCB HARLOW BUTLER PTY (LTD) FOR SUPPORTING THE NELSON MANDELA FOUNDATION'S HIV/AIDS AND EDUCATION PROGRAMMES, SPEAKING AT THE NELSON MANDELA FOUNDATION, JOHANNESBURG, SOUTH AFRICA, 27 FEBRUARY 2004

A fundamental concern for others in our individual and community lives would go a long way in making the world the better place we so passionately dreamt of.

SIXTH NELSON MANDELA ANNUAL LECTURE, KLIPTOWN, SOWETO, SOUTH AFRICA, 12 JULY 2008

Sexuality

When I went to prison, I resigned myself to the fact that I had no opportunity for sexual expression and I could deal with that.

FROM A CONVERSATION WITH RICHARD STENGEL, 9 MARCH 1993

Slavery

The institution of slavery also helped to strengthen the belief that Africa had no history, it had no culture.

FROM THE DOCUMENTARY *THE LAST MILE: MANDELA, AFRICA AND DEMOCRACY*, 1992

I can assure you that it was a devastating experience.

AFTER VISITING GOREE ISLAND, SENEGAL, WHERE AFRICANS WERE SENT TO THE AMERICAS AS SLAVES, FROM THE DOCUMENTARY *THE LAST MILE: MANDELA, AFRICA AND DEMOCRACY*, 1992

We have had men who were so arrogant that they wanted to conquer the world and turn human beings into their slaves. But the people always put an end to such men and women.

ADDRESS TO THE PARLIAMENT OF THE WORLD'S RELIGIONS, CAPE TOWN, SOUTH AFRICA, DECEMBER 1999

Smoking

When my friends were smoking, I could take a cigarette and just put it in my mouth, you know? And there was a bit of modernity you know in smoking, but I left smoking, I think I was younger than sixteen, I think I left smoking in 1934... I used to smoke very strong tobacco.

FROM A CONVERSATION WITH RICHARD STENGEL, 3 MAY 1993

Socialism

We all accept the need for some form of socialism to enable our people to catch up with the advanced countries of this world and to overcome their legacy of extreme poverty. But this does not mean we are Marxists.

SPEECH FROM THE DOCK, RIVONIA TRIAL, PALACE OF JUSTICE, PRETORIA, SOUTH AFRICA, 20 APRIL 1964

Today I am attracted by the idea of a classless society, an attraction which springs in part from Marxist reading and, in part, from my admiration of the structure and organisation of early African societies in this country. The land, then the main means of production, belonged to the tribe. There were no rich or poor and there was no exploitation.

IBID

Solidarity

The people are increasingly becoming alive to the necessity of the solidarity of all democratic forces regardless of race, party affiliation, religious belief, and ideological conviction.

FROM AN ARTICLE ENTITLED 'PEOPLE ARE DESTROYED', *LIBERATION*, OCTOBER 1955

I am also here today as a representative of the millions of people across the globe, the anti-apartheid movement, the governments and organisations that joined with us, not to fight against South Africa as a country or any of its peoples, but to oppose an inhuman system and pursue a speedy end to the apartheid crime against humanity.

NOBEL PEACE PRIZE AWARD CEREMONY, OSLO, NORWAY, 10 DECEMBER 1993

We can never celebrate the achievement of freedom and democracy without deeply remembering the role of our international solidarity partners across the world in helping to bring about that change. Without their moral and material support, we could not have achieved freedom in the manner and in the time that we did.

MESSAGE TO THE ROME CONFERENCE ON AFRICA, APRIL 2004

The values of human solidarity that once drove our quest for a humane society seem to have been replaced, or are being threatened, by a crass materialism and pursuit of social goals of instant gratification. One of the challenges of our time, without being pietistic or moralistic, is to re-instil in the consciousness of our people that sense of human solidarity, of being in the world for one another and because of and through others.

FIFTH STEVE BIKO LECTURE, UNIVERSITY OF CAPE TOWN, CAPE TOWN, SOUTH AFRICA, 10 SEPTEMBER 2004

Your voices carried across the water to inspire us in our prison cells far away. Tonight, we are free.

46664 CONCERT, HYDE PARK, LONDON, ENGLAND, 27 JUNE 2008

If a ninety-year-old may offer some unsolicited advice on this occasion, it would be that you, irrespective of your age, should place human solidarity, the concern for the other, at the centre of the values by which you live.

SIXTH NELSON MANDELA ANNUAL LECTURE, KLIPTOWN, SOWETO, SOUTH AFRICA, 12 JULY 2008

Solutions

For this solution to be just and lasting, it must result in the transformation of South Africa into a united, democratic and non-racial country. Anything less than this would condemn our country to worsening and endemic conflict. It would be an insult to the memory of the countless patriots in South Africa and the rest of our region, who have sacrificed even their lives, to bring us to the moment today when we can confidently say that the end of the apartheid system is in sight.

ADDRESS TO THE EUROPEAN PARLIAMENT, STRASBOURG, FRANCE, 13 JUNE 1990

In human affairs, no single person, organisation or social formation ever has a final or an absolutely correct position. It is through conversation, debate and critical discussion that we approach positions that may provide workable solutions.

MESSAGE TO THE EIGHTH NATIONAL CONGRESS OF COSATU (CONGRESS OF SOUTH AFRICAN TRADE UNION), MIDRAND, SOUTH AFRICA, 15–18 SEPTEMBER 2003

South Africa

It was blacks, the Abathwa, derogatorily referred to as Bushmen in white literature, who founded South Africa ages before Bartholomeu Dias saw our shores, and the Khoikhoi (the so-called Hottentots) who welcomed him when he landed.

FROM AN ESSAY ENTITLED 'WHITHER THE BLACK CONSCIOUSNESS MOVEMENT', WRITTEN ON ROBBEN ISLAND, 1978

To my compatriots, I have no hesitation in saying that each one of us is as intimately attached to the soil of this beautiful country as are the famous jacaranda trees of Pretoria and the mimosa trees of the bushveld.

INAUGURATION AS PRESIDENT OF SOUTH AFRICA, UNION BUILDINGS, PRETORIA, SOUTH AFRICA, 10 MAY 1994

South Africa: As One Nation

We can neither heal nor build, if such healing and building are perceived as [a] one-way process, with the victims of past injustices forgiving and the beneficiaries merely content in gratitude. Together we must set out to correct the defects of the past.

STATE OF THE NATION ADDRESS, PARLIAMENT, CAPE TOWN, SOUTH AFRICA, 9 FEBRUARY 1995

The call now is for each of us to ask ourselves: are we doing all we can to help build the country of our dreams?

INTERCULTURAL EID CELEBRATION, JOHANNESBURG, SOUTH AFRICA, 30 JANUARY 1998

Today the ANC and through it the African people are able and required to set the tone and national agenda for our country. The real challenge is to formulate and present this in a way that unites all South Africans – black and white – to share and work together in the common objective of eradicating poverty and creating a prosperous, non-racist and non-sexist South Africa.

ON THE DEATH OF WALTER SISULU, SOUTH AFRICA, 5 MAY 2003

Our nation comes from a history of deep division and strife; let us never, through our deeds or words, take our people back down that road.

ANC RALLY FOR HIS NINETIETH BIRTHDAY, LOFTUS VERSFELD STADIUM, PRETORIA, SOUTH AFRICA, 2 AUGUST 2008

South Africa: Challenges

It is easy to resist but what is very difficult is now to be proactive and to try and help to solve the problems of South Africa.

FROM THE DOCUMENTARY *LEGENDS: NELSON MANDELA*, 2005

We are a winning nation! We acknowledge our problems and challenges and then proceed to tackle them with determination and in a spirit of optimism. We have overcome much in order to be where we are.

VIDEO MESSAGE, 20 OCTOBER 2007

South Africa: Democratic Nation

We are proud to be able to count within our ranks Africans, coloureds, Indians and whites. We are 'one nation in one country'.

SPEAKING IN BLOEMFONTEIN, SOUTH AFRICA, CIRCA 1990

The basic issue in this country is whether blacks are going to have the right of self-determination.

SPEAKING IN SOWETO, SOUTH AFRICA, CIRCA 1990

We have a vision of South Africa as a united, democratic, non-sexist and non-racial country. We see ourselves as not aligned to any military blocs. At the same time, we shall be firmly aligned with regard to the fundamental and universal issues of human rights for all people, the right and possibility of every individual to full and unfettered development, the right of every country to determine its future, protection of the environment and peace in a world that should be free of regional conflicts and the threat of a nuclear war.

ADDRESS TO THE SWEDISH PARLIAMENT, STOCKHOLM, SWEDEN, 13 MARCH 1990

We must all strive to be inspired by a deep-seated love of our country, without regard to race, colour, gender or station in life. We must strive to be moved by a generosity of spirit that will enable us to outgrow the hatred and conflicts of the past. We must anchor all our efforts in the common determination to build a South African society that will be the envy of the world.

CHRISTMAS MESSAGE, 25 DECEMBER 1990

It was the right of all the people of South Africa, both black and white jointly, to decide the future of our country.

PRESS CONFERENCE WITH OLIVER TAMBO AND WALTER SISULU, JOHANNESBURG, SOUTH AFRICA, 8 JANUARY 1991

We live with the hope that as she battles to remake herself, South Africa will be like a microcosm of the new world that is striving to be born.

NOBEL PEACE PRIZE AWARD CEREMONY, OSLO, NORWAY, 10 DECEMBER 1993

We have moved from an era of pessimism, division, limited opportunities, turmoil and conflict. We are starting a new era of hope, of reconciliation and of nation building.

AFTER VOTING FOR THE FIRST TIME, OHLANGE HIGH SCHOOL, SOUTH AFRICA, 27 APRIL 1994

Tomorrow, the entire ANC leadership and I will be back at our desks. We are rolling up our sleeves to begin tackling the problems our country faces. We ask you all to join us – go back to your jobs in the morning. Let's get South Africa working. For we must, together and without delay, begin to build a better life for all South Africans. This means creating jobs, building houses, providing education and bringing peace and security for all.

ANC ELECTION VICTORY CELEBRATION, CARLTON HOTEL, JOHANNESBURG, SOUTH AFRICA, 2 MAY 1994

Out of the experience of an extraordinary human disaster that lasted too long, must be born a society of which all humanity will be proud.

INAUGURATION AS PRESIDENT OF SOUTH AFRICA, UNION BUILDINGS, PRETORIA, SOUTH AFRICA, 10 MAY 1994

Our daily deeds as ordinary South Africans must produce an actual South African reality that will reinforce humanity's belief in justice, strengthen its confidence in the nobility of the human soul and sustain all our hopes for a glorious life for all.

IBID

We enter into a covenant that we shall build a society in which all South Africans, both black and white, will be able to walk tall, without any fear in their hearts, assured of their inalienable right to human dignity – a rainbow nation at peace with itself and the world.

IBID

We must construct that people-centred society of freedom in such a manner that it guarantees the political liberties and the human rights of all our citizens.

FIRST STATE OF THE NATION ADDRESS, PARLIAMENT, CAPE TOWN, SOUTH AFRICA, 24 MAY 1994

To see Afrikaner farmers conversing in those queues with their employees and in a relaxed atmosphere, you could see that a new South Africa has dawned.

FROM THE DOCUMENTARY *COUNTDOWN TO FREEDOM: TEN DAYS THAT CHANGED SOUTH AFRICA*, 1994

We in South Africa are convinced that it is both possible and practicable to reach our goal of a better life for all in the shortest possible time. We derive our confidence from the knowledge that this is a vision shared by the overwhelming majority of South Africans across the colour and political divides.

RAJIV GANDHI FOUNDATION LECTURE, NEW DELHI, INDIA, 25 JANUARY 1995

The time of conflict in our land is over. We must embrace one another on the basis of justice and nurture the extended family to which we all belong.

BEYERS NAUDE'S EIGHTIETH BIRTHDAY, JOHANNESBURG, SOUTH AFRICA, 23 MAY 1995

Together, we have it in our power to change South Africa for the better.

WOMEN'S DAY MESSAGE, 9 AUGUST 1995

Yes, South Africa is not only on the right road, we are well on our way to making this the country of our dreams.

STATE OF THE NATION ADDRESS, PARLIAMENT, CAPE TOWN, SOUTH AFRICA, 9 FEBRUARY 1996

South Africa is well on its way to a new and better life. This we will achieve only if we shed the temptation to proceed casually along the road, only if we fully take the opportunities that beckon.

IBID

Time and time again the prophets of doom have been confounded by the capacity and determination of South Africans to solve their problems and to realise their shared vision of a united, peaceful and prosperous country.

INTER-FAITH COMMISSIONING SERVICE FOR THE TRC (TRUTH AND RECONCILIATION COMMISSION), ST GEORGE'S CATHEDRAL, CAPE TOWN, SOUTH AFRICA, 13 FEBRUARY 1996

It is our privilege as South Africans to be living at a time when our nation is emerging from the darkest night into the bright dawn of freedom and democracy.

ADOPTION OF THE NEW CONSTITUTION, CONSTITUTIONAL ASSEMBLY, CAPE TOWN, SOUTH AFRICA, 8 MAY 1996

And so it has come to pass, that South Africa today undergoes her rebirth, cleansed of a horrible past, matured from a tentative beginning and reaching out to the future with confidence.

IBID

I stand before you as a representative of a nation being born: a rainbow people defining their being in the recognition of each other's worth, and in the joint efforts to reach for the stars. Indeed, the irony of our late-coming into the court of free nations is that we are able to appropriate the best in human civilisation, to discard the worst, and to synthesise the rich experience of humanity with the specifics of our own unique past.

ADDRESS TO THE CBI (CONFEDERATION OF BRITISH INDUSTRY) CONFERENCE, LONDON, 10 JULY 1996

South Africans defied the prophets of doom by putting division and conflict behind them. Problems we do have, yes. But we pride ourselves on the giant steps we have taken to eradicate racism and injustice as well as religious and other forms of intolerance.

INTERNATIONAL LEADERSHIP REUNION DINNER, CAPE TOWN, SOUTH AFRICA, 20 OCTOBER 1996

There could be no peace, no lasting security, no prosperity in this land unless all enjoyed freedom and justice as equals. Out of such experience was born the vision of a free South Africa, of a nation united in diversity and working together to build a better life for all. Out of the many Sharpevilles which haunt our history was born the unshakeable determination that respect for human life, liberty and well-being must be enshrined as rights beyond the power of any force to diminish.

SIGNING OF THE NEW CONSTITUTION, SHARPEVILLE, VEREENIGING, SOUTH AFRICA, 10 DECEMBER 1996

As we close a chapter of exclusion and a chapter of heroic struggle, we reaffirm our determination to build a society of which each of us can be proud, as South Africans, as Africans, and as citizens of the world.

IBID

Part of building a new nation means building a spirit of tolerance, love and respect amongst the people of this country.

LUNCH FOR THE SPONSORS OF HIS BIRTHDAY PARTY FOR CHILDREN WITH LIFE-THREATENING DISEASES, SOUTH AFRICA, 4 JULY 1997

In time, we must bestow on South Africa the greatest gift – a more humane society. We are confident that by forging a new and prosperous nation, we are continuing the fight in which Steve Biko paid the supreme sacrifice.

COMMEMORATION OF THE TWENTIETH ANNIVERSARY OF THE DEATH IN POLICE DETENTION OF STEVE BIKO, EAST LONDON, SOUTH AFRICA, 1 SEPTEMBER 1997

Although you are bestowing an honorary doctorate on me, I do know that it is not any personal achievement that is being given recognition. Rather it is the triumph of the whole South African nation. They have turned apartheid's desert of division and conflict into a society where all can work together to make the people of our rainbow nation blossom. I humbly accept the award on their behalf, in the fervent hope that what we have achieved will serve as a symbol of peace and reconciliation, and of hope, wherever communities and societies are in the grip of conflict.

UPON RECEIVING AN HONORARY DOCTORATE FROM BEN-GURION UNIVERSITY OF THE NEGEV, CAPE TOWN, SOUTH AFRICA, 19 SEPTEMBER 1997

History will never repeat for us this moment of time and opportunity when so many of us are granted the privilege to participate in the creation of a new world.

OPENING OF THE FIFTIETH ANC NATIONAL CONFERENCE, NORTH-WEST UNIVERSITY, MAFIKENG CAMPUS, SOUTH AFRICA, 16 DECEMBER 1997

Quite often reference is made to the 'miracle' of South Africa's peaceful transition. It needs to be stated that the miracle happened because of, amongst other things, hard work over many decades to build and sustain a political culture of tolerance and non-racialism.

CLOSING SESSION OF THE FIFTIETH ANC NATIONAL CONFERENCE, NORTH-WEST UNIVERSITY, MAFIKENG CAMPUS, SOUTH AFRICA, 20 DECEMBER 1997

And so the time has come to make way for a new generation, secure in the knowledge that, despite our numerous mistakes, we sought to serve the cause of freedom; if we stumbled on occasion, the bruises sustained were the mark of the lessons that we had to learn to make our humble contribution to the birth of our nation: so our people can start, after the interregnum of defeat and humiliation, to build our [their] lives afresh as masters of their own collective destiny.
IBID

If we say with confidence that South Africa will succeed, it is in part because we know there is the Constitutional Court, the Public Protector, the Human Rights Commission, the Electoral Commission which has started its challenging work and the Attorney-General, all of which will assist in ensuring that what we do is not only constitutional, legal and legitimate, but that it is seen to be so by all and sundry, including the weakest among us.
STATE OF THE NATION ADDRESS, PARLIAMENT, CAPE TOWN, SOUTH AFRICA, 6 FEBRUARY 1998

Our confidence derives from the fact that, by joining hands, South Africans have overcome problems others thought would forever haunt us. As we destroyed apartheid so too can we defeat poverty and discrimination if we are united.
TENTH ANNIVERSARY OF THE SOWETAN'S NATION-BUILDING INITIATIVE, JOHANNESBURG, SOUTH AFRICA, 30 JUNE 1998

We can never be complacent, because the legacies of our past still run very deeply through our society. Nation-building must therefore first and foremost be about South Africans joining hands across all the racial and tribal distinctions to abolish poverty, unemployment, corruption, crime and civil strife.
IBID

There is so much to be thankful for. But if I were to speak of one thing in particular which brings me joy on my eightieth birthday, it is the way in which the people of South Africa are uniting around shared goals.
EIGHTIETH BIRTHDAY CELEBRATION, GALLAGHER ESTATE, MIDRAND, SOUTH AFRICA, 19 JULY 1998

Now that we are free, South Africa is forging a proud new identity in which all our diverse religions, cultures and languages are accorded equal rights.
SUMMIT OF THE GULF COOPERATION COUNCIL, ABU DHABI, UNITED ARAB EMIRATES, 7 DECEMBER 1998

For a country that not many years ago was the polecat of the world, South Africa has truly undergone a revolution in its relations with the international community. The doors of the world have opened to South Africa, precisely because of our success in achieving things that humanity as a whole holds dear. Of this we should be proud.
STATE OF THE NATION ADDRESS, PARLIAMENT, CAPE TOWN, SOUTH AFRICA, 5 FEBRUARY 1999

South Africans from every sector had reached out across the divisions of centuries, and averted a blood-bath which most observers believed inevitable. So much so that our smooth transition was hailed widely as a miracle.
FAREWELL BANQUET HOSTED BY PRESIDENT THABO MBEKI, PRETORIA, SOUTH AFRICA, 16 JUNE 1999

South Africa is a country bursting with untapped potential and great possibility.
ADDRESS TO RECIPIENTS OF THE NELSON MANDELA SCHOLARSHIP, SOUTH AFRICA, AUGUST 2002

I often think that the most fundamental challenge to South Africans in our post-apartheid era is to establish that sense of caring as the key characteristic of our new society.

ADDRESS AT FUND-RAISING EVENT, SOUTH AFRICA, SEPTEMBER 2002

Part of the potential greatness of this country resides in the manner in which we identify, acknowledge and talk about the problems and challenges we face.

ADDRESS TO RECIPIENTS OF THE NELSON MANDELA SCHOLARSHIP, SOUTH AFRICA, AUGUST 2003

We must recommit to our fellow South Africans. Reach out – a simple smile, a greeting, a helping hand or an act of courtesy says: I am nothing without you. I am richer for you. I respect you for who you are. Let's recommit to work towards our common goal: a nation where all of us are winners, all of us have shelter, food and education. Let's build a nation of champions.

UNVEILING OF WALTER SISULU'S TOMBSTONE, NEWCLARE CEMETERY, JOHANNESBURG, SOUTH AFRICA, 16 DECEMBER 2003

South Africa, the country that inspired the Mahatma [Gandhi] and that was inspired by the Mahatma, chose a path of peace in the face of all the prophets of doom. We chose his path, the route of negotiation and compromise. And we hope that we honoured his memory. And that, in remembrance of that great tradition, others will follow.

MESSAGE TO THE GLOBAL CONVENTION ON PEACE AND NON-VIOLENCE, NEW DELHI, INDIA, 31 JANUARY 2004

As South Africans we have worked hard and worked in unity to overcome our past and to transform our society into one in which all people enjoy that greatest of protections, namely of their dignity. We have worked hard to make a living reality out of the aspirational values of our Constitution – those of human dignity, equality, human rights and freedom, non-racialism and non-sexism.

DINNER TO CELEBRATE THE OFFICIAL OPENING OF THE CONSTITUTIONAL COURT BUILDING, CONSTITUTIONAL COURT, JOHANNESBURG, SOUTH AFRICA, 19 MARCH 2004

As a nation we have risen from the destructiveness and divisions of our past. In our transition we have not destroyed and broken down wantonly. We have in many cases taken the old forms and structures and imbued that with new values of humaneness and human solidarity.

IBID

We are solidly one nation, united in our diversity, held together by our common commitment to the Constitution. We have indeed put our racially divided past firmly behind us and face the future with the confidence of a united, non-racial, democratic country.

VIDEO MESSAGE TO MARK TEN YEARS OF DEMOCRACY IN SOUTH AFRICA, APRIL 2004

We, the people of South Africa, the preamble to our Constitution states, believe that South Africa belongs to all who live in it, united in our diversity.

JOINT SITTING OF PARLIAMENT TO MARK TEN YEARS OF DEMOCRACY, PARLIAMENT, CAPE TOWN, SOUTH AFRICA, 10 MAY 2004

We are warmed by the spirit of generosity that continues to characterise our nation and national efforts.

IBID

We today live in a country whose economy is sound and consistently growing. We live in a modern and stable democracy within which we constitutionally and legally live out our differences and tensions united in our diversity.

FOURTH ANNUAL NELSON MANDELA LECTURE, WITS GREAT HALL, JOHANNESBURG, SOUTH AFRICA, 29 JULY 2006

South Africa continues to be an example of what can be achieved in circumstances of conflict if there is the will and commitment to finding peaceful solutions. We are, in spite of our differences and tensions, a remarkably reconciled nation.

SEVENTY-FIFTH BIRTHDAY OF ARCHBISHOP DESMOND TUTU, JOHANNESBURG, SOUTH AFRICA, 8 OCTOBER 2006

We are now ready to begin the great task of building our country.

FROM THE DOCUMENTARY *HEADLINERS AND LEGENDS: NELSON MANDELA*, 2006

We are one country, we are one people.

IBID

South Africa: Healing Process

The whole South African nation has been a victim, and it is in that context that we should address the restoration of dignity and the issue of reparation. The healing process is meant for the individual, the family and the community. However, above all, the healing process involves the nation, because it is the nation itself that needs to redeem and reconstruct itself.

INTER-FAITH COMMISSIONING SERVICE FOR THE TRC (TRUTH AND RECONCILIATION COMMISSION), ST GEORGE'S CATHEDRAL, CAPE TOWN, SOUTH AFRICA, 13 FEBRUARY 1996

South Africa: Jewish Community

The Jewish community has made a major contribution to the well-being of South Africa in every sphere: enriching our culture; helping build our economy; and giving impetus to our intellectual achievements. The community has given our nation many who participated in the struggle for democracy, some at great cost and sacrifice.

MESSAGE FOR JEWISH NEW YEAR (ROSH HASHANAH), SOUTH AFRICA, 13 SEPTEMBER 1996

South Africa: Muslim Community

Our country can proudly claim Muslims as brothers and sisters, compatriots, freedom fighters and leaders, revered by our nation. They have written their names on the roll of honour with blood, sweat and tears.

INTERCULTURAL EID CELEBRATION, JOHANNESBURG, SOUTH AFRICA, 30 JANUARY 1998

South Africa: Nationalisation

Where do we get the capital for development, for the improvement of the living conditions of the people if we do not nationalise?

AT HOME, SOWETO, SOUTH AFRICA, 14 FEBRUARY 1990

We have not decided to nationalise the entire economy of the country, the economy of this country is going to remain exactly as it is except the sectors that we have mentioned like the mines, the financial institutions and monopoly industries, that is all.

IBID

We ourselves have no alternative if we want to address the problems and the grievances of the black people in this country.

AT HIS HOUSE, SPEAKING IN SUPPORT OF PRO-NATIONALISING BANKS AND MINES. HE LATER CHANGED HIS VIEW AFTER BUSINESS INDICATED THEY WOULD NOT INVEST IN A COUNTRY WITH SUCH A POLICY (SEE ENTRY DATED 28 OCTOBER 1993, BELOW), SOWETO, SOUTH AFRICA, 14 FEBRUARY 1990

The only way we can raise the resources for development is to nationalise certain sectors of the economy.

IBID

Nationalisation is part of the history of this country. After all, many sectors of our economy are today nationalised. It is only now that the government is thinking of changing the whole approach on our economic system, that they are calling for privatisation.

SABC (SOUTH AFRICAN BROADCASTING CORPORATION), JOHANNESBURG, SOUTH AFRICA, 15 FEBRUARY 1990

The view that the only words in the economic vocabulary that the ANC knows are nationalisation and redistribution is mistaken. There are many issues we shall have to consider as we discuss the question of democratisation and deracialisation of economic power.

CONFERENCE CONVENED BY THE CONSULTATIVE BUSINESS MOVEMENT ON THE THEME 'OPTIONS FOR BUILDING AN ECONOMIC FUTURE', SOUTH AFRICA, 23 MAY 1990

The ANC has no blueprint that decrees that these or other assets will be nationalised, or that such nationalisation would take this or the other form. But we do say that this option should also be part of the ongoing debate, subject to critical analysis as any other and viewed in the context of the realities of South African society.

IBID

The ANC holds no ideological positions which dictate that it must adopt a policy of nationalisation. But the ANC also holds the view that there is no self-regulating mechanism within the South African economy which will, on its own, ensure growth with equity.

ADDRESS TO THE JOINT SESSION OF THE HOUSE OF CONGRESS, WASHINGTON DC, USA, 26 JUNE 1990

A general statement that the land shall belong to all the people of South Africa, that's not nationalisation. It can mean individual ownership and we have never discussed the matter at all and that is the truth.

FROM A CONVERSATION WITH RICHARD STENGEL, 22 DECEMBER 1992

There was already a furious reaction in South Africa to the statement I made from prison where I said nationalisation was still our policy.

FROM A CONVERSATION WITH RICHARD STENGEL, 22 APRIL 1993

What is important is that we understand that it is not going to be possible for us to attract investments both from overseas and from the country itself if there is a danger that people's properties would be confiscated.

FROM AN INTERVIEW WITH THE BBC (UK) (SEE THIRD ENTRY UNDER NATIONALISATION DATED 14 FEBRUARY 1990, ABOVE), 28 OCTOBER 1993

It is quite clear now that throughout the world nationalisation is not a popular option.

FROM AN INTERVIEW WITH THE BBC (UK), 1993

NELSON MANDELA BY HIMSELF

When I was released from prison, I announced my belief in nationalisation as a cornerstone of our economic policy. As I moved around the world and heard the opinions of leading businesspeople and economists about how to grow an economy, I was persuaded and convinced about the free market. The question is how we match those demands of the free market with the burning social issues of the world.

SPEECH AT THE MILTON S EISENHOWER SYMPOSIUM, JOHNS HOPKINS UNIVERSITY, BALTIMORE, USA, 12 NOVEMBER 2003

South Africa: People

I am proud of what I am, of my country and people, our history and tradition, language, music and art and firmly believe that Africans have something distinct to offer to world culture.

FROM AN UNPUBLISHED AUTOBIOGRAPHICAL MANUSCRIPT, WRITTEN ON ROBBEN ISLAND, 1975

My country is rich in minerals and gems that lie beneath its soil but I have always known that its greatest wealth is its people, finer and truer than minerals and diamonds.

BRAM FISCHER MEMORIAL LECTURE, MARKET THEATRE, JOHANNESBURG, SOUTH AFRICA, 9 JUNE 1995

South Africans are a daring people who do not shy away from a challenge, no matter how formidable.

SUMMIT ON RURAL SAFETY AND SECURITY, MIDRAND, SOUTH AFRICA, 10 OCTOBER 1998

South Africans are competent to deal with issues of reconciliation, reparation and transformation amongst themselves without outside interference, instigation or instruction. We have dealt with our political transition in that manner and we are capable of dealing with other aspects of our transformation in similar ways.

DONATION OF THE RHODES BUILDING BY DE BEERS GROUP TO THE MANDELA RHODES FOUNDATION, CAPE TOWN, SOUTH AFRICA, AUGUST 2003

We must be careful not to project our unique circumstances too much on other situations. People can often take offence at what may be perceived as South African arrogance if we were to do that.

FROM AN INTERVIEW WITH LORIE KARNATH FOR NOBEL LAUREATES, APRIL 2004

South Africa: Places

Alexandra

Alexandra! That is a remarkable place. To some it is a township with a dubious reputation; famous more for its notorious gangs, slums, braziers and smoke. To others it is a perfect haven, where a person may build a dream house on his own plot of ground and to be loved in his castle. To me it is my other home.

FROM A LETTER TO ONICA MASHEGO, WRITTEN ON ROBBEN ISLAND, 8 NOVEMBER 1970

Life was cheap and the gun and the knife ruled at night.

FROM AN UNPUBLISHED AUTOBIOGRAPHICAL MANUSCRIPT, WRITTEN ON ROBBEN ISLAND, 1975

Whenever I think about the Dark City I become homesick. It was there that I stayed when I first came to Johannesburg. Some of my best friends lived in that city.

FROM A LETTER TO REBECCA KOTANE, WRITTEN ON ROBBEN ISLAND, 7 OCTOBER 1979

Alexandra is immortalised in the hearts of countless veterans, dead and alive, and it is only right that even the physical form of that heritage should never be allowed to disappear from the public eye.

FROM A LETTER TO THE REVEREND SAM BUTI, WRITTEN IN POLLSMOOR PRISON, CAPE TOWN, SOUTH AFRICA, 29 JUNE 1983

I am looking forward to the day when Alexandra, as well as the communities that surround it, become the united and organised community that I remember as my home.

RALLY, BLOEMFONTEIN, SOUTH AFRICA, 25 FEBRUARY 1995

Bloemfontein

The ANC is a child of Bloemfontein. The umbilical cord of the ANC is buried here.

RALLY, BLOEMFONTEIN, SOUTH AFRICA, 25 FEBRUARY 1990

Cape Town

Perhaps it was history that ordained that it be here, at the Cape of Good Hope, that we should lay the foundation stone of our new nation. For it was here at this Cape, over three centuries ago, that there began the fateful convergence of the peoples of Africa, Europe and Asia on these shores.

ADDRESS TO THE PEOPLE OF CAPE TOWN AFTER BEING ELECTED PRESIDENT, CITY HALL, CAPE TOWN, SOUTH AFRICA, 9 MAY 1994

In Cape Town resides part of the souls of many nations and cultures, priceless threads in the rich diversity of our African nation. This legacy of our history is both a strength and a challenge.

UPON RECEIVING THE FREEDOM OF THE CITY OF CAPE TOWN, CAPE TOWN, SOUTH AFRICA, 27 NOVEMBER 1997

If Cape Town's Robben Island was for centuries the symbol of repression, this City has also been the scene of stirring resistance from the very start of colonial occupation to the triumph of our people over oppression.

IBID

Cape Town's greatness lies not only in its contribution to our economy but in its involvement in our country's history. It was here, three centuries ago, that sailors from Europe triggered off the chain of dispossession whose consequence we are still grappling with today.

IBID

This City hosted me and my colleagues for over twenty-six years. It was the people of Cape Town who welcomed me on my first day of freedom.

IBID

Cape Town, more than any other city in South Africa, has been home to people from different cultures for a long, long time. The many people who know Cape Town as their home can trace their ancestries from across the world. Muslim and Jew, Christian and Hindu, coloured, African, Indian and white: all these and others have brought to the Cape a part of the soul of many peoples and cultures in many parts of the world.

OPENING OF THE 'ONE CITY MANY CULTURES' PROJECT, CAPE TOWN, SOUTH AFRICA, 1 MARCH 1999

Johannesburg

Johannesburg has always been the mecca for enterprising people, and it was a very important school of life, and the conditions there were such as to stimulate people to consider, you know, joining the Movement for the liberation of the African people.

FROM A CONVERSATION WITH RICHARD STENGEL, CIRCA APRIL 1993

Long live this town of vibrancy and activity. We know that it will transcend our history of division. We know that it is becoming one of the leading spaces of national unity in our country. We know that it is the centre of prosperity in our country, providing the opportunity to create that better life for all our people.

CITY OF JOHANNESBURG'S CELEBRATION OF SOUTH AFRICA'S TEN YEARS OF DEMOCRACY, ORLANDO COMMUNITY HALL, SOWETO, JOHANNESBURG, SOUTH AFRICA, 23 JULY 2004

Kholvad House

We had no real offices those days and we met at his place. And Dr [Yusuf] Dadoo also would meet many people in that flat. And it was originally the flat of Ismail Meer, a colleague of mine at Varsity, and I spent a lot of time there when I was preparing for exams and even slept there.

FROM A CONVERSATION WITH RICHARD STENGEL, 17 MARCH 1993

We closed our office because Comrade Oliver Tambo went into exile, and I was in the Treason Trial every day. I couldn't run an office; we closed the office. So I continued, however, to practise, and I then used the flat as my office.

IBID

I hope the record will be accurate, because it shows what other groups did for all of us.

FROM A CONVERSATION WITH AHMED KATHRADA ABOUT KHOLVAD HOUSE AND NON-RACIALISM, CIRCA 2009

Langa

I miss Langa very badly and sometimes wish I could stand on Table Mountain, just as I did in 1948, and see even if merely its distant outline.

FROM A LETTER TO DR MZOBANZI MBOYA, SOUTH AFRICA, 1 MARCH 1988

Liliesleaf

I naturally found Rivonia an ideal place for the man who lived the life of an outlaw. Up to that time I had been compelled to live indoors during the daytime and could only venture out under cover of darkness. But at Liliesleaf I could live differently, and work far more efficiently.

SPEECH FROM THE DOCK, RIVONIA TRIAL, PALACE OF JUSTICE, PRETORIA, SOUTH AFRICA, 20 APRIL 1964

Up to the time of my arrest, Liliesleaf Farm was the headquarters of neither the African National Congress nor Umkhonto. With the exception of myself, none of the officials or members of these bodies lived there, no meetings of the governing bodies were ever held there, and no activities connected with them were either organised or directed from there.

IBID

[Liliesleaf] could be regarded as the headquarters of Umkhonto we Sizwe but there was no decision either formal or informally to make either Rivonia or Trevallyn the headquarters of Umkhonto.

FROM A CONVERSATION WITH RICHARD STENGEL, 17 APRIL 1993

Mqhekezweni

Few things convince me that the universe is fast ageing more than the dilapidated condition of the once-stately buildings of the Mqhekezweni of my childhood. A lot of history lies locked up in those silent walls.

FROM A LETTER TO AMINA AND PETER FRENSE, WRITTEN IN VICTOR VERSTER PRISON, PAARL, SOUTH AFRICA, 21 AUGUST 1989

When I left my village, from Mqhekezweni, the passenger train passed very rarely through our area and the day it was going to pass was known and the village would come out and look at it as it passed, because it was something unusual, something unknown.

FROM A CONVERSATION WITH RICHARD STENGEL, 13 JANUARY 1993

Paarl

I feel perfectly at home and as one who has been adopted with open arms by the residents of this famous town.

FROM A LETTER TO THE PAARL ADVICE OFFICE, WRITTEN IN VICTOR VERSTER PRISON, PAARL, SOUTH AFRICA, 21 AUGUST 1989

Qunu

When I went back home to Qunu in 1990, it was an emotional moment, because it was my first time to see my mother's grave.

FROM A CONVERSATION WITH RICHARD STENGEL, 13 JANUARY 1993

The way people talk, and even *now* is something different for me to go... to Qunu – the people there, you know, there is a *different* dimension altogether and I get, you know, so pleased when I listen to them talk; their mannerisms, it reminds me of my younger days.

FROM A CONVERSATION WITH RICHARD STENGEL, 10 MARCH 1993

It arouses a great deal of emotion for me to be here because it would be fair to say part of myself lies buried here.

FROM A BBC (UK) DOCUMENTARY, TALKING ABOUT HIS FAMILY'S ANCESTRAL GRAVES IN QUNU, SOUTH AFRICA, 1996

Wherever I die I'll be buried here – this is where I am going to be buried.

FROM A BBC (UK) DOCUMENTARY, SPEAKING FROM QUNU, SOUTH AFRICA, 1996

I look forward to that period when I will be able to wake up with the sun: to walk the hills and valleys of my country village, Qunu, in peace and tranquility.

CLOSING SESSION OF THE FIFTIETH ANC NATIONAL CONFERENCE, NORTH-WEST UNIVERSITY, MAFIKENG CAMPUS, SOUTH AFRICA, 20 DECEMBER 1997

Soweto

The police handled the riots with total disregard for human life. They cruelly shot down schoolchildren, tortured those who fell into their hands and ill-treated those who were jailed.

FROM AN ESSAY ENTITLED 'WHITHER THE BLACK CONSCIOUSNESS MOVEMENT', WRITTEN ON ROBBEN ISLAND, 1978

South Africa: Racial Oppression

South Africa is known throughout the world as a country where the most fierce forms of colour discrimination are practised, and where the peaceful struggles of the African people for freedom are violently suppressed. It is a country torn from top to bottom by fierce racial strife and conflicts and where the blood of African patriots frequently flows.

ADDRESS ON BEHALF OF THE ANC DELEGATION TO THE PAFMECA (PAN-AFRICAN FREEDOM MOVEMENT OF EAST AND CENTRAL AFRICA) CONFERENCE, ADDIS ABABA, ETHIOPIA, 3 FEBRUARY 1962

There are numerous other South African patriots, known and unknown, who have been sacrificed in various ways on the altar of African freedom.

IBID

We fight against two features which are the hallmarks of African life in South Africa and which are entrenched by legislation which we seek to have repealed. These features are poverty and lack of human dignity.

SPEECH FROM THE DOCK, RIVONIA TRIAL, PALACE OF JUSTICE, PRETORIA, SOUTH AFRICA, 20 APRIL 1964

South Africa and the African continent are part of a larger world and the people of my country and those of Africa are part of the human race. Their problems must be seen from the point of view of their uniqueness as individual peoples and from the point of view of the history of mankind as a whole.

FROM AN UNPUBLISHED AUTOBIOGRAPHICAL MANUSCRIPT, WRITTEN ON ROBBEN ISLAND, 1975

It is present South Africa that is a country of racial oppression, imprisonment without trial, torture and harsh sentences and the threat of internment camps lies not in the distant past, but in the immediate future.

FROM A LETTER TO GENERAL DU PREEZ, COMMISSIONER OF PRISONS, WRITTEN ON ROBBEN ISLAND, 12 JULY 1976

A new South Africa has to eliminate the racial hatred and suspicion caused by apartheid and offer guarantees to all its citizens of peace, security and prosperity.

WELCOME HOME RALLY, SOCCER CITY, SOWETO, SOUTH AFRICA, 13 FEBRUARY 1990

South Africa: Reputation

The time has come that we abandon this terrible past which made our country an object of hatred by the nations of the world.

CHRISTMAS MESSAGE, 25 DECEMBER 1990

A united, non-racial, non-sexist and democratic South Africa will become the jewel of this planet.

OPENING OF THE GANDHI HALL, LENASIA, SOUTH AFRICA, 27 SEPTEMBER 1992

That spiritual and physical oneness we all share with this common homeland explains the depth of the pain we all carried in our hearts as we saw our country tear itself apart in a terrible conflict, and as we saw it spurned, outlawed and isolated by the peoples of the world, precisely because it has become the universal base of the pernicious ideology and practice of racism and racial oppression.

SPEAKING AT THE UNION BUILDINGS, PRETORIA, SOUTH AFRICA, 10 MAY 1994

It has been an inspiration to serve a nation that has helped renew the world's hope that all conflicts, no matter how intractable, are capable of peaceful resolution.

FAREWELL BANQUET HOSTED BY PRESIDENT THABO MBEKI, PRETORIA, SOUTH AFRICA, 16 JUNE 1999

We, the people of South Africa and the freedom movements of our people, have suffered many moments and eras of deep despondency when it must have appeared that the so-much-longed-for emancipation was never to be attained, at least not in our various and respective lifetimes.

FROM AN ARTICLE IN THE *SUNDAY TIMES* (SOUTH AFRICA) MARKING TEN YEARS OF DEMOCRACY, APRIL 2004

South Africa: War

We must never again allow our nation's resources, scientists and engineers to be used to support an ideology by producing weapons of mass destruction.

SOUTH AFRICAN INSTITUTION OF MECHANICAL ENGINEERS CENTENARY CONFERENCE, SOUTH AFRICA, 30 AUGUST 1993

Speaking

Long speeches, the shaking of fists, the banging of tables and strongly worded resolutions out of touch with the objective conditions do not bring about mass action and can do a great deal of harm to the organisation and the struggle we serve.

PRESIDENTIAL ADDRESS TO THE ANC TRANSVAAL CONGRESS, ALSO KNOWN AS THE 'NO EASY WALK TO FREEDOM' SPEECH, TRANSVAAL, SOUTH AFRICA, 21 SEPTEMBER 1953

There is a stage in the life of every social reformer when he will thunder on platforms primarily to relieve himself of the scraps of undigested information that has accumulated in his head; an attempt to impress the crowds rather than to start a calm and simple exposition of principles and ideas whose universal truth is made evident by personal experience and deeper study.

FROM A LETTER TO WINNIE MANDELA, WRITTEN ON ROBBEN ISLAND, 20 JUNE 1970

Gossiping about others is certainly a vice, a virtue when about oneself.

FROM A DIARY ENTRY, WRITTEN ON ROBBEN ISLAND, 18 JANUARY 1977

The masses like to see somebody who is responsible and who speaks in a responsible manner. They like that, and so I avoid rabble-rousing speeches.

FROM A CONVERSATION WITH RICHARD STENGEL, 3 FEBRUARY 1993

One cannot speak to a mass of people as one addresses an audience of two dozen. Yet, I have always tried to take the same care to explain matters to great audiences as to small ones.

FROM *LONG WALK TO FREEDOM*, 1994

Sport

Taking part in sports like running, swimming and tennis will keep you healthy, strong and bright.

FROM A LETTER TO DUMANI MANDELA, WRITTEN IN VICTOR VERSTER PRISON, PAARL, SOUTH AFRICA, 28 FEBRUARY 1989

Soccer is one of the sporting disciplines in which Africa is rising to demonstrate her excellence, for too long latent in her womb.

OPENING OF THE AFRICAN CUP OF NATIONS TOURNAMENT, JOHANNESBURG, SOUTH AFRICA, 13 JANUARY 1996

Sport has the power to overcome old divisions and create the bond of common aspirations.

BANQUET FOR THE AFRICAN CUP OF NATIONS, SOUTH AFRICA, 1 MARCH 1996

They are our treasured possessions, jewels in our country's crown. They will know that their triumphs are celebrated by the entire rainbow nation whose banner they have raised high amongst the nations of the world.

PRESIDENT'S SPORT AWARDS, PRETORIA, SOUTH AFRICA, 4 OCTOBER 1996

Who could doubt that sport is a crucial window for the propagation of fair play and justice? After all, fair play is a value that is essential to sport!

SPEAKING AT THE INTERNATIONAL FAIR PLAY AWARDS, PRETORIA, SOUTH AFRICA, 25 JUNE 1997

Reconstruction and reconciliation, nation-building and development must go hand-in-hand. In this process sport is a great force for unity and reconciliation.

IBID

Though we live in a world in which the good that is in people generally prevails, sadly there are also those who exploit magnanimity and openness. We have, therefore, constantly to affirm and celebrate good deeds and social virtues. In this respect, sport today plays a pre-eminent role in expounding what is good and exemplifying what is healthy.

IBID

Sport has the power to change the world. It has the power to inspire, it has the power to unite people in a way that little else does. It speaks to youth in a language they understand.

PRESENTING THE INAUGURAL LAUREUS LIFETIME ACHIEVEMENT AWARD, SPORTING CLUB, MONACO, MONTE CARLO, 25 MAY 2000

Sport can create hope, where once there was only despair. It is more powerful than governments in breaking down racial barriers. It laughs in the face of all types of discrimination.

IBID

The Special Olympics give telling testimony to the indestructibility of the human spirit and of our capacity to overcome hardships and obstacles.

SPECIAL OLYMPICS SUMMER GAMES OPENING CEREMONY, DUBLIN, IRELAND, 21 JUNE 2003

Sport reaches areas far beyond the reach of politicians.

FROM THE DOCUMENTARY MANDELA: THE LIVING LEGEND, 2003

We are ready for Soccer World Cup 2010 and now only wait for FIFA's final nod that we can go ahead full steam with our preparations.

FAREWELL BANQUET FOR SOUTH AFRICA'S 2010 SOCCER WORLD CUP BID COMMITTEE, VODAWORLD, MIDRAND, SOUTH AFRICA, 10 MAY 2004

In Africa, soccer enjoys great popularity and has a particular place in the hearts of people.

SPEAKING AT THE NELSON MANDELA FOUNDATION, JOHANNESBURG, SOUTH AFRICA, DECEMBER 2009

FIFA World Cup

I feel like a young man of fifteen.

UPON SOUTH AFRICA BEING VOTED AS HOST OF THE 2010 FIFA WORLD CUP, GERMANY, 2004

Rugby World Cup Final

I went around the stadium – I didn't expect such an ovation.

FROM THE DOCUMENTARY *MANDELA: THE LIVING LEGEND*, 2003

The cumulative effect was to allay the fears of the whites and also, by the way, of the blacks because there were many who said, 'Well this old man is selling out' and who booed me when I said, 'Let us now support rugby, let's regard these boys as our boys'.

IBID

Stay-at-Home

One of the most significant factors about the stay-at-home was the wide support it received from students and the militant and stirring demonstrations it inspired amongst them.

STATEMENT ON BEHALF OF THE NATIONAL ACTION COUNCIL FOLLOWING THE 29–31 MAY 1961 STAY-AT-HOME IN SUPPORT OF A NATIONAL CONVENTION, 1961

In spite of the magnificent courage shown by our people, numerical response fell below expectations. Mistakes were committed and weaknesses and shortcomings were discovered. They must be attended to. We must make adjustments in our methods and style of work to meet contingencies which we did not anticipate. Only in this way shall we build more strength and increase our striking power.

IBID

The strike at the end of May was only the beginning of our campaign. We are now launching a full-scale, countrywide campaign of non-cooperation with the Verwoerd Government, until we have won an elected National Convention, representing all the people of this country, with the power to draw up and enforce a new democratic constitution.

IBID

Succession

Well, you know I am a country boy and I have hunted and lived, you know, in forests and so on and I have seen big trees. And if you look under it nothing is growing but once that tree falls you find new trees from underneath it, growing and becoming as tall as the previous tree.

SPEAKING AT SHELL HOUSE (OFFICE OF THE ANC), JOHANNESBURG, SOUTH AFRICA, 28 OCTOBER 1993

Suffering

The suffering of the people of any single country affects all of us no matter where we find ourselves. That is why it is so important that multilateral bodies assume collective responsibility for finding fair and just solutions to problems in the world, taking into account equally the considerations of the weak and the mighty, the rich and the poor, developed and developing nations alike.

BANQUET HOSTED BY MUAMMAR QADDAFI, LIBYA, 22 OCTOBER 1997

We recognise today the many men, women and children who sacrificed freedom and even life itself, who have been left with disabilities, who have lost families. We think of the suffering of communities and the trauma of the nation as a whole.

SPECIAL DEBATE ON THE TRC (TRUTH AND RECONCILIATION COMMISSION) REPORT, PARLIAMENT, CAPE TOWN, SOUTH AFRICA, 25 FEBRUARY 1999

The suffering inflicted, and more often than not on the most vulnerable sectors of society, demeans all of us as humanity. That it is invariably women, children, the aged and disabled who suffer in these conflicts stands to the added shame of humankind.

GLOBAL CONFERENCE ON PEACE THROUGH TOURISM, GRAND HYATT AMMAN BALLROOM, AMMAN, JORDAN, NOVEMBER 2000

Superstition

Despite remarkable coincidences, it is far better never to be superstitious.

FROM A LETTER TO PROFESSOR WA JOUBERT, WRITTEN IN VICTOR VERSTER PRISON, PAARL, SOUTH AFRICA, 22 MAY 1989

It is indeed reassuring that the world has crawled or is crawling out of the superstitions of previous centuries. Otherwise many gurus would accept purely fortuitous occurrences for causal connections.

FROM A LETTER TO DR MAMPHELA RAMPHELE, WRITTEN IN VICTOR VERSTER PRISON, PAARL, SOUTH AFRICA, 19 SEPTEMBER 1989

I was not superstitious at all.

FROM A CONVERSATION WITH RICHARD STENGEL, 30 MARCH 1993

Support

We can also say that very big people, very important people who were not known, you know, to have identified themselves with the movement used to be generous and to support us.

FROM A CONVERSATION WITH AHMED KATHRADA, CIRCA 1993/94

It is best to rely on the freely given support of the people; otherwise that support is weak and fleeting. The organisation should be a haven, not a prison.

FROM LONG WALK TO FREEDOM, 1994

Suspicion

As we judge others so are we judged by others. The suspicious will always be tormented by suspicion.

FROM A LETTER TO WINNIE MANDELA, WRITTEN ON ROBBEN ISLAND, 9 DECEMBER 1979

Technology

In a world in which breathtaking advances in technology and communication have shortened the space between erstwhile prohibitively distant lands; where outdated beliefs and imaginary differences among peoples were being rapidly eradicated; where exclusiveness was giving way to cooperation and interdependence, we too found ourselves obliged to shed our narrow outlook and adjust to fresh realities.

FROM A LETTER TO MRS MANORAMA BHALLA, SECRETARY, INDIAN COUNCIL FOR CULTURAL RELATIONS, WRITTEN ON ROBBEN ISLAND, 3 AUGUST 1980

Television has revolutionised South Africa's social life in important respects. It has even softened the grim atmosphere of a maximum security prison and literally brought the world right into the cell, inducing the feeling that, in whatever circumstances man may find himself, life is always worthwhile and fulfilling.

FROM A LETTER TO EFFIE SCHULTZ, WRITTEN IN POLLSMOOR PRISON, CAPE TOWN, SOUTH AFRICA, 1 APRIL 1987

The camera has the ability to give one and the same person different faces.

FROM A LETTER TO DR MAMPHELA RAMPHELE, WRITTEN IN POLLSMOOR PRISON, CAPE TOWN, SOUTH AFRICA, 1 MARCH 1988

Thriftiness

Thrift, especially on the part of a young lady, is a virtue; taken to extremes, however, many people may equate it with self-denial and misery as dangerous as anorexia.

FROM A LETTER TO ELAINE KEARNS, WRITTEN IN VICTOR VERSTER PRISON, PAARL, SOUTH AFRICA, 14 FEBRUARY 1989

Time

I never think of the time I have lost. I just carry out a programme because it's there. It's mapped out for me.

FROM A CONVERSATION WITH RICHARD STENGEL, 3 MAY 1993

Timing

If you wait for textbook conditions, they will never occur.

FROM *LONG WALK TO FREEDOM*, 1994

Time is short – for if we do not act now, in concert, the brushfire crises that are proliferating around the world may yet become an uncontrollable conflagration.

STATEMENT ON BUILDING A GLOBAL PARTNERSHIP FOR CHILDREN, 6 MAY 2000

Tolerance

The ANC has on countless occasions emphasised the importance of tolerance in the course of our political work. The right of other parties to canvass and put forward their views without interference from other political organisations, that is our standpoint. It has always been our standpoint.

PRESS CONFERENCE, CAPE TOWN, SOUTH AFRICA, 4 MAY 1990

Bridge the chasm, use tolerance and compassion, be inclusive not exclusive, build dignity and pride, encourage freedom of expression to create a civil society for unity and peace.

OPENING OF THE CULTURAL DEVELOPMENT CONGRESS AT THE CIVIC THEATRE, JOHANNESBURG, SOUTH AFRICA, 25 APRIL 1993

The challenge for each one of you is to take up these ideals of tolerance and respect for others and put them to practical use in your schools, your communities and throughout your lives.

RECORDED MESSAGE FOR THE ROUND SQUARE CAMPAIGN, SOUTH AFRICA, 4 OCTOBER 1996

Let tolerance for one another's views create the peaceful conditions which give space for the best in all of us to find expression and to flourish.

SIGNING OF THE NEW CONSTITUTION, SHARPEVILLE, VEREENIGING, SOUTH AFRICA, 10 DECEMBER 1996

What is critical is not that we should have the same views on everything, nor that we should refrain from expressing our differences in a robust way. Rather it is that we should be tolerant of one another's views and as leaders work towards uniting our nation on the basis of the founding consensus which underpinned our negotiated transition to democracy and the adoption of our new constitution.

ADDRESS AT THE OPENING OF THE PRESIDENT'S BUDGET DEBATE, PARLIAMENT, CAPE TOWN, SOUTH AFRICA, 2 MARCH 1999

Trade Unions

You must make every home, every shack and every mud structure where our people live, a branch of the trade union movement and never surrender.

PRESIDENTIAL ADDRESS TO THE ANC TRANSVAAL CONGRESS, ALSO KNOWN AS THE 'NO EASY WALK TO FREEDOM' SPEECH, TRANSVAAL, SOUTH AFRICA, 21 SEPTEMBER 1953

Why should we continue enriching those who steal the products of our sweat and blood, who exploit us and refuse us the right to organise trade unions?

FROM THE 'STRUGGLE IS MY LIFE' PRESS STATEMENT, EXPLAINING HIS DECISION TO CARRY ON HIS POLITICAL WORK UNDERGROUND IN ACCORDANCE WITH THE ADVICE OF THE NATIONAL ACTION COUNCIL, SOUTH AFRICA, 26 JUNE 1961

The trade union movement has since the early twenties played an important role in our affairs. Today it has become one of the most dynamic instruments of progress with a solid mass rarely seen before, and using strategies which are certain to bring rich rewards in the end.

FROM A LETTER TO SAM NDOU, WRITTEN IN VICTOR VERSTER PRISON, PAARL, SOUTH AFRICA, 21 AUGUST 1989

The present trade union leaders are indeed the standard-bearers of traditions which are born of decades of hard work and sacrifice.

FROM A LETTER TO CHRIS DLAMINI, WRITTEN IN VICTOR VERSTER PRISON, PAARL, SOUTH AFRICA, 21 AUGUST 1989

In the new South Africa we want to create workers who will have to continue to organise, in order to defend and assert their interests as against those of the employers.

MAY DAY RALLY, SOUTH AFRICA, 1 MAY 1991

We salute you for your tireless and dedicated service to the millions of workers around our country. We urge you not to tire, not to be dismayed when times are tough and to be resilient in these challenging times.

MESSAGE TO THE NINTH NATIONAL CONGRESS OF COSATU (CONGRESS OF SOUTH AFRICAN TRADE UNIONS), MIDRAND, SOUTH AFRICA, 18 SEPTEMBER 2006

Traditional Structures

All people throughout the world have at one time or another had clans and some clans were certainly mightier and better known in history than ours… ours is the whole world, our umbrella and the broad steel blade that removes all obstacles.

FROM A LETTER TO MRS N THULARE, WRITTEN ON ROBBEN ISLAND, 19 JULY 1977

Treason Trial

Hardly anybody believed that we would be convicted. In fact in the case itself, people read and finished books, novels; they were not concerned with the proceedings.

FROM A CONVERSATION WITH RICHARD STENGEL, 30 MARCH 1993

Well the main occupation of Duma Nokwe and myself, we were trained lawyers, was to prepare the evidence of the accused.

FROM A CONVERSATION WITH RICHARD STENGEL, 4 APRIL 1993

Tribalism

In this regard, we need to recall the clarion call made by Pixley ka Seme at the founding of the ANC eighty years ago when he said that 'we must bury the demon of tribalism'.

FUNERAL OF REGGIE HADEBE, SOUTH AFRICA, 7 NOVEMBER 1992

Truth

Distortions have misled many innocent people because they are weaved around concrete facts and events which those who still have a conscience would never deny.

FROM A LETTER TO WINNIE MANDELA, WRITTEN ON ROBBEN ISLAND, 9 DECEMBER 1979

No single person, no body of opinion, no political doctrine, no religious doctrine can claim a monopoly on truth.

ADDRESS TO THE INTERNATIONAL FEDERATION OF NEWSPAPER PUBLISHERS, PRAGUE, CZECH REPUBLIC, 26 MAY 1992

Truth and Reconciliation Commission

As the Truth and Reconciliation Commission inches its way towards this truth, we are all bound to agonise over the price in terms of justice that the victims have to pay. But we can draw solace from the conviction that the half-truths of a lowly interrogator cannot and should not hide the culpability of the commanders and the political leaders who gave the orders. For we do know, that what they desperately sought to get from him was his contact with the leadership of the liberation movement. In time, the truth will out!

COMMEMORATION OF THE TWENTIETH ANNIVERSARY OF THE DEATH IN POLICE DETENTION OF STEVE BIKO, EAST LONDON, SOUTH AFRICA, 1 SEPTEMBER 1997

While the Truth and Reconciliation Commission is taking us on a difficult journey, it is one that has helped us understand our painful past. Incomplete and imperfect as the process may be, it shall leave us less burdened by the past and unshackled to pursue a glorious future.

NEW YEAR MESSAGE, 31 DECEMBER 1998

Captured in halls through the length and breadth of the country and besides the unmarked graves of fallen heroes was the resilience of the human spirit of South Africa's people. The tears shed and the voices choking with emotion reminded us once more that the freedom we have gained we should never take for granted.

SPECIAL DEBATE ON THE TRC (TRUTH AND RECONCILIATION COMMISSION) REPORT, PARLIAMENT, CAPE TOWN, SOUTH AFRICA, 25 FEBRUARY 1999

Tuberculosis

The world has made defeating AIDS a top priority. This is a blessing. But TB remains ignored. Today we are calling on the world to recognise that we can't fight AIDS unless we do much more to fight TB as well.

CLOSING ADDRESS TO THE XV INTERNATIONAL AIDS CONFERENCE, BANGKOK, THAILAND, 16 JULY 2004

Ubuntu

Umuntu ngumuntu ngabantu – it means you must serve your fellow man. You see? You must respect and serve your fellow man faithfully. That's what, because without their support you can never progress. That's what it means.

FROM A CONVERSATION WITH RICHARD STENGEL, 29 APRIL OR 3 MAY 1993

As with other aspects of its heritage, African traditional religion is increasingly recognised for its contribution to the world. No longer seen as despised superstition which had to be superseded by superior forms of belief, today its enrichment of humanity's spiritual heritage is acknowledged. The spirit of Ubuntu – that profound African sense that we are human only through the humanity of other human beings – is not a parochial phenomenon, but has added globally to our common search for a better world.

LECTURE AT THE OXFORD CENTRE FOR ISLAMIC STUDIES, SHELDONIAN THEATRE, OXFORD, ENGLAND, 11 JULY 1997

In Africa we have a concept known as ubuntu, based upon the recognition that we are only people because of other people.

CLOSING ADDRESS TO THE XIV INTERNATIONAL AIDS CONFERENCE, BARCELONA, SPAIN, 12 JULY 2002

United Democratic Front

The United Democratic Front is one of the pillars of the Mass Democratic Movement.

FROM A LETTER TO DULLAH OMAR, WRITTEN IN VICTOR VERSTER PRISON, PAARL, SOUTH AFRICA, 21 AUGUST 1989

United Nations

The United Nations understood this very well that racism in our country could not but feed racism in other parts of the world as well. The universal struggle against apartheid was therefore not an act of charity arising out of pity for our people, but an affirmation of our common humanity. We believe that that act of affirmation requires that this Organisation should once more turn its focused and sustained attention to the basics of everything that makes for a better world for all humanity.

ADDRESS TO THE FORTY-NINTH UNITED NATIONS GENERAL ASSEMBLY, NEW YORK CITY, USA, 3 OCTOBER 1994

When the secretary-generals were white, we never had the question of any country ignoring the United Nations. But now that we have got the black secretary-generals, like Boutros Boutros-Ghali and now Kofi Annan, certain countries that believe in white supremacy are ignoring the United Nations. We have to combat that without reservation.

PRESS CONFERENCE, JAKARTA, INDONESIA, 30 SEPTEMBER 2002

No country, however powerful it may be, is entitled to act outside the United Nations. The United Nations was established in order that countries, irrespective of the continent from which they come, should act through an organised and disciplined body. The United Nations is here to promote peace in the world, and any country that acts outside the United Nations is making a serious mistake.

IBID

The world today needs respectful and equitable partnerships between nations everywhere. We also need international institutions that equitably serve the needs of nations.

RECORDED MESSAGE OF ACCEPTANCE OF HIS COMMENCEMENT, MICHIGAN STATE UNIVERSITY, 29 APRIL 2008

United States of America

The stand you took established the understanding among the millions of our people that here we have friends, here we have fighters against racism who feel hurt because we are hurt, who seek our success because they too seek the victory of democracy over tyranny. And here I speak not only about you, members of the United States Congress, but also of the millions of people throughout this great land who stood up and engaged the apartheid system in struggle.

ADDRESS TO THE JOINT SESSION OF THE HOUSE OF CONGRESS, WASHINGTON DC, USA, 26 JUNE 1990

We could not have made an acquaintance through literature with human giants such as George Washington, Abraham Lincoln and Thomas Jefferson and not been moved to act as they were moved to act. We could not have heard of and admired John Brown, Sojourner Truth, Frederick Douglass, WEB DuBois, Marcus Garvey, Martin Luther King Jr, and others, and not be moved to act as they were moved to act. We could not have known of your Declaration of Independence and not elected to join in the struggle to guarantee the people life, liberty and the pursuit of happiness.

IBID

American security is very professional, highly professional, and they brief you on how to move and that the most dangerous moment is when you leave any place to your car and when you leave the car to your place. And they insist, you know, on a swift movement. And also when you travel from one place to the other, you are surrounded by security. It's difficult to stop and talk to people as one would like when you visit a new place.

FROM A CONVERSATION WITH RICHARD STENGEL, 22 APRIL 1993

NELSON MANDELA BY HIMSELF

If there is a country that has committed unspeakable atrocities in the world, it is the United States of America. They don't care for human beings.

SPEAKING AT A CONFERENCE OF THE INTERNATIONAL WOMEN'S FORUM, TOKYO, JAPAN, 30 JANUARY 2003

What I am condemning is that one power, with a president who has no foresight, who cannot think properly, is now wanting to plunge the world into a holocaust. I am happy that the people of the world – especially those of the United States of America – are standing up and opposing their own president. I hope that that opposition will one day make him understand that he [George W Bush] has made the greatest mistake of his life in trying to bring about carnage and to police the world, without any authority of the international body. It is something we have to condemn without reservation.

IBID

I have taken issue with the American political leadership where I thought they were acting contrary to the best values in American life and the American Constitution. For example, I strongly opposed the unilateral action taken outside of the United Nations with regards to Iraq. This has, however, not diminished my respect for America's leadership role in the world or my appreciation for the role its leaders play in the world.

SPEECH AT THE MILTON S EISENHOWER SYMPOSIUM, JOHNS HOPKINS UNIVERSITY, BALTIMORE, USA, 12 NOVEMBER 2003

I think the United States has become drunk with power.

FROM THE DOCUMENTARY *MANDELA: THE LIVING LEGEND*, 2003

United Women's Congress

The United Women's Congress has become one of the people's effective weapons in the struggle for human dignity and justice.

FROM A LETTER TO THE UNITED WOMEN'S CONGRESS, WRITTEN IN VICTOR VERSTER PRISON, PAARL, SOUTH AFRICA, 21 AUGUST 1989

Unity

Our main task is to link up and confront the enemy with a mighty force that enjoys the undivided loyalty of the oppressed people as a whole.

FROM AN ESSAY ENTITLED 'CLEAR THE OBSTACLES AND CONFRONT THE ENEMY', WRITTEN ON ROBBEN ISLAND, 1976

Unity between the ANC and the PAC [Pan Africanist Congress] has been blocked by differences over the Freedom Charter, the role of communists and other national groups and allegations of extreme nationalism.

IBID

Here in prison, policy differences do not prevent us from presenting a united front against the enemy.

IBID

A united liberation movement that enjoys the solid support of the oppressed people as a whole, which does not have rivalries to divert its attention, and which can devote all its resources to the single objective of crushing the enemy will be a turning point in the history of our country.

IBID

The unity we are advocating is a unity of existing political organisations in the movement, of those who are already waging the armed struggle, those who are still preparing to do so and even those who have no such plans.

IBID

Only a united movement can successfully undertake the task of uniting the country.

IBID

The first condition for victory is black unity. Every effort to divide the blacks, to woo and pit one black group against another, must be vigorously repulsed.

STATEMENT ABOUT THE 1976 SOWETO UPRISING, SMUGGLED OUT OF ROBBEN ISLAND PRISON AND RELEASED BY THE ANC IN EXILE, 1980

Our struggle is growing sharper. This is not the time for the luxury of division and disunity. At all levels and in every walk of life we must close ranks. Within the ranks of the people, differences must be submerged to the achievement of a single goal – the complete overthrow of apartheid and racist domination.

IBID

One of the most challenging tasks facing the leadership today is that of national unity. At no other time in the history of the liberation movement has it been so crucial for our people to speak with one voice and for freedom fighters to pool their efforts.

FROM A LETTER TO MANGOSUTHU BUTHELEZI, WRITTEN IN VICTOR VERSTER PRISON, PAARL, SOUTH AFRICA, 3 FEBRUARY 1989

We are united, but we take into account the fact that there are other political organisations whose members have sacrificed like all of us. We feel it is only fair to recognise their contributions and seek unity with them.

BRIEFING TO THE FIFTH SESSION OF THE OAU'S (ORGANISATION OF AFRICAN UNITY) AD HOC COMMITTEE ON SOUTHERN AFRICA, 8 SEPTEMBER 1990

We understand it still that there is no easy road to freedom. We know it well that none of us acting alone can achieve success. We must therefore act together as a united people, for national reconciliation, for nation building, for the birth of a new world.

INAUGURATION AS PRESIDENT OF SOUTH AFRICA, UNION BUILDINGS, PRETORIA, SOUTH AFRICA, 10 MAY 1994

That both black and white in our country today can say we are to one another brother and sister, a united rainbow nation that derives its strengths from the bonding of its many races and colours, constitutes a celebration of the oneness of the human race.

ADDRESS TO THE JOINT SESSION OF THE HOUSE OF CONGRESS, WASHINGTON DC, USA, 6 OCTOBER 1994

In the end, what will unite us most strongly and provide the surest foundation for our new nation, is joint action to build a future for all our people, regardless of our political affiliations.

UPON RECEIVING THE FREEDOM OF THE CITY OF BOKSBURG, BOKSBURG, SOUTH AFRICA, 26 JUNE 1997

We will have to travel a difficult road before we can truly unite the majority of our people, without regard to race, colour and gender, around a common patriotism, one of whose critical elements must be the establishment of a caring society.

CLOSING SESSION OF THE FIFTIETH ANC NATIONAL CONFERENCE, NORTH-WEST UNIVERSITY, MAFIKENG CAMPUS, SOUTH AFRICA, 20 DECEMBER 1997

An unswerving commitment to non-racialism, to unity in action and to the safe-guarding of the interests of all oppressed people became the cornerstones of our movement as we confronted the challenges of the apartheid era. These should remain the cornerstones of our endeavours to build a united, democratic nation.

MESSAGE TO THE YUSUF DADOO CENTENARY CELEBRATIONS, UNIVERSITY OF JOHANNESBURG, SOUTH AFRICA, SEPTEMBER 2009

Values

Permanent values in social life and thought cannot be created by people who are indifferent or hostile to the aspirations of a nation.

FROM A LETTER TO WINNIE MANDELA, WRITTEN ON ROBBEN ISLAND, 23 JUNE 1969

Vanity

The trouble, of course, is that most successful men are prone to some form of vanity. There comes a stage in their lives when they consider it permissible to be egotistic and to brag to the public at large about their unique achievements.

FROM A LETTER TO FATIMA MEER, WRITTEN ON ROBBEN ISLAND, 1 MARCH 1971

Vengeance

It could have been that we inscribed vengeance on our banners of battle and resolved to meet brutality with brutality. But we understood that oppression dehumanises the oppressor as it hurts the oppressed. We understood that to emulate the barbarity of the tyrant would also transform us into savages. We knew that we would sully and degrade our cause if we allowed that it should, at any stage, borrow anything from the practices of the oppressor. We had to refuse that our long sacrifice should make a stone of our hearts.

STATEMENT TO THE PARLIAMENT OF THE REPUBLIC OF IRELAND, DUBLIN, IRELAND, 2 JULY 1990

Victory

Victory in a great cause is measured not only by reaching the final goal. It is also a triumph to live up to expectations in your lifetime.

FROM A LETTER TO THE REVEREND FRANK CHIKANE, WRITTEN IN VICTOR VERSTER PRISON, PAARL, SOUTH AFRICA, 21 AUGUST 1989

We do not pursue any goals which would result in some emerging as winners and others as losers. We are striving to proceed in a manner and towards a result, which will ensure that all our people, both black and white, emerge as victors.

ADDRESS TO THE EUROPEAN PARLIAMENT, STRASBOURG, FRANCE, JUNE 1990

The order of the day to all our comrades and our people is: gird your loins for the final assault. Victory is in sight! As a united people no force on earth can defeat us.

RALLY AT THE END OF THE ANC NATIONAL CONSULTATIVE CONFERENCE, SOCCER CITY, SOWETO, SOUTH AFRICA, 16 DECEMBER 1990

We can't lose because the people of the world will not allow us to lose.

FROM THE DOCUMENTARY *MANDELA IN AMERICA*, 1990

These countless human beings, both inside and outside our country, had the nobility of spirit to stand in the path of tyranny and injustice, without seeking selfish gain. They recognised that an injury to one is an injury to all and therefore acted together in defence of justice and a common human decency. Because of their courage and persistence for many years, we can, today, even set the dates when all humanity will join together to celebrate one of the outstanding human victories of our century.

NOBEL PEACE PRIZE AWARD CEREMONY, OSLO, NORWAY, 10 DECEMBER 1993

Today we are entering a new era for our country and its people. Today we celebrate not the victory of a party, but a victory for all the people of South Africa.

RALLY TO CELEBRATE HIS ELECTION AS PRESIDENT, CITY HALL, CAPE TOWN, SOUTH AFRICA, 9 MAY 1994

Together with the peoples of the world, we celebrated a victory that belonged to the world. It was a victory that flowed from, and affirmed, a shared commitment to our common humanity.

FAREWELL BANQUET HOSTED BY PRESIDENT THABO MBEKI, PRETORIA, SOUTH AFRICA, 16 JUNE 1999

I have always been confident that we'll win but there were times when the apartheid regime appeared to be stronger and I had doubts.

FROM THE DOCUMENTARY MANDELA: THE LIVING LEGEND, 2003

Violence

Already there are indications in this country that people, my people, Africans, are turning to deliberate acts of violence and of force against the government, in order to persuade the government in the only language which this government shows, by its own behaviour, that it understands.

IN MITIGATION OF SENTENCE AFTER BEING CONVICTED OF INCITING WORKERS TO STRIKE AND LEAVING THE COUNTRY ILLEGALLY, OLD SYNAGOGUE, PRETORIA, SOUTH AFRICA, 7 NOVEMBER 1962

Government violence can only do one thing and that is to breed counter-violence. We have warned repeatedly that the government, by resorting continually to violence, will breed, in this country, counter-violence against the people, till ultimately, if there is no dawning of sanity on the part of the government, ultimately the dispute will finish up by being settled in violence and force.

IBID

The government behaved in a way no civilised government should dare behave when faced with peaceful, disciplined, sensible and democratic views of its own population. It ordered the mobilisation of its armed forces to attempt to cow and terrorise our peaceful protest. It arrested people known to be active in politics.

IBID

The continued suppression of our aspirations and reliance on rule through coercion drives our people more and more to violence.

FROM A LETTER TO THE MINISTER OF JUSTICE, WRITTEN ON ROBBEN ISLAND, 18 APRIL 1969

Whether or not evil strife and bloodshed are to occur in this country rests entirely on the government.

FROM A LETTER TO THE MINISTER OF JUSTICE, WRITTEN ON ROBBEN ISLAND, 22 APRIL 1969

From our rulers, we can expect nothing. They are the ones who give orders to the soldier crouching over his rifle; theirs is the spirit that moves the finger that caresses the trigger.

STATEMENT ABOUT THE 1976 SOWETO UPRISING, SMUGGLED OUT OF ROBBEN ISLAND PRISON AND RELEASED BY THE ANC IN EXILE, 1980

The gun has played an important part in our history. The resistance of the black man to white colonial intruders was crushed by the gun. Our struggle to liberate ourselves from white domination is held in check by force of arms.

IBID

The position of the ANC on the question of violence is very simple. The organisation has no vested interest in violence. It abhors any action which may cause loss of life, destruction of property and misery to the people. It has worked long and patiently for a South Africa of common values and for an undivided and peaceful non-racial state. But we consider the armed struggle a legitimate form of defence against a morally repugnant system of government which will not allow even peaceful forms of protest.

FROM A MEMORANDUM TO PW BOTHA, WRITTEN IN VICTOR VERSTER PRISON, PAARL, SOUTH AFRICA, CIRCA JUNE/JULY 1989

Great anger and violence can never build a nation.

RALLY, KINGS PARK STADIUM, DURBAN, SOUTH AFRICA, 25 FEBRUARY 1990

If we had channels, peaceful channels of communication, we would never have thought of resorting to violence. If there was not the violence of apartheid, there would never have been violence from our side.

AT HOME, SOWETO, SOUTH AFRICA, FEBRUARY 1990

We know that many people who want peace are praying every day that this violence should come to an end. We are also praying because we know that when you come back from work you never know whether you will reach your own homes. You never know whether you will be able to find your beloved wives and children alive because the government and police are just not interested.

SPEAKING AT KAGISO, WEST RAND, SOUTH AFRICA, CIRCA 1991

We were dealing with a brutal government which did not hesitate to use bullets, live bullets against our ordinary civilians, unarmed and defenceless.

FROM A CONVERSATION WITH RICHARD STENGEL, 5 APRIL 1993

Continuously, we have to fight to defeat the primitive tendency towards the glorification of arms, the adulation of force, born of the illusion that injustice can be perpetuated by the capacity to kill, or that disputes are necessarily best resolved by resort to violent means.

ADDRESS TO THE FIFTY-THIRD UNITED NATIONS GENERAL ASSEMBLY, NEW YORK CITY, USA, 21 SEPTEMBER 1998

When we dehumanise and demonise our opponents, we abandon the possibility of peacefully resolving our differences, and seek to justify violence against them.

AWARD OF A NATIONAL ORDER TO PRINCE BANDAR BIN SULTAN, SAUDI ARABIAN AMBASSADOR TO THE UNITED STATES AND TO PROFESSOR JAKES GERWEL, CAPE TOWN, SOUTH AFRICA, 11 MAY 1999

Vision

This is a lesson for all of us to live our lives by: that the ways in which we will achieve our goals are bound by context, changing with circumstances even while remaining steadfast in our commitment to our vision.

UPON RECEIVING THE CHRIS HANI AWARD AT THE TENTH SACP (SOUTH AFRICAN COMMUNIST PARTY) NATIONAL CONGRESS, JOHANNESBURG, SOUTH AFRICA, 1 JULY 1998

Ours is a vision of a just and democratic South Africa in which all its people will enjoy a full and rewarding life.

FROM THE VIDEO *THE NELSON MANDELA FOUNDATION*, 2006

Voting

We fight for and visualise a future in which all shall, without regard to race, colour, creed or sex, have the right to vote and to be voted into all effective organs of state.

ADDRESS TO THE JOINT SESSION OF THE HOUSE OF CONGRESS, WASHINGTON DC, USA, 26 JUNE 1990

I have come back after twenty-seven years; I still cannot vote. That is the issue in South Africa and, until all the people of South Africa can vote and determine their own destiny, there is no question whatsoever of reviewing our strategies. Sanctions and isolation of South Africa must be maintained.

BRIEFING TO THE FIFTH SESSION OF THE OAU'S (ORGANISATION OF AFRICAN UNITY) AD HOC COMMITTEE ON SOUTHERN AFRICA, 8 SEPTEMBER 1990

A vote without food, shelter and health care would be to create the appearance of equality while actual inequality is entrenched. We do not want freedom without bread, nor do we want bread without freedom.

INVESTITURE, CLARK UNIVERSITY, ATLANTA, USA, 10 JULY 1993

Our feeling of joy is mixed with a feeling of sadness because many of the comrades who struggled and sacrificed in the cause of the struggle will not be there to see the realisation of their fondest dreams. And that is the feeling that I have as I approach this historic day.

FROM THE DOCUMENTARY *COUNTDOWN TO FREEDOM: TEN DAYS THAT CHANGED SOUTH AFRICA*, 1994

Well, I haven't made a decision.

FROM THE DOCUMENTARY *COUNTDOWN TO FREEDOM: TEN DAYS THAT CHANGED SOUTH AFRICA*, WHEN ASKED WHO HE WAS GOING TO VOTE FOR, 1994

I marked an X in the box next to the letters ANC and then slipped my folded ballot paper into a simple wooden box. I had cast the first vote of my life.

FROM *LONG WALK TO FREEDOM*, 1994

This is for all South Africans an unforgettable occasion. It is the realisation of hopes and dreams that we have cherished over decades, the dreams of a South Africa which represents all South Africans.

AFTER VOTING FOR THE FIRST TIME, OHLANGE HIGH SCHOOL, SOUTH AFRICA, 27 APRIL 1994

We sincerely hope that by the mere casting of a vote the result will give hope to all South Africans and will make us, all South Africans, realise that this is our country, we are one nation.

IBID

It is the realisation of hopes and dreams that we have cherished over decades.
IBID

I waited for over seventy years to cast my first vote. I chose to do it near the grave of John Dube, the first President of the ANC, the African patriot that had helped found the organisation in 1912. I voted not for myself alone but for many who took part in our struggle.
BRAM FISCHER MEMORIAL LECTURE, MARKET THEATRE, JOHANNESBURG, SOUTH AFRICA, 9 JUNE 1995

I felt that with me when I voted were Oliver Tambo, Chris Hani, Chief Albert Luthuli and Bram Fischer. I felt that Josiah Gumede, GM Naicker, Dr Abdullah Abdurahman, Lilian Ngoyi, Helen Joseph, Yusuf Dadoo, Moses Kotane, Steve Biko and many others were there. I felt that each one of them held my hand that made the cross, helped me to fold the ballot paper and push it into the ballot box.
IBID

If anything symbolises to the world the miracle of our transition, and earned us their admiration, it is the image of the patient queues of voters of April 1994 as South Africans in their millions, from every community and background, asserted their determination that, whatever the difficulties, the people shall govern so that we should never relive our experience of oppression, injustice and inhumanity.
ADDRESS AT THE OPENING OF THE PRESIDENT'S BUDGET DEBATE, PARLIAMENT, CAPE TOWN, SOUTH AFRICA, 2 MARCH 1999

We were turning a new page in the history of South Africa. This was in my mind as I cast that ballot paper.
FROM THE DOCUMENTARY *MANDELA: THE LIVING LEGEND*, 2003

Standing on the sidelines, failing to go to the polls is a neglect of the democratic duty. And in our case in South Africa, it can be read to signal disregard for the hard and painful struggles that went into bringing about democracy.
ANC ELECTION RALLY, FNB (FIRST NATIONAL BANK) STADIUM, SOWETO, 4 APRIL 2004

You, the people, will express yourself at the polls – expressing in the most resounding way your ability to see with your own eyes, hear with your own ears, and think with your own brains.
IBID

I hope to have more years voting, and even if I go to the grave I will wake up and come and vote.
AFTER VOTING, 1 MARCH 2006

War

My message to those of you involved in this battle of brother against brother is this: take your guns, your knives and your pangas, and throw them into the sea. Close down the death factories. End this war now!
RALLY, KINGS PARK STADIUM, DURBAN, SOUTH AFRICA, 25 FEBRUARY 1990

I have lived through almost the entire twentieth century, in a country and continent where we had to devote almost all of that life to struggling against a social and political legacy left by events of the nineteenth century. To see young political leaders of the developed world in the twenty-first century act in ways that undermine some of the noblest attempts of humanity to deal with those historical legacies, pains me greatly and makes me worry immensely about our future.

SPEAKING ABOUT PRIME MINISTER TONY BLAIR AND PRESIDENT GEORGE W BUSH AND THE INVASION OF IRAQ, BRITISH RED CROSS HUMANITY LECTURE, QUEEN ELIZABETH II CONFERENCE CENTRE, LONDON, ENGLAND, 10 JULY 2003

The history of the world, also in the last two centuries, had unfortunately been a story of too many wars with all the attendant cruelty of humankind against humankind. The twenty-first century, which so many hoped would at last be the century of the triumph of world peace and global caring, has not started too promisingly. Conflicts still plague many areas on the globe, and we have seen the emergence of unilateral superpower military interventions.

IBID

Too much of our planet is still embroiled in destructive conflict, strife and war. And unfortunately none of us can escape blame for the situation in which humankind finds itself.

MESSAGE TO THE GLOBAL CONVENTION ON PEACE AND NON-VIOLENCE, NEW DELHI, INDIA, 31 JANUARY 2004

Water

All over the world water is regarded as precious as life itself. Here in South Africa it is even more than life. And yet for forty-eight years and more, millions of our people were not regarded as worthy of this simple but basic necessity. We have had to await the coming of democracy.

COMMISSIONING OF THE MORETELE WATER PROJECT, SEKAMPANENG, SOUTH AFRICA, 14 OCTOBER 1995

Wish

If I were to be granted one wish on this occasion, it would be that all South Africans should rededicate ourselves to turning this into the land of our dreams: a place that is free of hatred and discrimination; a place from which hunger and homelessness have been banished; a safe place for our children to grow into our future leaders.

EIGHTIETH BIRTHDAY CELEBRATION, GALLAGHER ESTATE, MIDRAND, SOUTH AFRICA, 19 JULY 1998

My wish is that South Africans never give up on the belief in goodness, that they cherish that faith in human beings as a cornerstone of our democracy.

JOINT SITTING OF PARLIAMENT TO MARK TEN YEARS OF DEMOCRACY, PARLIAMENT, CAPE TOWN, SOUTH AFRICA, 10 MAY 2004

Women

South Africa has produced a rich crop of eminent women who have played an independent role in our history.

FROM A LETTER TO HELEN SUZMAN, WRITTEN ON ROBBEN ISLAND, 1 MARCH 1974

I've never regarded women as in any way less competent than men.

FROM A LETTER TO ADVOCATE FELICITY KENTRIDGE, WRITTEN ON ROBBEN ISLAND, 9 MAY 1976

I pay tribute to the mothers and wives and sisters of our nation. You are the rock-hard foundation of our struggle. Apartheid has inflicted more pain on you than on anyone else.

FIRST SPEECH AFTER HIS RELEASE, CITY HALL, CAPE TOWN, SOUTH AFRICA, 11 FEBRUARY 1990

We salute the mothers of the cadres of Umkhonto we Sizwe, whose children have fallen in battle both inside and outside South Africa. We pay tribute to the mothers of all those who died in the course of the struggle for freedom and against the apartheid system. We commend also those white mothers who stood by their sons for refusing to be conscripted into the apartheid army. We salute the wives and mothers whose husbands and sons still remain in prison despite the solemn undertakings of the apartheid regime. We salute those brave daughters of this country who are presently in prison for their commitment to a just, non-racial and democratic South Africa.

IBID

Freedom cannot be achieved unless the women have been emancipated from all forms of oppression.

FIRST STATE OF THE NATION ADDRESS, PARLIAMENT, CAPE TOWN, SOUTH AFRICA, 24 MAY 1994

The fight against apartheid liberated all South Africans – Africans, coloureds, Indians, and whites – the struggle for gender equality will benefit both men and women. The prosperous future to which we aspire calls for a united front of all South Africans across both the colour and gender divides.

ADDRESS TO THE NATIONAL CONFERENCE OF COMMITMENTS: GENDER AND WOMEN EMPOWERMENT, KEMPTON PARK, SOUTH AFRICA, 23 FEBRUARY 1996

The cause of women's emancipation is part of our national struggle against outdated practices and prejudices. It is a struggle that demands equal effort from both men and women alike.

IBID

As long as we take the view that these are problems for women alone to solve, we cannot expect to reverse the high incidence of rape and child abuse. Domestic violence will not be eradicated. We will not defeat this scourge that affects each and every one of us, until we succeed in mobilising the whole of our society to fight it.

SPEAKING AT A NATIONAL MEN'S MARCH, PRETORIA, SOUTH AFRICA, 22 NOVEMBER 1997

Too many women continue to bear the brunt of social and economic deprivation, in the rural as well as urban areas. Domestic violence, rape, abuse of women remain disgraceful blots on the reputation of a country that is called a miracle nation in other respects. The suffering of children invariably impacts more greatly on women than on men.

SPEAKING AT A DINNER CELEBRATING WOMEN'S MONTH, JOHANNESBURG COUNTRY CLUB, JOHANNESBURG, SOUTH AFRICA, 25 AUGUST 2003

No longer are we allowed to put the national question above gender issues; in fact, we are no longer allowed to think of the national question as something apart from the role and place of women in society.

IBID

We have women, we've had women, in Thembuland taking leading positions, ruling the country and the mother of Mandela was such a person.

FROM AN INTERVIEW WITH TIM COUZENS, VERNE HARRIS AND MAC MAHARAJ FOR
MANDELA: THE AUTHORISED PORTRAIT, 2006, 13 AUGUST 2005

Well, in prison we had the privilege of reading, and expanding our thinking.
Women throughout the world have led their own countries.
IBID

Words

The real meaning of the spoken word has to be demonstrated by practical deeds.
ADDRESS TO THE FRENCH NATIONAL ASSEMBLY, BOURBON PALACE, PARIS, FRANCE, 7 JUNE 1990

This whole question of [the] written speech introduces a great deal of artificiality.
SPEAKING AT SHELL HOUSE (OFFICE OF THE ANC), JOHANNESBURG, SOUTH AFRICA, 28 OCTOBER 1993

It is never my custom to use words lightly. If twenty-seven years in prison have done
anything to us, it was to use the silence of solitude to make us understand how precious
words are and how real speech is in its impact on the way people live and die.
CLOSING ADDRESS AT THE XIII INTERNATIONAL AIDS CONFERENCE, DURBAN, SOUTH AFRICA, 14 JULY 2000

A statement on major policy matters should not be made without being processed
and cleared, no matter what the status of a comrade is.
FROM A NOTEBOOK, DATE UNKNOWN

Work

Jobs, jobs and jobs are the dividing line in many families between a decent life
and a wretched existence. They are, to many, the difference between self-esteem
and helplessness.
PRESIDENT'S BUDGET DEBATE, PARLIAMENT, CAPE TOWN, SOUTH AFRICA, 20 JUNE 1996

Workers

In the struggle against apartheid, the black workers will strike the most decisive
blows. Without their participation, the impact of the liberation movement must
remain limited. Fortunately they are in the centre of the battle against racial
discrimination and constitute the mighty force that will lead the way to
a democratic South Africa.
FROM AN ESSAY ENTITLED 'CLEAR THE OBSTACLES AND CONFRONT THE ENEMY', WRITTEN ON
ROBBEN ISLAND, 1976

Our people need proper housing, not ghettos like Soweto. Workers need a living
wage – and the right to join unions of their own choice and to participate in
determining policies that affect their lives.
RALLY AT THE END OF THE ANC NATIONAL CONSULTATIVE CONFERENCE, SOCCER CITY, SOWETO,
SOUTH AFRICA, 16 FEBRUARY 1990

World

A new world will be won not by those who stand at a distance with their arms
folded, but by those who are in the arena, whose garments are torn by storms
and whose bodies are maimed in the course of the contest.
FROM A LETTER TO WINNIE MANDELA, WRITTEN ON ROBBEN ISLAND, 23 JUNE 1969

The universe we inhabit as human beings is becoming a common home that shows growing disrespect for the rigidities imposed on humanity by national boundaries.

ADDRESS TO THE HOUSE OF COMMONS, LONDON, ENGLAND, 5 MAY 1993

Is the time, therefore, not upon us when we should cease to treat tyranny, instability and poverty anywhere on our globe as being peripheral to our interests and to our future?

ADDRESS TO THE JOINT SESSION OF THE HOUSE OF CONGRESS, WASHINGTON DC, USA, 6 OCTOBER 1994

We operate in a world which is searching for a better life – without the imprisonment of dogma.

CLOSING SESSION OF THE FIFTIETH ANC NATIONAL CONFERENCE, NORTH-WEST UNIVERSITY, MAFIKENG CAMPUS, SOUTH AFRICA, 20 DECEMBER 1997

The world remains beset by so much suffering, poverty and deprivation. It is in your hands to make of our world a better one for all, especially the poor, vulnerable and marginalised.

NINETIETH BIRTHDAY DINNER, HYDE PARK, LONDON, ENGLAND, 25 JUNE 2008

Writing

When I look back at some of my early writings and speeches I am appalled by their pedantry, artificiality and lack of originality. The urge to impress is clearly noticeable.

FROM A LETTER TO WINNIE MANDELA, WRITTEN ON ROBBEN ISLAND, 20 JUNE 1970

The utmost caution becomes particularly necessary where an autobiography is written clandestinely in prison, where one deals with political colleagues who themselves live under the hardships and tensions of prison life, who are in daily contact with officials who have a mania for persecuting prisoners.

FROM AN UNPUBLISHED AUTOBIOGRAPHICAL MANUSCRIPT, WRITTEN ON ROBBEN ISLAND, 1975

Writing is a prestigious profession which puts one right in the centre of the world, and to remain on top, one has to work really hard, the aim being a good and original theme, simplicity in expression and the use of the irreplaceable word.

FROM A LETTER TO ZINDZI MANDELA, WRITTEN ON ROBBEN ISLAND, 4 SEPTEMBER 1977

You should cultivate that habit carefully by having a particular day of the week or month reserved for writing letters. It's always better to draft a letter and then go over it to check its mistakes and to improve your formulations.

FROM A LETTER TO MAKAZIWE MANDELA, WRITTEN ON ROBBEN ISLAND, 13 MAY 1979

A good pen can also remind us of the happiest moments in our lives, bring noble ideas into our dens, our blood and our souls. It can turn tragedy into hope and victory.

FROM A LETTER TO ZINDZI MANDELA, WRITTEN ON ROBBEN ISLAND, 10 FEBRUARY 1980

Writing a letter in prison can be a costly and frustrating exercise. Some of the letters are referred to the prison headquarters in Pretoria for approval, a process which invariably involves lengthy delays, at times stretching over several months. When the reply comes at long last it is usually a curt 'not approved' and, as a general practice, no reasons whatsoever are given for the decision.

FROM A LETTER TO PROFESSOR SAMUEL DASH, WRITTEN IN POLLSMOOR PRISON, CAPE TOWN, SOUTH AFRICA, 12 MAY 1986

Writing letters to friends used to be one of my favourite hobbies and each letter gave me a lot of pleasure. Pressure of work now makes it impossible for me to engage in this hobby.

FROM A NOTEBOOK, CIRCA 1993

Under the apartheid regime it was a common practice for the authorities to take documents from those they regarded as enemies. Sometimes they used these documents as evidence in court cases. Sometimes they used them in various forms of intimidation. Sometimes they just destroyed them. For all of us who were part of the struggles for justice and freedom in this country, committing information to paper was a very risky business.

LAUNCH OF THE NELSON MANDELA CENTRE OF MEMORY, JOHANNESBURG, SOUTH AFRICA, 21 SEPTEMBER 2004

Xenophobia

We cannot blame other people for our troubles. We are not victims of the influx of foreign people into South Africa. We must remember that it was mainly due to the aggressive and hostile policies of the apartheid regime that the economic development of our neighbours was undermined.

RALLY, ALEXANDRA STADIUM, JOHANNESBURG, SOUTH AFRICA, 19 AUGUST 1995

During the years I lived here, the people of Alexandra ignored tribal and ethnic distinctions. Instead of being Xhosas, or Sothos, or Zulus, or Shangaans, we were Alexandrans. We were one people, and we undermined the distinctions that the apartheid government tried so hard to impose. It saddens and angers me to see the rising hatred of foreigners.

IBID

The current apparent rise of an intolerant and xenophobic right wing in Western Europe does not send encouraging signs about us having entrenched the freedom from fear in the world.

UPON RECEIVING THE FRANKLIN D ROOSEVELT FOUR FREEDOMS AWARD, 8 JUNE 2002

Youth

The involvement of students in the freedom struggle is crucial and the emergence of a vigorous student movement is to be welcomed.

FROM AN ESSAY ENTITLED 'WHITHER THE BLACK CONSCIOUSNESS MOVEMENT', WRITTEN ON ROBBEN ISLAND, 1978

The initiative taken by white students on many public questions, affecting blacks mainly, pricked the conscience of black students who realised the irony of sitting with folded arms while their white colleagues were on the attack.

IBID

At no time have the oppressed people, especially the youth, displayed such unity in action, such resistance to racial oppression and such prolonged demonstrations in the face of brutal military and police action.

FROM A LETTER TO PRESIDENT PW BOTHA, WRITTEN IN POLLSMOOR PRISON, CAPE TOWN, SOUTH AFRICA, 13 FEBRUARY 1985

South Africa is producing determined young people whose level of awareness is remarkably high.

FROM A LETTER TO HILDA BERNSTEIN, WRITTEN IN POLLSMOOR PRISON, CAPE TOWN, SOUTH AFRICA, 8 JULY 1985

The courage of members of the Cape Youth Congress seems to grow with danger. Their determination in the face of the most challenging odds has already produced young national heroes, whose lives are used by the rest of the youth as models on which to mould their own lives.

FROM A LETTER TO THE CAPE YOUTH CONGRESS, WRITTEN IN VICTOR VERSTER PRISON, PAARL, SOUTH AFRICA, 21 AUGUST 1989

A cause which enjoys the solid support of the youth throughout the country is bound to succeed in the end. That support ensures that the sacred ideals for which so many have sacrificed will never be forgotten: that those who hold them firmly will die rich in spirit, even though they may be poor in material terms.

FROM A LETTER TO PETER MOKABA, WRITTEN IN VICTOR VERSTER PRISON, PAARL, SOUTH AFRICA, 21 AUGUST 1989

Young people throughout the world, especially students, are determined to build a new world of happiness and hope in their lifetime.

FROM A LETTER TO THE PAARL STUDENTS ASSOCIATION, WRITTEN IN VICTOR VERSTER PRISON, PAARL, SOUTH AFRICA, 21 AUGUST 1989

I pay tribute to the endless heroism of youth, you, the young lions. You, the young lions, have energised our entire struggle.

FIRST SPEECH AFTER HIS RELEASE, CITY HALL, CAPE TOWN, SOUTH AFRICA, 11 FEBRUARY 1990

To the youth of South Africa we have a special message: you have lost a great hero. You have repeatedly shown that your love of freedom is greater than that most precious gift, life itself. But you are the leaders of tomorrow. Your country, your people, your organisation need you to act with wisdom. A particular responsibility rests on your shoulders.

TELEVISED ADDRESS TO THE NATION AFTER THE ASSASSINATION OF CHRIS HANI, SOUTH AFRICA, 13 APRIL 1993

There can be no process more important for the future of South Africa than the realisation of the potential of our youth. Freedom would be hollow if it did not bring about their liberation from the heavy weight that restrained their energy, dampened their enthusiasm for life and cast an angry shadow on their self-esteem.

ANNUAL GOLD AWARD CEREMONY OF THE PRESIDENT'S AWARD, SOUTH AFRICA, 25 NOVEMBER 1994

The youth at whom we have directed most of our awareness campaign on this golden jubilee, should marvel at the nobility of our intentions. They are also bound to wonder why it should be, that poverty still pervades the greater part of the globe; that wars continue to rage; and that many in positions of power and privilege pursue cold-hearted philosophies which terrifyingly proclaim: I am not your brother's keeper! For, no one, in the North or the South, can escape the cold fact that we are a single humanity.

SPECIAL COMMEMORATIVE MEETING OF THE UNITED NATIONS GENERAL ASSEMBLY ON THE FIFTIETH ANNIVERSARY OF THE UNITED NATIONS, NEW YORK CITY, USA, 23 OCTOBER 1995

The youth of South Africa made a crucial contribution to the struggle for liberation, and I have no doubt in my mind that they have what it will take to put the injustices of the past behind them.

OPENING OF THE YOUNG CHRISTIAN WORKERS WORLD COUNCIL, OUKASIE, SOUTH AFRICA, 26 NOVEMBER 1995

You jolted the nation from its slumber, and rejected the slave education that the apartheid regime had implemented, with the hope of making blacks accept their slavery. You changed the course of history, and accelerated the downfall of the apartheid system.

SOUTH AFRICAN YOUTH DAY, SOUTH AFRICA, 16 JUNE 1996

The working youth is critical to our future. The economy depends on you. With your hard work and efforts at improving your skills, you can make ours one of the most prosperous nations in the world.

IBID

Herein lies a profound lesson for young South Africans. For the moral of your own achievements is that, with application, determination and discipline, we can all rise to positions of responsibility. Today the doors of learning are wide open, and young South Africans from all communities should take up the challenge.

SEVENTY-FIFTH ANNIVERSARY OF THE SOUTH AFRICAN RESERVE BANK, PRETORIA, SOUTH AFRICA, 28 JUNE 1996

I admire young people who are concerned with the affairs of their community and nation, perhaps because I also became involved in struggle whilst I was still at school. With such youth we can be sure that the ideals we celebrate today will never be extinguished. Young people are capable, when aroused, of bringing down the towers of oppression and raising the banners of freedom.

ANNIVERSARY OF BASTILLE DAY, PARIS, FRANCE, 14 JULY 1996

This past century has seen more than its share of miseries and injustice amongst the peoples of the world but the younger generations being educated in our schools have every reason to expect a better world.

RECORDED MESSAGE FOR THE ROUND SQUARE CAMPAIGN, SOUTH AFRICA, 4 OCTOBER 1996

Our youth is our future. Whether our country will rise from the ashes of apartheid to become one of the world's success stories will, to a large extent, depend on what we invest in educating and training our youth.

SPEAKING AT DAMELIN BUSINESS COLLEGE, JOHANNESBURG, SOUTH AFRICA, 13 FEBRUARY 1997

It is vital that our youth lead the efforts to create the conditions in which our people can sleep peacefully at night and our children can go to school without fear.

UPON RECEIVING AN HONORARY DOCTORATE FROM THE UNIVERSITY OF KWAZULU-NATAL, KWAZULU-NATAL, SOUTH AFRICA, 30 MAY 1998

The future belongs to our youth. As some of us near the end of our political careers, younger people must take over. They must seek and cherish the most basic condition for peace, namely unity in our diversity, and find lasting ways to that goal.

IBID

It is normally invidious to single out individuals. But today, 16 June, is the day on which we South Africans commemorate the contribution of our youth to the achievement of democracy, and rededicate ourselves to creating a just society.

UPON BEING AWARDED THE FREEDOM OF THE CITY AND COUNTY OF CARDIFF, WALES, 16 JUNE 1998

Many of today's younger generation are independent and clear thinkers with their own set of values.

FROM A PERSONAL FILE, DATE UNKNOWN

In a world that so often decries the apathy of its youth, we can open our arms for the millions of adolescents eager to contribute their new ideas and bounding enthusiasm.

STATEMENT ON BUILDING A GLOBAL PARTNERSHIP FOR CHILDREN, 6 MAY 2000

The struggle for true and universal human emancipation still lies ahead of the children, youth and future generations of our planet.

LAUNCH OF THE ROBERT F WAGNER GRADUATE SCHOOL OF PUBLIC SERVICE AFRICAN PUBLIC SERVICE FELLOWSHIP FUND, NEW YORK UNIVERSITY, NEW YORK CITY, USA, 7 MAY 2002

Our youth had suffered gravely under the cruelty of apartheid. Their bravery and sense of sacrifice, however, outmatched the cruelties of the apartheid regime.

REBURIAL CEREMONY FOR ANTON LEMBEDE, MBUMBULU, SOUTH AFRICA, 27 OCTOBER 2002

It is up to the youth to decisively and finally break our society out of the constricting and divisive definitions of our past.

IBID

The history of the ANC Youth League stands as testimony to the constructive role the organised youth of a country can and should play in helping to shape the course of that society.

RALLY TO CELEBRATE THE FIFTY-EIGHTH ANNIVERSARY OF THE ANC YOUTH LEAGUE, SOUTH AFRICA, 27 OCTOBER 2002

South African youth played an enormously important and heroic role in the defeat of apartheid. It was often with great sadness that we observed how they sacrificed the innocence of their youth to resist the might of the apartheid state; our sadness was, however, always mixed with even greater admiration for the courage and commitment of the young people of our country.

YOUTH FORUM ON HIV/AIDS, UNIVERSITY OF THE WITWATERSRAND, JOHANNESBURG, SOUTH AFRICA, 22 SEPTEMBER 2003

One of our challenges as we build and extend democracy is the need to ensure that our youth know where we come from, what we have done to break the shackles of our oppression, and how we have pursued the journey to freedom and dignity for all.

LAUNCH OF THE NELSON MANDELA FOUNDATION'S CENTRE OF MEMORY, JOHANNESBURG, SOUTH AFRICA, 21 SEPTEMBER 2004

To the youth of today, I also have a wish to make: be the scriptwriters of your destiny and feature yourselves as stars that showed the way towards a brighter future.

BIRTHDAY CELEBRATION FOR THE NELSON MANDELA CHILDREN'S FUND, FRENCH INTERNATIONAL SCHOOL, JOHANNESBURG, SOUTH AFRICA, 9 JULY 2008

The display of leadership by our youth today gives me a comfort that not all is lost.

IBID

Zionism

If Zionism means the demand by the Jewish community for their own homeland, for their own state, which they could regard as their home, then I support it. But if Zionism means that they must conquer territories from other countries and occupy them, then I oppose it.

FROM A CONVERSATION WITH RICHARD STENGEL, 13 JANUARY 1993

Supplementary Information

Biography

Nelson Mandela was born in the Transkei, South Africa, on 18 July 1918. He joined the African National Congress in 1944 and was engaged in resistance against the ruling National Party's apartheid policies for many years before being arrested in August 1962. Mandela was incarcerated for over 27 years, during which time his reputation as a potent symbol of resistance to the anti-apartheid movement grew steadily. Released from prison in 1990, Mandela won the Nobel Peace Prize in 1993 and was inaugurated as the first democratically elected president of South Africa in 1994. He is the author of the international bestsellers *Long Walk to Freedom* and *Conversations with Myself*.

Timeline

1918: Rolihlahla Mandela is born on 18 July at Mvezo in the Transkei to Nosekeni Fanny and Nkosi Mphakanyiswa Gadla Mandela.

1925: Attends primary school near the village of Qunu. His teacher gives him the name 'Nelson'.

1927: Following the death of his father, Mandela is entrusted to the care of Chief Jongintaba Dalindyebo, the regent of the Thembu people. He goes to live with him in Mqhekezweni at The Great Place.

1934: Undergoes the traditional circumcision ritual, initiating him into manhood. He attends Clarkebury Boarding Institute in Engcobo.

1937: Attends Healdtown, a Wesleyan College in Fort Beaufort.

1939: Enrols at the University College of Fort Hare, Alice, the only black university in South Africa. Meets Oliver Tambo.

1940: Expelled from Fort Hare for embarking on protest action.

1941: Escapes an arranged marriage and moves to Johannesburg where he finds work in the gold mines as a night watchman. Meets Walter Sisulu, who finds him employment as an articled clerk at the law firm Witkin, Sidelsky and Eidelman.

1942: Continues studying for his Bachelor of Arts degree (BA) by correspondence through the UNISA (University of South Africa). Begins to attend ANC (African National Congress) meetings informally.

1943: Graduates with a BA and enrols for a Bachelor of Laws degree (LLB) at the University of the Witwatersrand.

1944: Co-founds the ANCYL (ANC Youth League). Marries Evelyn Ntoko Mase and they have four children: Thembekile (1945–69); Makaziwe (1947), who died at nine months old; Makgatho (1950–2005); and Makaziwe (1954).

1948: Elected national secretary of the ANCYL, and onto the Transvaal National Executive of the ANC.

1951: Elected president of the ANCYL.

1952: Elected ANC president of the Transvaal province and is automatically a deputy president of the ANC. Public spokesperson and national volunteer-in-chief of the Defiance Campaign, which begins on 26 June 1952. He is arrested on a number of occasions and spends several days in jail. He is convicted with nineteen others under the Suppression of Communism Act and sentenced to nine months' imprisonment with hard labour, suspended for two years, and also receives the first in a series of banning orders preventing him from participating in any political activity. With Oliver Tambo he opens Mandela and Tambo, South Africa's first African law partnership.

1953: Devises the M-Plan for the ANC's future underground operations.

1955: The Freedom Charter is adopted at the Congress of the People in Kliptown. Mandela, along with other banned comrades, watches the proceedings in secret, from the roof of a nearby shop.

1956: Arrested and charged with treason along with 155 members of the Congress Alliance. The trial continues for four and a half years.

1958: Divorces Evelyn Mase. Marries Nomzamo Winifred Madikizela and they have two daughters: Zenani (1959) and Zindziswa (1960).

1960: Following the Sharpeville Massacre on 21 March, the government declares a state of emergency and Mandela is detained. On 8 April, the ANC and PAC (Pan Africanist Congress) are banned.

1961: Acquitted in the last group of thirty in the 1956 Treason Trial; all the other accused had charges withdrawn at different stages of the trial. In April, Mandela goes underground, and appears at the All-in African Congress in Pietermaritzburg as the main speaker and demands a national convention to draw up a new constitution for South Africa. In June the armed wing of the ANC, Umkhonto we Sizwe (MK), is formed with Mandela as its first commander-in-chief, and launched on 16 December with a series of explosions.

1962: In January, Mandela departs South Africa to undergo military training and to garner support for the ANC. He leaves the country clandestinely through Botswana (then Bechuanaland) and re-enters South Africa from there in July. He receives military training in Ethiopia and in Morocco, close to the border of Algeria. In total he visits twelve African states, and also spends two weeks in London, England, with Oliver Tambo. On 5 August he is arrested near Howick in KwaZulu-Natal, and is sentenced to five years' imprisonment on 7 November for leaving the country without a passport and inciting workers to strike.

1963: Mandela is transferred to Robben Island Prison in May before being suddenly returned to Pretoria Central Prison two weeks later. On 11 July, police raid Liliesleaf Farm in Rivonia and arrest almost all of the High Command of MK. In October, Mandela is put on trial for sabotage with nine others in what becomes known as the Rivonia Trial. James Kantor has charges withdrawn and Rusty Bernstein is acquitted.

1964: In June, Mandela, Walter Sisulu, Ahmed Kathrada, Govan Mbeki, Raymond Mhlaba, Denis Goldberg, Andrew Mlangeni and Elias Motsoaledi are convicted and sentenced to life imprisonment. All except Goldberg, who serves his sentence in Pretoria, are taken to Robben Island Prison.

1968:   Mandela's mother dies on 26 September. His request to attend her funeral is refused.

1969:   Mandela's eldest son, Madiba Thembekile (Thembi), is killed in a car accident on 13 July. Mandela's letter to the prison authorities requesting permission to attend his funeral is ignored.

1975:   Begins writing his autobiography in secret. Sisulu and Kathrada review the manuscript and make comments. Mac Maharaj and Laloo Chiba transcribe it into tiny handwriting, and Chiba conceals it inside Maharaj's exercise books. It is smuggled out by Maharaj when he is released in 1976.

1982:   Mandela along with Walter Sisulu, Raymond Mhlaba, Andrew Mlangeni and, later, Ahmed Kathrada are sent to Pollsmoor Prison. They share a large communal cell on the top floor of a cell block.

1984:   Rejects an offer by his nephew KD Matanzima, the president of the so-called independent state (or bantustan) of Transkei, to be released into the Transkei.

1985:   Rejects President PW Botha's offer to release him if he renounces violence as a political strategy. On 10 February his statement of rejection is read out to a rally in Soweto by his daughter, Zindzi. In November, Mandela undergoes prostate surgery in the Volks Hospital. He is visited in hospital by the minister of justice, Kobie Coetsee. On his return to prison, he is held alone. Begins exploratory talks with members of the government over the creation of conditions for negotiations with the ANC.

1988:   A twelve-hour pop concert to celebrate Mandela's seventieth birthday, held at Wembley Stadium, London, England, is broadcast to sixty-seven countries. Contracts tuberculosis and is admitted to Tygerberg Hospital, then Constantiaberg Medi-Clinic. He is discharged in December and moved to Victor Verster Prison, near Paarl.

1989:   Graduates with an LLB degree through the University of South Africa.

1990:   The ANC is unbanned on 2 February. Mandela is released from prison on 11 February.

1991:   Elected ANC president at the first ANC national conference in South Africa since its banning in 1960.

1993:   Awarded the Nobel Peace Prize with President FW de Klerk.

1994:   Votes for the first time in his life in South Africa's first democratic elections on 27 April. On 9 May, he is elected first president of a democratic South Africa and, on 10 May, he is inaugurated as president in Pretoria. His autobiography, *Long Walk to Freedom*, is published.

1996:	Divorces Winnie Mandela.
1998:	Marries Graça Machel on his eightieth birthday.
1999:	Steps down after one term as president.
2001:	Diagnosed with prostate cancer.
2004:	Announces he is stepping down from public life.
2005:	Makgatho, Mandela's second-born son, dies in January. Mandela publicly announces that his son has died of AIDS complications.
2006:	Publishes *Mandela: The Authorised Portrait*.
2007:	Witnesses the installation of grandson Mandla Mandela as chief of the Mvezo Traditional Council.
2008:	Turns ninety years old. Asks the emerging generations to continue the fight for social justice.
2009:	Mandela's birthday, 18 July, is endorsed by the United Nations as International Nelson Mandela Day.
2010:	His great-granddaughter, Zenani Mandela, is killed in a car accident in June. Publishes *Conversations with Myself* in October.
2011:	Hospitalised for a lung infection.
2012:	Hospitalised for an abdominal complaint. Post-presidential office closed. Celebrates his 94th birthday.

Select Bibliography

Books:

Daymond, MJ and Corinne Sandwith (eds), *Africa South: Viewpoints 1956–1961*, University of KwaZulu-Natal Press, Scottsville, 2011

Mandela, Nelson, *Conversations with Myself*, Macmillan Publishers, London, 2010

Mandela, Nelson, *Long Walk to Freedom*, Little, Brown and Company, London, 1994

Meer, Fatima, *Higher than Hope*, Skotaville Publishers, Johannesburg, 1988

Nelson Mandela Foundation, *A Prisoner in the Garden: Opening Nelson Mandela's Prison Archive*, Penguin, Johannesburg, 2005

Nicol, Mike, *Mandela: The Authorised Portrait*, PQ Blackwell, Auckland, 2006

Villa-Vicencio, Charles, *The Spirit of Freedom: South African Leaders on Religion and Politics*, University of California Press, Berkeley and Los Angeles, California, 2006

Documentaries:

Countdown to Freedom: Ten Days that Changed South Africa, directed by Danny Schecter, Globalvision, USA, 1994

Headliners and Legends, 'Nelson Mandela', MSNBC, USA, 2006

The Last Mile: Mandela, Africa and Democracy, directed by Jennifer Pogrund, South Africa, 1992

Legends: Nelson Mandela, directed by Walter Sucher, SWR, Germany, 2005

Mandela at 90, directed by Clifford Bestall, Giant Media Productions, UK, 2008

Mandela in America, directed by Danny Schecter, Globalvision, USA, 1990

Mandela: Son of Africa, Father of a Nation, directed by Joe Menell and Angus Gibson, Clinica Estetico and Island Pictures, USA, 1996

Mandela: The Living Legend, directed by Dominic Allan, BBC Television (UK), UK, 2003

Nelson Mandela Life Story, Imani Media for the Nelson Mandela Foundation, South Africa, 2008

A South African Love Story: Walter and Albertina, directed by Toni Strasburg, XOXA Productions and Quest Star Communication, South Africa, 2004

Viva Madiba: A Hero for All Seasons, directed by Catherine Meyburgh and Danny Schecter (consulting director), Videovision Entertainment, South Africa, 2010

Website:

www.nelsonmandela.org

Acknowledgements

We would like to acknowledge Nelson Rolihlahla Mandela for his wise words throughout his long and rich life; for the wisdom they bestow, the bravery they inspire and for the warmth they impart. The Mandela family's ongoing support is appreciated.

The Nelson Mandela Centre of Memory has provided a platform for work around the life and times and legacy of Nelson Mandela, which has created the space for, among other projects, the creation of books such as this one. In this regard, thanks are due to: the chairman of the Board of the Nelson Mandela Foundation, Professor GJ Gerwel; the Board of Trustees of the Nelson Mandela Foundation – Ahmed Kathrada, Chris Liebenberg, Irene Menell, Kgalema Motlanthe, Futhi Mtoba, Professor Njabulo Ndebele, Dr Mamphela Ramphele, Tokyo Sexwale; and the chief executive of the Nelson Mandela Foundation, Achmat Dangor.

Verne Harris heads the Centre of Memory and it was his support that created the opportunity for this book to be published. If it were not for the enthusiasm and energy of Geoff Blackwell and Ruth Hobday of PQ Blackwell, this collection would not have seen the light of day.

Our team members in the Centre of Memory also provided essential support. They are Lee Davies, Boniswa Nyati, Lucia Raadschelders, Zanele Riba and Razia Saleh. Our colleagues Yase Godlo, Zelda la Grange, Thoko Mavuso, Vimla Naidoo and Maretha Slabbert provided invaluable assistance.

We would also like to extend our gratitude to Ahmed Kathrada and Richard Stengel for donating to us many hours of recorded interviews with Mandela – which were made in the course of producing his autobiography *Long Walk to Freedom* and Anthony Sampson's authorised biography, *Mandela: The Authorised Biography* – and the South African National Archives.

We are also grateful to Rachel Clare, Sarah Anderson, Jo Garden, Helene Dehmer, Anant Singh and Nilesh Singh, Dr PR Anderson, Jennifer Pogrund, Anton Swart, Kerry Harris, Gail Behrmann, John Battersby, Professor Charles Villa-Vicencio and Beata Lipman.

The work of all those who aim to preserve accurately Madiba's words and legacy is appreciated. Special thanks in relation to this project are due to Imani Media, Sara Halfpenny, Richard Atkinson and Brian Widlake.